ROCHDALE AFC

A Who's Who
1939 to 1973

Steven Phillipps

A *SoccerData* Publication

Published in Great Britain by Tony Brown,
4 Adrian Close, Toton, Nottingham NG9 6FL.
Telephone 0115 973 6086. E-mail soccer@innotts.co.uk
www.soccerdata.com

First published 2014

© Steven Phillipps 2014

All rights reserved. No part of this publication may be reproduced, stored in a retrieval system, or transmitted in any form, or by any means, electronic, mechanical, photocopying, recording or otherwise without the prior permission in writing of the Copyright holders, nor be otherwise circulated in any form or binding or cover other than in which it is published and without a similar condition including this condition being imposed on the subsequent publisher.

Cover design by Bob Budd.

The team group on the front cover dates from a cold day in January 1962.
Back row, L to R: Albert Emptage (trainer), Stan Hepton, Ted Burgin, Jock McKay, Norman Bodell, Ray Aspden, Brian Birch, Lou Bimpson, Jim Thompson, Tony Collins (manager).
Front row: Jock Winton, Stan Milburn, Doug Wragg, Ron Phoenix, Joe Richardson, Ronnie Cairns, Colin Whitaker, Peter Whyke, John Hardman.

Printed and bound by 4Edge, Hockley, Essex
www.4edge.co.uk

ISBN: 978-1-905891-83-2

PREFACE

At the time of writing, Rochdale have completed 107 seasons as a professional club and as noted in the first part of this work (covering 1907 – 1939), over 1800 players have now appeared in their first team in competitive games. The second period of a third of a century in the club's history (1939 to 1973) saw them play throughout the Second World War and complete the whole history of Division 3 (North). A very brief stay in the new national Division 3 preceded a decade in Division 4 until their first promotion as a Football League club. Remarkably, it also saw them become the only club from the fourth tier of the game to reach a national Cup Final until 2013. The wartime years inevitably saw large numbers of guests supplementing a handful of existing players and numerous local lads, or servicemen stationed nearby, drafted into the side, many with little other senior football experience. As in the first volume, in the interests of providing as complete a record as possible, I have therefore included details which, while likely true, are not completely certain (and are clearly marked as such). Also continuing the form of the previous volume, the players are ordered in the text in the order in which they made first team appearances for Rochdale, so that there is also an underlying narrative history of the club over the years in question. In the present volume, in a few cases this causes a slight anomaly if a player made an odd wartime appearance well before the time that he was primarily associated with the club. A total of 522 players are included herein, ranging from full internationals to players picked out of the crowd at wartime games. Towards the end of the period covered, substitutes were introduced and all players chosen as No. 12 are included, even if they never had the chance to leave the bench.

Steven Phillipps
September 2014

ACKNOWLEDGEMENTS

The details contained within these pages have been acquired over a period of many years with the help of many Rochdale followers and statisticians of other clubs, and I thank them all. I particularly wish to acknowledge the invaluable input from Jim Creasy and Peter Holme and Gordon Small at the Football Museum for their help with wartime players, Garth Dykes for supplying both information and photographs and Tony Brown for readily agreeing to publish these volumes.

ROCHDALE AFC HISTORY 1939 to 1973

War Years

The Football League was immediately put in abeyance on the outbreak of war just three games into the 1939-40 season. After an interval of a couple of months, replacement regional leagues were introduced and Rochdale joined the League North, in its various incarnations, for the duration. A low key campaign for Dale, of just 28 games, did not end until June 3rd.

The second wartime season saw more of the scores sometimes associated with the 'scratch' nature of some of the teams, Dale defeating Southport 10-0, Bolton reserve Wally Sidebottom – later to lose his life serving in the navy – scoring five times. On the other hand, they lost 11-0 at Huddersfield and by an aggregate of 15-2 in the War Cup to Manchester City. Despite appearances by well known players, including internationalists such as Everton's Jim Cunliffe, Dale continued to have limited playing success until 1942-43 when they finished 21st of 54 clubs in the season's second championship and 2nd in the League North Cup qualifying competition. The following term they rose to 13th of 50 clubs in the first championship, Jack Harker remarkably netting nine goals in the two games against Southport on successive weekends, but they were well down the pack in 1944-45.

Jim Cunliffe

After VE day, it was decided to run an approximation to the real FL programme in 1945-46, with Rochdale placed in Division 3 North West. An excellent first half of the season gave Dale second place (to Accrington Stanley) in a closely contested league, and they followed this up with another second place (this time behind Rotherham) in the shorter Division 3 North second championship. They also reached the third round of the revived FA Cup. Further, they produced their first post-war star, selling Jim Constantine to Manchester City for £1000, while manager Ted Goodier spent a new record £1500 on Huddersfield reserve centre half Walter Birch.

Division Three North

Under the chairmanship of Mr Fletcher Bolton and with Ted Goodier at the helm for his ninth season, Dale made a distinctly below par start to post-war FL games, picking up just two points from the first eight matches. However they then beat Carlisle 6-0 thanks to a hat-trick from part-timer Joe Hargreaves and went on to finish in a more than creditable 6th place, Hargreaves taking his tally to 25 in all games. The Reserves were also successful, winning the Lancashire Junior Cup, the club's first trophy for over 30 years. The post-war boom in attendances resulted in Dale playing in front of 22,000 at Hull in the league and 23,000 at Charlton – the eventual winners – in the FA Cup. The season's best at Spotland was 13,555 for the visit of runaway leaders Doncaster and the home average of 7634 was the best yet. Another record was the transfer of Billy Woods to Bradford for £4500.

For the first time there were no debutants in the side for the opening fixture of 1947-48, but the season as a whole was rather the reverse of the previous one, with a decent start ruined by six consecutive defeats in March. Dale eventually finished 12th, poor away form and a lack of goals preventing a challenge nearer the top. Goodier continued to do good business in the transfer market, though, free signings Norman Kirkman and Dick Withington both joining Chesterfield for £4000, and the spectator boom produced an average home gate of 8294, almost 13,000 seeing the derby against Oldham.

After an unexpected opening day drubbing at Hartlepool, 1948-49 brought further steady improvement, Dale finishing 7th in very tight league. Indeed, they were only two points off 4th place, thanks in no small part to eight wins in nine mid-season games, but 14 home wins (the third best in the division) were again counterbalanced by a shortage of away goals. A crowd of 36,509, easily the most ever at a Dale game, watched the match at runaway leaders Hull. The average Spotland gate rose again to a new record 8640. Dale captured the Lancashire Cup for the first time, new centre forward Jack Connor scoring the only goal of the final against Blackpool. The outgoing transfer record was beaten again when Jackie Moss moved to Leeds for £7,000.

The next campaign proved to be Rochdale's best since the 1920s. Connor and inside partner Jack Livesey netted 16 goals each as Dale claimed third spot, just four points behind champions Doncaster and Livesey's hat-trick helped them to their best post-war victory, 7-1 against Mansfield. On Boxing Day they had led the table for the first time in 20 years. The defence (usually Churchill in goal, veterans Watson and Hubbick at full back and Birch at centre half) kept 21 clean sheets in 42 games and conceded only 13 goals at home. Over 23,000 fans saw the game at Oldham and 14,500 the return at Spotland, which resulted in Dale's 10th home win in succession (they went 17 games unbeaten at home). But even this was dwarfed by Spotland's biggest crowd ever, 24,231 cramming in to see the FA Cup tie against Third (South) leaders Notts County, who featured the England centre forward Tommy Lawton in their attack.

Season 1950-51 also started well, with the Dale top after the first few games, but subsequently was rather hit and miss as they finished 11th, though they did progress to meet Chelsea in the third round of the Cup. Former top scorer Connor had been sold to Bradford and Livesey also departed in the summer. Tommy Dryburgh's move to Leicester equalled the record fee received of £7000 and helped compensate for a slump in attendances to below 4000 by the end of the season. Indeed, there was enough left in the coffers to finally pay of the mortgage on the ground taken out in 1914.

A largely new side for the new season had some promising spells, but fell away badly in the second half of the campaign, going 13 games without a win and sliding down to a disappointing 21st place finish, just four points above the re-election zone. Attendances were variable to say the least, with 21,526 turning up to see Leeds in the third round of the Cup but only 1226 to see Scunthorpe in the League. (The week before the latter game, 13,646 had seen Dale's visit to leaders Lincoln). In June 1952 Ted Goodier resigned after 14 years in charge and was replaced as boss by former Manchester United man Jack Warner, who became player-manager (and Dale's oldest FL player up to that point).

His tenure started unpromisingly with three defeats and the side spent most of the season towards the foot of the table - indeed after 31 games they had only 18 points. In November and December Dale had seven successive away fixtures and lost all of them. As usual the derby games against Oldham drew large attendances, 23,000 at Boundary Park and 15,000 at Spotland, where Dale managed to beat the eventual champions. Indeed, Dale did rally as the season wore on and a victory on the final day kept them one place above the re-election line. The other key game had been a couple of weeks earlier when they ended a run of 17 consecutive away defeats.

Harry Catterick

Nevertheless, Warner, too, resigned and new chairman Fred Ratcliffe (the FL's youngest chairman) appointed Crewe boss Harry Catterick as the next incumbent. His reign started catastrophically with a 7-0 defeat at Carlisle and only one win in the first 12 matches. Bringing in new men, including former England centre forward Jack Haines for a record £2000, Catterick gradually turned things round and five successive victories in January and February gave the side sufficient cushion to survive a late season slump and still finish 19th. February 1954 had also seen the use of floodlights for the first time at Spotland (beating the likes of Old Trafford, Anfield and Goodison Park in this regard) for a friendly against St. Mirren. Walter Birch retired during the season after a record 243 FL appearances and Bill Watson also decided to call it a day after reaching the 200 mark.

After another slow start, 1954-55 saw Dale continue to edge in the right direction, Eric Gemmel's 22 goals assisting them to a 12th place finish. Crowds everywhere were still good, with around 11,500 seeing the victory over champions Barnsley and the goalless draw with 2nd place Accrington at Spotland and even more attending the away games. Almost 17,000 saw the third round FA Cup tie against Charlton.

The most noteworthy game, though, was surely that at Carlisle when three Dale defenders all contrived to put the ball past their own 'keeper in a 7-2 defeat. An interesting aside saw Dale face continental opposition for the first time when they beat touring Columbia Wien in a friendly.

Catterick kept faith with basically the same squad for the next campaign and they again finished 12th despite a number of heavy defeats, the worst 7-2 at Chesterfield. Don Partridge, the last link with Dale's wartime sides left at the end of the season after becoming the first player to figure in ten successive league campaigns. Crowds had sunk to around 2500 by the end of season and a £10,000 annual loss was recorded for the first time.

The close season of 1956 saw many more changes to the squad, in particular several signings from the manager's old club Everton, but no change in the side's mid-table status, though Dale did record a 6-1 away win at Crewe. Goal scoring generally was not a problem with Frank Lord hitting two hat-tricks in the space of four games. During one unbeaten run of games, three successive home crowds exceeded 10,000 and almost 20,000 attended the away game at Derby.

Despite these figures, and against the wishes of many of those affected, especially in the Northern Section, the FL had decided to introduce national Third and Fourth Divisions from 1958 to add variety to the lower divisions; Rochdale played seven of their original companions in every single season from 1921 up to the end of the regional third divisions. It was therefore particularly important that Dale at least managed to finish in the top half of the Third North in the upcoming season. In fact, Dale were comfortably placed for most of the season, sitting 4th in mid-March, but after failing to win any of the last 11 games just scraped into 10th place on goal average. The home league game against neighbours Bury attracted a remarkable crowd of 18,728. During the good run, Dave Pearson hit four against Halifax and Jim Dailey went one better with a nap hand in a 7-0 demolition of Hartlepools. Even more amazing, though, was the 5-4 success against Darlington, Dale coming back from 4-1 down and both full backs, Harold Rudman and Charlie Ferguson, scoring in the last three minutes. The season also saw Dale revert to their old black and white striped shirts instead of the blue they had worn since the war

THIRD AND FOURTH

With Division 3 (South) considered to have been at a higher level than the Northern Section, Dale were always likely to be up against it in the combined top halves of the two divisions, and to add to their problems Harry Catterick left on the eve of the season to take over at Sheffield Wednesday. It was October before Wednesday trainer Jack Marshall made the reverse journey to become Dale boss, and by then the side was in a run which saw them win only twice in the first 18 fixtures (the game at champions to be Plymouth being watched by almost 27,000 fans). Indeed, victories proved elusive throughout the campaign – they did not record any away from home – and they finished last, 13 points from safety.

Down in Division 4 with a largely new squad, Marshall's side, including new record capture Ron Cairns, a £2500 buy from Blackburn, had a mixed season after a promising start, finishing 12th with 18 wins and 18 losses. In October 1959 they had finally ended a run of 38 away games without a win. Remarkably, the top scorer was veteran full back Stan Milburn who hit a hat-trick in his first game at centre forward and ended with 15 goals. Playing in the bottom tier, average crowds dipped to a shade over 4000, the worst since the 1930s.

Now playing in all white, Dale slipped downwards to 17th in 1960-61, despite the inside trio of Hepton, Lord and Cairns netting 56 times between them, only one win coming in the last 11 games. In September Jack Marshall had accepted the manager's job at Blackburn, with Tony Collins promoted to player-manager. In a taste of thing to come, Collins masterminded victories over second division Scunthorpe and third division Southend in the new Football League Cup, Dale's first successes against higher division sides since they had joined the FL.

A rather different looking team began the following term and remarkably the same players figured in all the first eight games as Dale got off to a good start. Even more remarkably, Dale launched into a run in the Football League Cup which saw them famously defeat first division giants Blackburn Rovers in the two-legged semi-final. Though beaten by Norwich in the final (again over two legs), they were the only fourth tier side to reach a national cup final until 2013. This had been a tactical triumph for the manager who deployed effectively a four man defence, dropping another player back alongside the centre half, when faced with higher division opponents. Dale played 61 games using a squad of only 18 players and towards the end of the season had beaten the earlier record by going unchanged for nine games.

Dale had finished 12th despite the cup distractions, and in 1962-63 they were able to mount a serious challenge towards the top of the table, until a poor run in April set them back. They eventually finished in 7th place, six points off the promotion places, but with an outstanding home record of 16 wins and only one defeat. (Nevertheless, crowds were poor, at least partly because of some of the worst winter weather for many years, numbers twice dipping below 2000). It was therefore surprising that the side slipped all the way back to 20th the following term. After 12 games without a win, only a final day victory over champions Gillingham kept Dale out of the bottom four on goal average.

The summer of 1964 saw the arrival of the player generally ranked as Rochdale's greatest ever, Reg Jenkins. Dale mounted a concerted challenge and were in the top six or seven throughout the campaign, indeed Reg's new post-war record 25 league goals kept Dale in the promotion hunt until the penultimate game of the season. They had to settle for 6th in the end, but their tally of 58 points would have guaranteed promotion in any other season up to the introduction of three points for a win.

A startling decline in 1965-66 – coinciding with the general introduction of a 4-2-4 system – saw Dale plummet into the re-election places for the first time since 1934. After a bright, if inconsistent, start, they had a dismal run from February onwards, picking up one point from eight games, and they eventually lost 10 home games, the worst since the dire days of 1931-32.

The following campaign was an almost exact replica, with Dale again 21st. Things had started badly when the long serving Ray Aspden was injured in a pre-season game and was not able to play again, finishing with 346 senior appearances for Dale. (At the other end of the scale, 18 year old Paul Crossley was sold to Preston for a new record £8000 after just 15 games). In the end, it came down to the final two league games; Dale and Notts County both lost each of them, but County remained out of the bottom four on goal average.

Reg Jenkins

When 1967-68 looked to be heading the same way, Tony Collins resigned and was replaced by former Charlton boss Bob Stokoe. The improvement wasn't dramatic, but in spite of a number of fairly dismal results, thanks to two wins in the last three games Dale did manage to creep up to 19th, when a third successive re-election application might have strained even the 'old pals act' that many considered to operate in the re-election voting.

A number of youngsters had been introduced before Collins' departure and Stokoe had added a couple of experienced hands, but otherwise there was a complete clear-out ahead of the next campaign, Dale also raising some cash by selling goalkeeper Les Green to Derby for another new record of £8500. In fact, even though it was Stokoe's new signings who did the trick, he had moved on to Carlisle and his assistant Len Richley had taken over, before a tremendous run from Boxing Day onwards saw Rochdale claim their first ever Football League promotion. A 15 match unbeaten run and only two defeats in 24 games saw third place confirmed by a final day 3-0 success against Southend, with Reg Jenkins bagging two of the goals. Only 14 different players – including new record £5000 signing Tony Buck – appeared during this run, and only 16 all season. The defence of 'keeper Harker and back four of (usually) Smith, Ryder, Parry and Ashworth conceded only 35 goals, just 11 of them at home, with Harker keeping 20 clean sheets, the best since Harry Moody in 1924. The games against the eventual top two, Doncaster and Halifax both attracted 12,000 crowds to Spotland.

Up in Division 3, Dale made a storming start, winning eight games in succession from the end of September to move to the top of the table. Remarkably, they fielded the same starting eleven in 15 games in a row. They found it harder going subsequently, though, and the broken leg suffered by Tony Buck was a key blow, despite fellow striker Reg Jenkins netting 20 times in the league. Dale, now being managed by former coach Dick Conner after Richley resigned, eventually finished 9th, still their equal best at this level. Earlier in the season, local discovery Steve Melledew had been sold to league champions Everton for £15,000. Average gates were the best for many years at 6424.

The 1970-71 campaign was rather the reverse, with only one win in the first twelve games, but again Boxing Day signalled an upturn in fortunes and they ended in 16th place despite a succession of injuries to key players, including those to Graham Smith and Derek Ryder which ended a record run of 96 games for the full back pairing. A shortage of home goals and wins had been the main problem; away from Spotland they picked up only one point fewer than Aston Villa in fourth place. The main feature of the season had been the run to the fourth round of the FA Cup, including the famous 2-1 defeat of first division Coventry City on a Monday afternoon, after the top flight side refused to play under Spotland's now aging floodlights. (The lights were replaced the following season). Dale also won the Lancashire Senior Cup for the second time, defeating neighbours Oldham 3-2 in the final.

The following term was rather a struggle, particularly after the sale of young striker Dave Cross to Norwich for easily a new record of £40,000, and especially on the road, where they picked up just one victory. Cross was subsequently replaced by record incoming transfer Jack Howarth, an £8000 buy from Aldershot. Even though they failed to win any of their last 14 games, they did scrape together enough draws to finish in 18th, just a point above the drop zone. The penultimate game, a draw away to promoted Brighton was watched by a remarkable crowd of 34,766.

Season 1972-73 started brightly with the side top of the table after 10 games but they were unable to keep this up, a solid defence – they played out no fewer than 10 goalless draws – being unable to counterbalance a lack of goals at the other end. Oddly, despite this, they scored four against promoted Notts County, Reg Jenkins scoring the last two of his club record 141 goals, and then lost 6-0 to Plymouth in successive home games, the latter equalling their worst ever home defeat. At the other end of his career to Reg, Paul Fielding became the club's youngest ever player a week before his 17th birthday. In the end, Dale were 13th, but only five points behind the side in 7th. Nevertheless, the Board, mindful of supporters' lack of enthusiasm for Dick Conner's perceived defensive tactics (the attendance had dipped as low as 1588 for one late season game), decided not to renew his contract and to find a new manager. In the period between managers, Reg Jenkins slipped away quietly back to his native Cornwall with 359 Dale games under his belt, and most of his experienced colleagues would soon depart too, Graham Smith after a new record 373 appearances, 317 of them in the league, signalling the start of a new Dale era.

March 1949. Back, players only: Watson, Partridge, Churchill, McGeachie, Birch. Front: Arthur, Livesey, Hubbick, Connor, Hood, Dryburgh.

1959. Back: Powell, Bodell, Milburn, Jones, Bushby, Edwards. Front: Barnes, Spencer, Anderson, Cairns Collins

1961-62. Back: Milburn, Hepton, Aspden, Burgin, Thompson, Winton. Front: Wragg, Richardson, Bimpson, Cairns, Whitaker

1966-67. Back: Emptage (trainer), Hardman, Taylor, Williamson, Jones, Smith, Russell, Storf, Collins (manager). Front: Richardson, Connor, Calloway, Pennington, Lister, Aspden, Collins, Crossley.

NOTES TO WHO'S WHO

In the following section, players are listed in the order of their Rochdale competitive debuts. An alphabetical Table of the players, with the seasons played and appearances and goals in the various competitions is appended. Games counted for these purposes are the Football League, the FA Cup (including the 1945-46 season), the Football League Cup (from 1960-61), the Lancashire Senior Cup (1939-40 and 1945-46 onwards) and the wartime Football League North (1939-45), Division 3 North (West) in 1945-46, and War League Cup (1939-41; in later years league games doubled as War League cup ties), all jointly given as 'WL'. 'Other' games include the short lived Northern Floodlit Cup (1963) and the pre-season Charity Rose Bowl games against Oldham Athletic (from 1962). Substitute appearances are denoted by + signs. If a player was named as substitute, but without making an appearance, this is denoted +0.

In the individual players' career details, FL appearances for any club are given in square brackets. In addition, wartime games (including the War League Cup) are denoted by WL, and those in the Scottish League (generally only for matches in the Scottish first division) by ScL (or ScWL for wartime games). After the formation of the Alliance League, later renamed the Football Conference, at the top of the non-league game, appearances at this level are denoted 'Conf'. Appearances in the North American Soccer League are given as NASL. A £ sign indicates that a fee was paid for the player's transfer, but the amount is not known. Under 'Honours', players (or managers) who were with a club at some point during a season in which a championship or promotion was obtained, but were no longer with the club at the end of that season (or were guest players), have the relevant honour in brackets, as do players who were unused substitutes in cup finals etc. In the dates of birth, if no precise date is known, JFM signifies the first quarter of the year (January, February, March) and so forth. Probable but unconfirmed details (particularly for wartime players, where information is sometimes scarce) are contained in curly brackets {}.

1971-72. Back: Madden (coach), Jenkins, Cross, Clarke, Jones, Godfrey, Ashworth, Parry, Blair, Connor (manager). Middle: Whitehead, Gowans, Downes, Buck, Butler, Riley, Ryder, Smith. Front: Arrowsmith, Simpson, Williams, Mandzuk

John (Jack) Ellis 1939-40

Born: Tyldesley 25.1.12 5'11" 12st
Goalkeeper
WL Apps 2
Career: Tyldesley U. Juniors, Atherton 1.30, Winsford U., West Bromwich A. 5.30, Wigan B. am 11.30, Wolverhampton W. 2.32 [26], Bristol R. 5.34 [86], Hull C. 5.38 [32], Clapton Orient 7.39 to 1941-42 [2 WL], Dale guest 10.39 [2 WL], Wrexham guest 11.41 [9 WL], Winsford U., Stockport Co. guest 9.44 [2 WL], Stalybridge Celtic, Mossley 9.46, Winsford U. player-manager, Leeds U. scout.
Honours: Division 3(S) Cup winners 1935

Dale's first wartime goalkeeper, Jack guested for them in the initial two Regional League North West Division games in October 1939. Having just signed for Clapton that summer, he had been a FL player throughout the 1930s and had accumulated 150 senior appearances. His most productive spell had come during four years with Bristol Rovers, even though he broke a collar bone in his first season and had the misfortune to enter the record books as their goalie the day Joe Payne scored 10 for Luton in a 12-0 win! While at Hull he had the opposite experience when his side beat Carlisle 11-1. During the war he served as an RAF policeman.

Willie Harker 1939-41
Born: Brierfield 21.12.10 5'8" 11st7
Half back
WL Apps/Gls 12/1
Career: Brierfield Tuesdays, Burnley am 5.29, Nelson am 9.8.30 [18/5], Burnley 21.5.31 [24/7], Torquay U. 2.6.33 [9/-], Accrington St. 9.6.34 [62/33], Portsmouth 13.2.36 (£1450 for 2 players), Stockport Co. 18.9.36 [35/3], Dale 7.6.39 to 10.40 (exchange for T. Doyle) [12/1 WL], Accrington St. guest 3.40 [1/1 WL]
Honours: Division 3(N) champions 1937

Willie signed for Dale in the summer of 1939 but was not chosen for any of the three FL games before war broke out. He had started out with Nelson in their disastrous final FL season – his debut came in an 8-1 defeat at Southport and he scored in another 8-1 loss at Carlisle - and then figured in the second division with Burnley. Known as a "penetrating forward who combines foraging and definite attacking in nice proportions", he scored five for Accrington Stanley against Gateshead in November 1935, including a six minute hat-trick, but subsequently dropped back into the half back line with Stockport following a brief unproductive spell at Portsmouth. Although figuring only twice in their Third North championship winning campaign, Willie did play in the crucial final game of the season against second placed Lincoln which won them the title. He played all across the intermediate line for Dale in a dozen appearances during the first two wartime campaigns, scoring their first goal in the North West Regional League (and also guested against them for his former club Accrington). The son of a publican, and formerly a butcher's apprentice, after the war he, too, was a licensee, in Oswaldtwistle.

Thomas Bernard (Tommy) Olsen 1939-40
Born: Tirphil 13.1.13 5'9" 10st4
Outside/inside left
WL Apps/Gls 13/1 Total Apps/Gls 14/1
Career: Tirphil School, Aberaman Juniors, New Tredegar, Swansea T. 1.30 [195/50], Bury 6.39 to 8.42 £1000 [7/4 WL], Dale guest 10.39 [13/1 WL], Manchester U. guest 5.41 [2/- WL]
Honours: Tredegar Schoolboys, Wales Schools 1927, Wales XI v Birmingham 11.41, South Wales & Monmouthshire Cup winners, West Wales Cup winners, Welsh FA Cup final 1938

Of Scandinavian descent, Tommy was born in South Wales – he was "a great pal" of Manchester United's Welsh international Jack Warner, the future Dale manager – and spent almost 10 years with Swansea. After nearly 200 league games, in which he netted a half century of goals, he moved to Bury just before war broke out. He appeared regularly as a guest for Dale in 1939-40, usually on the left wing, though he was better known as an inside forward. Despite few senior appearances over the next couple of years while serving in the RAF, he played for Wales in a representative game in 1941. He kept a grocery shop back in Swansea and was a keen fisherman.

George William Nevin 1939-40

Born: Lintz, Co. Durham 16.12.07 5'11" 12st7
Left back
WL Apps/Gls 1/0
Career: Leazes Council School, Lintz Institute, Dipton U., Lintz Colliery, Newcastle U. am 8.25, Sunderland am 3.26, Dipton U., White-le-Head Rangers, Newcastle U. 12.28 £100 [6/-],

Sheffield W. 5.30 [2/-], Manchester U. 12.33 [4/-], Sheffield W. 3.34, Burnley 5.35 [26/-], Lincoln 5.37 [8/-], Dale 6.39 [1/- WL]

George was 31 when he signed for Dale in the summer of 1939, but though he had been with five FL clubs since Newcastle bought him for £100 back in 1928 he had made only 46 senior appearances, almost half of them with Burnley in the second division in 1935-36, being considered "a good steady reserve". He was even less used at Spotland, not appearing in the aborted league campaign and playing just one wartime league match, against Southport in October 1939. A former miner, George was the nephew of Jack Nevin who played for Barrow and Crewe amongst others in the 1920s.

Arthur Warburton 1939-41, 1943-44

Born: Whitefield 10.9.09
5'8" 10st7
Left half/inside right
WL Apps/Gls 30/0
Total Apps/Gls 31/0
Career: Sedgley Park, Manchester U. am 2.29, pro 5.29 [35/10], Burnley 12.33 [25/4], Nelson 5.34, Fulham 10.34 [46/6], Queens Park R. 6.38 [17/-], Dale guest 10.39 to 10.40 and 4.44 [30/- WL], Middlesbrough guest 11.41 and 1942-43 [9/2 WL], Bradford PA guest 10.42 [1/- WL], Lincoln C. guest 8.43 [1/1 WL], Bury guest 8.45 [1/- WL], Southport 29.10.45 to 12.45 [1/- WL]

Arthur had an up and down career, first moving from minor football to Manchester United, for whom he scored on his top flight debut in 1930. "The schemer rather than the scorer", most of his United games unfortunately came the following term, when they lost 12 games in a row and were relegated and by 1934 he had dropped back to Lancashire Combination football. He soon returned to the FL with Fulham, however, and was with QPR in the last peacetime season. He appeared widely as a wartime guest for northern sides, playing at Spotland in three different seasons. He signed for Southport in 1945 after leaving the RAF, where he had been a PT Instructor, and played in the revived FA Cup, but was not retained for the return to proper league football.

William James (Bill) Carey 1939-41
Born: Manchester 21.9.13   6'0" 12st7
Goalkeeper
WL Apps 22   Total Apps 23
Career: Sedgley Park, Hereford U., Aston Villa 5.36 [4], Bury cs.39, Dale guest 11.39 to 9.40 [22 WL], Manchester U. guest 4.40 [1 WL], Manchester C. guest 9.41 [9 WL], Southport guest 1944-45 [6 WL], Coventry C. guest 1944-45 [8 WL], Aston Villa 11.45 [1 WL], Mossley 8.47
Honours: Division 2 champions 1938

Coincidentally having started out at Sedgley Park like fellow Dale guest Arthur Warburton, Bill's FL career had consisted of just four appearances for Aston Villa by the time war broke out, though he did keep clean sheets in all three games he played in Villa's second division championship winning campaign. He also played in an FA Cup tie for Villa against Charlton in front of a 64,000 crowd at neutral Highbury. Having signed for Bury in the summer of 1939, he never actually played for them, but appeared in the majority of Rochdale's games in the first wartime season and a few at the start of the following term, later guesting for several other sides.

Tom Holland (Tommy) Chester 1939-40

Born: Glasgow 7.11.07
5'10" 11st12
Right back
WL Apps/Gls 5/0
Career: East Bank Academy, Cambuslang Rangers, Bellshill Ath., Baillieston Juniors, Bury 12.26 [249/-], Burnley 3.37 [51/1], Notts Co. 6.39 [4/- WL], Dale guest 11.39 [5/- WL], Halifax T. guest 4.40 to 1942 [38/- WL]
Honours: Scottish Schoolboys

A Dale guest in 1939-40, Tommy had been at Gigg Lane for ten years and actually first came into the Bury side in 1927 in place of First World War Rochdale player Fred Heap. A former bricklayer, he was virtually an ever-present at right back in three seasons in the 1930s, playing "coolly, methodically and stylishly" with "good powers of recovery". He "timed his tackles admirably and judged his passes to a nicety". He moved on to Burnley after losing his place in the side and had just arrived at Notts County when war broke out. After representing Dale, he played quite frequently in the wartime leagues for Halifax. He was also an expert billiards player.

Alfred James (Alfie) Anderson 1939-40

Born: Old Cumnock 5.11.14
5'6" 10st2
Outside right
WL Aps/Gls 10/1
Total Apps/Gls 11/1
Career: Yoker Ath., Hibernian 9.34 [74/8], Bolton W. 1.37 [52/4], St Johnstone trial 1938-39, Third Lanark 2.39, Dale guest 11.39 [10/1 WL], New Brighton

guest 3.40 [2/- WL], Tranmere R. pro 10.11.40 [4/1 WL], Wrexham guest 3.41 [6/1 WL], Everton guest 9.41 to 1.43 [41/8 WL], (RAF), Crewe A. guest 1.43 to 9.43 [15/4 WL]

Alfie was an old fashioned Scottish winger who had made his mark with Hibs before a transfer to Bolton Wanderers in 1937, where he was the regular outside left for the next season and a half. Before agreeing to play for Dale in wartime games, he insisted that they insure him against any injury that might prevent him from carrying out his trade as an upholsterer, but this didn't stop him guesting for several other sides, too, figuring regularly for Everton in 1941-42. He later worked as a photographer at an engineering works back in Chesterfield.

Arthur Richardson 1939-40
Born: Wigan 15.1.13 5'9" 11st
Centre forward
WL Apps/Goals 15/15
Career: Calderstones, Burnley 10.36 [11/2], Chesterfield 7.38 £475 [4/1], Rochdale 4.39 [15/15 WL], Bolton W. guest 4.41 [1/- WL]

After three seasons on the fringes of Burnley and Chesterfield's second division sides, Arthur signed for Dale in the summer of 1939 but made no FL appearances for them. He quickly made a mark in wartime games, though, scoring in six of his first seven games including a hat-trick at Oldham. He finished with 15 goals in as many games at centre forward, but was not seen again after the end of that season.

Ernest (Ernie) Robson 1939-42
Born: Gateshead c.1910 5'11" 11st4
Goalkeeper
WL Apps 12
Career: Close Works, Gateshead am 1.35, pro 11.35 [7/4], Aldershot 1.36 [72/4], Dale 3.7.39 [12 WL]

Though he made a dozen appearances in goal for Dale during the war, Ernie was actually signed from Aldershot as a centre half in July 1939, though without making any first team appearances prior to the Regional League games. He had been a regular in the Shots' defence between 1936 and 1938 but didn't play at all in his final season with them. Earlier he had been a centre forward in his Gateshead days, scoring in four of his seven league games.

William John Shadwell 1939-40

Born: Bury 10.9.14
5'8" 11st
Left half
WL Apps/Gls 1/0
Career: Turton, Manchester C. am 4.33, pro 24.5.33 [2/-], Exeter C. 13.7.36 [85/2], Dale guest 1.40 [1/- WL], Mansfield T. guest 1943-44 [3/- WL]

John made a couple of first division appearances for Manchester City as understudy to Jackie Bray, but the remainder of his FL experience came after a move to Exeter. He made a single guest appearance for Dale in a 5-1 home defeat by Blackburn in January 1940.

J. Taylor 1939-40
Right back
WL Apps/Gls 7/0
Career: Dale 2.40 [7/- WL]

A right back, he played seven games for Dale in the North West Regional League between February and May 1940 but unfortunately Dale didn't win any of them.

Clifton (Cliff) Chadwick 1939-40
Born: Bolton 26.1.14 5'6" 10st10
Outside right
WL Apps/Gls 1/0
Career: Turton, Fleetwood, Bolton W. trial, Oldham A. 26.10.33 [18/6], Middlesbrough 22.2.34 £1000 [93/27, 19/3 WL], Dale guest 2.40 [1/- WL], Oldham A. guest 2.40 to 12.40 [22/6 WL], Bolton W. guest 4.40 to 1.44 [85/31 WL], Nottingham F. guest 11.41 [1/- WL], Manchester U. guest 9.42 and 9.44 and 5.45 [27/7 WL], Hull C. 9.46 £650 [23/7], Darlington 7.47 [37/5], Stockton 8.48
Honours: Bolton Schoolboys, Lancashire Schoolboys, League North Cup final 1945

A diminutive yet assertive winger, Cliff was a regular top flight performer in the late 1930s, making around 100 appearances for Middlesbrough after a £1000 transfer only four months after turning pro at Oldham. He played just the once for Dale in February 1940 but guested for numerous other Lancashire clubs during the war, particularly prominently with Bolton. Described as "a pocket Hercules" he was quite a prolific goalscorer getting close to a century in all games. He resumed his career after the war – during which he trained paratroops and carried out missions to drop saboteurs behind enemy lines - with a couple of seasons in the Third North. His favoured recreation was motoring.

John (Jack) Hall 1939-42
Born: Prestwich 23.10.12 5'10" 11st
Goalkeeper
WL Apps 38
Career: Failsworth, Newton Heath Loco, Manchester U. 9.32 [67], Tottenham H. 6.36 [53, 9 WL], Stockport Co. guest 10.39 [8 WL], Hyde U. 1.40, Dale guest 3.40 et seq. [38 WL], Hartlepools U. guest 1939-40 [3 WL], Oldham A. guest 2.42 [3 WL], Bolton W. guest 11.42 [2 WL], Blackburn R. guest 11.42 [1 WL], Nottingham F. guest 12.45 [1 WL], Stalybridge Celtic 5.46, Runcorn 1946, Stalybridge Celtic
Honours: Division 2 champions 1936

An experienced goalkeeper by the outbreak of war, Jack had a tough start in the Manchester United side that just avoided relegation to Division 3 in 1934. Two years later, though, his "wonderful agility and clever anticipation" helped to maintain the second best defensive record in the whole FL as United won promotion. However he then surprisingly moved to Spurs, back in Division 2. Following his trade as an electrician, Jack was able to play on through the war and assisted numerous sides, mostly near home in Lancashire. He first turned out for Dale in March 1940 and was their regular goalie for most of the following campaign, having the misfortune to be on the wrong end of the 15-2 aggregate defeat by Manchester City in the Lancashire Cup. (Earlier, while guesting for Stockport, he had conceded 6, 7 and 8 goals in successive games!). Well into his thirties by the end of the war he moved into non-league football and worked for Ferranti.

Alphonso (Alf) Ainsworth 1939-42, 1944-45

Born: Manchester 31.7.13
5'6" 10st6
Inside forward
WL Apps/Gls 16/3
Career: Ashton Ath., Manchester U. am 1933, pro 13.2.34 [2/-], Great Harwood, New Brighton £100 14.9.35 to 10.39 [150/39, 2/1 WL], Accrington St. guest 11.39 [4/1 WL], Dale guest 3.40 et seq. [16/3 WL], Southport guest 1942-43 [1/- WL], Oldham A. 9.42 to 9.43 [27/2 WL], Bury guest 11.43 [3/2 WL], New Brighton 10.8.46 [28/9], Cowdenbeath trial 1947, Congleton T. 12.47, Ashton U. 12.48
Honours: Palatine League champions 1933

Considered one of most skilful ball players in the lower divisions, Alf had a long association with New Brighton. After joining from Manchester United his "judicious passing... was one of the biggest influences in a greatly improved attack", and he helped them rise from the bottom of the league in his first season to mid table respectability by 1938-39 when he scored 16 times. Guesting for several Lancashire sides during the war, he made scattered appearances for Dale over several seasons, and re-signed for the Rakers in 1946.

Duncan Morton Colquhoun 1939-43

Born: Glenfruin, Helensburgh 24.7.15
5'7" 10st5
Outside right
WL Apps/Gls 41/7
Career: Helensburgh, Dunoon Ath. 3.33, Partick Thistle trial, Fulham trial 1932-33, Millwall 29.11.33, Raith Rovers 6.34, Dumbarton 11.34, Sheffield W. trial 23.12.34, Hartlepools U. trial 20.1.35, King's Park 1935, Queen of the South Wanderers 1935, Hibernian, Wigan Ath. 10.35, Blantyre Victoria, Bristol C. 10.37 [3/-], Southport 14.6.38 [36/10], Bradford C. 10.5.39, Dale guest 3.40 et seq. [41/7 WL], Partick Thistle guest, Walsall guest 11.42 [1/- WL], Blackpool guest 12.42 [2/1 WL], Stockport Co. guest 12.42 to 10.43 [4/- WL], Pwllheli T. 1943-44, Wigan Ath. 1945, Hurst 3.46, Wigan Ath. 5.46, player-manager 1948, Runcorn cs.49, Crompton's Rec. player-manager, Prescot Cables, Dale trainer 1951, Wigan A. trainer, coach and physio 1952 to 1985 (caretaker manager 1970)
Honours: Lancashire Senior Cup final 1936, Cheshire League champions 1937, Cheshire County Cup winners 1937, Lancashire Combination champions 1949

Another small Scottish winger, Duncan played for several smaller clubs in Scotland and had trials with several clubs south of the border (appearing in the Third North Cup for Hartlepools) before making his league debut with Bristol City in 1937 and playing one full season with Southport before the war. He guested for Dale (amongst others) on a number of occasions in the regional leagues, but in 1945 signed for one of his earlier clubs, Wigan Athletic, with whom he had remarkably reached the 1936 Lancashire Senior Cup final by defeating Manchester United, and received a benefit with them, eventually becoming player-manager. After a brief spell as trainer at Spotland he followed his Dale boss Ted Goodier back to Wigan and stayed on in various capacities for over 30 years until he retired at the age of 70 (he lived to the age of 90), by which time they had finally made it into the Football League.

Albert Thomas ('Sam') Earl 1939-40, 1947-48

Born: Gateshead 10.2.15
5'9" 11st5
Inside left
FL Apps/Gls 4/1
Total Apps/Gls 7/1
Career: Dunstan CWS, Bury am 4.31, pro 28.3.32 [35/7], Rhyl Ath loan 11.36, signed 2.37, York C. 3.7.37 [58/9], Hartlepools U. 7.39 [3/- WL], Dale guest 3.40 [1/- WL], Stockport Co. 23.8.46 [42/12], Dale 8.11.47 (exchange for T. Barkas) [4/1], New Brighton 6.3.48 [9/1], Northwich Victoria 8.48
Honours: England schoolboy trials, North v South, Midlands 1928-29, Lancashire Senior Cup final 1935

A star schoolboy footballer who had England trials alongside Stanley Matthews, Sam, as he was always known, in reference to the West Ham player, was signed by Bury when he was 17, making a number of second division appearances at centre forward or outside right and playing in the Lancashire Cup Final. He subsequently became a regular at York, mostly at inside right, and played the expunged 1939-40 league games for Hartlepools, guesting once for Dale later in the season. After a productive season and a half with Stockport after the war, he joined Dale when Tommy Barkas moved the other way, but only stayed a few months, ending the season with bottom club New Brighton.

William (Bill) Byrom 1939-48
Born: Blackburn 30.3.15
Full back
FL Apps/Gls 30/0   Total Apps/Gls 118/0
Career: Burnley 8.37, Queens Park R. 5.39 [1/- WL], Dale guest 1939-1946 [85/- WL], Manchester U. guest 4.43 [2/- WL], Dale 6.46 £100 [30/-], Stalybridge Celtic 8.48
Honours: (War League South Division 'B' champions 1940), Lancashire Junior Cup winners 1947

Although a Lancastrian, Bill was on QPR's books when war broke out. However, he played for them only once and spent most of the wartime seasons guesting for Dale, signing for them for the princely sum of £100 in 1946. Finally making his league debut at the age of 31, he spent two peacetime seasons with Dale, playing in either full back position, his best run in the side coming after Norman Kirkman was sold in December 1947. Earlier that year he had been a member of the Dale reserve side that won the Lancashire Junior Cup.

James Sydney Dean (Syd) Rawlings 1939-41

Born: Wombwell 5.5.13
5'8" 10st3
Outside/inside right
WL Apps/Gls 22/6
Career: Preston NE cs.31, Dick, Kerrs' 1932, Preston NE pro 3.32 [12/1], Huddersfield T. 2.34 [11/2], West Bromwich A. 3.35 [10/1], Northampton T. 6.36 [48/18], Millwall 12.37 [53/27, 13/1 WL], Preston NE guest 1939-40 [2/- WL], Dale guest 3.40 to 4.41 [22/6 WL], Clapton O. guest 1940-41 [6/3 WL], Bury guest 8.41 [2/- WL], Liverpool guest 3.43 [1/- WL], Southport guest 1942-44 [64/19 WL], Everton guest 8.44, signed 11.45 [45/14 WL], Stockport Co. guest 5.46 [1/- WL], Plymouth A. 5.46 to 1948 [56/20]
Honours: Division 3S champions 1938, League South Cup final 1945

The son of First World War Rochdale star Archie, Syd followed him into Dick, Kerrs' side and to many of his former FL clubs before also following him to Spotland for a number of wartime games. Indeed Syd figured in all divisions of the Football League, signing for Huddersfield when they were runners-up to Arsenal, but was one of the many players to lose the middle years of their careers to the war. Generally playing on the right wing, he had an excellent scoring rate with well over 100 goals in senior games. He played at Wembley for Millwall in the 1945 League South Cup Final. He died at the age of only 43 not long after finishing playing.

Douglas James (Doug) Redwood 1939-40
Born: Ebbw Vale 24.10.18
5'7" 10st4
Outside left
WL Apps/Goals 7/3
Career: Ebbw Vale, Cardiff C. 10.35 [13/-], Walsall 5.37 [27/6], Dale 6.39 [7/3 WL], Birmingham guest 1943-44 [1/- WL], Walsall guest 10.44 [3/- WL], Darlaston 8.46, Hednesford T., Stafford Rangers 8.47, Tamworth 8.49
Honours: Welsh schoolboy international

Joining Cardiff when he was just 17, Doug's most productive spell came in a couple of seasons at Walsall before he signed for Dale on the eve of the war. He didn't appear in any of their FL games at the start of the 1939-40 season but played a few games in the North West Regional League and also guested back at Walsall towards the end of the war.

Alick Robinson 1939-40

Born: Leigh 17.6.06
5'8" 11st
Right back
WL Apps/Gls 3/0
Career: Hindley Green, Bury 4.26 [169/4], Burnley 10.33 £2500 [204/8, 83/- WL], Bury guest 1939-46 [46/-], Dale guest 5.40 [3/- WL], Millwall guest 1943-45 [7/- WL], Bury trainer, Accrington St. trainer-coach 6.49
Honours: Football League v Irish League 1935, 1936, FL XI v Wales & Ireland (Jubilee game) 1935, North West Regional League champions 1940, Lancashire Cup final 1940

A highly experienced and popular full back "who never passes haphazardly and is always ready to start an attack", Alick played the best part of 400 games for Bury and Bolton over a 13 year period and twice represented the Football League. He only had three games for the Dale at the end of the 1939-40 season after Bury had already won the divisional championship, but as an auxiliary fireman during hostilities, he had the chance to play quite regularly for both Burnley and Bury again, taking his tally of senior games well past the 500 mark before retiring to take up the post of trainer at Gigg Lane. Earlier he had worked in the pit and was an all-round sportsman, being an excellent shot and baseball player.

Archibald (Archie) Livingstone 1939-40

Born: Pencaitland, Edinburgh 15.11.15 5'8" 11st4
Inside right
WL Apps/Gls 2/2
Career: Musselburgh Lewisvale c.1932, Ormiston Primrose, Dundee, Newcastle U. 5.35 £35 [33/5], Bury 6.38 £500 [24/8, 87/28 WL], Dale guest 5.40 [2/2 WL], York C. guest 12.41 to 8.42 [9/4 WL], (coaching in Turkey 1942), Wrexham guest 1.43 to 1944-45 [57/20 WL], Liverpool guest 5.43 [1/- WL], Brentford guest 3.45 [1/- WL], Accrington St. guest 5.45 [2/- WL], Fulham guest 2.44 [4/- WL], Peterborough U. 8.45, Everton 5.46 [4/2], Southport 17.6.47 £1000 [23/2], Glenavon player-coach 8.48, Dundee 9.49, Worksop T.
Honours: Scotland wartime international v England 1943, Lancashire XI v Everton 1946, North West Regional League champions 1940, Lancashire Cup final 1940

A slater by trade in Scotland, Archie had arrived at Bury from Newcastle for a sizeable fee just a year prior to World War II and most of his appearances for them actually came in the regional leagues where he was a regular scorer, despite playing much of the time at right half. He guested for several other sides, including very briefly the Dale, while working in an aircraft factory and then serving in the Lancashire Fusiliers, and once scored seven goals in a game for Wrexham. He was also a Scottish wartime international and did some coaching in Turkey while stationed there during the war. Towards the end of the war he played for a Lancashire representative side in a match against Everton in aid of Lancashire CCC and subsequently signed for the Toffees, grabbing a couple of goals in the top flight during the first post-war season. He also appeared for Southport in the Third North before moving into coaching. He suffered badly from jaundice originally contracted while in the army and died at the early age of 45.

Donald Frederick (Don) Carter 1939-40

Born: Midsomer Norton 11.9.21 5'8" 11st
Outside left
WL Apps/Gls 3/1
Career: Welton School, Norton St Johns, Stourbridge 4.38, Bury 28.1.39 [56/27, 143/71 WL], Dale guest 5.40 [3/1 WL], Manchester U. guest 6.40 [1/- WL], Oldham A. guest 5.42 [1/- WL], Albion R. guest 1941-42 [2/2 ScWL], Burnley guest 1942-43 [1/- WL], Bristol C. guest 1943-44 [1/1 WL], Manchester C. guest 3.44 [1/- WL], Bolton W. guest 4.44 [1/1 WL], Blackburn R. 12.6.48 £5000 [2/-], New Brighton 6.11.48 [105/19], Northwich Victoria cs.51
Honours: Somerset County Schools, North West Regional League champions 1940, Lancashire Cup final 1940, 1947

Don moved from his Somerset home to Bury in 1939 and spent the remainder of his career in the North West, guesting for most of the sides in Lancashire, including Dale, during the war. He spent almost 10 years on the books at Gigg Lane, but most of his appearances were necessarily in the wartime leagues when he played and scored on a regular basis (including four against Dale on Christmas Day 1942) despite first serving in the RAF as a wireless operator and then in 1943 transferring to the Tank Corps. A hard working forward, he appeared mostly on the left wing, from where he netted twice on his debut in a 5-0 victory over Burnley, but was able to play inside too. Blackburn signed him for a sizeable fee in 1948 but he stayed only a few months before New Brighton's record fee took him to a much more productive stint with them.

John (Jack) McGowan 1939-40
Centre half
WL Apps/Gls 1/0
Career: Bury 1939 [18/- WL], Dale guest 5.40 [1/- WL], York C. guest 1940-41 [1/- WL].
Honours: North West Regional League champions 1940, Lancashire Cup final 1940

Like several Bury colleagues he appeared for Dale in 1940 after the Shakers had already won the regional league title. Then working as a postman like team mate Reg Halton (q.v.), Jack had played in virtually all their league games and in June appeared in the Lancashire Senior Cup Final, but never played for them again after joining up.

Thomas (Tom) Burdett 1939-40
Born: Hartlepool 22.10.15 5'10" 11st7
Inside left/outside right
WL Apps/Gls 2/2
Career: Station Town Council School, Wingate Juniors 2.30, Station Town Welfare, Wheatley Hill Juniors, Blyth Spartans 2.33, Hull C. 6.33 [3/-], Fulham 6.35, Lincoln 6.36 [27/12], Bury 5.39 to 1944-45 [43/32 WL], Dale guest 5.40 [2/2 WL], Manchester U. guest 5.40 [2/2 WL], Manchester C. guest 5.40 [1/1 WL], Bradford C. guest 10.40 [1/- WL], Hull C. guest 1940-41 [7/5 WL], Leicester C. guest 1942-43 [1/- WL], Luton T. guest 1943-44 [1/- WL]
Honours: North West Regional League champions 1940, Lancashire Cup final 1940

More usually a centre forward, Tom played two games for Dale somewhat out of position, but still scored twice. Indeed, while he had had a somewhat undistinguished FL career before the war despite 22 Midland League goals for Hull Reserves in 1934-35, he had an excellent record in the wartime leagues for his own club Bury and various other sides, netting 25 league goals, plus 14 in other games, in 1939-40 alone. Unfortunately, he had to retire through injury before peacetime football resumed.

Reginald Lloyd (Reg) Halton 1939-40

Born: Leek 11.7.16
5'11" 11st4
Centre half
WL Apps/Gls 1/0
Career: Stafford R., Buxton 8.34, Cheddleton Mental Hospital, Manchester U. 10.36 [4/1], Notts Co. 6.37 [6/-], Bury 11.37 £ [114/19, 76/15 WL], Dale guest 6.40 [1/- WL], York C. 9.40 to 1945 [14/2 WL], Fulham guest 1940-44 [4/2 WL], Aldershot guest 1941-42 [50/17 WL], Millwall guest 3.42 [3/- WL], Southampton guest 1943-44 [6/- WL], Portsmouth guest 1944-45 and 1945-46 [5/1 WL], Arsenal guest 11.45, Chesterfield 12.48 [61/10], Leicester C. 9.50 [64/3], Scarborough T. player-coach 2.53, Goole T. 1.54, Symington 5.54, Brush Sports 10.54. Leek T. manager 1968-69
Cricket for Staffordshire, professional for Scarborough
Honours: North West Regional League champions 1940, Lancashire Cup final 1940, 1947

The sixth Bury regular to play for Dale in May and June 1940, Reg was then working as a postman but later had quite an eventful career after joining up. He played with numerous international players while stationed at Aldershot, captaining the side after Joe Mercer and Stan Cullis were posted elsewhere, and guested in the famous game between Arsenal and Moscow Dynamo in November 1945. Originally an outside left (he scored on his Manchester United debut in that position) he later became a wing half with a "cool and calculating style", who could also play at centre half. After the war he played on into the 1950s and was also a notable minor counties cricketer (having trials with Lancashire and Worcestershire), as well as playing golf, table tennis, snooker and billiards.

Eric Eastwood 1940-41
Born: Heywood 24.3.16 5'9" 11st8
Right back
WL Apps/Gls 3/0
Career: Oxford Grove School, Chorley Road Congregational, Little Lever, West Houghton, Manchester C. trial 1932, Heywood St. James, Darwen 3.35, Manchester C. am 14.4.35, pro 6.35 [16/-, 163/- WL], Bolton W. guest 10.39 to 3.41 and 4.42 [29/1 WL], Dale guest 8.40 [3/- WL], Manchester U. guest 5.43 [3/- WL], Wrexham guest 2.46 [3/- WL], Port Vale 27.3.47 to 4.50 [28/1]
Honours: Bolton Schools

A schoolboy 100 yards champion and a product of the Heywood St. James club which has produced several Rochdale players over the years, Eric spent the majority of his career with Manchester City. Though only managing 16 FL appearances either side of the war, he played over 160 games for them in the regional leagues, first as a full back and later at centre half. He guested for Dale in the first three games of the 1940-41 season. Eric's grandfather was a director of Bolton Wanderers and his father Percy was also on Bolton's books as a player, while brother Jimmy was another Dale player.

John (Jack) Connor 1940-41

Born: Ashton-u-Lyne 1.2.14
5'9" 11st
Left back/left half
WL Apps/Goals 17/0
Career: Mossley United Methodists, Mossley 11.32, Bolton W. 10.34 £325 [29/-, 71/5 WL], Dale guest 8.40 [17/- WL], Hurst 9.45 to 12.45, Mossley 10.46 £100, Tranmere R. 6.47 to 1949 [46/3]

A regular for Mossley in the Cheshire League when he was 18, Jack spent over a decade with Bolton and though losing the middle of his career to the war managed exactly 100 appearances in all games. He spent the first half of 1940-41 at Rochdale, playing in all their games until the turn of the year, mostly at left back, though he was more usually a left half at Bolton (and to add to the versatility sometimes turned out for them at centre half or on the left wing). He resumed his FL career in 1947 at Tranmere.

James Nathaniel (Jim) Cunliffe 1940-45, 1946-47

Born: Blackrod 5.7.12 5'10" 11st3
Inside right
FL Apps/Gls 2/0   Total Apps/Goals 92/47
Career: Adlington, Everton 5.30 [174/73, 3/1 WL], Bolton W. guest 11.39 to 5.40, 1.41 to 3.41, [27/8 WL], Dale guest 8.40 to 12.40, 8.41 to 4.45 [90/47 WL], Stoke C. guest 1944-45 [1/- WL], Dale trial 9.46 [2/-]
Honours: England v Belgium 1936, Empire Exhibition Cup final 1938, Division 1 champions 1939

Considered at the time to be the most cultured player ever to turn out for Rochdale, Jim (aka Nat) followed his cousin Arthur (q.v.) into the Adlington village side before giving up his apprenticeship as a plater to join Everton. "A nice type of youngster who is expected to develop along the right lines", he scored on his FL debut against Aston Villa in 1933 and the following season obtained a regular place in the absence of the injured Dixie Dean. Jim subsequently partnered Dean in the Everton attack and by the end of 1935-36, when he scored 23 league goals including four against both Stoke and West Brom, he had also made his England debut at inside right against Belgium. In 1938 he played in the Empire Exhibition Cup Final, a forerunner of international club championships, when Everton lost to Celtic, but an injury saw him struggle to keep his first team place and he figured only seven times in Everton's league title winning side. He guested for Bolton in the early war years, first arriving at Spotland in August 1940. He top scored with 10 goals including three against Bolton in 1941-42 and doubled that the following term, netting 20 goals, including a hat-trick against Stockport, and played regularly by wartime standards for four seasons. Back at Goodison Park in 1946 after a lengthy illness, he was deemed no longer fit enough for the rigours of league football and had a trial at Rochdale, who, sadly, came to the same conclusion after just two games. A third member of the Cunliffe family, a nephew also called Jim, appeared for Stockport in 1960.

George Samuel Hunt 1940-41

Born: Barnsley 22.2.10
5'9" 11st4
Centre forward
WL Apps/Gls 5/0
Career: Barnsley Central School, Regent St, Congregationals, Barnsley trial, Sheffield U. trial 1927, Port Vale trial 1928, Regent St. Congregationals, Chesterfield 9.29 [14/9], Tottenham H. 6.30 £1500 [185/127], Arsenal 10.37 £7500 [18/3], Bolton W. 2.38 £4000 [45/24, 174/83 WL], Dale guest 8.40 [5/- WL], Liverpool guest 1940-41 [7/5 WL], Sheffield W. 11.46 [32/8], Bolton W. coach, trainer and scout 5.48 to 9.68
Honours: England 3 caps 1933 v Scotland, Italy, Switzerland, The Rest v England 1933, Division 2 promotion 1933, Division 1 champions 1938, Lancashire Senior Cup joint winners 1939, War League North Cup winners 1945, War Cup winners 1945

After trials with several other league clubs, George was eventually signed by Chesterfield who then sold him to Spurs the following summer. A "persistent, courageous forward", "unstoppable in front of goal", he scored at a rate of two goals every three games at White Hart Lane, netting 34 times in their promotion campaign, and became their record FL goalscorer. He won three full caps for England, netting against Scotland, before an unusual move to Spurs' rivals Arsenal. He stayed only four months though before joining Bolton, where he once more scored on a regular basis as the replacement for ex-Dale centre forward Jack Milsom. Playing throughout the war, he added another century of goals to that scored for Tottenham, though he did not get on the score sheet during a brief stint with Dale. He later had an even longer association with Bolton, first on their coaching staff and then as a scout. Oddly, though already transferred to Bolton, he played enough games for Arsenal to qualify for a league championship medal at the end of the 1937-38 season. Away from the game, he was keen on golf, tennis and motoring. His grandfather, Sam, had played for Barnsley back in 1899.

Wiliam (Billy) Graham 1940-41

Born: Hetton-le-Hole 3.10.14
5'7" 10st6
Inside left
WL Apps/Gls 2/0
Career: Eppleton School, Houghton Secondary School, Hetton Juniors, Burnley trial 1932, Blyth Spartans 5.32, Burnley 9.32 [5/2], Bury 5.35 [81/29], Norwich C. 1.39 [17/4, 6/2 WL], Halifax T. guest 4.40 and 1945-46 [7/1 WL], Dale guest 9.40 [2/- WL], Bury guest 9.41, 10.42 and 8.45 [3/- WL], Chester guest 10.41 [2/- WL], Wrexham guest 1941-43 [15/11 WL], Barry T. 11.46, Holywell T. player-coach 1949

Another of the many former Bury men to turn out at Spotland during the war, Billy had scored fairly regularly in his three seasons at Gigg Lane but actually spent the end of the last pre-war campaign with Norwich. Occasional regional league appearances included the first two games of 1940-41 for Dale but after the war he joined Barry Town.

Walter (Wally) Sidebottom 1940-41

Born: Hunslet JFM.21
Outside/inside left
WL Apps/Gls 17/11
Career: John O'Gaunt's FC, Bolton W. am 5.37, pro 5.38 [1/-, 37/13 WL], Dale guest 9.40 [17/11 WL], k.i.a. 23.10.43

Wally played in only one peacetime FL game for Bolton, against Huddersfield in February 1939, but appeared in all Wanderers North West Regional League games the following year. As Bolton did not play any games in the first half of 1940-41, he guested for Dale alongside teammates Connor, Eastwood and Hunt and bagged 11 goals for them, including five in a 10-0 trouncing of Southport. Tragically he did not live to fulfil this promise as, after joining the navy as an Able Seaman, he was drowned when the cruiser HMS Charybdis was torpedoed in the English Channel in a disastrous operation in which "so many errors [were made] both ashore and afloat that the incident was an illustration to the Royal Naval tactical school for many years as an example of what not to do". The islanders of Guernsey hold a commemorative service each year for the men lost.

Joseph Thomas (Joe) Taylor 1940-41

Born: Wednesbury 11.4.10 5'9" 11st8
Centre half
WL Apps/Gls 2/0
Career: Wednesbury FC, Leamington T. 12.30, West Bromwich A. am 3.31, Shrewsbury T. 27.7.32, Luton T. 11.5.34 [1/-], Carlisle U. 28.9.35 [58/11], Stockport Co. 8.2.37 £400 [19/4], Oldham A. £200 5.7.38 to 1946 [13/6, 153/20 WL], Dale guest 9.40 [2/- WL], Halifax T. guest 4.44 [3/- WL], Ashton U. 2.48
Honours: Shropshire Senior Cup winners 1933

In his younger days a top class goalscorer - he netted 115 goals in 2 seasons with non-league Shrewsbury – Joe progressed to playing anywhere on the left of the forward or half back lines with his league clubs. He scored six times in the last six peacetime games for Oldham and played for the Latics throughout the war, retiring in 1946 to become a licensee. His two games as a guest for Dale were in the unaccustomed position of centre half. He had originally been a sheet iron roller and enjoyed golf, bowls, swimming, sprinting and dog fancying.

Reginald Charles (Reg) Mountford 1940-41

Born: Darlington 16.7.08
5'9" 11st
Right back
WL Apps/Gls 4/0
Career: Darlington GS, Darlington GSOB, Cockfield 1928, Darlington am 8.28, pro 1.29 [12/3], Huddersfield T. 5.29 to 1943 [236/7, 39/4 WL], Dale guest 9.40 [4/- WL], Norwich C. guest 1941-42 [1/- WL], Chelsea guest 9.42 to 1944 [25/- WL], Crystal Palace guest 10.43 to 1945 [61/2 WL], Brentford guest 1.45 [1/- WL], Southampton guest 1945-46 [1/- WL], Boldklubben Frem (Denmark) manager 5.46, Danish national coach, Bristol C. coach to 1953
Honours: FA Cup final 1938, War League North East winners 1940, England v Scotland 1941, RAF v Glasgow Rangers 1941, v Army in Scotland 1941-42

Starting out with Darlington – for whom he scored a hat-trick against Rochdale when tried at centre forward – Reg was a stalwart defender for Huddersfield in the decade up to World War II, though he only became an automatic choice, usually at left back, in the late thirties. A "sturdy back, who kicks cleanly and accurately", he played in about half their games when they finished runners up to Arsenal in Division 1 in 1934 and appeared in the 1938 Cup Final. Yet another ex-miner, he also played for the Terriers in the first part of the war, as well as turning out for Dale a few times, while serving as an ARP Warden. He subsequently moved to London, becoming a regular performer for Chelsea and Crystal Palace, also figuring in representative games, including an England – Scotland match, and coaching schools teams. After the war he coached the Danish national side, who beat Great Britain for the bronze medal in the 1948 Olympics. Reg's father had been prominent in the football, cricket and rugby clubs in Darlington.

Harry Ross Sutherland 1940-41
Born: Salford 30.7.15
Outside right
WL Apps/Goals 1/0
Career: Sedgeley Park, Mossley 1937-38, Leeds U. 7.38 [3/1, 5/1 WL], Accrington St. guest 12.39 [2/1 WL], Dale guest 10.40 [1/- WL], Doncaster R. guest 9.42 [5/3 WL], York C. guest 10.44 [2/1 WL], Exeter C. 5.47 [14/3], Bournemouth & B.A. 7.48 to 5.49, Hakoah (Australia) to 1955, Altona City (Melbourne) coach
Honours: Dockerty Cup winners 1955

Harry made a goal-scoring FL debut at centre forward for Leeds in the last pre-war season, but was able to make only a handful of appearances for them and as a guest player during hostilities. His one Dale game was on the right wing as former England international George Hunt was in the centre. He managed a few more league games after moving to Exeter in 1947 but didn't make the first team at Bournemouth and later emigrated to Australia, helping Hakoah to win a Victoria state cup when he was 40.

Vincent (Vince) Kershaw 1940-41
Born: {Rochdale?}
Outside right
WL Apps/Gls 5/1
Career: Dale 10.40 [5/1]

Vince scored on his Dale debut on the right wing at Southport in October 1940 and played a few further games, sharing the position with Syd Rawlings and Percy Taylor, over the next three months.

Thomas (Tom) Jones 1940-41, 1942-45
Born: Little Hulton AMJ.16
6'0" 12st2
Centre half
WL Apps/Gls 59/1
Career: Little Hulton, Accrington St. am 5.5.37, pro 25.8.37 [10/1], Oldham A. 14.1.39 [1/-, 8/- WL], Blackburn R. guest 2.40 [3/- WL], Accrington St. guest 12.39 and 1941-42 [9/1 WL], Dale guest 11.40 and 1942-45 [59/1 WL]

"Tall and fast with nice constructive ideas", Tom had just begun his FL career when war broke out. He alternated periods playing with Oldham, Accrington and Dale, but in 1945 tragically lost both feet when wounded just before the end of the war in Europe. His three former clubs got together to play benefit games for him the following season. His elder brother Bill also played for Accrington.

Alfred (Alf) Bellis 1940-42

Born Ellesmere Port 8.10.20
5'6" 9st
Outside left
WL Apps/Gls 9/2
Career: Ellesmere Port School, Shell Juniors, Burnell's Ironworks, West Bromwich A. trial 1.38, Port Vale 3.38 [82/18, 57/28 WL], Dale guest 11.40 [9/2 WL], Manchester U. guest 8.40 and 10.42 to 5.45 [52/18 WL], Manchester C. guest 4.43 [1/- WL], Lincoln C. guest 2.44 [4/1 WL], Notts Co. guest 1.45 [1/- WL], Ellesmere Port T. 1945 (loan), Bury 10.1.48 (exchange for W. Keeley) [95/18], Swansea T. 8.51 [41/11], Chesterfield 7.53 [13/3], Rhyl Ath. cs.54, Colwyn Bay U., Penmaenmawr

Alf joined Port Vale from his works side when he was 17, scoring on his debut, against the Dale, in April 1938, and played regularly for Vale before, during and after World War II. A frequent scorer from the wing for Vale, he was a wartime guest for a number of sides in the North West, including Rochdale (who scored 20 goals in his first four games for them), and in 1948 he signed for Bury, continuing as a FL player for another six seasons. One of the longest surviving pre-war players, he lived to be 92.

Errington Ridley Liddell ('Ike') Keen
1940-41

Born: Walker-on-Tyne 4.9.10
5'8" 10st6
Left half
WL Apps/Goals 19/0
Career: Newcastle U. jnr 1925, Nuns Moor, Meldon Villa, Newcastle U. Swifts, Newcastle U. 9.27 [1/-], Derby Co. 9.30 [219/4], Chelmsford C. 5.38, Hereford player-manager 7.39, Brighton & H.A. guest 4.40 [1/- WL], Notts Co. guest 8.40 and 1943-44 [4/- WL], Dale guest 11.40 [19/- WL], Everton guest 10.41 [26/- WL], Fulham guest 1941-42 [2/- WL], Millwall guest 1.42 [9/- WL], Liverpool guest 8.42 [17/- WL], Charlton A. guest 1943-44 [3/- WL], Lincoln C. guest 11.43 to 1945-46 [5/- WL], Leeds U. 12.45, Bacup Borough 7.46, Hong Kong coach, IFK Norrkoping (Sweden) coach 1949-50, Basiktas (Turkey) coach.
Honours England 4 caps 1933 to 1937, Football League v Scottish League 1937, England v The Rest 1933, (War League North Second Championship winners 1943)

The splendidly named Keen was usually known as Ike, though he was also nicknamed Eric and 'Snowy'. Coming through the junior ranks at Newcastle he made his debut in October 1930 but was almost immediately allowed to join Derby where he accumulated well over 200 appearances over the next eight years. Noted for being quick in the tackle, he won four England caps while with Derby but perhaps surprisingly dropped into non-league football just a year after his final cap when he was still only 27 and became Hereford player-manager a year later. He guested for a number of league sides during the war, being one of Dale's more regular performers in 1940-41. After the war he was with Bacup Borough before heading for Hong Kong as a coach. He was the nephew of James Keen, a league pro with several clubs including Newcastle in the early '20s. Ike worked in the tea trade even while playing in the first division.

Michael (Micky) Fenton 1940-41

Born Stockton 30.10.13
5'9" 11st
Centre forward
WL Apps/Gls 1/0
Career: South Bank Princess St. Juniors, Potrack Shamrocks, South Bank East End, Wolverhampton W. trial, Middlesbrough am 2.33, pro 3.33, player-coach 1.49 to cs.51 [240/147; 55/67 WL], Notts Co. guest 8.40 [2/1 WL], Dale guest 11.40 [1/- WL], (RAF), Blackpool guest 1.45 to 1945-46 [21/18 WL], Port Vale guest 1944-45 [1/- WL], Wolverhampton W. guest 3.45 [2/3 WL], Middlesbrough coach cs. 51 to cs.66
Honours: Stockton Schools, England v Scotland 1938, FA tour to South Africa 1939 (3 tests) British Empire Army XI v Scottish FA 1940, RAF v British Army, Civil Defence 1941, Inter Allied Services Cup final, British Empire Services XI v Scottish FA, FA Services XI v Switzerland 1945, England wartime international v Wales 1945

Another England international in the wartime Dale line-up – he played alongside Jim Cunliffe and Ike Keen in a 1-0 win at Burnley – Micky was a tremendous servant for Middlesbrough over a period of 33 years. Though losing seven years to the war, when he served with the RAF in North Africa, he still made 240 FL appearances for them, turning out until he was 37, and would have scored 150 goals if those in August 1939 had not been expunged from the record. In 1938-39 he netted 34 goals as Boro finished 4th in the first division and his wartime strike record was even better, at more than a goal a game. Exceptionally quick and hard to knock off the ball, his single England cap came against Scotland in 1938, though he also played against South Africa in three 'tests', netting a hat-trick in one of them, and in various wartime representative games. After retiring he served the Boro for another 15 years as coach.

Dennis Isherwood 1940-41
Born: Northwich 9.1.24
Inside right
WL Apps/Gls 1/0
Career: Crewe A. [4/1 WL], Dale guest 12.40 [1/- WL], Wolverhampton W. 1943-44 guest [2/- WL], Port Vale guest 1944-45 [1/1 WL], Wrexham 8.44 [17/6 WL], Chester 4.46 [1/- WL, 3/-], Northwich Victoria 1947, Wellington T., Winsford U., Macclesfield, Runcorn, Congleton T., Stafford Rangers, Sandbach Ramblers manager

Although on Crewe's books, his first wartime league game was for Dale in a 3-0 defeat by Bury, just before his 17th birthday. Dennis did subsequently appear for the Alex, and other clubs, either at inside or outside right and later made three peacetime FL appearances for Chester before a tour of senior non-league football in and around Cheshire.

John James (Jack) Robinson   1940-41
Born: Oswaldwistle 23.4.18   5'10"   11st7
Right half
WL Apps/Gls 1/0
Career: Sacred Heart, Accrington St. am 7.3.35, pro 17.5.35 [16], Manchester C. 17.4.37 (£1350 for two players) [2, 60 WL], Accrington St. guest 10.39 [7 WL], Blackburn R. guest 11.39 and 12.40 [9 WL], Liverpool guest 11.40 and 3.41 [2 WL], Dale guest 1.41 [1/- WL], Bolton W. guest 3.42 [1 WL], Raith Rovers guest 10.42, Manchester U. guest 5.43 [1 WL], Doncaster R. guest 8.43 to 1945-46 [60 WL], Bury 26.11.46 [12], Southend U. 7.8.47 to 4.48 [6]

Actually City's reserve goalkeeper, he turned out for Dale at right half against his own team when Dale turned up at Maine Road several players short in January 1941, City beating the scratch side 9-1. Jack was on the books of league clubs for 13 years, but was never a regular for any of them after a promising start with Stanley and lost the middle years of his career to the war, though he did play quite frequently for City and later Doncaster in the regional leagues. He retired soon after the war due to a shoulder injury.

B. Rothwell   1940-41
Centre half
WL Apps/Gls 1/0
Career: Dale 1.41 [1/- WL]

Rothwell was a local footballer, picked up on the ground when Dale were short handed at Manchester City in the Lancashire Cup in the first game of 1941. He played centre half and City's centre forward Jack Currier helped himself to five goals in a 9-1 win. However, it clearly wasn't all Rothwell's fault as Currier scored another five in the return leg the following week when regular centre half Tom Jones was playing.

Percy Taylor   1940-45
Outside right
WL Apps/Gls 40/9
Career: Dale 1.41 [40/9 WL]

Percy also made his debut in the 1-9 debacle at Manchester City, but subsequently became a regular on the right wing for Dale and reappeared at intervals throughout the war.

James Harrison   1937-38, 1940-41, 1943-45
Born: Little Hulton 24.5.13
Outside left/centre forward
WL Apps/Gls 22/5
Career: Border Regiment, Hibernian 11.36 [20/5 ScL], Dale trial 1937-38, Cardiff C. 3.38 [1/-], Chorley 5.38, Dale guest 1.41 and 1943-45 [22/5 WL], Stockport Co. guest 2.43 [4/- WL], Chorley 1945

A fairly regular performer in the top flight in Scotland in 1936-37, he made a solitary FL appearance during two months at Cardiff following an unsuccessful trial at Spotland and then joined non-league Chorley. Despite making his wartime debut for Dale in the 9-1 cup defeat by Manchester City in 1941, he had considerably better luck when he reappeared, mostly on the left wing, three years later, as he scored four times in six games and Dale won the first three games of this stint 4-1, 5-0 and 5-0.

Harry Seddon   1940-41, 1944-45
Born: {Stockport OND.20?}
Outside left
WL Apps/Gls 8/1
Career: Stockport Co. c 1939 and 1942 to 1944 [12/1 WL], Accrington St. guest 1939-40 and 1944-45 [5/1 WL], Dale 1.41 and guest 3.45 [8/1 WL], Preston NE 1944 [7/2 WL]

Another player whose Dale debut was in the 1-9 defeat by City, Harry interspersed further appearances for Rochdale with games for his other clubs Stockport and Preston, playing at full back and wing half as well as inside forward or on the wing.

John Charles (Jack) Johnson   1940-41
Born South Kirkby 3.10.05   5'9"   11st12
Right back
WL Apps/Gls 1/0
Career: South Kirkby Colliery, Denaby U. 5.26, Sheffield W. 30.4.27, Bournemouth 1.6.28 [11/7], Portsmouth 8.30, Rotherham U. 7.11.30 [90/3], Barnsley 6.9.33 [9/-], Carlisle U 9.6.34 [139/2], Accrington St. 9.6.38 to 1945 [39/-, 32/2 WL], Dale guest 1.41 [1/- WL]
Honours: Division 3(N) champions 1934, Division 3(N) Cup final 1939

A highly experienced Third North defender, playing mainly as a centre half, Jack had accumulated most of his FL appearances in three seasons at Rotherham and four at Carlisle, while he was also a near everpresent for Stanley in the last pre-war campaign. He had played a few games for Barnsley the year they won the Third North championship, but the following year his new club Carlisle finished bottom of the FL (he was the only professional retained at the end of the season), as did Accrington in 1939. His one game for Dale was at right back in the second leg of the Lancashire Cup tie which Manchester City won 6-1 at Spotland.

John Wood 1940-42
Centre forward/left back
WL Apps/Gls 5/1
Career: Charlton A., Dale 15.1.41 [5/1 WL]

Previously on Charlton Athletic's books, John netted Dale's goal on his debut in the Manchester City cup tie. Reported to have played at left back in a couple of games, he may actually have played in the front line, with Duff reverting to the defence.

Maurice Reeday 1940-41

Born: Darwen 28.8.09
5'9" 11st7
Left back
WL Apps/Gls 1/0
Career: Clitheroe 8.30, Wigan B. 7.31, Bacup Borough 8.31, Darwen, Blackpool 9.5.34, Accrington St. 6.5.36 [22/-], Leicester C. 11.3.37 £1200 [74/2, 4/- WL], Accrington St. guest 10.39 [21/- WL], Howard & Bulloughs guest, Dale guest 1.41 [1/- WL], Blackburn R. guest 9.40 to 9.41 [8/- WL], Burnley guest 11.43 [3/- WL], Accrington St. guest 9.44 [28/- WL], Nelson 9.46. Darwen player coach 10.47

Considered a full back of a class well above third division level when at Accrington, he earned them a sizeable fee when he moved to Leicester after less than a season in the FL. He played regularly in Division 1 for the last two pre-war seasons, being noted as "the man Stanley Matthews couldn't beat", though Leicester were relegated in 1939. Most of his wartime games were back at Accrington and he guested just the once for Dale, in a 5-0 win against Crewe. He became player-coach of his hometown side Darwen after the war.

Leslie Appleby (Les) Turner 1940-41
Born: Essington, Doncaster 25.11.09 5'10" 11st10
Centre half
WL Apps/Gls 4/0
Career: Warmsworth, Denaby U. am 8.28, Connisborough Welfare, Doncaster R. trial, Huddersfield T. 2.9.30, Crewe A. 11.7.32 [112/2], Doncaster R. 18.5.35 [13/-], New Brighton 16.7.38 [38/1], Dale guest 3.41 [4/- WL]

A regular during three seasons at Crewe – indeed he was an everpresent at left half in his debut season in the FL - Les had less opportunities with Doncaster in Division Two before a season at New Brighton when he was their most consistent performer. He made a few regional league appearances for Dale in 1941, one of them in the embarrassing 11-0 defeat at Huddersfield.

Walter Horrabin 1940-43
Born: {Leigh OND.19}
Centre forward
WL Apps/Gls 20/10
Career: Dale 3.41 [20/10 WL]

Making a remarkable start to his career, Walter scored four times on his Dale debut in a 5-2 victory at Crewe in March 1941. Unsurprisingly retained in the side, he netted eight times in nine games by the end of the season and made scattered appearances over the next two years.

A. Hughes 1940-41
Inside left
WL Apps/Gls 1/0
Career: Dale guest 3.41 [1/- WL]

Hughes guested just once for Dale, playing at inside left in the 5-2 win at Crewe.

Kenneth Heyes 1940-41
Goalkeeper
WL Apps 1
Career: {Bolton W., Hurst 1937-38?}, Dale 3.41 [1 WL]

Kenneth had the misfortune to play in goal in Dale's record 11-0 defeat by Huddersfield in March 1941, the only change to a defence that had conceded only one the week before.

Norman Kirkman 1940-42, 1946-48

Born: Bolton 6.6.20
5'11" 12st
Left back
FL Apps/Gls 53/0
Total Apps/Gls 66/0
Career: Folds Road School, Burnley am 1937, pro 9.39 [39/- WL], (RAF), Dale guest 1940-42 [6/- WL], Fulham guest 1942-43 [1/- WL], Brighton & HA guest 1942-43 [1/- WL],

24

Manchester U. guest 1.43 [1/- WL], Dale 10.46 [53/-], Chesterfield 12.47 £4000 [40/-], Leicester C. 8.49 £8500 [12/-], Southampton 7.50 [20/-], Exeter C. player-manager 3.52 [11/1], Bradford PA manager 3.53 to 1.55. Northwich Victoria manager 1965, Southampton scout, Newcastle U. scout
Honours: Lancashire Junior Cup winners 1947

Norman first appeared for Dale as a guest from Burnley in 1940. Though also playing for the Clarets during the war, when he served as a navigator in the RAF, he never appeared in their FL side and signed for Dale a couple of months into the first post-war season. He was everpresent throughout his stay (though somehow also qualifying to play for the Reserves in their Lancashire Junior Cup Final victory), before a big money transfer to Chesterfield. In 1949 he was the subject of an ever larger deal when he moved to Leicester for £8500 (one third of the then British record), but played only a small number of games before joining Southampton. In 1952 he became player-manager of Exeter when still only 31 and he subsequently managed Bradford for a couple of years.

Leslie (Les) Horton   1940-43, 1949-50

Born: Salford 12.7.21
5'8"   11st4
Inside right
WL Apps/Gls 15/0
Career: Tyldesley U., Dale 4.4.41 [15/- WL], Oldham A. 27.1.43 [57/7 WL, 79/2], Hartlepools U. guest 8.44 [12/8 WL], Carlisle U. 18.8.48 [66/-], Dale 3.4.50, York C. 3.7.50 [21/-], Halifax T. 17.3.51 [35/1], Ashton U. player-manager 8.52, Altrincham 1954, Chloride Recs manager 1955
Honours: Lancashire Schoolboys

Considered one of Oldham's best players of the immediate post-war period, being everpresent in the transitional 1945-46 season and then making 75 consecutive FL appearances up to March 1948, Les had spent two years on Dale's books during the war, generally playing at inside right. He became a wing half at Oldham but also figured at full back during his FL career and could turn his hand to most positions. He had a brief trial back at Spotland after leaving Carlisle, without making any senior appearances (though he did appear in Eric Wood's benefit game), and became player manager at Ashton United when he was still only 31.

Francis (Frank) Walkden   1940-41, 1946-47
Born: Aberdeen 21.6.21   5'10"   11st6
Outside left
FL Apps/Gls 1/0   Total Apps/Gls 2/0
Career: Bolton W. am, Dale guest 4.41 [1/- WL], Dale 11.46 to 4.47 [1/-]

Then a 19 year old Bolton amateur, Frank guested for Dale against Oldham in 1941, and after the war he spent a few months on the books at Spotland. His one and only FL game saw him deputise at outside left for Arthur Cunliffe in a goalless draw against Southport in December 1946.

George Henry Farrow   1940-41

Born: Whitburn 4.10.13
5'10"   12st13
Centre half
WL Apps/Gls 1/0
Career: Whitburn St Mary's, Whitburn, Aldershot trial c.8.28, Stockport Co. 10.30 [6/-], Wolverhampton W. 1.32 [11/-], Bournemouth & Boscombe A. 7.33 [107/12], Blackpool 6.36 [143/15, 155/38 WL], Manchester U. guest 9.40 [3/1 WL], Blackburn R. guest 3.41 [2/- WL], Dale guest 4.41 [1/- WL], Liverpool guest 6.41 [1/- WL], Sheffield U. 1.48 [1/-], Bacup Borough 7.48
Honours: Division 2 promotion 1937, League North winners 1942, 1943, 1944, League North Cup winners 1943, War Cup winners 1943, Lancashire Senior Cup winners 1937, 1942

Starting out at Stockport as a 17 year old, George made over a century of appearances in the Southern Section with Bournemouth before moving to Blackpool in 1936. Their regular right half for much of the next 12 seasons, he made around 150 senior appearances either side of the war and a similar number in the wartime leagues when the Tangerines were the country's outstanding team, winning a string of trophies. By contrast he played just once as a guest for Dale and once for his final league club Sheffield United. The possessor of a fierce shot, he was also a regular penalty taker and scored 13 times from half back in 1944-45. He was described by Blackpool teammate Stanley Matthews as "one of the greatest players who never played for England".

Clarke 1940-41
Right half
WL Apps/Gls 1/0
Career: Dale 4.41 [1/- WL]

Clarke was reported to have played right half for Dale in a three-all draw away to Bradford City in April 1941. However, he is not included in the team registered with the FL which included Jimmy Eastwood, as in the previous game.

John (Jackie) Chew 1940-41

Born: Blackburn 13.5.20
Inside left
WL Apps/Gls 1/0
Career: Blackburn R. am 1939 [23/3 WL], (RAF), Dale guest 5.41 [1/- WL], Burnley 5.45 [25/3 WL, 225/39], Leeds U. guest 1945-46 [6/1 WL], Bradford C. 6.54 [36/4], Darwen 1955 Cricket for East Lancashire 1939 to 1946, Rishton 1948 to 1971
Honours: FA Cup final 1947, Division 2 promotion 1947

Normally a winger, Jackie (probably) played once for Dale at inside left in a 5-0 defeat at Oldham in their last match of the 1940-41 season, after Blackburn had completed their fixtures. Later figuring over 250 times for Burnley, in 1947 he was a member of the Clarets side which won promotion to the first division and also reached the FA Cup Final, going down 1-0 to Charlton. He was noted for his pace and delivery of accurate crosses (and for his bandy legs which earned him the nickname 'Cowboy' from the Turf Moor fans) and had a decent scoring record from the wing. A more than useful cricketer, he played in the Lancashire League with East Lancashire and then Rishton, concentrating on this after his football career and helping them to the title in 1955 and the Worsley Cup in 1964 (scoring a half-century against an attack including West Indian paceman Charlie Griffiths). He played his last game when he was 51, when Rishton's 'pro' was former Lancashire and England bowler Ken Higgs, himself a former footballer. Jackie's son David often played alongside him for Rishton. [N.B. His Dale appearance wasn't registered with the FL, whose records have a rather different team to that reported in the press.]

William Charles (Bill) Gorman 1941-42

Born: Sligo 13.7.11
5'8" 10st4
Right back
WL Apps/Gls 8/0
Career: Dalmuir U., St. Anthony's, Clydebank St. James Parish Church, Shettleston Juniors 6.34, Bury 9.34 [52/-], Brentford £6000 12.38 to 1950 [128/-, 83/1 WL], Bury guest 12.40 and 1944-45 [43/- WL], Manchester U. guest 5.41 [2/- WL], Dale guest 8.41 [8/- WL], Bolton W. guest 9.42 to 5.44 [62/1 WL], Liverpool guest 3.44 [1/- WL], Halifax T. guest 3.45 [1/- WL], Deal T. player-manager 9.50 to 1.55, Bury scout, Manchester C. scout
Honours: Irish Free State 13 caps, N. Ireland 4 caps, Lancashire Senior Cup final 1944. As manager: Kent League champions 1954

Bill (also known sometimes as Willie) had the distinction of being an international for two countries, representing both Northern Ireland and the Republic – indeed he did so against England in the space of three days in September 1946! An engineer in Scotland, where he was brought up, he started out in the FL with Bury, and played for them again during the war. Most of his senior games, though, came during a 12 year association with Brentford, initially in Division 1, as a solid right back, Bill playing in the FL until he was 38. His brief spell at Spotland came at the start of the 1941-42 campaign, and he also guested with Bolton, among others, appearing for them in the second leg of the 1944 Lancashire Cup final against Liverpool. Totally bald by the age of 19, fans referred to him as 'Old Naked Brains'!

James Leslie (Jim) Treanor 1941-45
Born: Heap, Bury 11.10.13 6' 1" 11st7
Half back
WL Apps/Gls 44/1
Career: Bury GS, Winsford U. 10.31, Bury 16.8.33 [11/-], Accrington St. 20.9.35 [40/-], Hull C. 26.9.36 £500 to 5.39 [44/1], (army), Dale 8.41 to 2.45 [44/1 WL], Darlington guest 1943-44 [1/- WL], Chorley 9.45
Honours: Northern Command v Combined Universities 3.45

Jim had played over 100 FL games before the war, though he was really only an automatic choice during his one season at Accrington, where he was said to cover a tremendous amount of ground. Unusually tall for his day, at a shade over six feet, he used his height to great advantage. He worked for a cotton firm in Manchester before joining up as a sergeant wireless operator in the Royal Armoured Corps and figured quite regularly for

Dale during hostilities, especially during the 1941-42 season when he missed only one match and played in all the half back positions. He also figured in representative games in army football.

Andrew Davenport 1941-42
Centre half
WL Apps/Gls 5/0
Career: Dale 8.41 [5/- WL]

Andrew played the first five games of the 1941-42 season for Rochdale, only the opening game ending in a Dale victory.

Richard (Dick) Webster 1941-42

Born: Accrington 6.8.19
5'9" 11st8
Left half
WL Apps/Gls 7/1
Career: Baxenden Rovers Woodnook Amateurs, Accrington St. am 6.5.37, pro 18.11.37 [41/-], Sheffield U. 14.1.39 £1000 [5/- WL], Accrington St. guest 10.39 to 1941-42 [22/1 WL], Blackburn R. guest 9.40 and 9.43 [3/- WL], Dale guest 8.41 [7/1 WL], Burnley guest 10.42 to 1944-45 [81/2 WL], Accrington St. 8.45 £800 to 7.51 [39/- WL, 186/3]
Honours: Accrington Schoolboys, Division 3 North West first championship winners 1945-46

An Accrington lad, he signed pro for Stanley when he was 18 and was transferred to Sheffield United just over a year later for a reasonable fee. United won promotion to Division One that term but Dick never made their FL side. A plumber by trade, during the war he played for Stanley again in the various leagues they joined before a lengthy stint guesting for Burnley. In between he figured at left half in a number of games for Dale. Rejoining Stanley in 1945 for their record fee, he played in their Third North West championship winning side in the transitional season and made well over 200 senior appearances, by now mostly at full back, before retiring through injury. Stanley played a benefit game for him in March 1954

Thomas Anderson (Tom) Swinburne 1941-42
Born: East Rainton 9.8.15
5'9" 12st4
Goalkeeper
WL Apps 5
Career: East Rainton School, East Rainton Juniors, Hull C. trial, Herrington Colliery Welfare 12.32, Newcastle U. am 1.34, pro 4.34 [80, 42 WL], Grimsby T. guest 1940-41 [1 WL], Notts Co. guest 11.40 [1 WL], Dale guest 9.41 [5 WL], Bolton W. guest 12.41 [4 WL], Southport guest 1941-42 [3 WL], Consett 6.47
Honours: Wartime England international 1940

Tom was signed from his colliery team by Newcastle in 1934, making his Division One bow just after his 19th birthday. Quite a regular performer in the last two peacetime seasons – Newcastle only just avoiding the drop into the Third North in 1938 - his greatest honour was to represent England in a wartime international game on his home ground. He guested for several sides during the war including Dale. He had two sons who were also FL goalkeepers, Alan who figured for Oldham and 1970s Carlisle stalwart Trevor.

Alexander McLean (Alec) Davies 1941-42
Born: Dundonald 21.5.20
Centre forward
WL Apps/Gls 1/0
Career: Sheffield W. c.1939, pro 4.45 [1/- WL], Dale guest 9.41 [1/- WL], Chesterfield guest 1943-44 [1/1 WL], Lincoln C. 7.45 to 1949 [25/5 WL, 37/9]

Previously on Sheffield Wednesday's books, Alec guested for Dale in a 1-1 draw with Burnley in 1941. He signed pro back at Hillsborough at the end of the war but never played for them and soon moved on to Lincoln, playing in both the transitional 1945-46 campaign and in the FL proper. He later emigrated to New Zealand

Jack Smith 1941-42
Goalkeeper
WL Apps 1
Career: Dale am 26.8.41 [1 WL]

Jack kept goal for Dale in the 4-2 defeat at Halifax in September 1941, when the more regular 'keepers Swinburne and Hall were unavailable, just a few weeks after signing amateur forms.

S{amuel} Hanna 1941-42
Outside right
WL Apps/Gls 1/0
Career: Halifax T. 1940-42 [13/1 WL], Dale guest 9.41 [1/- WL]

When Dale turned up at Halifax a man short in September 1941, Hanna was loaned to the visitors for the afternoon, figuring on the right wing. He also played 10 times for his own club that season, alternating between inside left or centre forward and right back.

William Frederick (Bill) Whittaker   1941-42
Born: Northampton 18.4.11
Centre half
WL Apps/ Gls 2/0
Career: Nunhead, Kingstonian, Blackpool am 31.12.40 to 1942 [36/2 WL], Dale guest 10.41 [2/- WL], Liverpool guest 10.41 [9/- WL], Brentford guest 1942-43, Chelsea guest 1942-43 [4/- WL], Brentford am 31.8.43 [67/- WL], Fulham guest 1943-44 and 1944-45 [3/- WL], Burnley guest 1944-45 [4/- WL], Kingstonian c.1946
Honours: England Amateur international v Wales 1939, League North first champions 1941-42, Islington Corinthians (touring amateur select side), London Senior Cup final 1948

A pre-war amateur international, centre half Bill was quite a regular performer for Blackpool for two wartime seasons. He guested for Dale a couple of times in October 1941 but then returned to London, figuring primarily with Brentford. Bill's only official peacetime senior games were for the Bees in the 1945-46 FA Cup. His father Fred had been with Burnley in the 1900s and later served Northampton, Exeter (being a member of their famous tour side to Brazil in 1914) and Millwall, while his brother Geoff was also with Kingstonian but was better known as a county cricketer with Surrey either side of the war.

Frank Wright   1941-42
Centre forward
Apps/Gls 3/1
Career: Crystal Palace, Dale guest 10.41 [3/1 WL], Stockport Co. guest 12.42 [7/2 WL]

Frank, from Crystal Palace, made three guest appearances for Dale in October 1941, the first a 2-2 draw against Halifax in which he scored, but the other two against Preston having an aggregate score of 11-1.

David Jones   1941-42
Inside/centre forward
WL Apps/Gls 9/7
Career: Dale 10.41 [9/7 WL]

David had a successful, if brief, spell in the Dale side, scoring in each of his first three games and adding four more near the end of the 1941-42 season.

Leslie Mervyn (Les) Boulter   1941-42

Born: Ebbw Vale 31.8.13
5'9" 11st5
Inside left
WL Apps/Gls 1/0
Career: Cwmbetterment FC, Ebbw Vale Ex-Schoolboys, Cwm Athletic, Arsenal am 3.30, Charlton A. am 6.32, pro 9.32 [167/28], Brentford 1.39 £6000 [19/2, 26/12 WL], Cardiff C. guest 1939-40 [2/2 WL], Manchester C. guest 12.40 [1/- WL], Blackpool guest 3.41 [4/2 WL], Dale guest 10.41 [1/- WL], Bolton W. guest 2.42 [1/- WL], Fulham guest 12.44 [6/- WL], Yeovil T. 6.47, Pwllheli player manager 1948 to 1950, Charlton A. 'A' team manager 1959
Honours: Wales Schools v England, Scotland, Wales v N. Ireland 1939, Division Three South champions 1935, Division 2 promoted 1936

A former pit-boy in the Welsh Valleys, Les was a stylish player who "invariably masterminded his side's attacks". With Charlton he rose from the Third South to the first division in two years, the Addicks then finishing as runners up in the top flight. He was sold to Brentford, also then in Division 1, for a large fee in 1939 (the British record was still only £13,000 at the time), but surprisingly played only once for Wales, scoring against Ireland just after moving to Griffin Park. Despite serving in Canada with the RAF during the war, he guested for a number of sides including Rochdale. He was later player-manager of Pwllheli and then ran a grocery business in the town.

Ernest William (Ernie) Toser   1941-42
Born: Old Ford, Bow 30.11.13
Left half
WL Apps/Gls 1/0
Career: Smeed Road Junior School, Bow Central School, Eton Manor, Luton T. am 2.31, Dulwich Hamlet am 4.31, Southampton am 6.31, Dulwich Hamlet, Millwall 5.37 [2/-, 27/- WL], Clapton O. guest 1939-40 [1/- WL], Dale guest 10.41 [1/- WL], Bradford C. guest 11.41 [2/- WL], Aldershot guest 1944-45 [1/- WL], Fulham guest 10.44 [1/- WL], Notts Co. 9.46 [2/-], Bognor Regis T. 12.47, Dulwich Hamlet trainer 1948
Honours: England Schools

Having started out with amateurs Dulwich Hamlet, Ernie had managed just two FL games before war broke out, but was a regular for Millwall in the 1939-40 season. Thereafter he played just a handful of senior games, one of them for Dale in October 1941, unfortunately a 6-0 loss at Preston.

James Colin (Jimmy) Horton 1941-42
Born: Rotherham 2.11.09 5'10" 11st1
Right back
WL Apps/Gls 8/0
Career: Billsthorpe, Newark T. 8.32, Bradford C. 7.33 [3/-], Huddersfield T. trial, Boston U. 7.36, Manchester C. trial 9.36, Boston U., Aldershot 5.38 [3/-, 108/- WL], Dale guest 11.41 [8/- WL], Southport guest 1941-44 [6/- WL], Blackpool guest 11.42 [2/- WL], Burnley guest 1942-43 [1/- WL], Fulham guest 3.44 [1/- WL], Ebbw Vale 5.47

Jimmy made his FL debut when Bradford City beat Manchester United in their last game of 1934 but only managed six league appearances before war broke out, the latter three in April 1939. However, he was a regular with Aldershot during the war, despite the Shots' call on numerous international stars like Stan Cullis and Joe Mercer serving at the nearby army camp, though he became the first Aldershot player ever sent off during 1944-45. He also guested for other sides including the Dale. Aged 37 when peacetime football resumed, he dropped down to the non-league game.

Thomas Edward (Tom) Dooley 1941-44
Born: Accrington 15.12.14 5'9" 11st
Right half
WL Apps/Gls 21/1
Career: Baxendale Rovers, Bacup Borough am 8.33, Blackpool 11.10.34, Bacup Borough 8.37, Accrington St. 9.6.38 to 1946 [28/2, 24/4 WL], New Brighton guest 3.41 [1/- WL], Dale guest 11.41 et seq. [21/1 WL]
Honours: Accrington Schoolboys, Division 3(N) Cup final 1939

Although earlier on Blackpool's books, Tom only made his FL debut in the final pre-war season, playing regularly for Accrington at either wing half or inside forward. He made a number of wartime appearances for Dale, especially during 1941-42 but was subsequently posted to India.

Verdun Aubrey Jones 1941-43
Born: Edmonton 22.6.16 5'9" 11st7
Inside/centre forward
WL Apps/Gls 15/5
Career: Priory Albion (Hornsey), Aston Villa am 6.36, pro 9.36, Derby Co. 11.37 [2/-], Dale guest 11.41 [15/5 WL], Birmingham guest 10.43 [1/- WL], Southend U. 5.48

Managing just two pre-war league games with Derby, he guested with Dale quite frequently in 1941-42, along with (confusingly) several other players named Jones, and netted in each of his first three games, all of which ended in Dale victories. [N.B. 2 appearances are alternatively assigned to J. Jones.]

Fred Smith 1941-42
Outside left
WL Apps/Gls 11/1
Career: Dale 11.41 [11/1 WL]

Fred appeared quite regularly on the left wing for Dale from November 1941 to February 1942. Though Rochdale were unbeaten in his first seven games, unfortunately his last two games ended in 5-0 defeats.

Ronald (Ron) Wood 1941-42
Inside left
WL Apps/Gls 2/0
Career: Dale 11.41 [2/- WL]

Ron played twice at inside left for Dale, away to Bury and Bolton, his side scoring three times in each game, though he did not get on the scoresheet himself.

Harry Whitworth 1941-42, 1951-53

Born: Radcliffe 1.12.20
5'8" 10st7
Utility player
FL Apps/Gls 70/9
Total Apps/Gls 75/9
Career: Whitfield Juniors, Prestwich Central, Bury am 1937, pro 1941 [14/- WL], (navy), Dale guest 11.41 [1/- WL], Southampton guest 1943-44 [1/- WL], Bury re-signed 11.45 [13/2 WL, 112/14], Dale 7.51 [70/9], Northwich Victoria 17.8.53, Southport 23.9.53 [33/6], Crewe A. 7.54 [14/1], Rossendale U. 1954, Macclesfield T. cs.55 to 1957. Accrington St. reserve team player-trainer 8.59, coach 11.59

Harry progressed into the Bury side during the war, when he served as a Royal Navy petty officer and played some football in Holland. He made his debut in an archetypal wartime game, a 9-3 defeat at Burnley, and was then loaned to Dale for their match at Gigg Lane in November 1941, helping them beat his own club! He had accrued nearly 150 appearances, being everpresent, at right half or on the right wing, and scoring 9 goals in 1948-49, but had suffered with cartilage trouble before moving to Spotland in 1951. His second Dale appearance thus coming almost 10 years after his first, he became the utility man of the side over the next two years, appearing variously at full back, wing half and any forward position, indeed while playing No. 9, he scored a hat-trick in a 6-2 victory over Barrow. He left Rochdale for family reasons, opening a grocer's shop in Southport, and following a month at Northwich Victoria before Dale's demand for a £1000 fee was overruled by the FL, he quickly signed up with Southport. Subsequently appearing with Crewe, after playing non-league football he assisted, and then replaced, Harry Hubbick (q.v.) as Accrington trainer-coach before leaving the game to run a hotel.

Jeffrey (Jeff) Barker   1941-43
Born: Scunthorpe 16.10.15
Right half
WL Apps/Gls 3/0
Career: Brigg T., Sheffield U. pt 10.37, Goole T., Scunthorpe & Lindsey U. 6.35, Aston Villa 11.36 [3/-], Solihull T. guest 11.39, Watford guest 1940-41 [1/- WL], Dale guest 11.41 and 9.42 [3/- WL], Blackpool guest 12.41 [11/- WL], Burnley guest 1942-43 [1/- WL], Dundee U. guest 8.42 [1/- ScWL], Huddersfield T. guest 1942-45, signed 11.45 [86/1 WL, 67/-], Walsall guest 3.45 [1/- WL], Scunthorpe U. 8.48 [73/1], Goole T. 1951, Ashby Institute 1952 to 1956, Scunthorpe U. trainer-coach, junior coach, caretaker manager 11.74, groundsman
Honours: War League North winners 1945

Jeff was with his local club Scunthorpe in the mid-thirties, before a transfer to Aston Villa. After guesting for Dale odd times in the 1941-42 and 1942-43 seasons, he was transferred to Huddersfield at the end of the war, having helped them win the 1945 League North championship. He subsequently assisted Scunthorpe gain election to the league in 1950, making his FL debut for the Iron 15 years after first joining them! Appearing over 150 times in all, he later served them in various off-field capacities, including taking charge of three first team games when they were between managers in 1974. His son John was also a Scunthorpe stalwart for a decade from the mid-sixties.

James (Jimmy) Shields   1941-42
Born: {Glasgow}
Inside left
WL Apps/Gls 3/0
Career: Jordanhill College, St Mungos Academy, Arthurlie 1938, Celtic 15.6.39 to 1947 [3/- ScL], Dumbarton guest 1.40 and 8.40 [25/10 ScWL], (RAF), Dale guest 12.41 [3/- WL], Bolton W. guest 2.42 [1/- WL], Blackpool guest 11.42 [6/1 WL], Burnley guest 3.43 [1/- WL], Raith R. trial 5.47, Dumbarton 6.47 [2/1 ScL]

A forward on Celtic's books, Jimmy appeared three times as a guest for Dale, in successive games in December 1941, his debut coming in front of just 488 fans, Spotland's lowest attendance of the war. He managed three top flight appearances for Celtic after the war and worked as a PE teacher.

John Middleton   1941-42
Born: Mickley 15.4.10
Outside left
WL Apps/Gls 1/0
Career: Mickley School, Mickley, Swansea T. 2.29 [1/-], Mickley, Waterford 1932, Walker Celtic 6.32, Darlington 6.33 [77/22], Blackpool 4.35 [6/3], Norwich C. 6.37 [3/-], South Shields 7.38, Aldershot 1939-40 [1/- WL], Hartlepools U. 3.40 [8/2 WL], Stockport Co. guest 10.40 and 9.41 [4/3 WL], Dale guest 12.41 [1/- WL], Southport 12.41 [1/1 WL]

John spent a decade in and out of the first team at several FL clubs, netting double figures in goals in each of his two seasons at Darlington but totalling only 10 appearances elsewhere. Largely an inside right earlier in his career, he played on the wing in his single appearance for the Dale, and probably did not see much of the ball, as Blackburn Rovers romped to an 8-2 win. (His previous game, for Stockport, had been a 7-1 defeat, though he did get their goal!)

Clifford (Cliff) Pitt   1941-42

Born: Moston, Manchester 26.6.11
5'8"
Goalkeeper
WL Apps 7
Career: Newton Heath Parish Church WM Club, Acme, Bacup Borough 1932, Acme 1933, Southport am 9.1.34 [16], Ferguson Pailin 1934, Manchester C. am 10.34, pro 6.12.34, Manchester NE cs.37, Ashton National 6.38, Macclesfield T. 8.39 to 1940, Ashton National, Hurst 1.41, Manchester NE, Dale 4.42 [7 WL], Hurst/Ashton U. 10.46, Droylsden, Bangor C. 1946-47 to 1949. Oldham A. scout
Honours: Welsh League 1948

Cliff started as a free scoring centre forward before becoming a goalkeeper with engineering works side Acme in the Manchester League and he returned to them after a broken finger ended his time at Bacup after just 6 games. Despite three seasons as a part timer at Maine Road, understudying Frank Swift, his only FL games had come as an amateur with Southport in 1933-34, the run being ended when he was carried off unconscious at New Brighton. Nevertheless he figured for several non-league sides either side of the war, and turned out for Rochdale in 1942. He won representative honours for the Welsh League when he was 37. He was also a keen golfer.

William Harold (Willie) Mangham 1941-42, 1944-45
Born: Bolton 14.3.14
Right back
WL Apps/Gls 3/0
Career: Bolton W. [1/- WL], Accrington St. guest 10.41, Dale guest 1.42 and 8.44 [3/- WL].

All of Willie's games for FL clubs came during the war, three of them for Rochdale. Two were in January 1942 and one in August 1944, Dale conceding seven to Blackpool in the latter.

Samuel Allen Patton 1941-43
Born: 20.4.21
Full back
WL Apps/Gls 3/0
Career: Dale pro 17.2.42 [3/- WL]

Patton appeared three times for Dale, at left back, right half and right back in successive games in February 1942, the last an 8-2 home defeat by Liverpool, and though retained did not play the following term.

Robert Delaney 1941-42
Right half
WL Apps/Gls 1/0
Career: Dale am 17.2.42 [1/- WL], Southport 1942-43, am 3.1.44 [8/- WL]

Delaney appeared once for Dale in a 5-0 defeat at Manchester City in February 1942. He played further wartime games for Southport.

William (Willie) MacFadyen 1941-42

Born: Overtown 23.6.04
5'10" 12st
Inside right/outside left
WL Apps/Gls 2/0
Career: Wishaw YMCA, Motherwell cs.21 [278/249 ScL], Bo'ness loan 6.22, Clyde loan 10.24, Huddersfield T. 12.36 [48/19], Clapton Orient 5.39, Mossley 3.40, (RAF), Blackpool guest 3.41 [3/- WL], Halifax T. guest 10.41 [7/- WL], Nottingham F. guest 11.41 [1/- WL], Dale guest 2.42 [2/- WL], Huddersfield T. guest 1941-42 [1/- WL], Raith R. guest 1942-43 [1/- ScWL], Arbroath assistant trainer 1944, Dundee U. manager 10.45 to 8.54
Honours: Scotland v Austria and Wales 1933, Scottish League 1934, Scottish Division 1 champions 1932, Scottish FA Cup final 1931, 1933, FA Cup final 1938.

Originally a wing half, Willie became one of the great Scottish League goalscorers after switching to centre forward, netting almost 200 goals between 1930 (when he was already 26) and 1935. An amazing Scottish record 53 of them came in 34 games in 1931-32 when Motherwell were Scottish League champions. He also won two Scottish caps and represented the Scottish League (scoring in each of these games), but had less success in cup finals, three times ending on the losing side, with Motherwell and later south of the border with Huddersfield. Though in his late thirties he guested for several sides during the war, including two appearances for the Dale, and subsequently became a long serving manager of Dundee United (winning his first game in charge 7-0, but losing 12-1 to his old club Motherwell in 1954). He also worked as a masseur. His brother Ian was also with Motherwell and played in England with Bury.

William (Bill) Walsh 1941-42

Born: Blackpool AMJ.09
5'9" 11st
Centre forward
WL Apps/Gls 3/0
Career: South Shore Wednesday, Fleetwood, Bolton W. am 24.8.31, pro 9.10.31 Fleetwood 7.32, Oldham A. 15.11.33 £125 [77/48], Heart of Midlothian 11.5.36 £875 [36/26], Millwall 4.10.37 £2500 [42/19, 4/- WL], Oldham A. guest 5.40 and 11.40 [3/1 WL], Southampton guest 1939-40 [1/- WL], York C. guest 12.40 [3/- WL], Dale guest 2.42 [2/- WL], Notts Co. guest 1943-44 [8/3 WL], Blackpool guest 11.44 [4/5 WL], Blackburn R. guest 2.45 [1/- WL]
Honours: Division 3 South champions 1938

A centre forward whose "impulsive rushes unsettled opponents", Bill was the leading scorer in the Third North in 1935-36 with 32 goals for the Latics. He then scored another 22 league goals in one full season in Scotland as well as netting an amazing 8 goals when Hearts beat Kings Park 15-0 in the Scottish Cup. Back in England he won the Third South title with Millwall and then guested for numerous clubs including Dale during the war.

William Ronald (Roy) John 1941-42

Born: Briton Ferry 29.1.11 5'11" 11st10
Goalkeeper
WL Apps 2
Career: Neath Road Council School, Briton Ferry Ath., Swansea T. am 2.27, Cwmtillery U. 1927, Middlesbrough trial 9.27, Cardiff C. trial, Ebbw Vale trial, Newport Co. am, Manchester U. trial 1928, Walsall 5.28 [88/-], Stoke C. 4.32 [71], Preston NE 6.34 £1000, Sheffield U. 12.34 £1250 [28], Manchester U. 6.36 £600 [15], Newport Co. 3.37 £ [10], Swansea T. 7.37 to 1945 [40, 6 WL], (army), Dale guest 2.42 [2 WL], Burnley guest 1941-42 [1 WL], Blackburn R. guest 8.42 [5 WL], Southport guest 1942-43 [12 WL], Bolton W. guest 10.42 [5 WL], Blackpool guest 10.43 and 2.44 [2 WL], Derby Co. guest 1.44 [2 WL], Swansea T. guest 11.44 [1 WL], Briton Ferry Ath. to 1948
Cricket for Briton Ferry
Honours: Briton Ferry Schoolboys, Wales 14 caps 1931 to 1939, Red Cross international 11.39 v England, Wales v RAF 9.42, British Services tour to India 1945, Division 2 champions 1934, Welsh Cup final 1938

Roy had a somewhat eccentric career as he was centre forward for Briton Ferry Schoolboys, made his FL debut at full back for Walsall when he was 17, but made his name as a goalkeeper. Indeed he won the first of his Welsh caps just a few months after going in goal for the first time in an emergency in a practice match. A contemporary scribe reported him as "dashing and daring, a gay cavalier who laughs fortune in the face", and he was also notable for "5 o'clock shadow" as he never shaved before matches. He had a particularly successful time at Stoke, winning a second division championship medal and playing in front of the record 84,569 crowd at Maine Road in the 1934 cup quarter final. He had supposedly retired in November 1939, after captaining Wales in his last game for them, but made several comebacks including when he guested for Dale twice in 1942, his international pedigree not preventing Liverpool racking up eight goals in the second. At the end of the war he was in the Services touring party to India better known as 'Tommy Walker's XI'. He also kept wicket in Welsh League cricket.

Robert Francis Dudgeon (Bob) Ancell 1941-42

Born: Dumfries 16.6.11
5'10" 11st
Left back
WL Apps/Gls 1/1
Career: Mid Annandale Juniors, St. Mirren 2.30 [158/- ScL], Queen of the South loan 5.32, Newcastle U. 8.36 £2750 [97/1, 43/- WL], Carlisle U. guest 10.39 [1/- WL], (RAF), Blackburn R. guest 12.41 to 1943 [11/1 WL], Blackpool guest 1.42 [1/- WL], Aberdeen guest 1941-44 [41/7 ScWL], Dale guest 3.42 [1/1 WL], Derby Co. guest 10.43 [3/- WL], Burnley guest 9.45 [2/- WL], Dundee player-trainer 7.44 [19/2 ScWL, 58/- ScL], Aberdeen player coach 1948-49 [15/- ScL], Dundee 1949-50 [6/- ScL], Berwick R. player-manager 1950, Dunfermline manager 1952, Motherwell manager 7.55, Dundee manager 3.65 to 9.68, Dundee reserve team coach, Nottingham F. scout 10.69
Cricket for Backworth CC
Honours: Scottish FA Cup Final 1934, Scottish Division 2 promotion 1936, 1947, Scotland (2 caps) v Wales, Ireland 1937, Scotland v England wartime international 1940, Scottish Select v British Army 1941, 1942, RAF v Scottish Command 1943 (2), Scottish North East League Cup winners 1942-43, Mitchell Cup winners 1942-43, Aberdeen Select v British Army 1942. As manager: Scottish Division 2 promotion 1955, Scottish League Cup Final 1965

Bob was a slightly built but sound and capable "brainy" fullback who made his mark with St. Mirren (while working as a clerk and compositor), figuring in the 1934 Scottish Cup Final. After a big money move to Newcastle, he made nearly 100 FL appearances – being everpresent in 1938-39 - and won two full caps for Scotland as a "polished, skillful back". Given this background his guest appearance for Dale must have been quite a shock as Liverpool won 8-2 at Spotland, though Bob did score. The following year he scored twice from outside right for Aberdeen in a wartime cup final. An army PTI (his father had also been a PTI, at Dumfries College), he played in numerous wartime representative games and coached the Norwegian Free Army team who were based in Dumfries. Playing on after the war, he won promotion with Dundee (playing in two 10-0 victories in consecutive games!) and became player-manager of Berwick Rangers when he was 39. He went on to manage several other sides in the fifties and sixties – taking Dundee to the European Fairs Cup semi-final – and had a reputation for bringing on talented youngsters, such as Ian St John. He was also an excellent golfer. His brother Charlie played for Queen of the South.

Roland (Roly) Bartholomew 1941-43

Born: Great Harwood 15.1.15
5'6" 10st7
Outside left
WL Apps/Gls 11/6
Career: North Manchester Secondary School, Urmston OB, Leeds U. am cs.34, Bradford C. 5.35 [100/14], Grimsby T. 6.38 [12/4, 6/3 WL], Manchester U. guest 9.40 and 8.44 [6/- WL], Dale guest 3.42 [11/6 WL], Crewe A. guest 12.42 [8/1 WL], Droylsden 8.46
Honours: Division 3(N) Cup final 1938

A little winger with a good goalscoring record, Roly was a regular for three years at Bradford City, netting seven times in five FA Cup ties in 1937-38, before a move to Grimsby in the top flight, where he made his debut against Aston Villa. He scored regularly in his short spell at Spotland, netting in three of the last five games of 1941-42 and the first two of the next season. He didn't return to the senior game after the war and was employed as an electrical instrument maker.

Arthur Chesters 1941-46

Born: Salford 14.2.10
5'10" 12st Goalkeeper
WL Apps 69
Total Apps 75
Career: Irlam o' the Heights, Bangor C., Sedgley Park, Manchester U. am 5.29, pro 11.29 [9], Exeter C. 7.33 [95], Crystal Palace 4.37 [78, 5 WL], Fulham guest 1939-40 [1 WL], Brighton & HA guest 4.40 [7 WL], Leicester C. guest 2.41 [4 WL], Dale guest 3.42 and 3.43 to 4.45 [56 WL], Dale 9.45 [13 WL]
Honours: Division 3 South Cup winners 1934, (War League South section 'D' winners 1940)

After a promising start at Old Trafford – United beat Newcastle 5-0 on his debut a month after he signed pro – he had the misfortune to figure the following season when they lost the first twelve games of the season, Arthur conceding 22 goals in four consecutive games. He had several productive seasons in the Third South, helping Exeter beat neighbours Torquay in the first Division 3(S) Cup Final and Palace to second spot on the eve of the war. He guested quite regularly for Dale during the war, especially in 1943 to 1945 and signed for them in the transitional season, playing in all six games of Dale's run in the restored FA Cup. (Indeed, he was the only player to figure for Dale in these games who did not also make FL appearances for them). Away from the game, he was keen on tennis and billiards.

Gilbert (Gil) Richmond 1941-43

Born: Bolton 2.4.09 5'10" 12st1
Left back
WL Apps/Gls 14/0
Career: Clitheroe, Burnley am 11.29, Nelson 2.30, pro 3.30 [22/-], Clitheroe 6.31, Burnley 5.32 [176/1, 2/- WL], Dale guest 3.42 [14/- WL], Aldershot guest 1943-44 [1/- WL]. Coach in Sweden 1947

Gil had first played in the FL before Nelson lost their league status, later becoming a regular for Burnley for most of the 1930s. A "stylish and fearless" player, who "kicks a long ball and is a hard tackler", he accumulated approaching 200 senior appearances. In 1935 he was in the Clarets' second division side which reached the semi-finals of the FA Cup. Nearly all his wartime appearances were as a guest for Dale between March and November 1942, the last one a 5-0 defeat by his own club. Contrary to his on-field style, away from the game he was something of an artist, excelling at pencil sketches.

Stanley William (Stan) Cutting 1941-43

Born: St. Faith's 21.9.14
Wing half
WL Apps/Gls 13/1
Career: Sheringham FC, Norwich C. am 3.36, Southampton 5.37 [3/-], Exeter C. 7.39 to 1948 [8/- WL, 38/2], (RAF), Stockport Co. guest 8.41 to 1943 [31/2 WL], Dale guest 3.42 [13/1 WL], Millwall guest 1942-43 [1/- WL], Blackpool guest 10.43 [1/- WL]
Honours: Norwich and Norfolk Schoolboys, RAF Suez Zone v Cairo Zone

Although 25 the month war broke out, Stan had played just three times in the league. He had more opportunities during the wartime regional leagues and retuned to Exeter for a couple of seasons in 1946. He played regularly for Dale at the end of 1941-42 and in the first part of the following term after scoring on his debut in a victory over Manchester City. He served in the RAF in Egypt and later was a hotelier.

James Albert Thorpe 1941-43

Born: {Salford 28.6.20}
Centre forward
WL Apps/Gls 6/0
Career: Dale 3.42 [6/- WL]

A centre forward, he played in the last five games of 1941-42 and in one further game the following October. Although Dale won three of them, scoring freely, he did not get on the scoresheet himself.

Frank France 1941-43
Born: {Bolton AMJ.23?}
Outside right
WL Apps/Gls 2/0
Career: Dale 4.42 [2/- WL]

Frank played twice for Dale, at Bury in April 1942 and the following October at Oldham, when Duncan Colquhoun was unavailable.

David Oswald Edwards (Ossie) Jones
1941-42
Born: Ruabon 15.7.09
5'9" 11st10
Inside right
WL Apps/Gls 1/0
Career: Johnstown Council School, Afongoch Chums, Wrexham am 8.5.29 [1/-], Aberystwyth 1929, Llanerch Celts , Gylfa FC, Connah's Quay & Shotton 1930, Nottingham F. pro 10.31, Wrexham 8.7.32 [2/-], {Wellington T.?}, Oswestry T. cs.33, Macclesfield T. 7.34, Tranmere R. £100 5.36 [54/12], Watford 5.38 [2/-], Southport 21.11.38 [7/2], Crewe A. 5.39, (army), Dale guest 4.42 [1/- WL], Monsanto 1946
Honours: Division 3(N) champions 1938, Birmingham League champions 1933, Cheshire Senior Cup winners 1935

Ossie first played in the league as an amateur with Wrexham back in 1929, but only managed more than the odd game after joining Tranmere seven years later, helping them win the Third North in 1938. In the meantime he had reputedly gained 13 winners medals in various competitions and scored a remarkable 88 goals in 92 games for Cheshire League Macclesfield, including nine hat-tricks and five goals in one match. He guested in one match for Dale – a victory over the usually all conquering Blackpool side - while on leave from the Royal Artillery, with whom he played football in Egypt, Palestine and Sicily. He worked, and played, for chemical company Monsanto after the war and lived to the age of 92.

George James (Jim) Strong 1942-43

Born: Morpeth 7.6.16
Goalkeeper
WL Apps 28
Career: Choppington Welfare, Pegswood U. 10.33, Hartlepools U. 2.34 £15 [1], Chesterfield 7.34 [18], Portsmouth 3.35 £2000 [59], Ashington trial 8.38, Gillingham 8.38 £1000, Walsall 7.39 [1 WL], Blackpool guest 8.40 and 11.41 [25 WL], Southport guest 1941-42 [1 WL], Dale guest 8.42 [28 WL], (RAF), Burnley guest 1943-46, signed 1.46 £450 [95 WL, 264] to 5.54.
Honours: FA Cup final 1947, Division 2 promotion 1947, London Combination champions 1936, (League North champions 1941-42), Lancashire Senior Cup final 1946, winners 1950, 1952

Jim made his league debut for Hartlepools as a 17 year old but was released and a year later was signed by first division Portsmouth. He dropped down to play in the Southern League with Gillingham before returning to the FL just before war broke out. Everpresent for Blackpool in 1940-41, he then guested for Dale for most of the 1942-43 season, despite one run of four games when he conceded 20 goals. He then figured for Burnley and signed permanently for them at the end of the war. He appeared in the 1947 Cup Final and was everpresent in the side which was promoted from Division 2 the same season, eventually making more than 350 first team appearances at Turf Moor, including a record 220 in succession, retiring in May 1954.

Lewis (Lew) Bradford 1942-44
Born: Ashby-de-la-Zouch 24.11.16 5'9" 12st
Right back/centre half
WL Apps/Gls 72/0
Career: Preston NE 12.34 [46/- WL], Carlisle U. guest 1939-40 [1/- WL], Southport guest 1940-41 [24/- WL], Dale guest 8.42 to 5.44 [72/- WL], Blackburn R. guest 4.43 and 1944-45 [2/- WL], Burnley guest 1944-45 [12/- WL], Kilmarnock 8.45 [5/- ScL], Bradford C. 10.46 [68/1], Newport Co. 11.48 [24/-], Trowbridge 8.49, Bath C. 8.50

A long serving Preston reserve, Lew did not make his senior debut as a hard tackling full back until the wartime regional leagues. Given the circumstances, he had a remarkable record at Rochdale, not missing a single game in his two years playing for them. After a brief stint in Scotland, he eventually made his FL debut, appropriately in Bradford, when he was 30.

George Walton 1942-43

Born: Burnley 14.1.11
5'8" 10st7
Wing half
WL Apps/Gls 5/0
Career: St John's (Ivy Street), Duke Rovers, Burnley `A', Accrington St. trial 27.4.29, am 28.11.29, pro 18.5.31 [79/21], Bolton W. 13.2.33 £300 [26/1], Cardiff C. 23.10.36 £1550 [84/17], Walsall

19.8.39 to 1946 [7/2 WL], Bolton W. guest 11.39 [1/1 WL], Accrington St. guest 1.40 [8/- WL], Dale guest 8.42 [5/- WL]
Honours: Division 2 promoted 1935, Welsh Cup final 1939

A hard working inside forward who joined Accrington when he was 18, George was signed by Division 1 Bolton in 1933 and following their relegation he "proved a great asset" as a "smart ball player" in their promotion run two years later. He had more opportunities at Cardiff but joined Walsall on the eve of the war. A former weaver in a cotton mill, he appeared for each of his former clubs in the regional leagues as well as turning out as a wing half for Dale in the early part of 1942-43.

Thomas McCall (Tom) Smith 1942-43

Born: Fenwick 4.10.08 5'10" 11st3
Centre half
WL Apps/Gls 2/0
Career: Cumnock Juveniles, Sinclair Celtic, Cumnock Townhead Thistle, Kilmarnock 12.27 [244/4 ScL], Galston loan 1.29, Preston NE 12.36 to 1945 [44/-, 120/- WL], Dale guest 8.42 [2/- WL], Manchester U. guest 2.43 [1/- WL], Burnley guest 1943-44 [2/- WL], Kilmarnock manager 8.45 to 6.47
Honours: Scotland (2 caps) v England 1934, 1938, Scottish League v Football League 1937, Scottish FA tour to Canada and USA 1935, Scotland wartime international v England 1942, Scottish Cup final 1932, FA Cup winners 1938, War League Cup winners 1941, War League North winners 1941

A "commanding pivot", in a long career, Tom won numerous Scottish international honours and appeared in cup finals both sides of the border, captaining the winning Preston side in 1938. He broke his shin in a pre-season continental tour game, though, and was able to play only one more FL game the following term. However he came back to add well over 100 wartime league games to his tally, played in wartime internationals and a cup final, and guested twice for Dale in 1942-43. After the war he retired to become manager of Kilmarnock for whom he had made over 250 senior appearances in the twenties and thirties, following in the footsteps of his father Adam. He also worked for the Electricity Board.

N. Miller 1942-43
Inside left
WL Apps/Gls 1/0
Career: Dale 8.42 [1/- WL]

Miller played just the once for Dale, on the opening day of 1942-43, in a 1-1 draw at Southport.

Edward Ilderton (Ted) Goodall 1942-43
Born: South Shields 13.10.13 5'10" 11st5
Goalkeeper
WL Apps 3
Career: South Shields JIC, Middle Dock, Chester-le-Street, Jarrow, Chesterfield am 5.36, pro 8.36, North Shields 10.36, Hull C. 5.37 [26], Bolton W. 5.38 £3000 [12, 22 WL], Manchester U. guest 5.40 [2 WL], Bury guest 8.40 [6 WL], Chester guest 10.40 [1 WL], West Bromwich A. guest 12.40 [1 WL], Blackburn R. guest 4.41 [1 WL], Manchester C. guest 9.41 [2 WL], Dale guest 9.42 [3 WL]

A promising goalie who had had just one season in the league, Ted was bought by first division Bolton in 1938 for a sizeable fee, to understudy Stan Hanson. Working down the mines with teammate and other former Jarrow man Harry Hubbick (q.v.) during the war, he played in nearly all Wanderers' games in 1939-40, later guesting for a variety of other sides, his last senior games being for Dale. His debut for them was something of a shambles as Dale lost to Southport who had had to recruit two spectators to make up their team!

Frank Curran 1942-43
Born: Ryton-on-Tyne 31.5.17 5'8" 11st7
Inside left
WL Apps/Gls 1/0
Career: Emmaville School, Ryton Council School, Spen Black & White Juniors, Washington Colliery, Southport 8.8.35 [16/3], Accrington St. 13.2.37 (exchange for G. Pateman) [34/14], Bristol R. 14.6.38 [27/21], Bristol C. 17.5.39 £300 [19/10 WL], Bristol R. guest 1939-40 [1/2 WL], Swindon T. guest 5.40 [1/- WL], Southport guest 1940-42 [23/11 WL], Dale guest 9.42 [1/- WL], Everton guest 10.42 [7/9 WL], Oldham A. guest 11.43 [2/- WL], Stockport Co. guest 9.43 [1/1 WL], Tranmere R. guest 9.43 [1/1 WL], Accrington St. guest 8.44 [9/5 WL], Bristol R. 26.5.46 [10/3], Tranmere R. 17.6.47 [17/7], Shrewsbury T. 3.48, Ashton U. 4.48, Hyde U. 8.48, Ashton U. 12.48, Hyde U. cs.50, Darwen cs.52 to cs.53
Honours: Blaydon & District Boys, Gloucester Senior Cup 1945-46

Despite his north eastern origins, Frank had worked his way down the country to Bristol by the time war interrupted his career. A short but stocky inside forward, who was a "smart dribbler", his best season was undoubtedly 1938-39 when he hit

21 goals in only 27 games, including four against Swindon, to be easily Rovers' top scorer, though the side finished bottom of the league. Alternating between the Bristol clubs and a string of north west sides, he continued to score regularly during the war, though he did not find the net in his game for Dale. His final FL stint was at Tranmere in 1947-48 but he continued in non-league football for several more years, netting over 30 goals for Ashton. Three of his brothers were also footballers, Andy with Accrington and Blackpool, Jimmy with Barnsley and Southend and Jack who was an England amateur international, while his sister married Charlie Robinson, the 1930s Dale player. His other brother, Bertie, was a well known jockey.

Frank Gallimore   1942-43

Born: Winnington, Northwich 19.10.08
5'8" 11st3
Right back
WL Apps/Gls 6/0
Career: Bainton Victoria, Northwich Victoria 1926-27, Witton Albion 10.29, Preston NE 6.31 to 1942 [241/-, 70/- WL], Dale guest 9.42 [6/- WL]
Honours: FA Cup winners 1938, Charity Shield 1939, Lancashire Senior Cup joint winners 1939, War League Cup winners 1941, War League North winners 1941

A right back, and brother of Len who was a left back and also played a few games for Preston, Frank was a stalwart for North End throughout the 1930s, being everpresent in three separate seasons. Considered "a first class back in every way", he gained a cup winners medal at Wembley in 1938, in the first game to be broadcast in its entirety on television. He had the misfortune to score an own goal in the replay of the 1941 War Cup final, though Preston still beat Arsenal 2-1 to complete a league and cup double. His only senior games away from Deepdale were half a dozen guest appearances for Dale at the start of the 1942-43 campaign. He worked for ICI and was later a publican before emigrating to Canada.

Claude Arthur Garfoot   1942-43
Born: Nottingham 22.12.13
Right half
WL Apps/Goals 1/0
Career: Stockport Co. 9.41 [1/- WL], Dale 9.42 [1/- WL], Hurst 1.46

A wing half, Arthur made just two senior appearances in the wartime regional leagues, one for Stockport – a 7-1 defeat by Manchester United - and one for Dale against Halifax when Dale were missing several regulars.

A. Jones   1942-43
Outside right
WL Apps/Gls 1/1
Career: Dale 9.42 [1/1 WL]

Jones played at outside right in the 3-1 defeat by Halifax in September 1942, but he did at least have the honour of netting the Dale goal. [Though given as A. Jones in the team line-up, FL records show him as E. Jones].

Brown   1942-43
Inside right/outside left
WL Apps/Gls 2/0
Career: Dale 9.42 [2/- WL]

Brown managed two Dale games, one at inside right in the Halifax game and later one at outside left in a 6-3 victory over Bury, all the other four forwards getting on the scoresheet. He does not appear in FL records, however.

James Manning   1942-43
Inside left
WL Apps/Gls 1/0
Career: Huddersfield T. 1940-43 [7/1 WL], Halifax T. guest 4.42 [1/1 WL], Dale guest 9.42 [1/- WL]

Manning was a Huddersfield based player who was the fourth newcomer drafted in alongside Garfoot, Jones and Brown, when Dale were short of men for the game at home to Halifax, for whom he had played the previous year.

William Folds   1942-43
Born: {Fylde JFM.15}
Goalkeeper
WL Apps 1
Career: Leicester C., Dale guest 9.42 [1 WL]

A goalkeeper on Leicester's books, Folds figured just the once for Dale in a 3-0 defeat at Halifax.

Norman Richmond   1942-43
Born: {Rochdale JAS.24}
Inside right
WL Apps/Gls 1/0
Career: Dale 9.42 [1/- WL]

Another player who appeared only against Halifax in September 1942, Norman figured at inside right.

David Lloyd George Jones 1942-43
Inside/outside left
WL Apps/Gls 15/3
Career: Dale 9.42 [15/3 WL]

David also appeared first at Halifax, but unlike the others became a relatively regular performer, first at inside left and then on the left wing, Dale at one point winning six successive games in which he was in the team, scoring 22 goals in the process.

David Bebb 1942-43
Born: {Rochdale 23.6.20}
Winger
WL Apps/Gls 5/1
Career: Bury 1941-42 [10/1 WL], Dale 10.42 [5/1 WL]

Yet another debutant in the game at Halifax, David had figured a number of times for Bury in 1941-42 and then appeared five times for Dale, mostly at outside left, the following season.

Harold Whalley 1942-43
Born: Nelson 4.4.23
Inside left
WL Apps/Goals 1/0
Career: Burnley c.1940 [17/- WL], Blackburn R. guest 1.42 [2/- WL], Dale guest 10.42 [1/- WL], Barnoldswick T., Accrington St. 12.46 to 5.47 [3/-]

An outside left, Harold's first senior games came with his own club Burnley and as a guest for Blackburn in 1941-42. He appeared for Dale, at inside left, in the 5-1 home defeat by Blackburn the following season. After the war he made three FL appearances with Accrington.

Eric Wood 1942-51, 1952-53
Born: Bolton 13.3.20
Wing half/inside forward
FL Apps/Gls 148/15 Total Apps/Gls 266/55
Career: Bolton W. am, Dale am 1942, pro 8.43 [93/39 WL, 148/15], (local football 1951-52), Dale 'A' team player/coach 1952-53
Honours: Lancashire Junior Cup winners 1947, Lancashire Senior Cup winners 1949

Initially joining Dale from Bolton as an amateur and playing regularly in 1942-43, Eric turned pro the following year and accumulated nearly 100 wartime appearances in the various competitions, mostly playing as a goalscoring inside forward though he could also lead the line. Making his FL debut on the opening day of 1946-47, from January 1947 he was switched to play at wing half, Dale winning all the first five games he played in that position. Indeed, he notably formed the half-back line with Wally Birch and George McGeachie in 41 consecutive FL games in 1949 and 1950, as well as in the 1949 Lancashire Senior Cup success, though he still reverted to the forwards from time to time (as he had in the 1947 Lancashire Junior Cup final). He appeared in 140 FL games in the first four post-war seasons and was awarded a testimonial game in 1950 which attracted a crowd of over 6600 to see Tom Finney guest for Rochdale. Mostly a reserve the following season, he spent a year just playing local football before returning to Spotland as 'A' team player-coach. As well as his versatility as an outfield player, Eric was also a competent deputy between the sticks, twice taking over from injured keepers in league games.

Thompson 1942-43
Outside right
WL Apps/Gls 1/0
Career: Dale 10.42 [1/- WL]

Thompson apparently appeared on the right wing in a 5-0 defeat at Blackpool at the end of October 1942. However, he is not listed in the FL records.

Robert McFarlane Davidson (Bertie) Duffy

1942-43
Born: Dundee 19.4.13
5'9" 11st4
Left half
WL Apps/Gls 13/1
Career: Dundee St. Josephs 1932, Lochee Harp 1933, Celtic 5.10.35 to 4.47 [4/- ScL], Dundee loan 10.39, (RAF 1940), Fulham guest 1941-42 [6/- WL], Hamilton Ac. guest 1941-42, Bradford C. guest 5.42 and 3.44 [4/- WL], Huddersfield T. guest 1941-42 and 1942-43 [2/1 WL], Dale guest 11.42 [13/1 WL], Dundee U. guest 5.44 [1/- ScWL], Newcastle U. guest 1944-45 [21/- WL], Swansea T. guest 1944-45 [3/- WL], Port Vale guest 1944-45 [2/- WL], Leeds U. guest 8.45 [15/- WL]

A reserve half back with Glasgow Celtic, Bertie guested for Dale and other teams, particularly Newcastle and Leeds, during the war when he was a sergeant PTI in the RAF. At Spotland he alternated (confusingly) with Joe Duff in the left half spot for much of Rochdale's 1942-43 campaign. He rejoined Celtic in 1946 but did not add to his four pre-war Scottish League appearances.

Harry Gee 1942-44
Outside right
WL Apps/Goals 44/19
Career: Bolton W. 8.42 [4/2 WL], Dale guest 11.42 [44/19 WL], Birmingham 1943-44 [2/1 WL], Stockport Co. guest 4.44 to 9.45 [31/9 WL]

Harry was with Bolton and then Birmingham during the war but most of his appearances were as a guest at Rochdale and Stockport. Playing regularly for Dale for two seasons, he hit 11 goals in 25 games from the wing in 1943-44.

Jack Harker 1942-46
Centre forward
WL Apps/Gls 40/38
Career: {Chesterfield 1938?}, (RAF), Southport 1940-42 [45/39 WL], Bolton W. 8.42 [2/1 WL], Dale 11.42 to 9.45 [40/38 WL]

While serving in the RAF, Jack had a remarkable goalscoring record during the wartime regional leagues, netting virtually a goal a game. He hit 25 in 29 games at Southport in 1941-42 and another 25, in only 22 games, for Dale in 1943-44. The latter included nine goals in successive games against Southport and another four against Bolton, his two previous clubs, but he made only a handful of appearances after February 1944 and did not appear in any senior peacetime games. [A Jack Harker scored 10 in one game for Chesterfield 'A' in April 1938]

Harry Cload 1942-43
Bolton: Bolton 30.8.23
Outside left
WL Apps/Gls 8/4
Career: Halliwell, Bolton W. 1940-42 [9/1 WL], Dale 11.42 [8/4 WL]

Harry followed Bolton colleagues Gee and Harker into the Dale side in November 1942, scoring on his debut and then netting twice in a 4-4 draw at Bolton a couple of weeks later. He had earlier made his Bolton debut in the same match as a 15 year old Nat Lofthouse, both of them scoring in a 5-1 win.

Thomas (Tom) Breakwell 1942-44
Born: Stourport-on-Severn 3.7.15 5'10" 11st7
Wing half
WL Apps/Gls 20/0
Career: Palatine School, Whitegate Juniors (Blackpool), Lytham c.1930, Blackpool am 11.33, Central Juniors, Lytham 11.34, Bolton W. am 6.35, Bradford PA 5.36 [18/-], Wrexham 6.37 to cs.38 [3/-], Bradford City Police, (RAF 1942), Dale 12.42 [20/- WL], Fleetwood

Honours: West Yorkshire XI v South Yorkshire 1936

Tom appeared quite regularly in the second division in his one season at Park Avenue, but had been out of senior football for several years when he joined Rochdale in December 1942. He played in nearly all their remaining matches that season, usually at right half, and also appeared a few times the following term. He was in the police force in Bradford before joining the RAF as a Flying Officer in Halifax bombers. After the war he ran a butcher's, but in an interesting career change, then set up a medical supplies company.

Thomas (Tom) Wildsmith 1942-46
Born: Sheffield 8.1.13 5'11" 12st
Centre half/left back
WL Apps/Gls 21/0
Career: Hadfield Sports (Sheffield), Huddersfield T. am 5.31, Wolverhampton W. am 8.31, pro 6.32 [1/-], Bristol R. 6.34 [24/2], Doncaster R. 5.36 [4/-], Frickley Colliery 8.38, Southport 1942-43 [3/- WL], Dale 12.42 to 1945-46 [21/- WL]
Honours: Gloucestershire Senior Cup winners 1935, Western League champions 1936

Another player with little recent senior football, Tom, "a reliable, steady and consistent player", had last played for Doncaster, at right half, in the Division 3 North Cup early in 1937-38. He made scattered appearances for Dale between December 1942 and April 1944, mostly at centre half and was still figuring in the reserves during the transitional 1945-46 campaign.

Shaw 1942-43
Centre forward
WL Apps/Gls 1/0
Career: Dale 12.42 [1/- WL]

Shaw played just once for Dale, at centre forward when they lost 7-3 at Bury on Christmas Day 1942, though FL records do not include him.

George ('Spud') Murphy 1942-44

Born: Cwmfelinfach 22.7.15 5'9" 12st7
Utility player
WL Apps/Gls 6/3
Career: Pontllanfraith, Cwmfelinfach Colts, Bradford C. 10.34 [180/43, 126/41 WL], (RAF), Liverpool guest 3.40 and 5.43 [4/1 WL], Bradford PA guest 12.40 and 10.44 [8/3 WL], Blackpool guest 5.41 and

1942-43 [5/2 WL], Dale guest 1.43 [6/3 WL], Everton guest 10.43 [1/- WL], Notts Co. guest 11.43 [2/- WL], Hartlepools U. guest 10.44 [1/- WL], York C. guest 1944-45 [1/- WL], Lovells Ath. guest 1944-45 [?/3 WL], Hull C. 12.47 £1500 [15/9], Gainsborough Trinity cs.48, Scunthorpe U. 8.48, Scarborough 6.49, Goole T. 7.51
Honours: Monmouthshire Schools, Division 3(N) Cup final 1938, Wales wartime internationals v England 1943 (2)

George was the archetypal wartime player, reputedly figuring for eight sides in nine weeks (though it is not evident that he actually played for any more than four FL sides in any one season) and playing in virtually any position as needed. Indeed, in his first four games for Dale he figured at left back, left half, outside right and centre forward, grabbing a hat-trick against Burnley. He had already made well over a century of appearances for Bradford City before the war, and including wartime games (when he was serving in the RAF) and a further season and a half after the war, he totalled over 300 senior appearances for the Bantams. His most common positions were at full back or centre forward, where he was renowned for his "fearless assaults in the goalmouth" which earned him over 100 career goals.

Frederick Thomas Sweeney 1942-43
Born: Northwich 20.1.19
Left back
WL Apps/Goals 1/0
Career: Everton 1939 [4/2 WL], Stockport Co. guest 1.43 [1/- WL], Dale guest 1.43 [1/- WL], Grimsby T guest 1943-44 [2/- WL]

Sweeney played a few times for his own club Everton in 1939-40 and guested for Stockport against Dale and for Dale against Stockport on successive weekends in January 1943 (Dale winning the first 4-3 and the return 6-0).

Schofield 1942-43
Left half
WL Apps/Gls 1/0
Career: Dale 2.43 [1/- WL]

Schofield's one Dale appearance was at left half in a 1-1 draw at Burnley in February 1943.

John Foster (Jack) Blood 1942-43
Born: Bingham, Nottngham 2.10.14
Left back
WL Apps/Gls 3/0
Career: Johnson & Barnes (Nottingham), Notts Co. am 7.36, pro 6.38 [8/-], Exeter C. 5.39 to 1948 [31/1 WL, 39/1], Notts Co. guest 12.42 and 1944-45

[3/- WL], Dale guest 3.43 [3/- WL], Southport guest 1943-45 [46/1 WL], Liverpool guest 12.44 [5/- WL], Lovells Ath. guest 1944-45, Peterborough U. player/manager 1948 to 1950
Cricket for Nottinghamshire 2nd XI, South Devon

Jack signed for Notts County from a local works side when he was 23 and appeared for them in the Third (South). He signed for Exeter in 1939, playing in the three expunged games, and reappeared for them in 1946, but during the war mostly guested for sides in the north west, Dale included. He had a remarkable debut for Liverpool, when they beat Southport, one of his other clubs, 12-1. He was also a useful Minor Counties cricketer.

Frank Kitchener Marsh 1942-43

Born: Bolton 7.6.16
Outside left
WL Apps/Gls 1/0
Career: Crewe A. am, Stafford R. 1.36, Crewe A. am 7.36, Witton Albion 11.36, Bolton W. am 9.37, pro 5.38 [3/-], Chester 5.39 to 1948 [28/- WL, 69/2], Grimsby T. guest 1941-43 [2/- WL], Lincoln C. guest 1941-44 and 1945-46 [80/5 WL], Dale guest 3.43 [1/- WL], Port Vale guest 11.44 [2/- WL], Crewe A. guest 1944-45 [1/- WL], Mossley guest 1946, Macclesfield 1.49 to 1951
Honours: Third Division North Cup final 1946, Welsh Cup winners 1947

Originally a left winger, Frank had played a handful of league games before the war, figuring in Chester's last two (expunged) peacetime games, and he returned to Chester in 1946 for two seasons, by then playing at right half. He guested fairly regularly for Lincoln in the regional leagues and appeared for Dale at Blackburn in March 1943. He played regularly for Macclesfield in the Cheshire League for a couple of seasons after leaving Chester.

William Frederick (Billy) Burnicle [aka Burnikell] 1942-43
Born: Southwick, Co. Durham 9.12.10 5'9" 11st6
Wing half
WL Apps/Gls 1/0
Career: Newcastle U. jnr, Lincoln C. 7.29 [25/-], Bradford C. 7.33 [53/2], Aldershot 6.37 to 1939-40 [63/2, 2/- WL], Dale guest 3.43 [1/- WL], Watford guest 1944-45 [2/- WL], Helsingborgs IF (Sweden) coach 1947, Landskrona BOIS (Sweden) coach 1949 to 1951, Sudan national coach, Universidad Catolica (Chile) coach 1954, Halifax T. coach 2.56, caretaker manager 4.56 to 12.56, Orebro FK (Sweden) manager 1957 to 1959, Dagerfors IF (Sweden) manager 1960 to 1961

Honours: Division 3N champions 1932. As coach: Chilean first division champions 1954

Billy had first appeared in the league back in 1929 and accumulated around 150 appearances over the next decade, though he was an automatic choice only after joining Aldershot. Early in his career, it was noted that he was a "hard working defensive half-back" but still had "a good deal to learn in the matter of ball distribution". He played only a few times in the regional leagues and just once for Dale. After the war he was a long serving and well travelled coach, spending many years in Sweden, and was briefly in charge at Halifax in 1956. His leisure activity was noted as billiards. [NB. His true surname was a matter of doubt during his career, but his birth was registered as Burnikell, a not uncommon spelling in the Sunderland area.]

Byrne   1942-43
Outside left
WL Apps/Gls 1/0
Career: Dale 3.43 [1/- WL]

Byrne appeared on the left wing once for Dale, in a 1-0 victory over Oldham in March 1943.

Ellis Cornwell   1942-45
Born: Copull 14.11.13   5'8"   10st12
Full back
WL Apps/Gls 33/0
Career: Heskin Parish Church, Chorley 8.38, Dale 3.43 [33/ WL], Accrington St. 30.11.45 [24/- WL, 5/-], Rossendale U. 2.8.47, Mossley 1947-48
Honours: Division 3 North West (first championship) winners 1945-46

Originally a forward with Chorley, Ellis signed for Rochdale in 1943 and was a fairly regular performer at full back until the end of the war. When he was demobbed in 1945 he was transferred to Accrington, playing against Dale in the two Christmas fixtures. He helped Stanley win the first championship of the Third North West and played in the defeat over two legs by Manchester United in the third round of the FA Cup. He finally made his FL debut the following season at the age of 32 and played in Stanley's home defeat by Dale a few weeks later.

Herbert Palfreyman   1942-43
Born: {Stockbridge 2.4.15}
Left half/outside left
WL Apps/Gls 3/0
Career: Aldershot, Dale trial 3.43, pro 5.4.43 [3/- WL], Lovells Ath. guest 1943-44

Apparently from Aldershot, Palfreyman's only wartime league games were for Rochdale, at left half and then left wing in the last three matches of 1942-43.

Webb   1942-43
Left half
WL Apps/Gls 1/0
Career: Dale 4.43 [1/- WL]

Another left half, Webb played for Dale in the last game of the 1942-43 campaign, a 2-0 defeat at Burnley.

Albert Collinge   1942-43
Born: {Rochdale}
Outside right
WL Apps/Gls 1/0
Career: Dale 4.43 [1/- WL]

Like Webb, Collinge's only senior outing was in the final match of 1942-43, when he figured on the right wing in place of Harry Gee.

William (Bill) Fielding   1943-44

Born: Broadbottom, Hyde 17.6.15
5'11" 11st10
Goalkeeper
WL Apps 12
Career: Broadbottom YMCA, Hurst 8.34, Cardiff C. 5.36 [53], Hurst guest 11.39, Stockport Co. guest 5.40 to 1941-42 [41 WL], Dale guest 8.43 [12 WL], Bolton W. 6.44 [48 WL], Manchester U. (exchange for W. Wrigglesworth) 1.47 [6], Ashton U. 6.48 to 5.53. Ashton U. trainer 1958
Honours: Welsh Cup final 1939, League North Cup winners 1945, Football League War Cup winners 1945, Manchester Challenge Shield winners 1953

A regular with Hurst when he was only 19, Bill had made around 50 league appearances for Cardiff in the late thirties, but was one of the many players to loose the middle years of their careers to the war. After guesting with Stockport and Dale – where he conceded six goals to Blackpool in each of his first two games – he joined Bolton and played for them when they beat Manchester United in the League North Cup final and then Chelsea, the southern winners, in the Football League War Cup final. In the first post-war season he was transferred to Manchester United but, after playing in one cup tie, conceded six on his United league debut against Arsenal. He ended his career with a long spell back where he started, though Hurst had by then adopted their new name of Ashton United, taking his tally for the club past 300 Cheshire League games in his three spells. Also a good class cricketer, he had trials with Glamorgan during his Cardiff days. He was one of the last surviving pre-war Cardiff players, living until he was 90.

John McGahie   1943-44
Outside right
WL Apps/Gls 1/0
Career: Blackpool am 1943 [1/- WL], Dale guest 8.43 [1/- WL], Burnley guest 1943-44 [3/- WL], {Bristol R. 28.8.45 [12/- WL]}

A Blackpool reserve, John was loaned to Dale for the 6-1 defeat at Bloomfield Road on the opening day of the 1943-44 season. He only ever played once for his own club, too (at centre forward).

William (Billy) Rudd snr   1943-44
Born: {Dublin?}
Outside left
WL Apps/Gls 2/0
Career: (Ireland), Dale pro 3.5.43 [2/- WL], Witton Albion, Hurst 3.46 to 11.46

Previously figuring in Irish football, Billy was another player with a rather brief Dale career, as he played in the 6-1 defeat at Blackpool in the first game of 1943-44 and then in an 8-0 thrashing on the same ground the following March in the second championship. He played Cheshire League football after the war but tragically lost a leg in a work accident in 1948. However, he became more noted in the Rochdale club annals as the father of Billy jnr who starred in Dale's promotion team 25 years later. Billy's brother Jimmy was also a well known league pro with several lower division sides including York and Rotherham in the forties and early fifties.

Richard C. Maudsley   1943-44
Born: {Toxteth Park AMJ.18?}
Outside left
WL Apps/Gls 4/0
Career: Gillingham 22.10.37 to 15.12.38, Stockport Co. 1.41 and 1.42 [9/- WL], Blackburn R. guest 9.41 [15/3 WL], Southport 1941-42 [6/- WL], Bolton W. 9.42 [8/- WL], Millwall guest 1942-43 [1/- WL], Watford guest 1942-43 [1/- WL], Dale pro 8.9.43 to 14.1.44 [4/- WL], Blackpool 2.44 [3/- WL], Accrington St. 8.44 [6/2 WL], Port Vale 10.44 [3/- WL]

A versatile player, Richard was mainly an outside left for Stockport and an outside right for Blackburn, but sometimes turned out at inside forward and played all across the half back line for Bolton. He appeared in four games for Dale, signing just after the start of the 1943-44 campaign, and his wing play must have been appreciated by Jack Harker, as the centre forward scored 11 times in those games. This contrasted with his Stockport spell when he was twice in a side which conceded nine goals. After Dale cancelled his contract he signed for Blackpool.

George Haigh   1943-46
Born: Reddish JAS.15   5'11" 12st
Left half
WL Apps/Gls 60/3   Total Apps/Gls 61/3
Career: Norbury Sunday School, Stockport Co. 5.36 [2/-], Hyde U. 7.39, (RAF), Manchester U. guest 3.43 [1/- WL], Dale 9.43 [60/3 WL], Wigan A. 11.45, Lancaster C. 1946-47, Rossendale U. 1947

George had made a couple of league appearances at centre half for Stockport before the war, but the vast majority of his senior career appearances came in the later war years, as a guest at Spotland, playing nearly all the games in 1943-44 and 1944-45, at left half.

Edward Mulligan   1943-44
Inside forward/right half
WL Apps/Gls 3/1
Career: {Blackburn R. pro 3.11.41 [1/- WL]?}, Aston Villa, Dale pro 19.10.43 [3/1 WL], Walsall guest 1943-45 [11/2], {Wrexham pro 20.9.44 [1/- WL]?}

Mulligan, from Aston Villa, appeared in three Dale games between October 1943 and January 1944, scoring on his debut in a 4-3 defeat of Halifax.

William (Willie) Miller   1943-44
Outside left
WL Apps/Gls 7/0
Career: Bradford C. am 31.8.43 [1/- WL], Dale guest 10.43 and 2.44 [7/- WL]

Willie was an amateur on Bradford City's books and had a run of games on Rochdale's left wing, one of them against the Bantams, prior to a single appearance for his home club.

Arthur Emmanuel Joseph   1943-44
Born: Newport 11.4.15
Inside left
WL Apps/Gls 1/0
Career: Dale am 14.12.43 [1/- WL]

Arthur figured at inside left for Dale at Bradford City when Eric Wood was moved into the centre in the absence of Jack Harker.

Charles Windle   1943-44
Born: Barnsley 8.1.17
Inside right
WL Apps/Gls 1/0
Career: Rawmarsh Welfare, Bury 9.38, Exeter C. 7.39, Chesterfield guest 1941-42 [2/1 WL], Bury guest 10.43 [4/- WL], Dale guest 1.44 [1/- WL], Bristol R. 12.46 [7/1], Ashton U. 5.47

Charles had his official FL debut expunged when the 1939-40 season was abandoned, but managed a few games for Bristol Rovers in 1946-47. Between times he made a handful of regional league appearances, one of them for Dale at the start of 1944. [NB. His original surname was Davis, but he adopted the name of his mother's second husband.]

Roy Carrick   1943-44
Born: {Leigh 21.10.21}
Centre forward
WL Apps/Gls 1/0
Career: Dale am 1.44 [1/- WL], {Notts Co. guest 8.44 [1/- WL]?}

Roy was another player with a single wartime appearance for Dale, in the same game as Windle, at Blackburn in January 1944.

Ernest Morris   1943-45
Inside left
WL Apps/Gls 20/10
Career: Dale am 17.1.44, pro 15.2.44 [20/10 WL], Accrington St. 3.10.45 [5/2 WL]
Honours: Third Division North West (first championship) winners 1945-46

Ernie played fairly regularly for Rochdale for a season and a half, making his mark with two goals on his second appearance, a 3-1 victory over Burnley, which earned him a professional contract. In fact, all his Dale goals came in braces, two of them in successive games against his future employers Accrington in October 1944.

Leslie (Les) Lievesley   1943-44

Born: Staveley 1.7.11
5'10" 12st
Right half
WL Apps/Gls 1/0
Career: Rossington Main Colliery, Doncaster R. 7.29 [66/21], Manchester U. 2.32 [2/-], Chesterfield 3.33, Torquay U. 6.33 [131/4], Crystal Palace 4.37 to 1946 [75/3, 16/5 WL], Doncaster R. guest 3.40 [10/- WL], Queens Park R. guest 1940-41 [1/- WL], Millwall guest 1940-41 [1/- WL], York C. guest 1940-41 [10/- WL], Raith R. guest 1941-42 [3/- ScWL], Bolton W. guest 9.42 [2/- WL], Mansfield T. guest 1942-43 [2/- WL], Stockport Co. guest 1.43 to 1945 [64/1 WL], Dale guest 3.44 [1/- WL]. Coach in Holland, Spain 1946, Torino (Italy) coach 1947 (d. 4.5.49]
Honours: Division 3(S) Cup final 1934, War League South winners 1941, (Division 3S South section winners 1946)

Les came from a footballing family, his father Joe (Arsenal and Sheffield U.) and uncles Wilf (Manchester U. and Exeter) and Fred (Manchester C. and Southend) all being league professionals, while his brother Harold was briefly with Doncaster. He started out as a goalscoring forward, netting 12 times in 14 games in his first season in Doncaster's league side, but was later transformed to a wing half. Over 200 of his FL appearances came in six seasons in the Third (South) with Torquay and then Crystal Palace. Dale were one of nine sides he represented during the war and after the war he coached abroad and was tragically killed in the Superga air crash when with Torino.

Thomas Ivor (Tom) Sibley   1943-44, 1946-48
Born: Porth 27.10.20   5'8"   10st
Winger
FL Apps/Gls 23/3 Total Apps/Gls 29/6
Career: Ton Pentre, Blackpool Services, Birmingham 9.43 [4/- WL], Dale trial 3.44 [3/3 WL], Mossley 1945-46, Dale 3.47 £ [23/3], Barry T. 1948, Cheltenham T. 5.48

Tom had been with Birmingham when Ted Goodier was temporarily their manager, and Goodier gave him a trial at Spotland the following year, Tom scoring in all three games in which he played. He returned to Spotland in 1947 after a stint at Mossley, making his debut on the right flank in a 5-2 win over Hull. He played a number of further games that season and the following one, when he mostly played on the left, before heading back to Wales.

Michael O'Mahoney   1943-46
Born: {Prestwich JAS.17}
Inside right
WL Apps/Gls 3/0
Career: Dale 4.44 to 1945-46 [3/- WL]

Michael played just three times for Dale but his debut at inside right was noteworthy in that it saw a rare defeat for champions Blackpool, who had beaten Dale 8-0 just the week before. He did not

appear in the senior side after April 1944 but played in the reserves as a half back in 1945-46.
[NB. Other sources incorrectly claim that this is Matthew Augustine (Matt) O'Mahoney, the Ipswich T. player who was an international for both the Republic and N. Ireland.]

John Edwin (Jackie) Wharton 1943-44

Born: Bolton 18.6.20
5'5" 10st6
Outside left
WL Apps/Gls 3/1
Career: Duckworth's FC, Bolton W. am 1935, Plymouth A. am 10.35, pro 4.37 [11/2], Preston NE 7.39 £5500 (with J. Hunter) [128/40 WL, 25/7], Carlisle U. guest 1939-40 [1/- WL], Liverpool guest 5.42 [1/1 WL], Bolton W. guest 8.42 [26/3 WL], Blackburn R. guest 3.43 [30/3 WL], Dale guest 4.44 [3/1 WL], Manchester C. 3.47 £5000 [23/2], Blackburn R. 6.48 £ [129/14], Newport Co. 2.53 £4000 (with L. Graham) [74/10], Wigan A. cs.55
Honours: Division 2 champions 1947

A "nippy enthusiastic little left winger", Jackie scored in the first minute of his league debut in 1938. A large fee took him to Preston a year later and he played in the three games of the aborted league campaign. He played regularly for North End during the regional leagues, scoring 21 times in 1943-44, and guested for other Lancashire sides including the Dale (playing nearly 200 wartime games in total), but it was after the war that he really made his mark, playing well over 100 top flight games with Blackburn and helping them to reach the 1952 FA Cup semi final. His son Terry, another winger, starred for Wolves and Bolton in the 1960s and Jackie also moved to Wolverhampton where he was bar manager in a hotel.

Robert Griffith (Bob) Davies 1943-45

Born: Blaenau Ffestiniog 19.11.13
Centre half
WL Apps/Gls 2/0
Career: Blaenau Ffestiniog 1932, Nottingham F. 12.36 £55 [55/-, 33/- WL], Notts Co. guest 6.40 and 1945-46 [12/- WL], (RAF), Blackpool guest 2.44 and 8.44 [38/1 WL], Dale guest 4.44 [2/- WL], Wrexham guest 1944-45 [1/- WL], Leicester C. guest 10.45 [2/- WL], Nottingham F. reserve team coach 1947, physio 1954, Walsall physio 1974 (d. 5.78). Also physio to Nottinghamshire CCC.
Honours: Wartime Welsh international 6 caps v England, Scotland 1940-45, Wales XI v Western Command 1942

Bob starred for his local club and was selected for the Wales Amateur trial but turned pro with Forest before the game. A "dominant defender" in contention for a full cap for Wales, his league career spanned just 49 games before war broke out as he had suffered with cartilage problems and also caught pneumonia. Joining the RAF, he made 300 parachute jumps as an instructor and combined further games for Forest with guest appearances for the Dale amongst others. He also appeared in several wartime internationals against England and Scotland. He joined Forest's backroom staff after figuring in half a dozen games in 1946-47 and worked as a physio until his death at the age of 64.

John E. Banner 1943-45
Inside right
WL Apps/Gls 2/0
Career: Dale am 17.4.44 [2/- WL]

John made one appearance for Dale in April 1944 – as one of eight changes to the previous week's side - and another in March 1945 when Dale won at Tranmere.

S. Connor 1943-44
Outside right
WL Apps/Gls 1/0
Career: Dale 4.44 [1/- WL]

Connor appeared in the penultimate game of 1943-44 when Dale lost 1-0 to Tranmere Rovers.

James (Jimmy) Jones 1943-45
Outside left
WL Apps/Gls 16/2
Career: Bolton W. 10.36, South Liverpool 11.38, Torquay cs.39, Dale 4.44 [16/2 WL]

Jimmy had made his league debut for Torquay in the aborted 1939-40 campaign and did not appear in the FL again after the war so had his whole career expunged!. He figured fairly regularly for Dale between April 1944 and the end of the following campaign, usually at outside left, though he also figured on the other wing and at inside right.

J. Macauley 1943-45
Centre/right half
WL Apps/Gls 2/0
Career: {Bury 4.44 [1/- WL]?}, Dale 4.44 [2/- WL]

Macauley appeared at centre half in the last game of the 1943-44 season for Dale, a 4-1 win over Stockport, and then played at right half in the second game of the following term.

John William (Jack) Gallon 1943-45

Born: Burradon 12.2.14
5'8" 11st7
Inside right
WL Apps/Gls 23/5
Career: Burradon Council School, Burradon Welfare, Gateshead am 1931, Blyth Spartans 8.31, Bedlington U. 1932, Carlisle U. trial 1934, Birmingham trial 2.36, Carlisle U. trial 3.36, Bradford C. 4.36 [20/5], Bradford PA 2.38 (exchange for J. Robertson) [31/4], Swansea T. 6.39 to 1945-46 [10/- WL], Bristol C. guest 1939-40 [1/- WL], Hartlepools U. guest 3.40 [1/1 WL], Bradford C. guest 3.41 and 10.41 [4/- WL], Bolton W. guest 5.41 to 1.43 [8/1 WL], Burnley guest 1943-44 [2/- WL], Stockport Co. guest 9.43 [1/- WL], Manchester U. guest 2.44 and 4.45 [4/- WL], Dale guest 4.44 [23/5 WL], Port Vale guest 4.45 [1/- WL], Walsall guest 9.44 [2/- WL], Gateshead 3.46 [11/1 WL, 20/2], North Shields 4.47, Ashington 11.48. Leicester C. scout
Honours: Northumberland County FA

Jack had managed just over 50 league appearances in the last three seasons before the war and was much in demand as a guest player during the regional leagues, appearing for ten sides before reappearing with Swansea in 1945-46. He first played for the Dale in the last game of 1943-44 and was a regular for them the following term. He spent the first post-war season with Gateshead in the Third (North).

Walter Ainsworth 1944-45
Born: South Bank 12.2.16
Inside right/right half
WL Apps/Gls 7/3
Career: South Bank, Sheffield W., Lincoln C. 5.37, Cheltenham T. cs.38, Plymouth A. 2.39, Dale guest 8.44 [7/3 WL]

Walter's only pre-war senior appearance had come in 1937 when he played centre half for a Lincoln side beaten 7-2 by Doncaster in the Division 3 North Cup. He was on Plymouth's books when he played in the first five games for Dale at the start of the 1944-45 season at inside right, scoring three times, and then reappeared twice playing right half. One of his goals was on his debut, but Dale lost 3-7 to Blackpool.

Arthur Cunliffe 1944-45, 1945-47

Born: Blackrod 5.2.09
5'7" 11st5
Outside left
FL Apps/Gls 23/5 Total Apps/Gls 66/13
Career: Adlington 8.23, Chorley 8.27, Blackburn R. 1.28 [129/47], Aston Vila 5.33 £8500 (joint fee with R. Dix) [70/11], Middlesbrough 12.35 [27/5], Burnley 4.37 [9/-], Hull C. 6.38 [42/20, 27/10 WL], Aldershot guest 10.39 to 1941 and 1942-46 [63/16 WL], Brighton & HA guest 11.41 [19/2 WL], Reading guest 3.43 [2/2 WL], Fulham guest 1944-45 [2/- WL], Dale guest 8.44, loan 1945, pt 6.46 [32/5 WL, 23/5], reserve coach 2.47, trainer 7.47, Bournemouth trainer 7.50, physio 1971 to 1974
Honours: England (2 caps) v Ireland, Wales 1932-33, Possible v Probables (international trial) 1936, Lancashire Junior Cup winners 1947

A cousin of Jim (q.v.), and like him an England international, Arthur originally worked in a cotton mill but after joining Blackburn in 1928, when just 18, he had a "meteoric rise to fame" the following season, netting twice on his debut at outside left in a 5-4 win against Manchester U. and hitting a hat-trick in just his fifth game. "One of the game's fastest wingers", he was "cool while on the ball" and had "perfect ball control and footwork". He played well over 100 games and won two England caps before a notable transfer to Aston Villa, along with Ronnie Dix, again making a scoring debut in the last game of the 1932-33 season. After further transfers he arrived at Hull the year before war broke out and scored 19 goals, his best ever tally. A PTI at the nearby army camp, he was a wartime guest for an Aldershot side boosted by numerous other international players such as Stan Cullis and Joe Mercer. Eventually returning to the north west, he first guested for the Dale in 1944 and after a period on loan signed permanently for them in 1946, on part time terms (he was also a plumber's mate). He scored Dale's first post-war goal and later in the season became reserve team player-coach, leading them to success in the Lancashire Junior Cup. Subsequently first team trainer, in 1950 he began a long association with Bournemouth, remaining on their staff until he was 65, when he received a well deserved testimonial.

Albert Griffiths 1944-45
Centre forward
WL Apps/Gls 1/0
Career: Dale 4.9.44 [1/- WL]

Griffiths played at centre forward for Dale in the second game of 1944-45, a 3-0 defeat at Blackpool.

Jack Bradshaw 1944-45
Left half
WL Apps/Gls 2/0
Career: Dale 1.5.44 [2/- WL]

Jack made just the two first team appearances for Dale, at the beginning and end of 1944-45, replacing George Haigh at left half.

John (Jack) Bradley 1944-45

Born: Hemsworth 27.11.16
Inside left
WL Apps/Gls 1/0
Career: South Kirkby Colliery, Huddersfield T. am 11.35, Swindon T. 8.36 [25/6], Chelsea 6.38, Southampton 5.39 [59/44 WL, 49/22], Reading guest 1940-44 [49/32 WL], Dale guest 9.44 [1/- WL], Bolton W. £8000 10.47 [92/19], Norwich C. 11.50 [6/-], Yarmouth T. player-trainer 7.52 to 6.55

Jack had made his debut in the Third (South) at Swindon but did not make the first team during a year at Chelsea. He became a prolific scorer during wartime football, netting 21 times for Southampton in 1939-40, though he didn't net in his one Dale game. He continued this form in 1946 and was sold to Bolton for £8000 just before his 31st birthday, playing on for a further four seasons in the league. Moving to Yarmouth as player-trainer, he remained living on the Norfolk coast until he died at the grand old age of 96, having kept the Jolly Farmers pub in Great Yarmouth for many years.

Kenneth J. Atkinson 1944-45
Born: {Rochdale OND.20?}
Outside left
WL Apps/Gls 2/0
Career: Dale 9.44 [2/- WL]

One of eight changes to the side for the third game of the 1944-45 season, winger Ken managed a couple of games for Dale, a win and a loss against Blackburn Rovers.

Harold Acton 1944-45
Born: {Rochdale 1921?}
Centre forward
WL Apps/Gls 2/1
Career: Dale 9.44 [2/1 WL]

Harold had two games at centre forward for Dale in September and October 1944 when Dale used a different number nine in each of the first six games.

Matthew {R.} Muir 1944-45
Born: {Penrith AMJ.19?}
Wing half/full back
WL Apps/Gls 15/0
Career: Dale pro 25.9.44 [15/- WL], Crystal Palace guest 1944-45 [1/- WL], Tottenham H. guest 1944-45 [1/- WL], Fulham guest 1944-45 [1/- WL]

A versatile defender, Matthew first played for Dale at left half in two games against Burnley but later in the 1944-45 season he also figured at right half and in both full back positions.

Alfred George Chaney 1944-45
Born: Stockport 22.3.14
Centre forward
WL Apps/Gls 1/0
Career: Dale am 18.9.44 [1/- WL]

Another player with just one senior game to his credit, he was at centre forward for Dale in a 2-2 draw at Burnley.

Samuel Walker Grimsditch 1944-45
Born: Great Lever 10.8.20 5'10" 11st10
Goalkeeper
WL Apps 7
Career: Farnworth St. Thomas, Wigan A., Bolton W. am 1940, pro 23.3.41 [19 WL], Dale guest 9.44 [7 WL], Rossendale U., Southport 12.11.45 [24 WL, 10], Rossendale U. cs.47, Droylsden 1948, Stalybridge C. 1950

A former England junior swimming champion, Walker played as a full back at Farnworth but joined Bolton as an amateur goalkeeper during the war, making his debut in the same match as Nat Lofthouse, before turning pro. He guested for Dale in 1944-45, two of his first four games being against Bolton, and after a brief stint as a reinstated amateur signed for Southport, making his FL bow in 1946. He had a few further seasons as a non-league player before having to retire as a result of kick on the knee. His son Leslie was also a senior non-league player with the likes of Altrincham.

David (Davy) Cochrane 1944-45

Born: Portadown 14.8.20
5'3" 9st 10
Centre forward
WL Apps/Goals 2/1
Career: Portadown jnr, pro 19.8.35, Leeds U. £2000 11.37 [28/3, 11/7 WL], Portadown 7.40, Shamrock Rovers 1941-42, Linfield 1942, Crewe A. guest 11.43 [2/3 WL], Dale guest 9.44 [2/1 WL], Stockport Co. guest 12.44 [2/- WL], Shamrock Rovers 1945, Leeds U. 1946 to 10.50 [144/25], Marlborough U. 1951
Honours: N. Ireland (12 caps) 1938-1950, N. Ireland Regional League (8 caps), Irish League (4 caps), Irish FA v Army 1942, 1943, Ireland v Combined Services 1944 (2), Irish League v Combined Services 1944, Irish War-time League champions 1943, 1944, County Antrim Shield final 1943, Irish Cup winners 1945, final 1944, 1946, Gold Cup winners, Yorkshire XI v FA 1945

One of the most capped players ever to turn out for Dale, Davy represented the Irish League and the Northern Ireland Regional League as well as the full Irish side twelve times (despite his debut ending in a 7-0 defeat by England). He had turned pro when he was 15, was sold to Leeds aged 17 and was in the Irish side at 18. An outside right for Leeds and Ireland, noted for his "blistering pace", at odds with his tiny physique he played at centre forward in wartime games, netting for Dale against Burnley and hitting a hat-trick for Crewe in a 5-5 draw at Everton as well as a treble for Ireland against the Army. All told, in 1944-45 he netted 50 goals. He returned to Leeds for a further four seasons after the war but his career with N. Ireland ended on a demoralising note when they lost 9-2 to England in 1949. He decided to retire the following year and later ran a newsagents. Davy's father had also played for Linfield.

George Douglas (Doug) Cole 1944-45
Born: Hessle 2.7.16
Left back
WL Apps/Gls 2/0
Career: Hessle Old Boys, Birmingham trial 5.35, Sheffield W. am 10.35, Sheffield U. 5.37 [1/-], Chester 5.39 [72/2 WL, 20/-], Dale guest 10.44 [2/- WL], Plymouth A. guest 1945-46 [1/- WL], Stalybridge Celtic 1948

Primarily a wing half, though he also figured at full back later in his career, George had managed just one FL game before war broke out. Appearing quite frequently with his own club Chester throughout hostilities, he guested for Dale in October 1944 and February 1945. He also made a number of league appearances for Chester after the war.

Donald Strachan 1944-45
Born: Burnley AMJ.26
Inside left
WL Apps/Gls 6/0
Career: Preston NE 1944 [9/4 WL], Dale guest 10.44 [6/- WL]

Quite a successful goalscorer in his games for his own club Preston, Strachan did not find the net in six games for Rochdale scattered through the 1944-45 season.

Henry (Harry) Lowe 1944-45

Born: Skelmersdale 19.2.07 5'9" 11st7
Left back
WL Apps/Gls 5/0
Career Skelmersdale Mission, Southport am 4.5.26, pro 21.12.27 [72/-], Everton 9.6.30 £ [5/-], Preston NE 21.12.32 [182/-], Swindon T. 19.6.39, New Brighton guest 4.41 to 4.42 [26/- WL], Southport guest 1940-41 [2/- WL], Dale guest 10.44 [5/- WL], Skelmersdale U. 1946-47, Burscough trainer, Skelmersdale coach 1960s

Distinctly a veteran when he turned up as a Spotland guest Harry had already been a FL regular at Southport in the late twenties after working, appropriately, as a boot maker. He then spent most of the 1930s at Preston, impressing with his "unflurried positional sense" and "cool and calculating methods", being everpresent for three seasons and accumulating around 200 senior appearances at full back. He was still playing for Skelmersdale when he was 40 and was their coach in the early 1960s. His cousin Albert Rimmer also played for Southport.

Thomas (Tom) Cochrane 1944-45

Born: Newcastle 7.10.08
5'8" 11st11
Inside left
WL Apps/Gls 4/1
Career: St Peter's Albion, Washington Colliery, Sunderland trial 4.27, Hull C. trial, Sheffield W. trial, Leeds U. 8.27 [244/23], Middlesbrough 10.36 £2500 [80/16], Bradford PA 5.39

£1100 [7/1 WL], Darlington guest 1939-40 [6/3 WL], Bradford C. guest 1.41 to 4.43 [4/- WL], Middlesbrough guest 4.41 to 1942 [33/9 WL], Bristol C. guest 1943-44 [1/- WL], Dale guest 10.44 [4/1 WL], Hartlepools U. guest 11.44 [11/7 WL]
Honours: Division 2 promotion 1932

Another veteran from the 1920s who made his Dale debut in the same games as Harry Lowe, Tom had made over 250 senior appearances in eight years as Leeds' regular outside left in the top flight, after previously working as a bricklayer. Described as a player who "travels well with a ball, and has a remarkable body swerve when on the run", he also figured regularly in Division One after being sold to Middlesbrough. Joining Park Avenue in the summer before the war, he then guested for several sides, often in an inside position, until 1945. He worked for a boot and shoe maker.

John M. Reid 1944-46
Centre forward
WL Apps/Gls 13/7
Career: Dale 27.11.44 [13/7 WL], Accrington St. guest 3.45 [1/- WL]

John was quite a regular performer for Dale in 1944-45, mostly at centre forward though he also played inside and outside right, scoring half a dozen goals in the process. He also played and scored in the first match of 1945-46.

Sydney (Syd) Roberts 1944-45

Born: {Bootle 1911}
5'9" 10st4
Inside left
WL Apps/Gls 2/1
Career: Bootle JOC, Liverpool 7.28 [57/10], Shrewsbury T 8.37, Chester 1.38 [29/6], Northfleet 8.39, Crewe A. guest 2.43 [2/- WL], Dale trial 11.44 [2/1 WL]

Yet another highly experienced man to turn out for Dale in 1944-45, Syd came up through the ranks at Anfield after joining from the same Bootle junior side as Alf Hanson (q.v.) whom he eventually partnered in the Liverpool first team. Though it was said that he "gives wing men passes which they can take to best advantage and generally shows the touches which go to make a first class forward", he was more often in the reserves and after eight years he moved on to Shrewsbury before returning to the league with Chester. He scored on his Dale debut but played only one other game during a brief trial spell. He worked as a decorator.

Samuel Hansbrew (Sammy) Makin 1944-47
Born: Radcliffe 14.11.25
Outside right
FL Apps/Gls 5/1 Total Apps/Gls 39/9
Career: Moss Rovers, Dale 5.44 [31/7 WL, 5/1], Droylsden 4.47 (exchange for F. Chappell)

Sammy joined Dale from minor football when he was 18 and managed a number of appearances in the last two wartime seasons, largely at outside right though his first few games had been on the other flank, scoring twice against Crewe in his first appearance of 1945-46. His FL career comprised just the first five games in the first peacetime season, his single goal coming in the last of them, a home draw against New Brighton. He was then exchanged for Droylsden's ex-Manchester City goalkeeper Fred Chappell who never made the first team at Spotland.

Stanley Pickstock 1944-45
Born: {Liverpool 10.5.21?}
Inside right
WL Apps/Goals 1/1
Career: Liverpool 1940-41 [3/2 WL], Wolverhampton W. 1943-44 [2/- WL], Dale guest 12.44 [1/1 WL]

A guest from Wolves, Pickstock scored on his one Dale appearance, a 4-2 defeat at Halifax in December 1944.

James Young 1944-46
Outside left
WL Apps/Gls 2/1
Career: Dale pro 5.8.44 [2/1 WL]

Young was Dale's left winger in victories over Halifax and Accrington in Christmas week 1944, scoring in the former. He was still on the retained list in 1946.

James Joseph (Jimmy) Constantine 1944-46

Born: Ashton 16.2.20
Centre forward
WL Apps/Gls 13/7
Total Apps/Gls 14/8
Career: Ashton National, (army), Dale 12.44 [13/7 WL], Manchester C. 19.9.45 £1000 [34/29 WL, 18/12], Bury 7.8.47 £4000 [32/14], Millwall 5.48 (exchange for R. Kelly) [141/75], Tonbridge 7.52, player-trainer 1955-56 to 1962
Honours: Division 2 champions 1947, Kent Challenge Cup final 1950, winners 1951

Dale's most prominent discovery of the war years, former Grenadier Guardsman Jimmy scored five times in one week in September 1945 and was immediately sold to Manchester City for £1000. He added another 29 goals for City in the remainder of the transitional season, including a hat-trick in the FA Cup. A "fast forward, stong in the air", he maintained an excellent scoring record when called upon when league football resumed, netting a hat-trick on his FL debut, and helped City win the Division Two title. Bury paid their record fee for him in 1947 and over his whole FL career he hit 101 goals in just 191 games. After hat-tricks for both City and Bury at the Den, Millwall signed him themselves in 1948 and 'Connie' was top scorer in three of his four seasons with them. Down in non-league football, he hit 39 goals for Tonbridge in 1953-54 and 37 the following term. After retiring through injury in 1956, he nevertheless reappeared several times, finally finishing in 1962 and playing local soccer until he was 50.

Harry Revell 1944-45
Outside left
WL Apps/Gls 1/0
Career: Dale am 12.2.45 [1/- WL]

Harry was one of seven changes in the side that met Burnley in February 1945, but Dale lost 4-0 at home and a further eight changes followed for the next game.

Herbert Harry Coombs Hall 1944-45
Born: Morecambe JAS.24
Goalkeeper
WL Apps 2
Career: Bolton W. 1943 [38 WL], Dale guest 2.45 [2/- WL], Liverpool 5.45 to 12.45 [8 WL]
Honours: Lancashire Senior Cup final 1944

Hall was Bolton's regular 'keeper in 1943-44, appearing in both legs of their Lancashire Senior Cup final defeat by Liverpool, with whom he later guested, but played no senior peacetime games. He figured twice for Dale, both against Blackpool when they lost 6-3 and 4-0.

Charles M. Wilson 1944-45
Right half
WL Apps/Gls 1/0
Career: Grimsby T. 1941-42 [2/- WL], Millwall 1942-43 [1/- WL], Stockport Co. guest 1942-43, signed 1944-45 [24/- WL], Dale guest 2.45 [1/- WL], Burnley pro 26.7.45 [15/- WL], Clapton Orient 1945-46 [1/- WL]

Then on Stockport's books, though he made wartime appearances elsewhere, too, Charles made one guest appearance for Dale in February 1945 in the 6-3 loss to Blackpool. He joined Burnley for the transitional post-war season and appeared in the FA Cup, his only 'official' senior game.

James Chambers 1944-45
Born: Alcester 1.4.18
Centre half
WL Apps/Gls 1/0
Career: Britannia Batteries FC (Redditch), Worcester C., Bromsgrove Rovers 8.36, Bolton W. am 8.36, Swindon T. 5.37 [4/-], Worcester C. cs.39, Luton T. guest 1939-40 [6/- WL], Dale guest 2.45 [1/- WL], Norwich C. guest 1945-46 [1/- WL]

Transferred from Bromsgrove Rovers to first division Bolton after just one Birmingham Combination game, James appeared briefly in the FL before the war, with Swindon. He figured just once for Dale, again in the 6-3 defeat by Blackpool.

Jack Dixon Foxton 1944-45
Born: Salford 17.6.21
Left half
WL Apps/Gls 1/0
Career: Bolton W. 1943 [8/- WL], Dale guest 2.45 [1/- WL], Portsmouth 5.45 [19/- WL, 1/-], Swindon T. 9.48 to 1951 [49/-]

The eight changes Dale made for the game against Blackpool included a half back line all making their debuts for the club, and Jack, from Bolton Wanderers, took the left half spot. He subsequently signed for Portsmouth, making his league debut after the war.

Adolph Jonathan (Alf) Hanson 1944-46

Born: Bootle 27.2.12
5'8" 10st10
Outside left
WL Apps/Gls 17/11
Total Apps/Gls 19/11
Career: Bootle JOC, Everton trial 10.30, Runcorn 11.30, Stalybridge Celtic 1.31, Liverpool 11.31 [166/50], Chelsea 6.38 £7500 [37/8, 3/1 WL], New Brighton guest 10.39 to 4.41 [49/37 WL], Liverpool guest 5.40, 5.41 and 8.43 [16/3 WL], Chester guest 1940-41, 5.45 [3/2 WL], Wrexham guest 5.41 [1/- WL], Manchester C. guest 11.43 [1/- WL], Bolton W. guest 8.44 [5/1 WL], Tranmere R. guest 1944-45 [27/11 WL], Dale guest 2.45 to 1.46 [19/11 WL], Crewe A. guest 5.45 [1/- WL], Southport guest 1945-46 [13/1 WL], South Liverpool player-manager 1946, Shelbourne U. player-manager 1947-48, Ellesmere Port Town player-manager 2.49, Penmaenmawr 1950
Baseball international for England

Honours: England v Scotland 1941, Football League v British XI 1941, Lancashire Senior Cup winners 1933

A top notch winger throughout the 1930s, he was noted for his speed and pinpoint centres. He was also a more than useful goalscorer in his own right with a half century of goals for Liverpool (including the winner in the 1933 Lancs Cup Final) and was the subject of a huge transfer to Chelsea in 1938 (the British record set that year being only £13000). During the war he played for England (despite his unfortunate first name!) and for the Football League in what was called "the most freakish, goalfull representative match of all time", the FL winning 9-7 with Hanson netting twice. He appeared as a guest with a whole host of league clubs in the north west, turning out for Dale a number of times in both 1944-45 and 1945-46 and netting a hat-trick against Southport. He subsequently continued his career as player-manager of several non-league sides and was a plumber by trade. His younger brother Stan kept goal for Bolton for 20 years. [N.B. The son of a Norwegian sailor, Alf was actually born Adolf Hansen.]

Albert Hesketh 1944-45
Born: Preston 1920
Goalkeeper
WL Apps 1
Career: Preston N.E. [5 WL], Southport guest 1943-44 [1 WL], Dale guest 3.45 [1 WL]

A goalkeeper with the unfortunate Dale record of one match, eight goals conceded, he guested for them against Blackburn in March 1945 when Dale lost 8-0 at home. He managed five games for his home club Preston during the same season.

John Victor (Jack) Brinton 1944-45

Born: Avonmouth 11.7.16
5'7" 10st6
Outside left
WL Apps/Gls 2/1
Career: ShellMex & BP (Avonmouth), Avonmouth T., Bristol C. am cs.34, pro 8.35 [12/1], Newport Co. 7.37 [6/-], Derby Co. 1.38 £1000 [8/2, 2/- WL], (army), Chester guest 2.44 to 10.44 [9/5 WL], Crewe A. guest 1.45 [5/2 WL], Dale guest 3.45 [2/1 WL], Mansfield T. guest 1945-46 [1/1 WL], Newport Co. guest 1945-46 [3/3 WL], Swindon T. guest 10.45 [1/- WL], Stockport Co. 7.46 [58/9], Leyton Orient 8.48 [4/1], Street 1949, Chippenham T. 9.49

The younger brother of Bristol City stalwart Ernie, Jack followed him to Ashton Gate, but made the step up to Division 1 Derby on the back of a brief spell with Newport County and a cup hat-trick against Kidderminster. During the war he hit a hat-trick when Chester beat Crewe by the remarkable score of 9-5, but was also in the side when they lost 9-2 to Everton. Guesting briefly for Dale during his army service, he figured regularly for Stockport County after the war before returning to the West Country non-league scene and later working as the manager of the Port of Bristol.

Albert Edward (Eddie) Lyons
1944-45, 1953-55
Born: Rochdale 20.5.20
Left back
FL Apps/Gls 19/1 Total Apps/Gls 29/1
Career: Stockport Co. 1940 [54/- WL], Bury 12.44, pro 4.45 [14/- WL, 2/-], Dale guest 3.45 [5/- WL], Millwall 3.50 [6/-], Crewe A. 7.52 [23/-], Dale 12.53 [19/1], Dartford pt 7.55

Eddie first appeared for Dale during the war while on Bury's books and also played against them in the 1945-46 FA Cup. He only managed two FL games for the Shakers, though, and did not fare much better at Millwall. He did play more frequently for Crewe in 1952-53 and then followed Harry Catterick to Spotland. His Dale debut at left back was in a 4-0 defeat on Boxing Day 1953, but when he regained his place the following month Dale won five games in a row. In a 4-2 victory against Workington in March he scored the only goal of his career and by amazing coincidence his brother George – who had made his debut in the same game as Eddie - scored, too. Eddie appeared in only a handful of games the following term before retiring to open a business in London and play part time for Dartford.

Frederick L. (Fred) Whittaker 1944-45
Born: Bethnal Green AMJ.27
Right half
WL Apps/Gls 7/0
Career: Arsenal am 17.2.44, Dale guest 3.45 [7/- WL]

A young Arsenal amateur, Fred played wing half for Dale in seven games towards the end of the 1944-45 season.

James Wotherspoon 1944-45
Born: {Newburgh c.1921}
Centre forward
WL Apps/Gls 1/0
Career: {Raith R., Markinch Victoria Rangers, Raith R. guest 1939-40, 1941-42, re-signed 1944-45 [5/4 ScWL]}, Dale 3.45 [1/- WL]

Wotherspoon was Dale's centre forward in a 1-0 defeat by Blackburn, a considerable improvement on the 8-0 demolition by the same opposition the previous week. He is almost certainly the same player – a former blacksmith – who scored a hat-trick for Raith in his one Scottish Regional League East game in 1939-40, guesting from his junior club Markinch.

Albert Malam 1944-45

Born: Liverpool 20.1.13
5'6" 10st9
Inside left
WL Apps/Gls 2/0
Career: Loraine Street School, Bedford Amateurs, Everton trial, Liverpool trial 8.31, Colwyn Bay U. 3.32, Chesterfield 11.32 £50 [58/25], Huddersfield T. 9.34 £3000 [21/11], Doncaster R. 9.36 [95/26, 2/- WL], New Brighton guest 10.39 to 4.42 [81/37 WL], Tranmere R. guest 1939-40 and 1941-42 [2/2 WL], Newport Co. guest 1941-42, Manchester C. guest 3.42 and 8.42 [14/9 WL], Crewe A. guest 12.42 to 10.43 [33/14 WL], Wrexham guest 1943-44 [28/13 WL], Southport guest 1944-45 [27/9 WL], Dale guest 3.45 [2/- WL], Wrexham 2.46 [6/2 WL, 6/1], Runcorn player-manager 1.47
Honours: Liverpool Schoolboys, Lancashire Schoolboys

Despite a broken leg in 1935, Albert was an experienced pre-war performer in all three divisions – Huddersfield finishing third in the first division in 1936 when Albert hit a hat-trick in an 8-0 victory over Liverpool – and cost Doncaster their record fee. Remarkably, in the wartime conditions, he didn't miss a single match for New Brighton between his debut for them in October 1939 and when they ceased operations three years later, netting four times in a 10-1 victory over Tranmere. He continued to play regularly as a guest, though just twice for Dale, until transferred to Wrexham in 1946, playing a few league games the following term. His son Colin was a well known sports journalist.

Arthur L. Hughes 1944-45
Born: {Bolton JAS.26}
Outside right
WL Apps/Gls 1/0
Career: Bolton W. am 15.4.44 [1/- WL], Dale guest 3.45 [1/- WL]

Winger Hughes, from Bolton Wanderers, played in Dale's 1-0 win at Tranmere in March 1945.

Arthur Bailey 1944-45
Born: Beswick, Manchester 11.1.14 5'7" 11st4
Inside left
WL Apps/Gls 1/0
Career: Chapel-en-le-Frith, Manchester N.E. 1932-33, Oldham A. 22.5.33 [53/12], Stalybridge Celtic 19.2.37, Oldham A. 24.7.39 [137/52 WL], Droylsden guest 1.40, Wolverhampton W. guest 3.43 [1/- WL], Crewe A. guest 3.44 [1/- WL], Blackpool guest 3.44 [3/- WL], Manchester U. guest 4.44 [1/- WL], Dale guest 3.45 [1/- WL], Port Vale guest 1944-45 [2/- WL], Shrewsbury T. 8.45

A high scoring forward in non-league football, netting 40 goals in 1931-32, while working as a joiner, Arthur first appeared for Oldham in 1933. Leaving four years later, he re-signed for them in 1939, playing in their match on September 2nd that year. "Admired for the way he engineers attacks and paves the way to goal", he was a stalwart of their wartime teams and managed odd games for other sides, including one for Dale in March 1945.

Walter Francis Thorpe 1944-45
Born: Barton upon Irwell JAS.23
Goalkeeper
WL Apps 1
Career: Notts Co. am 27.3.44 [4 WL], Blackpool pro 27.6.44 [30 WL], Southport guest 1944-45 [15 WL], Manchester C. guest 2.45 and 1.46 [3 WL], Dale guest 4.45 [1/- WL]

A fairly regular performer between the sticks for Southport and Blackpool in the last two wartime seasons, Thorpe guested for Dale in April 1945.

James Bate 1944-45
Inside left
WL Apps/Goals 1/0
Career: Birmingham c.1939 [2/1 WL], Aston Villa 1942-43, pro 1944 [1/- WL], Dale guest 4.45 [1/- WL]

Aston Villa's Bate appeared for Dale in a 3-0 defeat at Stockport.

James (Jimmy) Gemmell 1944-45

Born: Sunderland 17.11.11
6'0" 11st3
Centre half
WL Apps/Gls 3/0
Career: Ouston Juniors, West Stanley 8.28, Annfield Plain 9.29, Bury 19.3.30 [255/-, 58/2 WL], Manchester U. guest 5.40 and 12.40 [3/- WL], Leicester C. 11.42 to 1945 [53/- WL], Dale guest 4.45

[3/- WL], Southport player-coach 24.8.45 to 1947 [34/- WL, 25/-]. Lincoln trainer 7.48, Coventry C. assistant trainer

Jimmy was a "robust and dour, long-kicking defender" who could nevertheless "race the fastest forwards", enabling him to play centre half or left back. He spent almost a decade at Bury, racking up over 250 appearances and missing just three games in one spell of three seasons. He guested for several sides during the war, when he worked in a factory making engines for Wellington and Lancaster bombers, appearing for Dale towards the end of 1944-45. He then spent a couple of seasons as Southport player-coach and later worked both in the engineering industry and back in the game as a trainer. His father, also Jimmy, was a Scottish inside forward recruited by Sunderland in the early 1900s and his sister married Aston Villa's Scottish international Billy Simpson.

James (Jimmy) Taylor 1944-45
Born: Ashton-in-Makerfield 7.4.25
Outside left
WL Apps/Gls 1/0
Career: Manchester C. 1942, pro 10.44 [34/3 WL], Dale guest 4.45 [1/- WL], Crewe A. 6.47 to 1949 [49/8]

Jimmy was a Manchester City youngster borrowed by Dale for their home defeat by Stockport in April 1945 when the team showed no fewer than 10 changes from the previous game, though the opposition and the result were the same. (This appearance was also given as "Thorpe"). After the war he had a couple of seasons in the league with Crewe.

Albert Mycock 1944-45
Born: Manchester 31.1.23 5'7" 11st6
Centre forward/inside right
WL Apps/Gls 2/0
Career: Goslings 1942, Manchester U. 5.44 [29/16 WL], Accrington St. guest 3.45 [1/- WL], Dale guest 4.45 [2/- WL], Crystal Palace 6.46 [59/9], Barrow 7.48 (exchange for J. Mullen) [42/4], Macclesfield 1949-50 to 1950-51

Scorer of 84 goals for Goslings in two years, Albert had a highly successful first season with Manchester United, netting 16 goals in 1944-45, and he also played two of the last three games of the season for Dale. When peacetime football returned he was transferred to Palace before returning to the north west with Barrow, generally playing on the wing rather than in his earlier inside position, and then netted 15 times in 23 Cheshire League games for Macclesfield.

Fred Olive 1944-46
Goalkeeper
WL Apps 3 Total Apps 4 Career: Dale 5.45 [3 WL]

Fred played in the final game of 1944-45 and the first three of the following season, Dale winning two and losing two.

William (Billy) Woods
1944-45, 1945-47, 1948-50
Born: Farnworth 12.3.26 5'8" 10st12
Inside forward
FL Apps/Gls 28/2 Total Apps/Gls 49/9
Career: Farnworth, Bolton W., Dale guest 4.45 [2/- WL], Moss Grove, Dale pt 8.5.45 [11/1 WL, 15/1], Bradford PA 18.1.47 £4120 [5/-], Dale 13.1.48 £1000 [13/1], Barrow 4.11.49 £1000 [16/4], Crewe A. 29.7.50, Accrington St. 11.11.50 (exchange for D. Travis and S. Parker) to 16.4.51 [3/-]
Honours: Lancashire Senior Cup winners 1949

Billy, a "flame-haired inside forward", was for a time Dale's most expensive outgoing transfer, and in fact renowned wheeler-dealer Ted Goodier managed to sell him twice, even though he only ever scored two league goals for Dale. He first guested briefly for Dale while on Bolton's books, before signing as a part-timer on VE Day 1945, when just turned 19 (he also worked as a mechanic). After some appearances in the interim tournaments the following term, he made his FL bow at the end of September 1946 in the 6-0 hammering of Carlisle that gave Dale their first post-war victory, in their 9th game. Though Billy himself was the only one of the forwards not to score, unsurprisingly he kept his place and had a terrific time in the FA Cup, scoring five times including a hat-trick against Hartlepools, as Dale twice more scored six goals before going out to eventual cup winners Charlton. Immediately after scoring a brilliant goal against the first division side, he was transferred to second division Bradford for £4500, a new club record, Park Avenue themselves having just collected £13,000 for the transfer of Len Shackleton to Newcastle. Two years later Dale bought him back for a cut-price £1000. but he again scored just one league goal before being sold for a second time, and after short stays with three other league clubs he disappeared from the scene when still only 25.

Jack Higham 1944-46
Inside right/right half
WL Apps/Gls 2/0
Career: Dale am 21.8.44 [2/- WL]

Jack made his debut at inside right in the last match of 1944-45, when Dale beat Chester, and appeared once more, the following October, at right half in a 5-0 win over Southport.

William Whittle 1944-46
Centre forward/right half
WL Apps/Gls 5/0
Career: Dale am 5.45 [5/- WL]

Another debutant, at centre forward, in the last game of the 1944-45 season, his other four games came at right half in April 1946 and included a 4-0 away win at Oldham. He was retained at the end of the season but made no more appearances.

Edric Alfred ('Syd') Pomphrey 1945-47
Born: Stretford 31.5.16
Right back
FL Apps/Gls 9/0   Total Apps/Gls 46/0
Career: Hyde U., Notts Co. 9.44 [10/- WL], Dale 10.45 [29/- WL, 9/-], Droylsden cs.47
Cricket for Rochdale CC.

Unsurprisingly never using his real first name, Syd turned out for Notts County before being Dale's regular right back in their Third Division North West campaign. He also started the first seven post-war games, but these produced just a solitary point and Syd played only twice more, deputising for Len Jackson. He was also a useful cricketer with Rochdale in the Central Lancashire League.

Robert Muir 1939-47
Born: St. Ninians 5'10" 12st10
Left back
WL Apps/Gls 1/0
Career: Rutherglen Glencairn, Celtic trial, Hamilton Ac. trial, Portsmouth 5.34 [1], Third Lanark 5.35 [104 ScL], Dale 3.7.39 [1/- WL], Kings Park guest 1939-40 [5 ScWL], {Partick Thistle guest 1942-43 [2 ScWL]?}, Brighton & HA guest 1944-45 [2 WL], Millwall guest {1941-42?} and 1944-45 [3 WL], Crystal Palace guest 1944-45 [1 WL]

Robert was a Scottish goalkeeper who had played one FL game for Portsmouth in 1934 and was a regular at Third Lanark for three seasons in the Scottish first division. Signed by Rochdale as reserve to Peter Robertson in 1939, he did not make any appearances for them in the regional leagues, though guesting for clubs back in Scotland and in the south of England. Bizarrely, he finally made his Dale debut at left back in the first Division 3 North West fixture of the transitional 1945-46 campaign, a 4-1 defeat by Wrexham. [NB. It is possible that this appearance should have been assigned to Matthew Muir]. He was retained as one of several reserve goalkeepers for 1946-47 but again without making the first team.

Joseph Michael (Joe or 'Mac') McCormick 1945-48
Born: Holywell 15.7.16
Wing half
FL Apps/Gls 66/0 Total Apps/Gls 109/1
Career: Bolton W. 10.37 [2/- WL], Crewe A. guest 11.44 [1/2 WL], Dale 5.45 [30/1 WL, 66/-], Boston U. 7.48, Scunthorpe U. 1949-50 [7/-], retired 1951

Although he had signed for Bolton in 1937, Joe — otherwise known as Mac — didn't make his debut for them until 1944-45, then spent the final wartime season as a regular for Rochdale. Thus, like many of his generation, his long delayed FL debut came when he was already 30. Skippering the side and equally at home in either wing half berth he spent two further seasons at Spotland, passing a century of appearances in all competitions, before dropping down to Midland League football. However, he made a brief reappearance in the FL following Scunthorpe's election in 1950.

Arthur Jones 1945-47
Born: Harpurhey 23.4.20
Outside right
FL Apps/Gls 1/0 Total Apps/Gls 16/3
Career: Goslings FC, Dale 5.45 [13/3 WL,   1/-], Hyde U. 4.47, Ashton U. 1950, {Rossendale U.?}, Macclesfield cs.53, Congleton T. 1954, Droylsden, Ashton U. 8.55
Honours: Cheshire Senior Cup winners 1954

Coming from the Goslings club in Manchester which also produced future Manchester United and England man Henry Cockburn during the war, Arthur figured quite successfully for Rochdale in 1945-46, scoring three times from his right wing berth as well as laying on chances for the likes of Jimmy Constantine and then Joe Hargreaves. On the resumption of league football, he was almost entirely consigned to the reserves, appearing only once, when he replaced Alex Carruthers for the Boxing Day game at Stockport in front of a 13,000 crowd, fellow reserve and namesake, Wally Jones scoring both Dale goals in a 5-2 defeat. A regular scorer in non-league football, he netted 24 times in 1953-54 for Macclesfield, including the winner in the Cheshire Cup Final.

Joseph (Joe) Meek 1945-46

Born: Hazlerigg 31.5.10
5'6" 11st7
Inside right
WL Apps/Gls 4/1
Career: Burradon Welfare, Pelaw CWS, Seaton Delaval cs.26, Bedlington U. 7.27, Liverpool trial 3.28, Crawcrook Albion, St. Peter's Albion, Stockton, Middlesbrough am 1929, Newcastle CWS, Gateshead am 1930, pro 1.31 [135/50], Bradford PA 10.34 [31/11], Tottenham H. 3.36 [45/15], Swansea T. 2.39 (exchange for J. Harris) [16/5], Newcastle U. guest 1939-40, 1941-42 [2/- WL], Lincoln C. guest 1940-42 [21/10 WL], Middlesbrough guest 8.40 [1/- WL], Southport guest 1940-41 [3/- WL], Grimsby T. guest 1941-42 [1/- WL], Nottingham F. guest 1941-42 [1/- WL], Dale guest 8.45 [4/1 WL], Burnley guest 1945-46 [3/- WL]. Burradon Welfare committee 1957

A survivor from the Third North in the early thirties, Joe had been an ever-present with the renamed Gateshead, when they missed promotion on goal average in 1931-32. He worked his way up to play around 100 games for Park Avenue, Spurs and Swansea, then all in Division Two, netting a hat-trick on his home debut for Spurs in an 8-0 win over Southampton (another Dale guest, George Hunt, also scoring three). Originally a left winger, he had changed flanks after injuring his left foot in a pit accident. He played odd games during the war, including four for Dale at the beginning of 1945-46 – the last lost 7-0 at Stockport – but was 35 by this time and did not resume his FL career at Swansea. In the 1950s he was on the committee at his original club Burradon Welfare.

George Lunn 1945-46
Born: Bolton-on-Dearne 28.6.15
Left back
WL Apps/Goals 1/0
Career: Frickley Colliery, Aston Villa 5.38, Fulham guest 1940-41 [1/- WL], Clapton O. guest 1940-41 [6/- WL], Watford guest 1940-41 [1/- WL], Northampton T. guest 1941-42 [1/- WL], Doncaster R. guest 1942-43 [1/- WL], Southport guest 1944-45 [5/- WL], Chester guest 9.44 and 12.45 [7/- WL], Stockport Co. guest 2.45 [1/- WL], Wrexham guest 1944-45 [1/- WL], Dale guest 8.45 [1/- WL], Birmingham 9.46, Watford 10.47 [5/-]

George was of the generation of players who lost most of their careers to the war, eventually making his FL debut in 1947 with Watford, when he was 32. Although on Villa's books, he never figured in their first team but guested for a variety of sides including Dale, either at centre half or full back.

Peter (Paddy) Molloy 1945-46

Born: Haslingden 20.4.09
5'9" 12st2
Wing half
WL Apps/ Gls 4/0
Total Apps/Gls 5/0
Career: King's Royal Rifles, Rossendale U. trial 4.28, Accrington St. 7.30, Park Royal FC, Fulham am 8.31, pro 12.31 [4/-], Bristol R. 5.33 [6/-], Cardiff C. 2.34 [23/-], Queens Park R. 7.35 [3/-], Stockport Co. 7.36 [10/-], Carlisle U. 5.37 [33/-], Bradford C. 5.38 to 1943-44 [25/-, 65/2 WL], Hartlepools U. guest 5.40 [1/- WL], Chelsea guest 1940-41 [2/- WL], Watford guest 1942-43 [1/- WL], Belfast Distillery 8.43, Clapton O. guest 1943-44 [1/- WL], Chester guest 3.44 [1/- WL], Accrington St. guest 1944-46 [26/- WL], Dale guest 9.45 [4/- WL], Ballymena U. 1945, Dundalk 1946, Kettering player-manager, Galatasary (Turkey) manager 1947, Notts Co. 4.48 [1/-], Turkey national coach, Watford 1951 to 1991 as trainer, coach, caretaker-manager, and physio
Honours: Division 3(N) champions 1937, Division 3(N) Cup winners 1939, N. Ireland Regional League winners 1944, Division 3 North West first championship winners 1945-46

Another real veteran still playing at the end of the war, Paddy had been largely a reserve at his various league clubs until signing for Carlisle in 1937. He played mainly for his own club Bradford City in the early war years, before moving to Distillery. He alternated between right and left half in a run of games for Dale in September 1945 until they lost 7-0 to Stockport. He figured in one last FL game in May 1948, just after his 39th birthday. After a stint as the national coach in Turkey he spent over 40 years on the staff at Watford until he was 82. Before starting his football career, he had boxed on a fairground attraction after leaving the army.

John Norman (Jack) Breedon 1945-46

Born South Hiendley 29.12.07
5'10" 11st3
Goalkeeper
WL Apps 4
Career: South Hiendley School, South Hiendley Amateurs, South Hiendley Bible Class, Hemsworth West End, South Hiendley Amateurs, Barnsley 9.28 [8],

Sheffield W. 11.30 £1000 [45], Manchester U. 7.35 [35, 171 WL], Bolton W. guest 3.42 [1 WL], Manchester C. guest 3.45 [1 WL], Dale guest 9.45 [4 WL], Burnley 10.45 [4 WL], Cliftonville cs.46, Halifax T. manager 7.47, Bradford PA scout 12.50, manager 1.55 to 10.55, Leeds U. scout 1960s
Honours: Division 2 champions 1936, promoted 1938, Lancashire Cup winners 1938, 1941, Sheffield v Glasgow 1932, League North Second Championship winners 1942

Approaching 38 when he turned out at Spotland, Jack had started out with Barnsley back in 1928. Although never really a FL regular, the former miner nevertheless earned transfers to Sheffield Wednesday, where he was said to be "one of the most promising goalkeepers in league football and certainly one of the most spectacular" and then Manchester United. He played frequently for United in 1938-39 in Division 1 and then through much of the war, notably saving a penalty in the Lancashire Cup Final defeat of Burnley in 1941. He was later manager of Halifax and Bradford Park Avenue, though both sides were struggling at the time.

Robert Griffiths   1945-46
Left back
WL Apps/Goals 1/0
Career: Dale 9.45 [1/- WL]

Griffiths was Dale's fourth left back in four games at the start of the 1945-46 season when he appeared against Oldham.

Fred Taylor   1945-46
Outside left
WL Apps/Goals 1/1 Total Apps/Gls 2/1
Career: Dale 9.45 [1/1 WL]

Fred made his debut against Manchester United in the Lancashire Cup but despite a goal against Oldham in the Third North West in September 1945, these were his only two senior appearances.

J. Clive   1945-46
Right back
WL Apps/Goals 1/0
Career: Dale 9.45 [1/- WL]

Another player with just one wartime Dale appearance, Clive played in a 4-2 victory over Stockport at the end of September 1945.

Donald (Don) Partridge   1945-56
Born: Bolton 22.10.25
Half back/full back
FL Apps/Gls 103/2 Total Apps/Gls 135/2
Career: Farnworth, Dale 10.45 to 1956 [15/- WL, 103/2], Bolton W. scout and junior team coach 1957-58
Honours: Lancashire Junior Cup winners 1947, 1951

Don was the archetypal one club man of the 1940s and '50s, spending a decade with Rochdale – indeed becoming the first player to make FL appearances for them in 10 different seasons and still the only one to do so for 10 seasons in succession – yet spending most of it in the 'stiffs'. He arrived from Farnworth part way through the transition Division Three North West campaign and then played half a dozen league games in 1946-47, as well as representing the Reserves in the Lancashire Junior Cup final. This set the pattern for the rest of his career as Don gradually accumulated 103 FL appearances, with only 1948-49 seeing him appear regularly (33 consecutive games) at wing half. He later figured more at centre half and also played at right back on occasions, winning a second Lancs Junior Cup medal before leaving to join Bolton's staff after just a single appearance in both 1954-55 and 1955-56.

John James (Jack) Brindle   1945-46, 1947-48
Born: Blackburn 12.7.17 5'11" 11st12
Inside right
FL Apps/Gls 1/0 Total Apps/Gls 25/10
Career: Blackburn R. am 1934 [2/- WL], Accrington St. guest 1940 to 1942, Burnley 13.3.43 [3/1 WL], Howard & Bullough 11.43, Dale 29.9.45 [18/9 WL], Chelsea 6.3.46 £1000 [2/- WL], Dale 9.8.47 £500 [1/-], New Brighton 6.3.48 [9/3], {Rhyl cs.48?}, Stalybridge Celtic 8.48

Jack had joined Blackburn as an amateur back in 1934 but did not play in any first team matches until odd wartime games in 1939 and 1940, subsequently guesting for Accrington, albeit in the Lancashire Combination. He was playing for a factory side when picked up by Dale but in a remarkable turn around of his fortunes, 9 goals in 18 league games saw him transferred to Chelsea for £1000. Although he did play for them in the transitional season, his FL debut came after he returned to Spotland, on Christmas Day 1947 in the 4-0 defeat at Bradford City. His only other league games came later that season after he joined New Brighton along with Sam Earl, his style being described as "robust, energetic, yet skilful".

John (Jack) Livesey 1945-46, 1947-51

Born: Preston 8.3.24
Inside forward
FL Apps/Gls 113/36 Total Apps/Gls 125/39
Career: Preston NE am, pro 4.44 [28/8 WL], Dale guest 9.45 [1/1 WL], Bury 5.46 [7/1], Doncaster R. 1.47 [3/-], Dale 4.48 [113/36], Southport 7.51 £1000 [31/9], Wigan A. cs.52, Nelson cs.54 to cs.55. Later scout for Bury
Honours: Preston schoolboys, Division 3N champions 1947, Lancashire Senior Cup winners 1949

Although he played one game for Dale as a guest in 1945-46, it was when he returned two seasons later that Jack made his mark. An important member of Dale's successful sides of 1949 and 1950 which won the Lancashire Cup and finished 3rd in the league, he had arrived at Spotland after short spells with Bury and Doncaster and played on the left wing in the final three games of 1947-48, scoring on his (second) debut. Nicknamed 'Scoops', apparently on account of his kicking action, he was soon switched to inside forward, forming a tremendous partnership with centre forward Jack Connor after the latter joined the club. They both scored in the victory over Manchester City that took Dale to the Lancashire Cup Final in 1949 and each of them netted 16 times in the league the following season, Jack netting hat-tricks against Gateshead and Mansfield (when Dale won 7-1 despite the absence of Connor). New Brighton may have been Jack's favourite opponents, though, as he netted first minute goals against them in successive seasons. Popular with the fans, and reputedly a great foil to their voluble boss in the dressing room, supporters were upset when Goodier sold him to Southport in 1951, soon after Connor's departure. He subsequently teamed up again with Goodier at Wigan, where he had an outstanding scoring record, 52 goals in 76 Lancashire Combination games, and later worked for a wine merchants for many years. Jack claimed to be the first professional player to wear contact lenses (in his spell at Doncaster), his poor eyesight having earlier cost him a chance with first division Preston after he had done well for them in wartime games (he also failed his army medical for the same reason).

Joseph Albert (Joe) Hargreaves 1945-48
Born: Accrington 30.10.15
Centre forward
FL Apps/Gls 35/24 Total Apps/Gls 68/51
Career: {Accrington St. 1941-42}, Rossendale U., Dale pt 10.45 [24/19 WL, 35/24], Stalybridge Celtic 8.48, Accrington St. coach 8.49
Cricket for Church CC
Honours: Lancashire Junior Cup winners 1947

Dale's top scorer in the last wartime and the first peacetime campaign, Joe was a late starter in senior football, being a week short of his 30th birthday when he reached Spotland via non-league football. He started in style, though, with two goals in each of his first three games and when the FL resumed he scored a hat-trick in Dale's first post-war victory (obtained only at the 9th attempt), a 6-0 beating of Carlisle. One of the still rather few Dale centre forward to hit 20 goals in a season, despite an apparently awkward looking style, Joe managed 23 in just 30 FL games in 1946-47, as well as two in cup ties. (Somehow he was also deemed eligible for the Reserves' Lancashire Junior Cup final, and scored in that, too). It could well have been more, but as a part timer he had to miss a number of games due to work commitments as a clerk, but in any case it stood as a post-war record for nearly 20 years. He also did not take any penalties, despite Dale missing all eight they were awarded that season, apparently because being stone deaf he could not hear the referee's signal to take the kick. After 51 goals in 68 games, or exactly three goals every four games, one of the best strike rates of any Dale forward, he returned to the non-league game, though he did later coach at Accrington Stanley. Also a top club cricketer, Joe played for Church in the Lancashire League from 1936 to 1959 and still holds the record as their highest scoring amateur with 138 against Colne in 1941. His grandson Bryn has played for Accrington CC.

Leonard (Len) Jackson 1945-49
Born: Stockport 10.5.23
Right back
FL Apps/Gls 61/0 Total Apps/Gls 75/0
Career: Manchester C. 1942, pro 1.45 [15/- WL], Dale pt 19.9.45 [5/- WL, 61/-], Northwich Victoria 12.48

After some wartime games for Manchester City, Len signed professional with them in 1945, but then moved to Dale as a part-timer (he was also a machinist) later the same year. Little used in 1945-46, he was given his FL debut at right back the following term after Dale had picked up just one point in seven games. The new full back partnership of Len and Norman Kirkman certainly worked, as Dale lost only one of the next 14 league and cup games and eventually finished 6th. Len remained a first choice throughout the following season, too, but after being in dispute with the club in the summer of 1948 was released following the arrival of Bill Watson.

Ernest (Ernie) Toseland 1945-46

Born: Northampton 17.3.05
5'6" 10st3
Outside right
WL Apps/Gls 3/2
Total Apps/Gls 4/2
Career: Guildhall U., Higham Ferrars T. c.1923, St Lawrence's Crescent, Shakespear U., Queens Park R. 5.25, Higham Ferrars T. 5.27., Coventry C. 4.28, [22/11], Manchester C. 1.3.29 [368/61], Sheffield W. 14.3.39 [12/2, 4/- WL], Manchester C. guest 11.39 and 11.45 [2/- WL], Manchester U. guest 5.40 [1/- WL], Stockport Co. guest 2.40 to 3.42 [46/5 WL], Dale guest 12.45 [3/2 WL], Droylsden guest 8.46, Mossley 1946-47
Honours: Football League v Irish League 1929, Charity Shield 1935, 1938, FA Cup final 1933, winners 1934, Lancashire Senior Cup winners 1930, final 1932

Even older than Jack Breedon, Ernie was turned 40 when he appeared for Dale. After playing rugby as a wing three-quarter at school, he had joined QPR way back in 1925. Making his mark at Coventry as a "flying winger" who "has good ball control and uses fine judgement in centring" despite breaking his collarbone on his debut, he was transferred to Manchester City, representing the FL the same year and playing in two FA Cup Finals. A "fine dribbler and very fast with the ball" known as 'Twinkle Toes Toseland', in exactly 10 years, he accumulated a massive tally of 409 league and cup games for City, in which he scored 75 times, including goals in the 1933 and 1934 FA Cup semi-finals. Ernie hadn't played at senior level for two and a half years when he scored the winning goal on his Dale debut in the last match of 1945, earning Rochdale second place in the Division Three North West first championship, but he was still a regular for Mossley in 1947, netting a dozen goals at the age of 42.

Joseph (Joe) Keddie 1945-46
Born: Newington, Edinburgh 1916 5'10" 12st2
Left half
WL Apps/Goals 1/0
Career: Niddrie Thistle, Hamilton Ac. 1936/37 [50/16 ScL], Heart of Midlothian guest 1939-40 [1/- ScWL], Hibernians guest 1939-40 [1/- ScWL], Glentoran 1940-42, Leith Ath. guest 1941-42 [1/- ScWL], (services), Dale 1.46 [1/- WL]
Honours: British Forces tours in India 1944, 1945

Joe had had two seasons as a regular for the Accies, as an inside forward, before the war and then spent two years in Ireland with Glentoran before being posted to India. In 1944 and 1945 he was a member of the Services touring teams generally known as 'Denis Compton's XI' and 'Tommy Walker's XI', figuring against select sides or for 'Scotland' against the English half of the tour party. He had a very brief trial at Spotland in 1946, playing left half in a defeat by Southport.

John Kirk 1945-47
Born: {Lancashire 1923}
Goalkeeper
WL Apps 5 Total Apps 6
Career: Dale am 1.46 [5 WL], Peterborough 1.47
Honours: Lancashire Amateurs, England Amateur Victory international 1946

John came into the Dale side for their victory over Manchester United in the Lancashire Cup in January 1946 and replaced Arthur Chesters for five Division 3 North West games. He was then chosen for Lancashire Amateurs and his performance earned him selection for the England Amateur Victory international against Wales. However, after missing games while on international duty, he never regained his Rochdale place and joined Peterborough half way through the following season.

Richard (Dick) Neilson 1945-46

Born: Blackhall 1.4.16
5'10" 11st6
Centre half
WL Apps/Gls 3/0
Career: Blackhall Council School, Easington Juniors, Blackhall Colliery Welfare, Dawdon Colliery 3.35, Manchester C. 26.9.35 [16/1, 25/- WL], Stockport Co. guest 11.39 to 11.40 [24/1 WL], Dale loan 1.46 [3/- WL], Droylsden player-coach 9.46, player-manager cs.47, Manchester C. 'A' team coach cs.48, junior coach to 1981
Honours: Blackhall Schoolboys

Another ex-Manchester City player, former colliery worker Dick had managed just 16 games in four seasons before the war. He played fairly regular both for City and Stockport in the first two seasons of regional league football and was loaned to Dale early in 1946 as cover for Jim Pearce. He later served Droylsden as player, coach and manager before returning to Maine Road, coaching their juniors until his retirement in 1981. His elder brother George was a regular with South Shields and Gateshead in the thirties.

W. Hamilton 1945-46
Left half
WL Apps/Gls 2/0
Career: St. Bernards 1941-42 [7/- ScWL], Dale 2.46 [2/- WL]

Hamilton, from Scottish club St Bernards, appeared twice for Dale in February and March 1946 when Don Partridge was not available.

Kenneth (Ken) Ashbridge 1945-47
Born: Burnley 12.11.16
Goalkeeper WL Apps 3
Career: Burnley Lads Club, Burnley am 9.35, pro 10.35 [1], Halifax T. trial 9.38, signed 10.38 [1], Dale guest 2.46 [3 WL]

Ken played in goal for Dale when John Kirk was away on representative duty, his first appearances for a league club since the 1930s and only his third in total. He was on the retained list in the summer of 1946 but did not play subsequently.

Norman ('Richie') Richardson 1945-46
Born: Hamsterley, Durham 15.4.15 5'9" 11st
Right half WL Apps/Gls 1/0
Career: Blackhall Mill School, Spen Juniors, Medomsley Juniors 1930, Bolton W. 9.5.33, New Brighton 20.2.36 [213/-], Bolton W. guest 11.39 [3/- WL], (army), Dale guest 2.46 [1/- WL], Chorley 5.51, Bangor C.
Honours: Derwent Valley Schools

A "sure footed defender with a deadly tackle" who was a stalwart New Brighton full back before and after the war, playing over 200 times for the Rakers, Norman had started out in the same Medomsley Juniors side as wartime Blackpool star Jock Dodds. He joined the Royal Scots Fusiliers during the war and served for four years in Burma. On his return 'Richie' guested for Dale in February 1946, New Brighton not resuming operations until that summer. He appeared in virtually every position for New Brighton and had a benefit in 1950. His older brother Jon played a few games for Wolves and was a full back in Linfield's Irish Cup winning sides in the 1930s.

James Walter (Wally) Birch 1945-54
Born: Ecclesfield 5.10.17 6'0" 12st
Centre half
FL Apps/Gls 243/10 Total Apps/Gls 280/13
Career: Sheffield W. jnr, Huddersfield T. am 1938, pro 5.39 [5/- WL], Mossley guest 1939-40, Leeds U. guest 1944-45 [1/- WL], Oldham A. guest 3.45 [6/- WL], Dale 3.46 £1500 [11/- WL, 243/10], retired injured 10.53
Cricket for Rochdale CC
Honours: Lancashire Senior Cup winners 1949

Wally had very little first team experience when Ted Goodier, himself a centre half in his playing days, splashed out the considerable sum of £1500, a new club record, to bring him to Spotland, even though he was not allowed to sign full-time immediately as he worked in an essential industry. "Long, lean and hard as nails", he played in the last few games of 1945-46 and became a fixture as a "tall, dependable pivot" for the next five seasons, Dale managing three top seven finishes in that time as well as winning the Lancashire Senior Cup. His battle with England centre forward Tommy Lawton was a particular talking point of the Notts County cup tie which attracted Rochdale's record crowd. Eventually knee injuries started to take their toll but he played on until 1953, finally totalling 243 FL appearances and 280 in all games to easily top the Dale's appearance record at the time, ahead of his 1920s counterpart David Parkes. Like his uncle Arnold, Chesterfield's renowned penalty taking goalkeeper (who had been on the wrong end of Dale's record 8-1 victory), Wally was reliable from 12 yards, converting seven spot-kicks in 1948-49 alone. (Another uncle, Wallace, was also a league pro with Luton and Accrington). Just before he retired, Dale played a testimonial game for him between Rochdale Past and Present and an All Star XI which included the likes of Manchester United's Roger Byrne and Johnny Carey. He ran a local hostelry immediately after leaving the game but later worked for the Inland Revenue. In the summers Wally was a useful performer with Rochdale cricket club and in later years he was secretary of the football club's former players' association, organising the annual reunions.

Charles (Charlie) Hurst 1945-46, 1946-47
Born: Denton 25.1.1.19
Right half
FL Apps/Gls 4/1 Total Apps/Gls 9/1
Career: Hyde U., Bristol R. 9.38, (army), Oldham A. 1.43 [83/5 WL], Dale guest 3.46 [5/- WL], Dale 6.46 [4/1], Mossley 1947, Chelmsford C. 4.47, Sudbury T. player-manager 1950-51
Honours: Suffolk Senior Cup winners

Joining up just after the war started, Charlie was one of those evacuated from Dunkirk. He played regularly at right half for Oldham from 1943 and guested briefly for Dale, subsequently signing up as a professional at Spotland in 1946. His FL career comprised just four games in the space of 10 days that September, none of which Dale won, though his goal against New Brighton did earn a point. He later managed at non-league level and worked as a toolmaker. Considerably more famously, his son Geoff was England's World Cup winning hero 20 years later, one of five members of the side with family connections to the Dale.

John Thomas Jones 1945-46

Born: Holywell 25.11.16
5'8" 11st4
Goalkeeper
WL Apps 2
Career: Flint Town Amateurs, Port Vale am 7.7.36, pro 14.12.36, [3], Northampton T. 5.37 [71, 2 WL], Wrexham guest 10.39 [17 WL], Notts Co. guest 1943-44 [2 WL], Arsenal guest 9.43 [1 WL], Brentford guest 9.43 [2 WL], Hull C. guest 12.44 [1 WL], Manchester C. guest 3.45 [2 WL], Dale guest 3.46 [2 WL], Oldham A. £250 4.8.48 to 7.49 [22]
Honours: Wales Schools

Another pre-war pro returning to the game in 1946, John played a couple of games for Dale before rejoining his own club Northampton. Nicknamed 'Jones the cap' on account of his headgear, he was a goalkeeper who made up for his small stature with his bravery. Oldham signed him for a small fee in 1948 but he left the league scene the following year.

Jack Dobson 1945-47
Born: Norden 26.1.26
Left half
WL Apps/Gls 5/0
Career: Norden YC, Dale am 1945 [5/- WL], Norden YCOB c.1947
Honours: Timson Cup Final 1951

A local lad from Norden, Jack played a number of games towards the end of Dale's 1945-46 campaign, mostly in the second championship in which they finished second to Rotherham. Indeed, Jack's five senior games resulted in four victories and a draw, probably one of the best records of any Dale player! Retained as an amateur for the first peacetime season, he later played in local football for several years but was subsequently much better known as a champion crown green bowls player.

John Walmsley 1945-46
Goalkeeper
WL Apps 1
Career: Preston N.E. am c.1942, pro 9.10.43 [14 WL], Manchester U. guest 11.43 [2 WL], Bury guest 12.43 [1 WL], Halifax T. guest 2.44 [2 WL], Burnley guest 1943-44 [1 WL], Accrington St. guest 8.44 [22 WL], Dale guest 3.46 [1 WL]

Preston reserve goalie Walmsley appeared for Dale in their win over Bury in March 1946. A couple of years earlier, his appearance for Bury had been less successful, as Dale put five past him. In between he had figured a number of times for his own club.

Joseph (Joe) Rodi 1945-47
Born: Glasgow 23.7.13 5'8"
Outside right/inside forward
FL Apps/Gls 9/3   Total Apps/Gls 16/8
Career: Holytown U., Glasgow Perthshire 1.36, East Fife 5.36, Heart of Midlothian trial, Glasgow Rangers trial, Montrose 8.37, Glentoran 5.38, Montrose 1939, Stenhousemuir guest 1939-40 [18/9 ScWL], Petershill guest 7.41, East Fife 1943-44 [2/- ScWL], Grimsby T. 4.45 [32/21 WL], Bradford PA guest 9.45 [1/2 WL], Boston U., Dale 3.46 to 1.47 [7/5 WL, 9/3]

Of Italian extraction, Joe had figured with Scottish lower league sides in the late 'thirties and remained playing in Scotland in the early war years. He later signed for Grimsby for whom he continued to score at an excellent rate until leaving briefly for Boston and then signing for Dale. Scoring in five of his seven games at the end of 1945-46, he appeared in the first peacetime league game in his usual inside left position – thus making his FL debut at the age of 33 – but soon lost his position to Tom Barkas and played his remaining games at outside right, scoring twice in a victory at Accrington. He subsequently emigrated to Canada. [NB. His birth seems to have been registered as Giuseppe, but he appears as Joseph in subsequent records.]

Robert Yates 1945-46
Goalkeeper
WL Apps 1
Career: Dale am 4.46 [1 WL]

Robert was an amateur goalie who played once in the first team, when Dale were beaten at home by Lincoln in April 1946.

William Ernest (Bill) Roberts 1945-49
Born: Flint 22.10.18
Goalkeeper
FL Apps 43   Total Apps 53
Career: (Wales), Dale 4.46 to cs.49 [5 WL, 43]
Honours: Lancashire Junior Cup winners 1947

Bill was signed from Welsh football near the end of the transitional 1945-46 season and played in the last five games of Dale's Division 3 North West campaign. When the Football League proper resumed, he was Dale's first post-war goalie, but he lost his place when they failed to win any of their first six games. He returned to the side in January with considerably more success - Dale winning six of the next seven games - but was injured at Gateshead in April, just after figuring in the (supposedly reserve) Lancashire Junior Cup winning side. He subsequently shared the goalkeeper's jersey with Charlie Briggs and then Les Bywater but appeared only twice after August 1948.

Samuel (Sam) Baum 1945-46
Born: Sunderland 4.5.14
Outside right
WL Apps/Gls 1/0
Career: Usworth Amateurs, Usworth Colliery, Bolton W. am 1.36, pro 5.36, Darwen loan 1936, Port Vale 3.38 [3/-], South Shields 12.38, Dale guest 4.46 [1/- WL]

A winger with a handful of league appearances for Port Vale before the war, Sam was given a trial at Spotland at the end of the 1945-46 season, figuring against Tranmere. He had not played any senior football during the war.

Clement (Clem) Smith 1945-46
Born: Wath-on-Dearne JAS.10
Inside right
WL Apps/Gls 1/0
Career: South Kirkby Colliery, Halifax T. 1935 [55/12], Chester cs.37 [26/3], Stoke C. 3.38 [28/9 15/6 WL], Halifax T. guest 8.41 and 8.44 to 3.46 [52/25 WL], Dale trial 4.46 [1/- WL]

An anonymous "Trialist", later noted as Smith of Stoke, Clem played at inside right in a nil-nil draw against Tranmere in April 1946. He had had four seasons as a league regular before the war, but was by now in his mid-thirties and despite seven goals in two games for Halifax earlier in the term did not reappear at league level.

Harry Nuttall 1945-47
Centre forward
WL Apps/Gls 1/0
Career: Dale am 4.46 [1/- WL]

The son of Jimmy and nephew of Harry, the former Dale players of the twenties and thirties, the younger Harry had a much less successful time with the club, being somewhat unkindly noted in the press as "undoubtedly a handicap" to the side during his single outing leading the attack as an amateur in April 1946. Even so, he was retained as an amateur for the following season.

John Henry (Jack) Howshall 1945-46
Born: Longton, Staffs 12.7.12   5'9" 11st4
Left half
WL Apps/Gls 1/0
Career: Dresden Juniors c.1926, Longton Juniors, Dresden Juniors, Stoke C. am 10.30, pro 23.11.31 [1/-], Chesterfield 4.6.34 [25/-], Southport 14.6.35 [51/-], Bristol R. 25.6.37 £350 [21/-], Accrington St. 26.7.38 [8/-], Carlisle U. 21.10.38 [32/-, 3/- WL], (RAF), Dale guest 5.46 [1/- WL], Northwich Victoria cs.46, Wigan A. 8.47

A "dour, red haired defender" with varied pre-war experience with six different FL sides, Jack had not played any league football during his RAF service in North Africa. He appeared for Dale in the final game of 1945-46 and moved into senior non-league football for the first normal peacetime season. His brother Tommy appeared with several league clubs during the war.

John Kindred 1945-46
Born: {Bolton 24.12.21?}
Outside right
WL Apps/Gls 1/0
Career: Dale trialist 5.46 [1/- WL]

A trialist, Kindred was listed as 'A.N. Other' in the match report for his sole appearance in May 1946 against Southport, when he figured on the right wing in the last game of the season.

William (Bill) Hallard 1946-47

Born: St. Helens 28.8.13
5'9" 11st
Left half
FL Apps/Gls 17/2 Total Apps/Gls 22/2
Career: (St. Helens junior football), Runcorn, Prescot Cables trial 8.34, Bury 19.8.35 [1/-], Bradford PA 12.6.37 [70/5, 34/2 WL], Chester guest 10.42 [4/3 WL], Everton guest 10.43 [5/- WL], Dale 6.46 [17/2], Accrington St. 15.3.47 to 5.47 [3/-]

Perhaps surprisingly, the only player to make his Dale debut when the Football League reconvened on August 31st 1946, Bill was already quite an experienced wing half or inside forward with second division Park Avenue before the war, appearing in their FA Cup 5th round tie against Sunderland in 1938 which attracted a crowd of 59,326. The following year, he was one of the Bradford players sent-off in an extremely rare (in that era) case of a side being reduced to nine men. He continued to play for them in the wartime competitions and was in their side which amazingly beat Manchester City 8-2 at Maine Road in the 1945-46 FA Cup. He was nearly 33 when he signed for Dale for the resumption of peacetime football but appeared regularly, mostly at left half, until January 1947 when Eric Wood was switched to the intermediate line, Bill ending the season at Accrington. He later became a licensee

Thomas Norton (Tom) West 1946-47
Born: Salford 8.12.16 5'10" 11st5
Centre forward
FL Apps/Gls 4/2   Total Apps/Gls 6/2
Career: McMahon's, Stockport Co. 3.38 [3/1], Oldham A. 10.45 [24/16 WL], Dale 6.46 [4/2], Nelson 6.47, Bacup Borough 1948-49

Tom had just begun his league career at Stockport when war broke out and he did not return to senior action until a successful goalscoring stint at Oldham in 1945-46. Joining Dale for the following season, he added just four FL appearances to his tally. One of several players used as cover for Joe Hargreaves at centre forward, both his goals came in a victory at Carlisle in February 1947, but the bad weather meant that Dale didn't play again for a month and by that time Tom was back in the reserves where he totalled 34 goals.

Thomas (Tommy) Hargreaves 1946-47
Born: Blackburn 29.10.17 5'11" 12st4
Centre half
FL Apps/Gls 7/0   Total Apps/Gls 7/0
Career: Crosshills FC, Blackburn R. 10.36 [4/2, 33/19 WL], Accrington St. guest 1939-40 [2/- WL], (army), Morton guest 3.43, Dale 5.46 [7/-], Nelson 5.47
Honours: Lancashire Junior Cup winners 1947

Tommy had appeared four times for Blackburn at centre forward in Division 2 in 1937-38, scoring in the first two of them, and also played successfully during the war, netting a hat-trick against Dale in June 1940. He joined Dale in 1946 and was used in his alternative role as a centre half, playing only when Wally Birch was absent. He also played in the Reserves' Lancashire Junior Cup winning campaign but then joined Nelson along with Tom West.

Thomas (Tommy) Barkas 1946-48

Born: Wardley Colliery, South Shields 27.3.12
5'7" 10st6
Inside right
FL Apps/Gls 44/17
Total Apps/Gls 51/19
Career: Boldon Christian Endeavour, Boldon Colliery Welfare 8.28, Hebburn Colliery, Washington Colliery, {North Shields}, Wardley Main, Boldon Colliery Welfare 8.30, Washington Colliery, Hebburn Colliery 11.31, Wolverhampton W. trial 1932, Washington Colliery 8.32, Bradford C. 9.32 [16/2], Halifax T. 12.34 [171/36, 104/30 WL], York C. guest 1939-40 [1/- WL], (RAF), Stockport Co. guest 9.44 and 4.45 [5/5 WL], Huddersfield T. guest 1944-45 [2/- WL], Hartlepools U guest 8.45 [1/- WL], Dale 9.46 £500 [44/17], Stockport Co. 8.11.47 (exchange for A.T. Earl) [44/18], Carlisle U. 2.49 [14/5], Scunthorpe U. 10.49
Honours: (League North champions 1945)

Tommy was the youngest of a large footballing family, his brothers Ned (Huddersfield and Birmingham), Harry (South Shields), Sam (Bradford C., Manchester C. and England), Frank (with Barnsley) and Jimmy (on West Brom's books) all being FL pros, as was his cousin Billy Felton (Sheffield W., Manchester C. and England). A product of Tyneside collieries football, he trialled with Wolves as a full back but had his big break when he joined Sam at Valley Parade. It was at Halifax that he became a league regular, though, appearing in the best part of 300 senior games between 1934 and 1946. An inside forward who was "ever ready to shoot" and could "bustle into the thick of the fray", he was no mean goalscorer and could also play on the wing. In September 1946, with no points on the board and needing a midfield general, Ted Goodier invested £500 in bringing him to Spotland to skipper the side. Though the improvement wasn't instant – none of the next five games were won either – by the end of the season Dale had risen to 6th and Tom had netted 18 times including a hat-trick against Accrington. He and Joe Hargreaves totalled 38 goals in the games in which both of them played and in addition they were somewhat oddly allowed to play in the Lancashire Junior Cup final – ostensibly for the reserves – and added three more between them. Part way into the following season, however, he was transferred to Stockport and ended his league career at Carlisle in 1949-50. While serving in the RAF in Malta as a corporal instructor during the war, he was awarded the British Empire Medal for his actions during a bombing raid.

William John (Bill) Henderson 1946-47

Born: Closeburn, Dumfries 21.2.20
6'2"
Goalkeeper
FL Apps 17
Total Apps 22
Career: Kello Rovers, Queen of the South 1938, Dale 9.7.46 [17], Southport 17.6.47 [20], Bacup Borough 24.9.48 to 22.10.48

Honours: British Forces touring party in India 1945, Tommy Walker's XI in India 1945, Scottish FA in India 1945-46

A tall Scottish goalie, noted as something of a 'character', Bill played some of his most productive football during the war when he was a military policeman. After figuring in army teams, he toured India twice with Tommy Walker's XI during the spring and autumn of 1945 and was then selected for the Scottish FA team, also to tour India. His only senior professional games came in the following two seasons, first at Rochdale and then at Southport, each time playing in around half their league matches. For Dale, all his appearances came consecutively from September to the New Year, when Bill Roberts was recalled. After leaving the game he worked for the Air Ministry and then at an aircraft factory, but he suffered badly from attacks of malaria originally contracted when serving in Burma and died at the age of only 45.

Alexander Neilson (Alex) Carruthers

1946-47
Born: Logan Lea, West Lothian 12.5.14
5'10" 11st4
Outside right
FL Apps/Gls 13/4 Total Apps/Gls 17/6
Career: West Calder Juniors, Heart of Midlothian 1934-35 [1/- ScL], Falkirk 5.35 [28/19 ScL], Bolton W. 2.37 £4000 [26/4], Falkirk 9.38 to 1942-43 [30/14 ScL, 52/26 ScWL], Heart of Midlothian guest 9.40, Airdrieonians guest 11.42 [5/1 ScWL], Dale 6.46 [13/4], Rossendale U. 8.47
Honours: Scottish Division 2 champions 1936, Reserve for Scotland 1939, Lancashire Junior Cup winners 1947

A "dashing winger" in the traditional Scottish style, Alex made his mark with Falkirk in the mid-thirties, helping them to promotion and scoring 19 goals in the top flight before a £4000 move to Bolton Wanderers towards the end of the 1936-37 season. He returned to Falkirk a year later and after regaining his goalscoring touch was twice the travelling reserve for Scotland. He continued to play for Falkirk at the start of the war, scoring 17 times in the Regional League in 1939-40, but signed for Dale in 1946. Though not making his debut on the right wing until mid-October, he immediately netted twice in a victory over Tranmere. He remained in the side until February when the weather prevented any games for a month (unusually all his last five games were victories) and was released in the summer.

Walter Schofield (Wally) Jones 1946-47

Born: Hurstead, Rochdale 9.1.25
Centre forward
FL Apps/Gls 2/2
Total Apps/Gls 2/2
Career: St. Chads, (navy), Dale am, pt 11.46 [2/2], Altrincham cs.47 to 10.52, Rugby league for Rochdale Hornets 1952 to 1956, coach to Spotland Rangers 1956 to 1958; cricket for Rochdale CC, Littleborough
Honours: Cheshire League Cup final 1948, 1949, Rest of Cheshire League v champions (Rhyl) 1948

A legendary figure in Rochdale sport despite only a brief FL career, Wally is the only man to have played football for Dale, rugby league for Hornets and cricket for Rochdale - having played rugby union at Rochdale Municipal High School and then later representing the town at crown green bowls! He joined Dale as an amateur after his demob from the Royal Navy and hit 29 goals, including three hat-tricks, in less than a season for the reserves, as well as his two goals in two FL games in December 1946. As he worked in the foreign section of Barclays Bank, he decided not to turn professional and signed for Altrincham, netting a five and a four in a total of 45 goals in his first season, adding 39 more the following term. "Quick, good in the air and able to shoot with either foot", after totalling 141 goals in 215 games for Alty he surprisingly opted to switch codes in 1952, running in 31 tries in 104 games on the wing for Hornets before finishing in 1956 because of a damaged shoulder. He was a reserve for Lancashire on one occasion and later coached local amateur side Spotland Rangers. In the summers he was a top class club cricketer, noted for his dazzling outfielding, who skippered Rochdale to the Central Lancashire League championship in 1948 and the Wood Cup final in 1951 and 1952, winning the latter. Sadly he was diagnosed with Parkinson's disease when he was only 48 and was confined to a wheelchair for many years.

Alan Moorhouse 1945-48
Born: Wardle, Rochdale 12.10.25
Outside left
FL Apps/Gls 17/3 Total Apps/Gls 17/3
Career: Blackburn R. am, Dale trial 1945-46, Dale am 1.47, pt 3.47 [17/3], Bedford T. cs.48, Scarborough 1952-53
Honours: Lancashire Junior Cup winners 1947

Local lad Alan had a trial in Dale's reserves in 1945-46 and made his league debut as an amateur in January 1947, replacing Arthur Cunliffe when the latter became reserve team coach. Scoring in successive games actually separated by a month because of the extreme winter weather, he played some further matches after signing on part-time terms (he worked as a railway fireman) and also scored the Reserves' goal in the first leg of the Lancashire Junior Cup final against South Liverpool which allowed a side suitably strengthened by first team players to clinch the cup in the second leg.

Ronald (Ron) Rothwell 1946-54
Born: Bury 10.7.20
Full back
FL Apps/Gls 48/0 Total Apps/Gls 54/0
Career: Dunfermline Ath., Dale am 10.46, pro 6.47 [48/-], Rossendale U. 1954, manager 1956-57
Honours: Lancashire Junior Cup winners 1951

Despite his Bury origins, Ron had been playing in Scotland before joining the Dale and, like Alan Moorhouse, making his debut while still an amateur. In Ron's case it was just the one game, in place of Len Jackson at right back, and it was not until a year later that he signed pro and played some further games, alternating between the two full back positions. Indeed, though he was with Dale for eight years in all, he was only a regular first teamer for a spell during 1948-49 when he played 20 games in succession. However, he did win a Lancashire Junior Cup winners medal with the Reserves in 1951. One of many Rochdale men to have figured with Rossendale United, he managed them in the late 'fifties.

Jack (Jackie) Moss 1946-49

Born: Blackrod 1.9.23
5'6" 10st13
Inside forward
FL Apps/Gls 58/17 Total Apps/Gls 64/17
Career: Horwich Central, Bury 12.42, pro 12.43 [56/11 WL, 7/2], Dale pt 1.47 [58/17], Leeds U. 1.49 £7000 [23/2], Halifax T. 1.51 [124/10], Lancaster C. 1954
Honours: Lancashire Junior Cup winners 1947

Remarkably, a native of the same small village, Blackrod near Chorley, as the Cunliffes, Jackie came through the ranks at Bury, making over 50 wartime appearances and being given his FL debut when peacetime football returned. Early in 1947 he was signed as a part-timer by Dale and gained a regular place at inside left once the winter weather relented. Like several other first teamers, he also appeared in the Lancashire Junior Cup Final, scoring one of the four goals in the second leg. He played about half the Dale's games the following term, but made a big impression at the start of 1948-49 and was transferred to second division Leeds for £7000, a club record. Surprisingly hard to knock off the ball, considering his apparently lightweight frame (presumably on account of his job as a blacksmith!), most of his league appearances came in a subsequent stint at Halifax. He was also a useful league cricketer.

John (Jack) Oakes 1946-47
Born: {Hamilton 16.1.21?} 5'9" 11st
Outside right
FL Apps/Gls 1/0 Total Apps/Gls 1/0
Career: {Queen of the South?} (RAF), Huddersfield T. 1945-46, Queen of the South 1946, Dale 2.47 to 4.47 [1/-]

Jack scored 23 goals as centre forward for Huddersfield's reserves in 1945-46 after leaving the RAF, before being transferred back to Queen of the South and then joining Dale in 1947. He played in just one game, replacing fellow Scot Carruthers on the right wing in a 4-1 defeat at Darlington in March that year. [He was possibly related to Jackie Oakes, also a winger and a stalwart of Queen of the South before and after a successful stint in England with Blackburn Rovers and Manchester City.]

Hugh O'Donnell 1946-48

Born: Buckhaven 15.2.13
5'9" 11st
Centre forward/outside left
FL Apps/Gls 40/14 Total Apps/Gls 44/16
Career: St Agatha's School (Leven), Dunbeath Violet Juniors, Wellesley Juniors 8.30, Blantyre Victoria 1931, Celtic 9.31, pro 3.32 [75/20], Preston NE 5.35 [136/29], Blackpool 3.39 [14/2, 98/32 WL], (RAF), Heart of Midlothian guest 3.40 [6/1 ScWL], Preston NE guest 1939-41 [23/8 WL], Manchester U. guest 9.40 [4/- WL], Manchester C. guest 9.41 [1/1 WL], Liverpool guest 9.41 [2/- WL], Burnley guest 9.42 [18/5 WL], Blackburn R. guest 3.43 [5/2 WL], Lincoln C. guest 9.43 [4/3 WL], Tranmere R. guest 1943-44 [1/- WL], Birmingham guest 2.45 [3/- WL], Dale 2.47 [40/14], Halifax T. 3.48 to 1948-49 [13/1]
Honours: Glasgow v Sheffield 1933, Scottish Cup winners 1933, FA Cup final 1937, winners 1938, North Regional League champions 1941, 1942, 1943, 1944, War League Cup winners 1941, RAF v British Army 1941

Hugh and his brother Frank (two of 15 children) famously played together with five clubs ranging from Dunbeath Violet to Preston North End. Hugh himself was a stocky goalscoring centre forward or winger who spent three seasons in the Celtic first team and four more in Preston's, playing in the Scottish Cup Final in 1933, his first full season, and in the English one in 1937 and 1938, when Mutch's famous last minute penalty won the match. The O'Donnells were said to "have contributed largely to the revival of the famous Lancashire club", North End finishing just 3 points behind champions Arsenal, their best performance since 1889. Just before war broke out Hugh, a "wonderful opportunist" was transferred to Blackpool, and while serving in the RAF became part of the Tangerines' all-conquering wartime teams alongside Jock Dodds, with whom he shared digs. He also guested for Preston, winners of the War League and cup in 1941, scoring four times in a 12-1 cup win (Andy Mclaren, q.v., got five of the others). He played for various RAF representative sides, on one occasion doing so at the last minute, wearing his service boots. Signed by Dale in 1947, when he was 34, he managed another season and a half as a regular, alternating between the centre and the right wing, with a final short stint at Halifax. Originally a miner, he also went in for boxing, golf and swimming and later worked as a publican in Preston, sadly being charged with receiving stolen cigarettes shortly before his death when he was only 52.

Cyril Lawrence 1946-50
Born: Salford 12.6.20   5'9"   11st
Centre forward/outside right
FL Apps/Gls 44/5   Total Apps/Gls 49/5
Career: Blackpool am 1939, pro 2.46 [2/- WL], Dale 4.47 £ [46/5], Wrexham 9.50 to 1952 [50/9]
Honours: (League North champions 1944), Lancashire Senior Cup winners 1949

Cyril managed a couple of games for Blackpool in wartime competitions, and arrived at Spotland from Bloomfield Road for a small fee a couple of months after Hugh O'Donnell. He appeared quite regularly on the right wing in the second half of the 1947-48 campaign but thereafter was largely a reserve, though he did play in the semi-final and final of the Lancs Cup in 1949. He subsequently had a couple of quite productive seasons at Wrexham.

Charles Edward (Charlie) Briggs 1946-48
Born: Newton, Bedfordshire 4.4.09   6'2"   14st
Goalkeeper
FL Apps 12   Total Apps 13
Career: Tottenham H. am 1930, Haywards Sports, Guildford C., Fulham 12.35, Guildford C., Crystal Palace 5.36, Guildford C., Bradford PA 5.37, Halifax T. 3.38 [56, 67 WL], (army), Aldershot guest 1939-45 [59 WL], Fulham guest 1941-42 [1 WL], Tottenham H. guest 1942-44 [3 WL], Brentford guest 10.43 [1 WL], Clyde 6.46, Dale 5.47 [12], Chesterfield 12.47
Honours: (League South champions 1944)

A very tall, solidly built custodian, Charlie was 38 when he arrived at Spotland and had joined his first club, Spurs, back in 1930, though his FL debut had not come until he reached Halifax eight years later. During the war he was stationed at Aldershot with the Royal Artillery and though he was injured in an air raid, this posting enabled him to turn out for the Shots' star-studded team with international players like Stan Cullis, Tommy Lawton and future Dale colleague Arthur Cunliffe who were also stationed there. He was particularly noted for a brilliant display in Aldershot's 2-0 cup win at Spurs in 1943-4. After a spell in Scotland immediately after the war, Charlie played a dozen games for the Dale at the end of 1946-47 and the beginning of 1947-48.

John (Jackie) Arthur 1946-54

Born: Edenfield 14.12.17
5'8"   11st10
Outside right
FL Apps/Gls 170/25   Total Apps/Gls 191/27
Career: Haslingden St. Mary's, Blackburn R. am 1936, Everton am 1936, Stockport Co. 5.38 [2/-], Shrewsbury T. 6.39, Everton 11.40 [13/2 WL], Wrexham guest 1945-46 [1/1 WL], Chester 5.46 [24/3], Dale 5.47 £ [170/25], 'A' team trainer-coach 1954, youth team coach 1955

Jackie made his FL debut for Stockport in a home defeat by Rochdale in April 1939, but rejoined his earlier club Everton during the war. He was transferred to Chester in 1946 and scored against Dale in both legs of their Lancashire Cup tie that season, but just before its rather late close (Dale played until June 7th), he was transferred to them for a small fee. Over the next five years he was generally the first choice on the right flank, though he could play in other forward positions, and eventually figured in nearly 200 games before becoming 'A' team coach in 1954, scoring in his final game (though he turned out against a Star XI in May 1956).

Austin ('Ossie') Collier 1946-48
Born: Dewsbury 24.7.14   5'7"   12st
Left half
FL Apps/Gls 6/0   Total Apps/Gls 6/0
Career: Upton Colliery 1935, Frickley Colliery 6.37, Mansfield T. 5.38 [21/-], York C. 5.39 [31/- WL,

11/-], (army), Partick Thistle guest 8.40 [24/- ScWL], Celtic guest 5.41 [3/- ScWL], Third Lanark guest 10.41 [15/- ScWL], East Fife guest 7.42 [4/- ScWL], Partick Thistle guest 1942-43 [12/- ScWL] and 1943-44, Aberdeen trial 8.43 [7/1 ScWL], Hibernian guest 1.44, Leeds U. guest 3.46 [1/- WL], Queen of the South 11.46 [17/- ScL], Dale 5.47 [6/-], Halifax T. 11.47 [1/-], Goole T. 8.48, Mansfield T., Scarborough 7.49, Halifax T. assistant trainer 1950, Ashton U cs.51 to 5.52, Halifax T. assistant trainer to 1955
Honours: Notts County Cup winners 1939, British Army v Polish Army 1940, v Norwegian Army 1940, v Scottish League 1941, v Rangers 1941, v NE League 1942, v Polish Army 1942, v French Army (in Italy) 1944; Army in Scotland v Army in England 1940, 1941, v RAF 1941, v Dutch Army 1942; Scottish Command v AA Command, v Northern Command, v Aberdeen 1942, v RAF 1943 (2), v Sumburgh Select 1943, v Army Select 1943, v Combined Services 1943 (2); Army v Scotland (international trial) 1942, v Scottish FA Select 1942; United Services

A collier by occupation as well as name, Ossie joined Mansfield for the last pre-war season, though he had moved to York before the FL programme was abandoned. Despite his lower league origins, he was a prominent player in services football, where his reported "lack of pace" was not a handicap. He appeared in numerous Army sides in representative games and guested for Celtic and Partick Thistle amongst others while stationed north of the border as a sergeant PTI in the Highland Light Infantry. He played for Scottish Command in a tour of the Orkneys and Shetlands in 1943 and for the Army against their French counterparts while in Italy the following year. After the war he returned to York but after losing his place due to injury spent the second half of 1946-47 back in Scotland, before signing for Dale for the end of this protracted season. He played only the first three games the following season at wing half before being left out and figured only once for Halifax after quickly moving on yet again. In the 'fifties he returned to the Shay as assistant trainer.

Richard Stanley (Dick) Withington 1947-48
Born: South Shields 8.4.21
Inside right
FL Apps/Gls 32/6 Total Apps/Gls 37/7
Career: South Shields Ex-Schoolboys, Blackpool 5.38 [12/2 WL], Dale 6.47 [32/6], Chesterfield 6.48 £4000 [6/-], Dartmouth, Bradford C. trial
Honours: (League North champions 1944)

Like Cyril Lawrence, Dick had been on Blackpool's books and played a few wartime league games, mostly in the 1945-46 season. He joined Dale in the summer of 1947 and did well enough as their regular inside right to rate a £4000 price tag when he moved to Chesterfield a year later, though he only ever played 6 games for them and was placed on the transfer list in July 1949. Before joining Blackpool he had played in the same junior side in South Shields as Tangerines legend Stan Mortensen.

Walter Berkeley (Wally) Cornock 1947-48
Born: Bondi, NSW 1.1.21
Goalkeeper
FL Apps 1   Total Apps 1
Career: Oldham A. am 1939-40 [3 WL], Royton Amateurs, Ashton National, Hurst 9.40, Oldham A. pro 1.41 [6 WL], Hereford U. 1946, Dale 11.47 [1], (Australia 1948-49)
Cricket for Royton, Rochdale, Leicestershire (26 first class matches 1948)

One of the few Australians to play league football prior to the Premier League era of multi-national squads, probably unsurprisingly Wally was actually primarily a cricketer. However, during the war, when he saw active service with the Australian forces in North Africa, he also played in goal for several clubs, having a spell as a pro with Oldham. After the war he turned out for Rochdale CC and made a single appearance for the Dale in November 1947, in a 2-0 home defeat by Hartlepools. (Unusually, at least for Dale, he was only the second entirely new player used up to that point in the season). He had earlier hit a record 197 for Royton and in 1948 was a regular in county cricket for Leicestershire as a middle-order batsman and left arm medium-pace bowler, before returning to Australia.

Noel Leslie (Les) Bywater 1947-49
Born: Lichfield 8.2.20
Goalkeeper
FL Apps 34   Total Apps 39
Career: Huddersfield T. 3.45 [2 WL], Luton T. guest 1945-46 [13 WL], Luton T. 9.46 [19], Dale 12.47 [34], retired 1949. Rochdale Police 1950, later manager
Honours: (League North champions 1945), Lancashire Senior Cup winners 1949, Lancashire Police v Yorkshire Police 1951

Les guested for Luton during the 1945-46 season and soon after peacetime football resumed he signed for them from Huddersfield. Half way through the following campaign he moved to Rochdale, taking over in goal from Roberts and Briggs. He suffered a fractured skull in a collision in a match at Gateshead soon afterwards, but made a rapid recovery and was playing again before the end of the season. Losing his place after a 6-1 defeat the following term, he returned for the last couple of games, gaining a Lancashire Cup winners medal in the process with a clean sheet against

Blackpool. He then retired to join the police, but was soon back playing for police representative sides and later managed the Rochdale Police team. He was subsequently better known as the owner of Bywater's Coaches, which were used by the Dale for travel to away games for many years. His son David played for Dale and Halifax's reserve sides before becoming a coach, while grandson Stephen won England youth honours while at Spotland before a big money move to West Ham.

Ronald (Ron) Johnston 1947-48
Born: Glasgow 3.4.21
Centre forward
FL Apps/Gls 17/7 Total Apps/Gls 19/7
Career: Albion R., Hartlepools U. guest 10.43 [5/5 WL], Glasgow Perthshire, Dale 11.47 [17/7], Exeter C. 6.48 [10/2], Weymouth, Headington U., Brighton & HA 11.50 [1/-]

The first of two signings from Glasgow Perthshire during 1947-48, Ron scored the winner against Darlington on his debut and in fact scored six times in his first seven FL games. He was unable to maintain this, though and moved to Exeter the following summer, later playing an odd game for Brighton.

James (Jimmy) Britton 1947-49
Born: Salford 27.5.20
Left half
FL Apps/Gls 20/0 Total Apps/Gls 22/0
Career: (navy), Lowestoft T., Bradford PA am 1944, pro 1.46 [3/- WL, 1/-], Hurst loan 4.46 to 10.46, Dale 12.47 [20/-], Mossley 1948-49, Rossendale U. 2.49

After service in the Royal Navy, Jimmy signed pro for Park Avenue in 1946 but managed just one FA Cup and one FL appearance before being freed. Despite a 4-0 defeat by the other Bradford club on his Dale debut on Christmas Day 1947 – he had only signed terms that morning when Ted Goodier had the team coach stop at his house in Halifax! - Jimmy was a regular selection at wing half for the remainder of the season, also going in goal when Bywater was injured at Gateshead. However, he only appeared twice in the league and twice in cup ties – at full back – the following season.

Charles William (Charlie) Longdon 1947-48
Born: Mansfield 6.5.17 5'9" 11st4
Left half/right back
FL Apps/Gls 2/0 Total Apps/Gls 2/0
Career: Folkestone T., Brighton & HA 5.39 [100/4 WL], Bournemouth & BA guest 1940-41 [2/- WL], Liverpool guest 8.40 [1/- WL], New Brighton guest 9.40 [20/- WL], Bristol C. guest 1943-44 [1/- WL], Chesterfield guest 1943-44 [1/- WL], Southport guest 1944-45 [1/- WL], Swansea T. guest 1944-45 [1/- WL], Mansfield T. guest 1945-46 [1/- WL], Bournemouth & BA 5.46 [9/1], Dale 7.47 [2/-], Bath C. 1948

Charlie arrived at Brighton on the eve of WWII and played 100 games for them in the regional league as well as guesting for a whole string of other clubs all around the country. He moved to Bournemouth for the resumption of league football (playing all his FL games as a forward) and then to Rochdale the following summer. However, it was Christmas Day before he got his chance in the first team in his usual half back role, and he played just once more, at right back, Dale losing 4-0 each time.

Alexander (Alex) Anderson 1947-48

Born: Gorbals, Glasgow 8.1.22
5'9" 11st
Goalkeeper
FL Apps 4 Total Apps 4
Career: Provanside Hibs, Petershill Juniors, Heart of Midlothian 1941, East Fife guest 1941-42 [1 ScWL]), Heart of Midlothian 'A' 1942-43 [1 ScWL], (army), Stirling Albion loan 1947 [3 ScL], Third Lanark loan 1947, Dale 27.2.48 [4], Dundalk cs.48, Southport 5.11.49 [21], Bangor C. cs.51, Runcorn cs.53, Lancaster C. 10.54 to 1957
Honours: East of Scotland Select v British Army, League of Ireland v Scottish League 1948, FA of Ireland Cup winners 1949

On Hearts' books during the war, playing for their 'A' side which figured in the Scottish North Eastern League alongside the senior sides of other clubs, Alex represented the East of Scotland before service in the army, when he was in Ceylon with the Royal Marines. After being demobbed he played a few first division games for Stirling Albion before arriving at Spotland as a cover for the injured Les Bywater, making him the Dale's fifth goalkeeper of the season. He was soon joined by his brother Eddie and the two played together in the Easter game at Carlisle, the first instance of Dale having two brothers in the same side in the FL. Unfortunately Dale lost 5-0 and neither Anderson played again. However, Alex's move to Dundalk proved a success and he won both an Irish Cup medal and representative honours for the League of Ireland. He subsequently had another spell in the Third North with Southport, notably making his debut in a heavy snowstorm in Bradford even though the game was in mid-April! Despite conceding six in that game he played fairly regularly the following term before again heading for Ireland. Alex was noted for wearing a yellow goalkeeping jersey, the colour officially reserved for internationals. He later worked as a painter and decorator.

Hugh Colvan 1947-48
Born: Port Glasgow 24.9.25
Inside right
FL Apps/Gls 1/0 Total Apps/Gls 1/0
Career: Hibernian 1943 [3/- ScWL], Raith R. 1945 [6/3 ScL], Arbroath 9.47 [6/1 ScL], Dale 2.48 [1/-], Derry C. 1948, Coleraine 1950, Yeovil T. 7.51, Coleraine 1952-53
Honours: Irish Cup winners 1949, 1953, Irish League v League of Ireland 1949, 1950

Another Scottish import, Hugh had played with Raith in the 1945-46 Scottish Cup and both Raith and Arbroath in the league, prior to signing for the Dale. His one FL outing came when Dale were without both Withington and Arthur and lost 2-1 at home to Mansfield. His career in Ireland was much more successful as he was top scorer for two seasons with Derry and scored in their 3-1 victory over Glentoran which gave them their first ever Irish Cup win. He also scored for the Irish League in their 1949 match against the League of Ireland. After a stint with top Southern League side Yeovil, scoring 15 times in 50 games, he won a second Irish Cup medal with Coleraine

Connor (Con) Gallacher 1947-48
Born: Derry 24.4.22 5'9" 11st4
Inside forward
FL Apps/Gls 6/1 Total Apps/Gls 6/1
Career: Lochee Harp, Middlesbrough 1.47 [1/-], Hull C. 5.47 [18/3], Dale 3.48 [6/1], Boston U. cs.48

Although starting with one top flight game for Middlesbrough, Irishman Con's entire FL career spanned only 16 months, most of it spent at Hull. He netted on his Dale debut, against Crewe, but Dale won only one of his six games and he wasn't retained at the end of the season.

Edward (Eddie or 'Jock') Anderson 1947-48
Born: Govanhill, Glasgow 23.9.17
Left back
FL Apps/Gls 1/0 Total Apps/Gls 1/0
Career: Cowdenbeath 1946 [10/- ScL], Stirling Albion 9.47 [18/- ScL], Dale trial 8.47, signed 3.48 [1/-], Prescot Cables 1948

Full back Eddie, or Jock as he was frequently called, had been with Stirling Albion with his brother Alex (q.v.) before following him to Spotland. Despite a reasonable number of games for his Scottish clubs, he made just the one appearance for Dale, in the side beaten 5-0 at Carlisle on Easter Saturday after Ted Goodier made seven changes from the match the previous day. (Seven more changes were made for the game on Easter Monday).

Michael Noel (Mike) Skivington 1947-48
Born: Glasgow 24.12.21
Centre half
FL Apps/Gls 1/0 Total Apps/Gls 1/0
Career: St Roch's, Alloa Ath. 9.45 [22/- ScL], Bury 6.47, Dale 1.48 [1/-], Dundalk cs.48, Leyton Orient 10.49 [5/-], Gillingham 7.50 [7/-], Brentford 9.51
Honours: League of Ireland v FL 1949, FA of Ireland Cup winners 1949, Dublin City Cup winners 1949

Another player with the shortest of Dale careers, Mike's first senior games had been with Alloa in the 1945-46 Scottish Cup, but his FL debut came, like compatriot Jock Anderson's, in the 5-0 hammering at Carlisle when future Dale centre forward Jack Connor netted a hat-trick and Mike put through his own goal. He headed off to Dundalk with Alex Anderson, and like him played for the League of Ireland, though Mike's international debut turned out the same way as his Dale one, as the Irish lost 5-0 to the Football League. Nevertheless his form with Dundalk, including two cup winners medals, earned him another stint in the FL with Leyton Orient and Gillingham.

David Alexander (Dave) Reid 1947-51
Born: Glasgow 3.1.23
Left half
FL Apps/Gls 36/2 Total Apps/Gls 38/2
Career: Glasgow Perthshire, Dale 1.48 [36/2], Bradford PA 9.50 £8000 [13/-], Workington 7.53 [8/1], Crewe A. 8.54 [3/-], Wellington T., Gainsborough Trinity, Mossley 1957-58

Dave followed Ron Johnston from Glasgow Perthshire to Spotland, one of six Scottish signings in 1947-48, and made his debut in peculiar circumstances in April 1948 when he played against Hartlepools wearing spectacles. Overcoming comments from the terraces when he missed an open goal that he should have worn stronger glasses, he scored the winner. (He later played in contact lenses). At this point an inside left, he subsequently played at left half for a spell at the start of the following term before being injured. Following 18 months out of the side, he returned late in 1949-50, Dale turning down Huddersfield's bid of £6000 for him. His continued good form early the following season prompted an £8000 move to Bradford, Dave presumably having impressed when Dale beat them 1-0 at Park Avenue in front of a 19,000 crowd. He made a number of appearances that season but thereafter was consigned to the reserves for the most part, as he was also in seasons at Workington and Crewe. Away from the game he played in the John Emsley Jazz Quartet.

William (Bill) Watson 1948-54
Born: South Hiendley, Yorks 29.5.16 5'10" 11st4
Right back
FL Apps/Gls 200/0 Total Apps/Gls 214/0
Career: Hiendley School, Monckton Colliery, Lincoln C. 2.35 [9/-], Chesterfield 6.35 [21/2 WL, 36/-], Dale 6.48 to cs.54 [200/-]
Honours: Lancashire Senior Cup winners 1949

Bill made his FL debut with Lincoln in March 1935 and was then transferred to Chesterfield along with his brother Arthur, but did not make their first team until eventually making his FL debut for them after the war, 11 years after signing. Then aged 32, he joined Dale in 1948 and, despite a disastrous debut when he put through his own goal in the course of a 6-1 defeat, proved a hugely dependable right back, missing only a handful of games in the next four seasons, and continuing to appear fairly regularly for two more, when he was sometimes used at centre half. Noted for his "excellent mobility and execution", he reached exactly 200 FL games for Dale, but never scored for them, the most appearances without a goal of any Dale outfield player. "A gentleman both on and off the field", he played in the Lancashire Cup Final and in the famous cup-ties against Notts County and Chelsea – though he missed the Leeds game in 1950-51 when he was skipper, due to injury - before retiring at the age of 38. [Oddly, he was reported in the Daily News Football Annual of 1939 to have signed for Rochdale – nine years before he actually did.]

Arnold Bonnell 1948-49
Born: Barnsley 23.3.21
Left back
FL Apps/Gls 5/0 Total Apps/Gls 6/0
Career: Barnsley am, pro 4.38 [7/-], Dale 7.48 [5/-], Shrewsbury T. 8.49

Arnold joined his local club Barnsley in 1938, but like Bill Watson at Chesterfield made a long delayed debut after the war. A left back, he joined Dale at the same time as Watson and made his debut in the opening game of 1948-49. He lost the place back to Ron Rothwell after only three games, following a 4-3 defeat at home to Darlington and only appeared twice more later in the season. He then played for Shrewsbury before their election to the FL.

Cecil Heydon 1948-49
Born: Birkenhead 24.5.19 5'10" 11st
Right half
FL Apps/Gls 1/0 Total Apps/Gls 1/0
Career: Victoria Social (Birkenhead), New Brighton am 31.12.37, pro 16.2.39 [1/-], Derby Co. 5.6.39 [1/- WL], Tranmere R. guest 1941-45 [13/3 WL], Doncaster R. guest 10.44 [6/- WL], Doncaster R. 3.10.45 [24/1 WL, 6/-], Dale 2.7.48 [1/-]
Honours: Division 3(N) champions 1947

After just one league game on the right wing for New Brighton, Cecil was transferred to first division Derby County in the last summer before the war. Having guested for Doncaster, he then signed for them, playing regularly at right half in the latter stages of the 1945-46 season, but infrequently when Rovers won the Third North title the following year. His Dale career was even more truncated, just the first game of 1948-49 when Dale lost 6-1 at Hartlepools.

Walter Booth Price 1948-49
Born: Neston 14.2.21
Centre half
FL Apps/Gls 1/0 Total Apps/Gls 1/0
Career; Tranmere R. 3.41 [34/2 WL, 2/-], Middlesbrough guest 1941-42 [2/- WL], Dale 7.48 [1/-]

Like Cyril Heydon, Walter was a native of the Wirral and had played with Tranmere during the war. He also played for them a couple of times in the first peacetime season before arriving at Spotland in 1948 and like Heydon playing only in the opening day hammering at Hartlepools, though he did later appear in a friendly against Halifax.

George Richard ('Diddler') Eastham
1948-49

Born: Blackpool 13.9.14
5'7" 9st6
Inside forward
FL Apps/Gls 2/0
Total Apps/Gls 5/0
Career: Cambridge Road Juniors (Blackpool), South Shore Wednesday, Bolton W. am 5.31, pro 8.32 [114/15], Brentford 6.37 £4000 [49/1], Blackpool 11.38 £5000 [45/9, 28/7 WL], Birmingham guest 9.40 [6/3 WL], Bolton W. guest 1.41 to 1942 [8/2 WL], York C. guest 2.41 [4/- WL], Brentford guest 3.41 [2/- WL], Mansfield T. guest 1941-42 [1/- WL], Millwall guest 1941-42 [2/1 WL], Queens Park R. guest 1941-42 [8/2 WL], (army), Swansea T. 8.47 [15/-], Dale 6.48 [2/-], Lincoln C. 12.48 [27/1], Hyde U. 9.50, Ards player-manager 7.53, manager cs.55, Accrington St. manager 10.58, Distillery manager 6.59, Ards manager 3.64, Stoke C. scout 3.70, Hellenic FC (South Africa) manager 1971, Glentoran manager 10.72 to 5.74

Honours: England v Holland 1935, Football League XI v Wales and Ireland (Jubilee match) 1935, The Rest v England 1935, Possibles v Probables 1936 (international trials), Lancashire Senior Cup winners 1934, War League North champions 1942. As manager: Gold Cup 1954, Irish League champions 1957, 1963, Irish Cup final 1963, winners 1969, 1973

Coming through the junior ranks at Bolton while working in a bakery, George made his debut when he was 19 and scored in that season's Lancashire Cup Final. By the time he was 21, he had played in an international trial, had appeared for both the Football League – scoring twice against a joint Irish and Welsh XI in a match celebrating the King's Jubilee – and England, and just missed a trip to Wembley when Wanderers lost in the FA Cup semi-final. He was also rumoured to be the subject of a £10,000 transfer bid, which would have almost equalled the then record. Nicknamed 'Diddler', he was a "very clever ball manipulator" and mazy dribbler, though thought by some fans to be "over elaborate". In 1937 he was bought by first division newcomers Brentford before joining home town club Blackpool. He guested for numerous clubs around his army service in South Africa, resuming his career at Bloomfield Road in 1946. He arrived at Willbutts Lane via Swansea in 1948 but appeared only twice before leaving for his final league club, Lincoln. In 1953 he became player-manager of Ards, leading them to a Gold Cup win in his first season, when he was almost 40, famously playing alongside his son, George jnr, who later played for Arsenal, Stoke and England (making them the only father and son to both win England caps). Ards won the league title in 1957, subsequently meeting Rheims in the European Cup. After a less successful time at Accrington and the first of two spells in South Africa, George returned to winning ways in Ireland with another championship – Distillery earning a 3-3 draw with Benfica in Europe the following year – and cup wins with both Ards, again, and Glentoran before he retired from management when he was 60 and subsequently moved to the USA. His brother Harry won a league championship medal with Liverpool and was with Tranmere for several years after the war.

Cyril Brown 1948-51
Born: Ashington 25.5.18
Inside left/left half
FL Apps/Gls 61/11 Total Apps/Gls 69/12
Career: Glentoran, Folkestone, Brentford 1.39 [5/2 WL], Ashington guest 11.39, Hartlepools U. guest 12.44 [14/14 WL], Sunderland guest 1945, signed 4.45 £2500 [31/9 WL], Notts Co. 8.46 £3500 [13/5], Boston U. 1947-48, Dale 8.48 [61/11], Peterborough U. cs.51

Despite his north east birthplace, Cyril took a roundabout route to Roker Park, Sunderland paying Brentford £2500 for him in 1945, though he never actually played for either club in the FL. He did figure in the FA Cup in 1945-46 before Notts County spent even more on him, but though he had a decent scoring record, netting on his debut and in his final two games, they let him leave for non-league Boston. Dale recruited him a year later and after a year largely in the reserves was their regular inside left when they finished 3rd in 1949-50, later appearing at left half. His most memorable performance was probably when he scored the opening goal of the famous cup tie against his former club Notts County, in front of the record Spotland attendance.

Thomas James Douglas (Tommy) Dryburgh
1948-50, 1957-58
Born: Kirkaldy 23.4.23   5'7"   11st7
Outside left
FL Apps/Gls 82/17 Total Apps/Gls 96/22
Career: (navy), Lochgelly Albert, Aldershot 25.6.47 [19/2], Dale 2.7.48 [77/17], Leicester C. 11.8.50 £7500 [95/29], Hull C. 14.5.54 [23/3], Kings Lynn 7.55, Lancaster C., Oldham A. 26.8.57 [1/-], Dale 7.11.57 [5/-], Morecambe, Lancaster C. 1958
Ice hockey for Kirkaldy Flyers c.1939
Honours: Lancashire Senior Cup winners 1949, Division 2 champions 1954

Almost certainly the only top class ice hockey player to appear for Dale – he had played for the well known Kirkaldy Flyers in his home town as a teenager – Tommy's football career only really began after his service in the navy. Moving south in 1947, he had a useful season at Aldershot before signing for Rochdale. A traditional tricky Scottish winger, he was such a success in his two seasons - helping them win the Lancashire Cup and finish 3rd in the league – that Leicester stepped in with a bid of £7500. A clever dribbler with a particularly good scoring ratio for a winger, he spent four seasons in their Division 2 side, netting four times in nine games in their 1954 promotion run, but was transferred to Hull before having the chance to play in the top division. He was brought back from the non-league game by Oldham in 1957 and returned to play a few further games for Dale later in the season.

Alan Middlebrough 1948-52
Born: Wardle, Rochdale 4.12.25
Centre forward
FL Apps/Gls 47/25 Total Apps/Gls 57/29
Career: Bolton W. 1943, pro 7.46 [15/9 WL, 5/1], Bradford C. 8.48 [4/-], Dale 10.48 to cs.52 [47/25]

Alan must rate as one of the most successful but under used of all Dale centre forwards, averaging a goal every other game for four seasons yet playing only 47 league games. A Rochdale lad, he first played for Bolton as an amateur during the war and after signing pro made a handful of first division appearances. After a brief spell at Valley Parade, Dale signed him just after the start of the 1948-49 season and he scored 3 times in 6 games before the signing of Jack Connor consigned him to the role of understudy. He grabbed a brace when standing in for Connor in the 7-1 win against Mansfield the following term and actually netted 10 times in 13 mid-season games in 1950-51. After Connor's departure he had more chances and scored a hat-trick against Darlington, but following another burst of 4 goals in 3 league games around the New Year of 1952 didn't find the net again and was released in the summer. Retiring from the game though still only 26, he returned to work in Bradford.

Thomas A. (Tom) Jones 1948-49
Born: {Rotherham JFM.23}
Left half
FL Apps/Gls 0/0 Total Apps/Gls 1/0
Career: Derby Co. am, pro 29.10.43 [33/3 WL], Dale £750 19.8.48 to 1949

One of Ted Goodier's deals that did not work out, Tom was signed from Derby for £750 but played only once, at left half, in a Lancashire Cup tie against Everton in November 1948, just after Dave Reid had been sidelined through injury. He had earlier made a number of wartime appearances for the Rams.

James (Jimmy) Cheetham 1948-49, 1954-55
Born: {Rochdale JAS.28}
Inside left
FL Apps/Gls 0/0 Total Apps/Gls 1/0
Career: (Rochdale Sunday Schools League), Dale 20.5.48, Bury 3.8.49 (exchange for W.H.J. Williams), Mossley 1950-51, Winsford 1950-51, Dale trial 29.9.54 to 12.54

Jimmy lived near Willbutts Lane and had two spells on Dale's books without making the breakthrough into the league side. His one first team game, like Tom Jones, was the Lancashire Cup draw against Everton, when he played at inside left. He joined neighbours Bury in an exchange for Bert Williams (q.v.), but again did not figure in the senior side and after a spell in non-league football had his second trial with Dale five years later.

Ronald (Ron) Hood 1948-49
Born: Cowdenbeath 18.11.22
Inside forward
FL Apps/Gls 9/1 Total Apps/Gls 9/1
Career: Kirkford, Hamilton Ac. 1941 to 1943-44 [26/8 ScWL], Aberdeen guest 1944-45 [1/1 ScWL], Dunfermline Ath. guest 1944-45 [6/2 ScWL], Aldershot 8.47 [14/8], Dale 11.48 [9/1], Shrewsbury T. 8.49, Cowdenbeath 1950-51 [9/5 ScL]

The first of another batch of mid-season Scottish signings in 1948-49, Ron had had an excellent scoring record in the games he played for Aldershot the previous year, but had refused terms for the new season and hadn't played prior to switching to Spotland. He played a couple of games in place of Jack Livesey and made further appearances after the departure of Jackie Moss, but managed only one goal, though it was in the 1-1 draw at runaway leaders Hull in front of a 36,500 crowd, the most ever to see a Dale game up to that time. He played for Shrewsbury the season before their entry to the FL and then returned to Scotland to play for his home town Cowdenbeath.

Alexander (Alex) Hawson 1948-49
Born: Auchincairn 23.10.23
Right half
FL Apps/Gls 1/0 Total Apps/Gls 1/0
Career: Aberdeen, Dale 12.48 [1/-], Burnley 1.49

Alex joined Dale from Aberdeen's reserve side but stayed only a month, playing in a friendly against Port Vale and the 1-0 home defeat by Hartlepools in December 1948. George McGeachie was signed the following week and Alex moved to Burnley but without adding to his single senior appearance.

George McGeachie 1948-51

Born: Calder 26.10.16
5'10" 11st
Wing half
FL Apps/Gls 90/6
Total Apps/Gls 101/6
Career: Gairdoch Juveniles, St. Johnstone 5.37 [25/1 ScL], Stenhousemuir guest 1939-40 [20/-ScWL], Falkirk guest 8.43 [17/3 ScWL], (army), Dundee U. guest 16.12.44 [15/-ScWL], New Brighton 17.7.46 [63/4], Leyton Orient 28.7.48, Ellesmere Port, {Ards}, Dale 12.48 [90/6], Crystal Palace 5.6.51 £1000 [46/5], Wigan Ath. cs.52 to 1.53

Honours: Lancashire Senior Cup winners 1949

A pre-war and wartime Scottish League player before his army service with the Argyle and Sutherland Highlanders, George appeared in St Johnstone's 8-2 Scottish Cup defeat by Celtic in 1945-46 but signed for New Brighton on the resumption of league football. After very brief spells with three other clubs at the start of 1948-49 he arrived at Spotland in time for the Christmas Day fixture against Stockport. An "inspirational footballer with rare fighting spirit", George partnered first Don Partridge and then, for a long spell, Eric Wood at wing half, chalking up just over 100 appearances. He appeared in the Lancashire Cup Final at the end of his first campaign and was a regular for most of the following season when Dale finished 3rd. Against his former side New Brighton in September 1950, he became one of very few Dale players to score two penalties in a game as Dale won 5-1 on their last visit to the Tower Ground. In the summer of 1951 Dale accepted a bid of £1000 from Crystal Palace for the 35 year old and he repaid their faith by being everpresent the following season, subsequently playing for Ted Goodier again at Wigan before retiring through ill health and becoming a greengrocer in Falkirk.

John Thomas (Jack) Connor   1948-51

Born: Todmorden 21.12.19
Centre forward
FL Apps/Gls 82/42
Total Apps/Gls 91/48
Career: (army), Ipswich 11.44 [2/- WL, 12/4], Lovells Ath. guest 1944-45 [?/2 WL], Carlisle U. guest 1945-46 [25/26 WL], Carlisle U. 12.46 [39/12], Ards 1948, Dale 12.48 [82/42], Bradford C. 4.51 £2000 [14/7], Stockport Co. 19.10.51 £2500 [206/132], Crewe A. 9.56 [27/4], Runcorn 1957-58, Dale scout 1959-60, Glossop manager 5.61, Stockport Co. pools promoter 1962, Dale pools manager 1966, Droylsden manager 1969-70, Glossop manager 1969-70, Stockport Co. pools promoter 1970 to 1978, Dale promotions manager 1980
Honours: Lancashire Cup winners 1949, Division 3(N) v 3(S) 1955

Though hailing from Todmorden, Jack's first club was Ipswich, but his army posting saw him turn out mostly for Carlisle, scoring prolifically in 1945-46. He played for both clubs again after the war, scoring twice on the first Saturday of peacetime football, but had spent the first half of 1948-49 in Ireland before signing up for Dale at the same time as George McGeachie. He netted a dozen goals in the second half of the season, scoring in both the semi-final and final of the Lancashire Cup, where he finally came out on top in a match-long battle with Blackpool's Scottish international goalkeeper George Farm. A traditional bustling centre forward, he and inside partner Jack Livesey netted 16 league goals each as Dale mounted a serious promotion challenge for the first time since the 1920s. In 1950-51 he hit another 16 in only 26 games, but with Dale out of the promotion picture, he was then sold to Bradford City for £2500. Though he scored a goal every other game for them, City sold him after only a few months, Jack famously having a message to meet Stockport officials relayed to him when in the cinema. Though Jack was now nearly 32, it was the County fans who saw the best of him as he terrorised Third North defences over the next five seasons, scoring a record 132 goals, with 30 or more in three successive seasons, leading the division's scoring charts in 1953-54 and being third highest scorer in the whole FL the following year (also scoring twice for the Third Division North representative team against their southern counterparts). He scored 17 hat-tricks for County, including three in successive games and two nap hands, but after falling out with the new manager in 1956, moved on for a final stint at Crewe where he took his total to 201 FL goals. He later scouted for Dale, managed non-league sides and was Pools promoter at both Edgeley Park and Spotland in the sixties and seventies. His son John was also a professional with Stockport.

Trevor Churchill   1948-53

Born: Barnsley 20.11.23
Goalkeeper
FL Apps 110   Total Apps 115
Career: Yorkshire Amateurs, Sheffield U. am 1941 [3 WL], Loughborough College, Reading 9.46 [10], Leicester C. 8.47, Dale 1.49 £400 [110], Swindon T. 5.53 [11]

At one time talked about as a possible successor to legendary England goalie Frank Swift, Trevor played for Sheffield United as an amateur in wartime games before going to Loughborough College to train to be a teacher. He made his FL debut for Reading in 1946 and was soon transferred to Leicester, but did not make their first team. He joined Dale for £400 early in 1949 and kept 8 clean sheets in 16 games. A regular again the following term, this time keeping 16 clean sheets as Dale challenged for promotion, he reputedly attracted a bid of £4000, but he had a long spell out injured in 1950-51 and played less frequently in subsequent years until transferred to Swindon in 1953. Throughout his career he continued to work as a schoolmaster.

Henry Edward (Harry) Hubbick 1948-51

Born: Jarrow 12.11.10
5'8" 11st
Left back
FL Apps/Gls 90/0
Total Apps/Gls 99/0
Career: Spennymoor, Jarrow, Blyth Spartans 6.33, Spennymoor 8.33, Arsenal trial 11.34, Burnley 2.35 [59/1], Bolton W. 2.37 [128/-, 233/1 WL], Bury guest 8.40 [17/- WL], Blackburn R. guest 5.41 [1/- WL], Blackpool guest 5.43 [2/- WL], Port Vale 10.47 [50/1], Dale 1.49 [90/-], Lancaster C. player-coach 1951, Caernarvon 8.52 to 11.52, Llandudno, Rhyl, Accrington St. trainer 1953, coach, acting manager 1958-59, Bury assistant trainer 11.59, Accrington St. trainer-coach cs.60, joint manager 12.61 to 3.62, Halifax T. trainer 1968, Preston NE trainer c. 1970, later kit man (d. 18.3.92)
Honours: Durham Senior Cup winners 1933, Lancashire Senior Cup final 1939, 1944, winners 1949, League North Cup winners 1943, 1945, War Cup winners 1943, 1945

Considerably senior even to his Dale full back partner Bill Watson, following non-league football in his native north east, Harry had been 24 by the time he made his FL debut for Burnley but remained associated with the game for the next 57 years! A long spell with Bolton followed, where in addition to well over 100 league games at left back, he accumulated what must have been one of the largest totals of wartime games anywhere — he was a collier at Haydock pit throughout the war - winning the War Cup with his own club in 1945 and as a guest for Blackpool in 1943. After a stint at Port Vale, he arrived at Rochdale when he was 38 yet played another 99 senior games (making his career total around 600), being 40 yrs 174 days old when making his last appearance (briefly a club record). Everpresent in 1949-50, he skippered Dale to their best season since the 1920s. Next becoming player-coach at Lancaster City, he finally finished playing in 1953 and joined the staff at Accrington, being their acting joint manager immediately prior to their demise in 1962. After working as Halifax trainer under Alan Ball (q.v.) when they gained promotion along with the Dale in 1969, he followed Ball to Preston, the Division 3 champions in 1971. After retiring as trainer he became kit-man and general factotum at Deepdale and continued working there until he died (at Deepdale) at the age of 81.

William Hubert J. (Bill or Bert) Williams 1949-50

Born: Manchester 24.9.25
Inside right
FL Apps/Gls 8/3 Total Apps/Gls 9/3
Career: Manchester U. 1943 [1/- WL], Bury 1.47 [1/-], Dale 8.49 (exchange for J. Cheetham) [8/3], Aldershot 6.50 (exchange for A. Steen) [6/4], Ramsgate 1951

Joining Manchester United when he was 18, Bert made his FL debut with Bury in May 1947, playing at centre forward in a 2-2 draw with Newcastle. Following 80 games in their reserves, he switched clubs with Jimmy Cheetham two years later, and was the only new face in the Dale side which opened the 1949-50 season. He spent most of the campaign as back-up to Jack Livesey and Cyril Brown for the inside forward positions, scoring twice when replacing the former against Bradford City in February. Another exchange deal saw him move on to Aldershot, where he again contributed several goals without becoming a regular.

Bennett (Benny) Nicol 1949-50
Born: Glasgow 10.3.21
Inside forward/outside right
FL Apps/Gls 5/1 Total Apps/Gls 7/1
Career: {Glasgow Ashfield, Falkirk guest 1943-44 [1/- ScWL]?}, Bolton W. 11.46, Winsford U., Dale 7.49 to cs.50 [5/1], (Scotland)

Another inside forward signing – he was the third No. 10 tried in the first week of the 1949-50 season - who could also play on the wing, Benny had joined Bolton after the war without making their league side. He only played seven times for Dale, scoring against Mansfield, before returning to play in Glasgow.

Konrad Kapler 1949-50

Born: Tychy, Poland 25.2.25
Outside left
FL Apps/Gls 4/0
Total Apps/Gls 4/0
Career: (Polish Army), Polish Eagles, Forres Mechanics, Celtic 1947-48 [7/- ScL], Dale 5.49 [4/-], Morecambe 1950, Congleton 1951, Altrincham cs.51, Stalybridge Celtic cs.57, Mossley cs.58, Ashton U. 1959-60
Honours: Polish junior international, Polish Army XI, Lancashire Junior Cup final 1951

Konrad was a pre-war Polish junior international who escaped the German invasion of his country to join the exiled Polish forces operating from Britain. A member of the Polish Grenadiers, he played for the Polish Army's representative side and their offshoot based in Scotland, the Polish Eagles. Remaining in Scotland after the war, he made several appearances for Celtic before joining the Dale – becoming their first non-British or Commonwealth born player - and playing a few games in place of Tommy Dryburgh on the left wing. Most of his career, though, was spent at the top end of the non-league game, appearing for Morecambe in the Lancashire Junior Cup Final against Dale's Reserves in 1951 and then spending six years as an automatic choice at Altrincham scoring 34 goals in 258 games. Continuing to live in Rochdale, he was still turning out for Ashton United, under Alan Ball (q.v.), in 1960.

Walter (Wally) Stanners 1949-50
Born: Carriden 2.1.21
Goalkeeper
FL Apps 5   Total Apps 7
Career: Bo'ness U., Bournemouth 7.47 [3], Dale 8.49 [5] to 1950, Dale trial 4.51

Wally must rate as one of the most unfortunate of Dale players, breaking his leg in just his fifth league game and never playing at the top level again. Although a Scot, his first senior games were in the Third South with Bournemouth before he joined Dale as understudy to Trevor Churchill. Given his chance in a Lancashire Cup tie in November 1949, he kept a clean sheet against Blackpool and shortly afterwards was handed his first league start, again keeping a clean sheet, as he did in the FA Cup at Rhyl. In three further league games he conceded only one goal and a fifth successive victory, against Southport, carried Rochdale to the top of the table in front of a Boxing Day crowd of 13,000. Disaster struck in the return the following day, however, as Wally was stretchered off after a collision just before half time. After recovering he had a try-out at Spotland at the end of the following season but was not re-engaged.

Albert (Bert) Lomas 1949-51

Born: Tyldesley 14.10.24
Goalkeeper
FL Apps 9   Total Apps 12
Career: Bolton W. am, Leeds U. 9.48 [1], Mossley 1949-50, Dale 5.50 [9], Chesterfield 7.51 [29], Wigan Ath. 1952
Honours: Lancashire Junior Cup winners 1951

After one senior game for Leeds - when immediately replaced by Harry Fearnley (q.v.) – Bert had been a regular for Mossley, playing around 50 games including their surprise cup run in 1949, and made his Dale bow in friendlies against Dunfermline and Arbroath in May 1950. In his one season at Spotland, Bert was second string to Trevor Churchill but had a decent run in the side in mid-season, unfortunately ended in the big cup tie against Chelsea, when in the narrow 3-2 defeat he let a shot from England centre forward Roy Bentley roll between his legs. His manager was quoted as saying that Bert "couldn't stop a pig in a ginnel" and that he wouldn't play again. True to his word, Goodier played Churchill in all the remaining games, though this did give Bert the chance to play in the Reserves' Lancashire Junior Cup success. He then moved to Chesterfield, where he played regularly, before Goodier relented and signed Bert for his new club Wigan.

Alan William Steen 1950-52

Born: Crewe 26.6.22
Outside left
FL Apps/Gls 45/8
Total Apps/Gls 49/9
Career: Wolverhampton W. am 3.37, pro 3.39 [1/1, 25/- WL], New Brighton guest 10.39 [1/- WL], (RAF), Wrexham guest 1940-42 [18/6 WL], Notts Co. guest 11.40 [3/- WL], Bolton W. guest 1.42 [2/- WL], Luton T. 5.46 [10/-], Northwich Victoria 7.47, South Liverpool 10.48, Aldershot 6.49 [10/-], Dale 6.50 (exchange for W.H.J. Williams) [45/8], Carlisle U. 12.51 £1250 [16/2], New Brighton 1952
Honours: Wallasey Schools, War League Midland Division champions 1940

A 'boy wonder' at Wolves, probably the first major club to operate what we call a youth policy, he made his debut at 16 years 9 months, on the opposite wing to Jimmy Mullen, also 16, in March 1939, scoring against Manchester United. He continued to play for Wolves and guest for other sides after joining the RAF as a wireless operator until his Halifax was shot down on a bombing raid over Germany in 1943. He parachuted to safety and went on the run, but ended up in Stalag Luft IVB, who could field a complete professional team (a prisoners' team photo is labelled 'England 1944'), and despite escaping twice remained a pow for the next two years. After the war he played for Luton but was then out of league football for a couple of years before returning with Aldershot. Dale signed him in exchange for Bert Williams in 1950, to replace Tommy Dryburgh on the left wing. A regular, and useful goalscorer, over the next 18 months, he was then the subject of one of Ted Goodier's legendary transfer dealings. Hearing that

Carlisle's outside left had suffered a broken leg, Goodier made Steen available for transfer, but somehow forgot to inform anyone except Carlisle, who were suitably tempted into concluding a rapid deal. Later working for Goodyear and then as a warehouse manager, despite suffering a heart attack when only in his forties, he lived to the age of 90, and was one of the last surviving pre-war FL players.

James Edward (Jim) Whitehouse 1950-52
Born: West Bromwich 19.9.24
Inside right
FL Apps/Gls 46/13 Total Apps/Gls 50/15
Career: (army), West Bromwich Hawthorns, West Bromwich A. 5.48, Walsall 6.49 [19/8], Dale 7.50 [46/13], Carlisle U. 10.51 £3500 [198/100], retired injured 1957

After serving with the North Staffordshire Regiment, Jim progressed from the West Brom nursery side, signing pro when he was 23. He made his FL debut with neighbours Walsall and had a very respectable goals return in his first season. Then signed by Ted Goodier, he initially formed the inside trio with Connor and Livesey, though several different partnerships were tried during the season. Early in 1951-52, he followed Connor and Livesey in being transferred to a rival Third North side, costing Carlisle a substantial fee. He repaid this many times over, though, netting over 20 goals from inside forward in each of his first three full seasons and becoming only the second Carlisle player to reach 100 goals. His 29 in 1952-53 included five against Scunthorpe in an 8-0 win on Christmas Day and four a fortnight later against the Dale. He retired through injury in 1957, later running a newsagents and then working in the Pirelli factory.

Gordon Ernest Medd 1950-51
Born: Birmingham 17.8.25
Outside left
FL Apps/Gls 5/1 Total Apps/Gls 5/1
Career: Worcester C., Birmingham am 1945, pro 10.46, Worcester C. 8.47, Walsall 6.49 [22/2], Dale 6.50 [5/1], York C. 1.51 [1/-]

Having played some 65 times in Birmingham's reserve sides, like Jim Whitehouse, Gordon made his FL debut with Walsall in 1949-50 and joined Dale the following summer. He had much less subsequent success than his colleague, despite a goal on his home debut in a 5-0 win, making just five appearances for Dale, and just one after moving to York where he had the misfortune to break his leg. He later worked as an insurance man.

William Arthur (Bill or 'Archie') Hughes
1950-51

Born: Colwyn Bay 2.2.19
6'2" 12st5
Goalkeeper
FL Apps 9 Total Apps 10
Career: Colwyn Bay U. 1935, Manchester U. trial, Larne 1937, Newry Town 1938, Huddersfield T. 5.39 [1 WL], West Ham U. guest 1943-44 [1 WL], Arsenal guest 1943-44 [2 WL], Tottenham H. guest 1944-45 [24 WL], Tottenham H. 12.45 [27 WL, 2], Blackburn R. 10.48 £7500 [27], Nelson 8.50, Dale 9.50 [9], Crystal Palace 2.51 (exchange for W. Blackshaw) [18], Canterbury C. 6.52
Honours: War League South champions 1945, Wales (5 caps) v England, N. Ireland, Poland, Belgium, Switzerland 1948-49, North Wales Coast FA 1937 (Welsh junior international)

Bill — or Archie as he was more usually known — went to the same school as another Welsh 'keeper, Cyril Sidlow and had been a Welsh junior international before the war. Indeed, he was Wales' regular 'keeper only a year or so before joining Rochdale, putting in "a masterly display" against England in the 1948-49 Home Internationals. After playing for his local club Colwyn Bay and representing the North Wales Coast FA, he had a stint in Ireland before joining Huddersfield on the eve of the war. He only played once for Huddersfield in the regional leagues - reputedly because they forgot they had signed him - but appeared frequently as a guest with Spurs when they won the War League South and they signed him permanently in 1945. Deputy to Ted Ditchburn, he played only twice in the league but "his consistent, fine ability" in the Football Combination resulted in a move to Blackburn, and soon afterwards the first of his five Welsh caps. However he was playing with Nelson when Dale signed him in 1950, and he only appeared nine times for them, as a stand-in for the injured Trevor Churchill, before being traded for Palace's Bill Blackshaw (who never played in the Rochdale first team). Outside the game, he was a trained engineer, working for Hotpoint, and he later owned a gents outfitters back in Old Colwyn.

Albert (Bert) Foulds 1950-51, 1951-53

Born: Salford 8.8.19
5'11" 12st2
Inside/centre forward
FL Apps/Gls 61/24
Total Apps/Gls 67/24
Career: Altrincham 11.38 to 1939, re-signed 3.47, Chester 8.48 [31/14], Yeovil T. 1949, Dale 9.50 [6/1], Scarborough 8.51,

Dale 11.51 [55/23], Crystal Palace 7.53 (exchange for F. Evans) [17/4], Crewe A. 1.1.54 [14/2], Congleton cs.54 to cs.55, Ashton U. 12.55
Honours: Lancashire Junior Cup winners

Originally a winger, Bert first signed for Altrincham before the war, rejoining them in 1947 and making his mark as a goalscoring inside forward, netting 28 times in 1947-48. He also top scored in a season with Chester and after a year with Yeovil in the Southern League, scoring 26 goals, signed for Dale in 1950. His first season was undistinguished, though he scored the Reserves' winning goal in the Lancashire Junior Cup Final, but after he scored a dozen goals for Scarborough at the start of the following term he was quickly re-signed. He was a regular scorer over the next season and a half, playing either centre or inside forward, and ended as top scorer in both campaigns, albeit with modest totals, though he netted a hat-trick away at Bradford City in September 1952. Traded for Crystal Palace's Fred Evans, he spent only a few months at Selhurst Park before a similarly short stop at Crewe.

Herbert Robert (Bob) Smyth 1950-51
Born: Manchester 28.2.21 5'10" 12st
Left half
FL Apps/Gls 3/1 Total Apps/Gls 4/1
Career: Manchester C. am, Bolton W., HMS Ganges, Ipswich T. 1944, pro 22.12.45, [7/1 WL, 2/-], Halifax T. 2.8.50 [2/-], Dale 30.9.50 [3/1], Accrington St. 26.1.51 to 16.4.51 [7/-]

After his naval service, Bob turned pro with Ipswich, but after a debut in the 1945 FA Cup made only two appearances, as a forward, in four peacetime seasons. After just a month at Halifax in 1950, he arrived at Spotland but again was limited to just three league games at left half, though he did score his one league goal in a 3-1 win against Accrington. Considered skillful on the ball with "good headwork", but perhaps lacking pace at league level, shortly afterwards he moved to Stanley for the remainder of the season and had the misfortune to play in their 9-1 defeat at Lincoln that led to manager Porter's resignation.

Henry (Harry) Boyle 1950-51, 1952-56

Born: Possil Park, Glasgow 22.4.24
5'9" 11st4
Left back
FL Apps/Gls 175/0
Total Apps/Gls 190/0
Career: Southbank St. Peter's, Grangetown St Mary's, Billingham Synthonia 1945, Middlesbrough am 23.11.45, Manchester U. am 3.5.46, Murton Colliery Welfare 1946, Southport 8.7.47 [88/-], Dale 24.6.50 [17/-], {Bacup Borough?}, Bangor C. cs.51, Dale 7.8.52 [158/-], Runcorn 7.56, Altrincham cs.57, Wigan Rovers reserve team coach 1959, Skelmersdale U. player-coach 1960 to 1962, Lancashire FA coach, Formby youth team coach 1963, visiting coach to Zambian national squad 1968, Marine manager, Ormskirk manager, Lancashire FA chief coach
Honours: Lancashire Senior Cup final 1948

Though born in Glasgow (his father was a cousin of Matt Busby), Harry came through the junior ranks in the north east before signing for Southport in 1947. He appeared nearly 100 times for them at left back, playing in their surprise appearance in the Lancashire Senior Cup Final, before moving to Spotland in 1950. Stand-in for Harry Hubbick in his first season, he left to play for Bangor City but re-signed for Dale a year later. This time he became undisputed first choice left back for four seasons, missing just one game in 1952-53 and in 1954-55 and taking his total appearances to 190 before leaving for non-league football. His most unfortunate game, though, must have been the Christmas Day fixture at Carlisle in 1954 when he, Danny Murphy and George Underwood all put through their own goal. He had already become a Lancashire FA coach while with the Dale, gaining his senior FA coaching badge in 1966, and subsequently coached in Zambia (along with Graham Taylor), turning down the post of coach of the national team. He was the Lancashire FA's senior coach for 21 years and received the LFA order of merit on his retirement. Still living in Southport, he ran a corner shop and was the organiser of the town's team that competed on the 1970s television show Jeux sans Frontieres. He also worked as a manager with National Girobank and later turned to writing poetry, with his first book published in 1990. He was included on a scroll of honour of Southport's 28 most famous citizens – including Grand National winner Red Rum! – to go in a time capsule in the Winter Gardens.

William Henry (Billy) Heaton 1950-51

Born: Leeds 26.8.18
Inside/outside left
FL Apps/Gls 5/0 Total Apps/Gls 6/0
Career: Ingram Road School (Leeds), Whitkirk, Leeds U. 12.37 [23/3 WL, 59/6], (army), Southampton 2.49 £8000 [15/-], Stalybridge Celtic, Dale 11.50 [5/-], Witton Albion 1951
Honours: Leeds City Boys, Yorkshire Schools, FA XI, British Forces tours in India and Far East February and September 1945, Lancashire Junior Cup winners 1951

Billy had originally signed for Leeds in 1937 and appeared for them in wartime games but made more of a mark in army football. He toured India and the far east with the two services teams usually referred to as Tommy Walker's XI and Denis Compton's XI and also played for an FA XI. Usually figuring on the left wing, he played fairly frequently for Leeds in the first three seasons after the war and was then transferred to Southampton for a sizeable fee, the Saints missing out on promotion to Division 1 on the last day of the season. Not figuring at all the following term, he left for Stalybridge Celtic and then joined Dale in November 1950. He appeared five times in the next couple of months, at inside or outside left, and then again in the final match of the season, also winning a Lancashire Junior Cup medal with the Reserves. He then left the senior game to take a job with a roofing company back in Leeds.

Kenneth (Ken) Crowther 1950-51

Born: Halifax 17.12.24
Right half
FL Apps/Gls 2/0
Total Apps/Gls 2/0
Career: Luddenden FC, Halifax T. am 8.42 [6/- WL], Burnley am 7.43, pro 9.45 [8/2 WL], Bradford PA 7.48 [6/1], Dale 8.50 [2/-], Nelson 1951
Honours: Lancashire Junior Cup winners 1951

Another man with a very brief Dale career in 1950-51, when fifteen new players were tried, Ken had earlier played a few games for Halifax and Burnley during the war but made his FL bow in Division 2 with Bradford in 1948. Two years later he joined Dale but figured just twice, at right half, when George McGeachie was absent, but also played inside left for the Reserves in the Lancashire Junior Cup Final.

Alexander Hogarth (Alex) McNichol 1950-51
Born: Baillieston 10.10.19
Inside left
FL Apps/Gls 17/3 Total Apps/Gls 17/3
Career: Dunfermline Ath. 1946-47 [2/- ScL], Aldershot 8.47 [109/20], Dale 1.51 [17/3], Ramsgate 1951, Dover 1951

Despite his Scottish origins, most of Alex's career was spent in the south of England. After a couple of appearances for Dunfermline, he was a consistent performer at inside forward for Aldershot for three and a half years, missing only one match in 1947-48 and scoring a hat-trick in a 6-4 loss at Port Vale in only his fifth game (he netted another treble in a 5-0 defeat of Ipswich in 1950). He spent the second half of 1950-51 with the Dale, taking the inside left berth, but was not retained at the end of the season and headed south again.

Alistair Reid Buchan 1950-54
Born: Aberdeen 27.5.26
Left half
FL Apps/Gls 107/2 Total Apps/Gls 113/2
Career: Huntley, Arbroath 1950 [5/1 ScL], Huntley, Dale 2.51 to 1954 [107/3].

Another Scot, Alistair had played briefly with Arbroath between spells with junior side Huntley. Arriving at Spotland midway through the 1950-51 season, he immediately established himself as first choice left half and had over 100 appearances to his credit over the next three years, even playing regularly when Jack Warner, himself a wing half became player manager. He eventually lost his place when Bill Morgan became Joe Lynn's regular wing half partner.

Eric R. Downes 1949-54
Born: Wigan 25.8.26
Centre half
FL Apps/Gls 54/0 Total Apps/Gls 60/0
Career: Chester am, Dale 5.49 [54/-], Horwich RMI 4.54
Honours: England amateur youth international, Lancashire Junior Cup winners 1951

Eric was originally on Chester's books as an amateur, during which time he became an England amateur youth international. He also obtained a B.Sc. degree from Manchester University before signing pro with Dale. He eventually made his FL debut in March 1951, when he was 24, and soon afterwards played for the Reserves in the Lancashire Junior Cup triumph. He proved a dependable stand-in at pivot for Walter Birch, though he could also play at left half, most of his appearances coming in season 1951-52. He also played a number of times in 1953-54 when Dale finally had to replace the stalwart Birch but unfortunately what turned out to be Eric's last two games resulted in 4-0 and 6-0 defeats and he was released following the signing of Bev Glover.

Eric Barber 1950-52
Born: Stockport 25.3.26
Outside right/centre forward
FL Apps/Gls 17/2 Total Apps/Gls 17/2
Career: {Manchester C. am 9.2.44 [3/- WL]?}, Sheffield U. 2.47, Stockport Co. 3.49, Macclesfield cs.49, Bolton W. £1500 1.3.50, Dale 14.4.51 [17/2], Macclesfield cs.52, Witton A. 10.55, Stalybridge Celtic

After being on the books of several other league clubs, Eric arrived at Willbutts Lane in time for the final five games of 1950-51, netting in the 2-0 victory over Wrexham which kept Dale in the top half of the table. He also appeared on the right wing in the first three games of the following season but all three were lost and Eric made only scattered appearances thereafter, some at centre forward as Dale tried to vary a rather shot-shy attack. He had earlier netted 25 times in a season for Macclesfield prior to a £1500 move to Bolton, and he returned to the Moss Rose after leaving Spotland, totalling 44 goals in 93 games in the Cheshire League. He worked as an electrical engineer.

Henry (Harry) Mills 1950-51
Born: Bishop Auckland 23.7.22
Centre forward
FL Apps/Gls 1/0 Total Apps/Gls 1/0
Career: Consett, Sheffield U. 6.46 [3/2], Rotherham U. 3.48 [6/3], Blyth Spartans 1948, Huddersfield T. 1948, Tunbridge Wells 1949, Dale 4.51 [1/-], Halifax T. 8.52

Though making few league appearances for any of them, Harry was on the books of four Yorkshire clubs, as well as playing just the once for the Dale in a 0-0 draw on the final day of the 1950-51 season. At Sheffield United, he had scored in each of his first two Division 1 games and at Rotherham scored three times in six games immediately after signing, as the Millers just missed promotion to Division 2.

Frederick Thomas (Fred) Fisher 1951-52
Born: Wednesbury 12.1.20 5'9" 11st2
Left back
FL Apps/Gls 1/0 Total Apps/Gls 2/0
Career: (Walsall works team), Fallings Heath FC, Grimsby T. 5.37 [166/-, 2/- WL], Darlaston 9.39, Walsall guest 1939-40 [1/- WL], Reading guest 1944-46 [22/- WL], Arsenal guest 1945-46 [1/- WL], Dale 6.51 [1/-], Boston U. 11.51 to 4.53. Grimsby T. scout 1964, Nottingham F. scout

Fred was 31 when signed by Rochdale as a possible successor to the even older Harry Hubbick, but in the event it was Alf Radford who was preferred at left back and Fred's only game was the first one of the season when Dale lost 4-0 at home to Carlisle. Most of Fred's senior football had been with Grimsby and despite losing seven years to the war, when he worked in a munitions factory near Reading, he played 166 FL games for them, many in Division 1, though he also played in their 8-0 defeat at Arsenal on the final day of 1947-48 as the Mariners went back down to Division 2. He later worked as a driving instructor and scouted both for Grimsby and for Notts Forest.

Henry William (Bill) Jennings 1951-52

Born: Norwich 7.1.20
Centre forward
FL Apps/Gls 3/1
Total Apps/Gls 3/1
Career: Northampton T. am 8.38, pro 10.38 [11/2, 19/2 WL], Grimsby T. guest 10.40 [19/9 WL], Ipswich T. 5.47 [102/41], Dale 6.51 [3/1], Crystal Palace trial 9.51

Yet another early fifties player with a very brief Rochdale career, Bill managed Dale's only goal in the first three games of season 1951-52, all of them defeats, before quickly moving on. He had made his league debut for Northampton as a youngster before the war, and after it topped 100 appearances for Ipswich. His best form undoubtedly came between 1947 and 1949 when he was twice top scorer, netting 23 times in his second season.

Joseph (Joe) Lynn 1951-56
Born: Seaton Sluice, Northumberland 31.1.25
Inside forward/wing half
FL Apps/Gls 193/23 Total Apps/Gls 208/24
Career: Cramlington, Huddersfield T. 5.47 [5/-], Exeter C. 6.50 [28/2], Dale 7.51 £ [193/23], Blyth Spartans cs.56

Easily the longest lasting of the new signings in 1951, Joe had played a handful of first division games in three years at Huddersfield and then been rather more of a regular in a season at Exeter. Ted Goodier signed him for a small fee and he soon became a consistent performer in the side, sometimes in his earlier position of inside forward but more often at wing half, and was a near everpresent in three of his five seasons at Spotland. All told, he surpassed 200 Rochdale appearances and was the skipper from 1953. He also became the side's penalty taker, netting seven times from the spot in 1954-55, at the time a club record (as was his total of eight goals from half back). He left league football when still only 31 and returned to the north east.

Arthur ('Alf') Radford 1951-52
Born: Rotherham 7.10.25
Left back
FL Apps/Gls 27/0 Total Apps/Gls 31/0
Career: Huddersfield T. 10.44 [3/- WL], Rotherham U. 5.47 [44/-], Dale 5.51 [27/-], Frickley Colliery 7.52, Swindon T. 8.52 [15/-]
Honours: (League North champions 1945)

Like Joe Lynn, Alf had been on Huddersfield's books, but he only made his FL debut after joining his home town club Rotherham. His best season was 1948-49 when he was the regular left back as the Millers finished runners up in the Third North, and he played a similar number of games for Dale three seasons later, though Ron Rothwell and Joe Coupe contested the left back slot. He left for Frickley Colliery the following close season, but almost immediately signed up for a further season in the FL with Swindon.

James (Jimmy) Hazzleton 1951-52
Born: Bolton 29.9.30 5'9" 11st
Inside left
FL Apps/Gls 11/1 Total Apps/Gls 12/1
Career: Leeds U. am, Atherton Collieries, Bury 14.5.50 to 14.3.51, Dale 14.8.51 [11/1], Accrington St. 12.7.52 to 1.5.53 [4/-]

Jimmy arrived at Spotland just after Bury colleague Harry Whitworth, though in his case without any first team experience. Although his first game for Rochdale ended in defeat, his home debut resulted in a 6-2 victory over Darlington, while his sole FL goal came in a 3-0 success against Lincoln in October 1951. He lost the inside left slot when Bert Foulds returned from Scarborough and played only twice more, at centre forward, before an even less productive season at Accrington.

James Walsh (Jim) Drury 1951-52
Born: Cumnock 29.5.24 5'10" 12st
Outside left
FL Apps/Gls 4/1 Total Apps/Gls 4/1
Career: Cumnock Academy, Cumnock Home Guard, Auchinleck PTE, Kilmarnock 5.45 [44/15 ScL], Stirling Albion £1000 12.48 [15/2 ScL], Dale 22.5.51 [4/1], Carlisle U. 14.8.52 [35/5], Southport 9.7.54 [24/2], Newton Stewart 12.55
Honours: (Scottish Division 2 promotion 1949), South of Scotland League champions 1956

Serving in, and playing for, the Home Guard in his home town after leaving Cumnock Academy, Jim was a 'Bevin Boy' at a nearby pit during the war and later worked in open-cast mines. He acquired considerable Scottish League experience, particularly with Kilmarnock, prior to his season at Rochdale, though suffering recurrent cartilage problems. He replaced Alan Steen for one early season game, but after the latter's departure it was Eric Betts who took the left wing position and Jim played just three more games the following April. He had better fortune when following Steen to Carlisle, and later at Southport, before returning north of the border and winning the South of Scotland League with Newton Stewart. He then worked at a power station before opening a grocer's back in Cumnock

Eric Hayton 1951-52
Born: Carlisle 14.1.22
Right half/inside left
FL Apps/Gls 12/0 Total Apps/Gls 13/0
Career: Carlisle U. 8.45 [9/1 WL, 49/5], Dale 5.51 [12/-], Workington 10.52 [19/-], (Carlisle local football cs.53)
Honours: Cumberland Schoolboys

One of the many transfers between Dale and Carlisle in the fifties, Eric had been a fringe player with the Cumbrians for five years, having first played in the 1945-46 FA Cup, but figured quite frequently in his final season, including in the FA Cup against Arsenal. Again largely a reserve despite Dale winning all his first three games, including the 6-2 victory over Darlington, he made a dozen appearances, shared between right half and inside left, before moving to league new boys Workington, one of only two sides to finish below the Dale in 1952-53. A varied career off the field had seen him work on the railways and as a fireman during war, while after his FL career he stayed in Carlisle working for an engineering firm and was well known as a greyhound trainer.

James Henry (Jimmy) Nicholls 1951-53
Born: Coseley 27.11.19
Goalkeeper
FL Apps 50 Total Apps 55
Career: Bilston Borough, Dudley T., East Bierley, (army), Bradford PA am 1940, pro 5.46 [4 WL, 36], Huddersfield T. guest 1940-41 [1 WL], Barnsley guest 1941-42 [4 WL], Halifax T. guest 11.41 [6 WL], Doncaster R. guest 2.42 [1 WL], Dale 8.51 to cs.53 [50]
Honours: Coseley Schoolboys, Canal Area XI (army)

Approaching the veteran stage when reaching Spotland, Jimmy had been with Park Avenue as an amateur but played very few games during the war when he served with the RASC in the Middle East. Turning pro when he was already 26, he had five more years largely in their reserves. He came into the Dale side in September 1951 when Churchill missed the game against Mansfield and shared the 'keeper's jersey with him for the next two years as Dale struggled in the lower reaches of the table. He kept a crucial clean sheet in the last game of 1952-53 – coincidentally a 1-0 win over Mansfield like his debut – which kept Dale out of the bottom two.

Robert (Bobby) Gilfillan 1951-54
Born: Dunfermline 14.3.26
Inside forward
FL Apps/Gls 62/11 Total Apps/Gls 65/11
Career: Jeanfield Swifts, Blackpool 7.47, Cowdenbeath 1949/50 [34/17 ScL], Dale 6.51 [63/11], Worcester C. cs.54

One of the many Scots in the Third North in the early fifties, Bobby had had a quite productive couple of seasons at Cowdenbeath prior to joining Dale. He made only one appearance at centre forward in the early part of the 1951-52 season and stood in briefly at left half before getting a run at inside left at the end of the season. A regular at inside forward the following term, he was also second to Bert Foulds in the goalscoring stakes with 10 including the winner in the last game of the campaign which saved Dale from a re-election application. His goalscoring deserted him the following term, though, and like Eric Downes he did not play again after appearing in the 4-0 Boxing Day defeat at Bradford City,

Joseph Norman (Joe) Coupe 1951-52
Born: Carlisle 15.7.24
Left back
FL Apps/Gls 8/0 Total Apps/Gls 8/0
Career: (army 1941), Swift Rovers, Carlisle U. 9.47 [31/-], Dale 10.51 [8/-], Workington 10.52 [6/-]

A schoolboy rugby player, Joe served in the Royal Marines as a corporal during the D-Day landing. He then played in minor football before signing up for his local club Carlisle in 1947. He was a regular in the first half of 1950-51, playing alongside Eric Hayton, but followed Hayton to Rochdale a year later. After having to share the left back spot with Radford and Rothwell, he moved on to Workington, again with Hayton, but soon returned to his original sport. A keen supporter of Workington Town, he was instrumental in the creation of Carlisle rugby league club. He was also a keen golfer.

Eric Betts 1951-53

Born: Coventry 27.6.25
5'10" 11st
Outside left
FL Apps/Gls 52/8
Total Apps/Gls 56/10
Career: Mansfield Villa, Nottingham F. am 19.10.43 and 12.5.45 pro 13.9.45 [7/2 WL], Mansfield T. 25.2.46 [10/2 WL, 19/5], Coventry C. 18.8.47, Nuneaton Borough 1947, Walsall 14.5.49 [30/3], West Ham U. 15.4.50 £5000 [3/1], Nuneaton Borough 8.51, Dale 13.10.51 [52/8], Crewe A. 12.2.53 £2000 [25/5], Wrexham 9.10.53 [53/21], Oldham A. 24.2.56 £350 [26/5], Bangor C. Later manager of Robinsons, Royal Abbey, Castleton Gabriels 1987-88 (d. 1990)

Starting out in wartime league football, Eric had a lengthy but somewhat variable career, at one time earning a £5000 move from Walsall to West Ham yet twice dropping into non-league football with Nuneaton Borough, the second time while on West Ham's transfer list. "Fast moving" and with a hard shot, he spent nearly 18 months as a regular on the left wing with Rochdale before being sold to Crewe for £2000. He had his best goalscoring returns after joining Wrexham with eight goals in only 13 games in 1953-54 and double figures the following year. Living in Rochdale after he retired, he later managed a number of local teams including Castleton Gabriels, while his son Dave played in Dale's youth and reserve sides before also becoming a stalwart of the local football scene with the likes of Tim Bobbin, Wheatsheaf and Industry.

Walter Keeley 1951-52

Born: Manchester 1.4.21
5'9" 10st12
Inside right
FL Apps/Gls 4/0
Total Apps/Gls 5/0
Career: (RAF), Accrington St. am 18.9.44, pro 11.12.44 [54/26 WL, 48/19], Manchester U. guest 3.45 and 9.45 [3/- WL], Bury 25.10.47 £3500 [7/-], Port Vale 10.1.48 (exchange for A. Bellis) [18/3], Accrington St. 24.9.48 £1500 [100/35], Dale 20.10.51 £300 [4/-], Fleetwood 2.52
Honours: Lancashire Senior Cup final 1945, Third Division North West (first championship) winners 1945-46

In the RAF during the war, Walter signed for Accrington in 1944, initially on amateur forms, and had an excellent scoring record at Peel Park, both in wartime football and in the first peacetime seasons. A "match-winning opportunist" inside forward, he played in the 1945 Lancashire Cup Final and netted 20 goals as Stanley won the Third Division North West. He also scored twice in Stanley's 8-4 victory over Lincoln in the last match of 1946-47. Whilst at Peel Park he also played one full game in goal, a 1-0 win against Southport, and covered for injuries to the goalkeepers on four other occasions, never conceding a goal. Bought by Bury for a sizeable fee, the Shakers traded him to Port Vale in exchange for Alf Bellis (q.v.) after only three months. Despite scoring twice on his Vale debut, early the following term they let him rejoin Stanley for a big fee by their standards and he reached a career total of 80 goals for them before suffering a broken leg. A final transfer to Rochdale late in 1951 saw him appear in four FL games at inside right but Dale lost them all and he was released three months later, then scoring five times on his Fleetwood debut. Walter's father had been a stalwart of Manchester North End in the years after World War I.

Francis Anthony (Frank) Tomlinson 1951-52

Born: Manchester 23.10.25
5'8"   10st10
Inside right
FL Apps/Gls 20/2 Total Apps/Gls 22/4
Career: Bolton W. am 1945-46 [2/- WL], Goslings FC, Manchester U. am, Goslings 1945-46, Oldham 16.11.46 [115/27], Dale 15.11.51 £ [20/2], Chester 22.8.52 [11/-], Ashton U. 1953-54, re-signed cs.55, Droylsden 1958-59. Bradford PA manager 2.70 to 12.70

A product of Goslings FC like earlier Dale player Arthur Jones, Frank played the bulk of his career with Oldham. An "enterprising winger" with "the ability to swerve past an opponent", he scored in each of his first three games in 1946 and appeared over 100 times until breaking his leg in September 1950. When he was transferred to Rochdale, the Latics used the small fee to pay him a benefit. He scored on his Dale debut in a 3-2 victory over Tranmere in November 1951 and played regularly at inside right until the last month of the season. In a lengthy stint with Ashton United he scored 40 goals in 160 games. He later worked for Hawker Siddeley and ran a sports centre for many years before surprisingly being appointed Bradford's manager just before the Park Avenue club's final demise.

James Alan Ball 1951-52

Born: Farnworth 23.9.24
5'8"   10st6
Inside left
FL Apps/Gls 5/1
Total Apps/Gls 5/1
Career: (Bolton Boys Federation), Southport am 17.8.42, pro 5.3.46 [18/3 WL, 2/-], Birmingham £ 20.5.47, Southport 1.48 £500 [40/10], Oldham 3.7.50 [7/-], Dale 2.2.52 [5/1], Ashton U. cs.52, Oswestry T. 1952, player-manager 1953-55, Borough United 1.58, Ashton U. manager 1959-60, Nantwich manager, Stoke C. coach, Halifax T. manager 12.67 to cs.70, Preston NE manager cs.70 to 2.73, Southport manager 1.74 to 7.75, Saab (Sweden) manager 1975, Halifax T. manager 2.76 to 11.77, Sirius (Sweden) manager, Upsalla (Sweden) manager, Blackpool scout 1980-81, Vester Haringe (Sweden) manager, Apoel Nicosia (Cyprus) coach 1981-82 (d. 2.1.82)
Honours: As manager, Birmingham League champions, Shropshire Senior Cup, Division 4 promotion 1969, Division 3 champions 1971

Father of England 1966 World Cup winner Alan jnr., Alan had a very lengthy association with the game, but with most of his success coming as manager rather than player. With Southport during and immediately after the war, he was transferred to Birmingham but then bought back by the Sandgrounders a few months later. Less productive stints with Oldham and Dale followed before he took over as Oswestry's player-manager when he was only 28, winning the Shropshire Cup and the Birmingham League. His first FL management position did not follow until 1967 but he took Halifax to promotion alongside the Dale 18 months later. Moving on to Preston he won the Third Division championship in his first season but was sacked a couple of years later. In 1975 he had his first stint in Sweden, with Saab, and returned there at intervals for the rest of his career. He had just been appointed coach to Apoel alongside much later Dale player Mike Ferguson when he was tragically killed in a car crash on Cyprus in 1982.

Norman Case 1948-49, 1951-52
Born: Prescot 1.9.25
Centre forward
FL Apps/Gls 2/0 Total Apps/Gls 2/0
Career: Sheffield U. 8.48, Leyton Orient 10.48, Dale 11.48, Ards, Sunderland 10.49 £3500 [4/2], Watford 12.50 £2000 [10/3], Yeovil T. 8.51, Dale 2.52 [2/-], Cheltenham T. 7.52
Honours: Irish League v Scottish League 1949

Norman first passed through Spotland briefly – playing only in a friendly against Halifax – when they became his third club of the 1948-49 season. Moving in the opposite direction to Jack Connor and George McGeachie, he was more successful during a stint with Ards, scoring for the Irish League against the Scots, albeit in an 8-1 defeat and securing a transfer to Sunderland. He scored twice on his first division debut but played only three more games before moving on and, while on Watford's transfer list, appearing regularly for Yeovil with the other former Rochdale and Irish League player Hugh Colvan. In his second stint he played two FL games for Dale in February 1952.

Tom Hindle 1951-52

Born: Keighley 22.2.21
5'8"   12st
Outside left
FL Apps/Gls 6/1
Total Apps/Gls 6/1
Career: Ignow Council School, Keighley T., Bradford PA trial, Leeds U. 9.43 [96/39 WL, 42/2], York C. 2.49 (exchange for J. Rudd) [19/3], Halifax T.

9.49 [85/17], Dale 3.52 [6/1], Wigan Ath. 7.52, Nelson cs.55, Salts (Saltaire) committee 9.59
Honours: Keighley Boys

During wartime, when he worked as an engineer, Tom was a regular for Leeds, netting an exceptional 26 goals in 1944-45, and he stayed with them when league football resumed, initially as an inside left before moving out to the wing. He also had a productive spell at Halifax before arriving at Willbutts Lane near the end of the 1951-52 season. He scored on his debut and played six times in total but was not retained, though he played for Ted Goodier again the following season at Wigan. He was later a committee member for top Yorkshire amateur side Salts. His brother Jack was with East Fife.

Harold (Harry) Potter 1952-54

Born: Tyldesley 20.5.23
Right back
FL Apps/Gls 52/0
Total Apps/Gls 56/0
Career: Winsford U., Shrewsbury T. 1948 [67/-], Dale 6.52 [52/-], Rhyl 1954

Ted Goodier's final signing before he resigned, Harry had played for Shrewsbury for four seasons before and after their election to the FL. He spent two years at Spotland, being preferred at right back to Bill Watson for much of 1952-53 and the first three months of the following term - Watson latterly being switched to centre half - but was then himself replaced, first by Fred Evans and then by Harry Boyle moving from left back.

John (Jack) Warner 1952-53

Born: Tonypandy 21.9.11 5'7" 10st7
Half back
FL Apps/Gls 21/0 Total Apps/Gls 22/0
Career: Trealaw Rangers, Treorchy Juniors, Aberaman 1932, Swansea T. 15.1.34 [132/8], Manchester U. 6.6.38 [105/1, 213/7 WL], Oldham A. player-coach 19.6.51 [35/2], Dale player-manager 5.7.52 to 7.5.53 [21/-]
Honours: Wales (2 caps) v England 1937, v France 1939, Victory international v Ireland 1946, League North Second Championship winners 1942, League North Cup final 1945, Charity Shield 1948, Lancashire Senior Cup winners 1941, 1946

A product of junior football in the Welsh valleys — he was born in the same street as three other FL players — Jack, nicknamed 'Nippy', was working in the pits when signed by Swansea in 1934, making well over 100 appearances for them as a wing half. An accurate passer who "tackled tenaciously and exhibited a calm assurance" in defence, though he rarely headed the ball, he won his first Welsh cap, against England, a few months before being transferred to Manchester United, winning a second cap just before the war. Continuing to play throughout the war, when he assisted with coaching the junior sides, he accumulated over 200 Regional League appearances and played in the League North Cup Final as well as a Victory international against Ireland. He also made over 100 FL appearances for United, and though losing his place before the 1948 FA Cup Final did play in the Charity Shield game at the start of the following season. After skippering United's reserve side, in 1951 he became player-coach at Oldham and, priding himself on his physical fitness, played in almost all their games, at the age of 40. The following July he became Dale's new player-manager and during the season turned out in all the half back positions, his final game coming when he was 41 years, 195 days old, making him Dale's oldest player until Tony Ford 50 years later. However, his appointment was judged "not a conspicuous success". Dale had struggled throughout and only escaped the re-election places with a victory on the last day of the season (in fact, they won four of the last six games) and Jack left the club, and professional football, the following week, subsequently becoming a bookmaker.

Alexander Duncan (Alex or 'Sandy') Lister
1952-53
Born: Glasgow 20.1.24
Inside/outside right
FL Apps/Gls 2/0 Total Apps/Gls 2/0
Career: Queen's Park 1943, Third Lanark 1945, Dundee U. trial 1946, signed 17.10.46 [24/16 ScL], Glentoran 5.49, Alloa Ath. 1950 [43/25 ScL], Dale 5.52 [2/-], Stenhousemuir cs.53 [2/- ScL]

Appearing for Third Lanark in the Scottish Cup in the transitional 1945-46 season, Sandy had an excellent strike rate in his first season with Dundee United in the Scottish 'B' Division, netting 18 times in 22 games, but spent most of the next two years in the reserves. After a spell in Ireland he repeated this goalscoring form with Alloa but was unable to make much impression during his sole spell in England, playing in Dale's opening game of 1952-53 at inside right but not being seen again until figuring on the wing in a 3-1 defeat at Oldham, in front of a 15,500 crowd, the following February.

Leslie (Les) Murray 1952-53
Born: Kinghorn, Fife 29.9.28
Inside right
FL Apps/Gls 16/3 Total Apps/Gls 16/3
Career: Lochgelly Albert, Raith Rovers 1949 [28/7 ScL], Arbroath 1951-52 [20/7 ScL], Dale 5.52 [16/3], Cowdenbeath cs.53 to 1958 [142/26 ScL], Grimsby Police XI

Another Scot in Dale's line-up, Les had figured fairly regularly with Raith Rovers and Arbroath over the previous three seasons before his arrival at Spotland. He had a run of games at inside right in September and October and reappeared late in the season at outside left, scoring in a 3-1 victory over Hartlepools (indeed, Dale won all three games in which he scored). He subsequently had a long stint with Cowdenbeath, retiring in 1958 to join the police (in Grimsby, who apparently were keen to recruit ex-professional footballers to strengthen their force's team) and then worked as a hotel manager for S&N.

Brian Sutton 1952-56
Born: Norden 8.12.34
6'1" 15st
Goalkeeper
FL Apps 13 Total Apps 13
Career: Norden School, Norden Youth Club, Dale am c.9.52, pro 10.52 [13], Rossendale U. 10.55, Darwen 1957-58, Macclesfield 1958-59
Honours: Rochdale Schools 1951

One of the first of a string of local lads to make the first team in the early fifties, Brian played for Rochdale Schools and joined Dale from his youth club side in Norden. He made his debut as a 17 year old, replacing Churchill in the wake of a 5-1 defeat and becoming Dale's youngest player up to that point, indeed he remained Dale's youngest goalkeeper until Stephen Bywater 45 years later. He kept a clean sheet in his first game and in two of the next four as well. After turning pro the following month he added a few further appearances that season but the arrival of Albert Morton and Graham Cordell relegated him back to the third team and his only other FL games came in September 1955, a 5-1 victory over Barrow but then the disastrous 7-2 defeat at Chesterfield the day Ray Aspden made his debut. By the time he played for Macclesfield in 1958 he weighed in at 15 stone.

Charles (Charlie) Hogan 1952-53

Born: Bury 23.4.26
5'6" 11st6
Winger
FL Apps/Gls 3/0
Total Apps/Gls 3/0
Career: Spartan Athletic 1941, Manchester C. 1942, (army), Bury am, pro 2.6.48 [1/-], Accrington St. 5.8.49 [56/4], Southport 8.51 [9/1], Dale 15.8.52 [3/-], Nelson cs.53, Wigan Ath. 9.53, Ashton U. 2.54

Charlie had played regularly in the Third North during two years at Accrington where he was noted for his "spirited play and clever ball control" on the right wing. However in only his second game for Southport he suffered a knee injury which required a cartilage operation and he was largely consigned to the reserves thereafter. One of Jack Warner's first signings, he played just three times for Dale, as stand-in for Betts and Whitworth on the wings, the last in a 5-0 defeat at Carlisle. The following year he played under the Dale's previous boss, Ted Goodier, at Wigan. After leaving the game, he had an unusually academic career for an ex-footballer. He worked for the Bury Times and ICI, qualified as a company secretary, lectured in further education colleges and obtained a university masters degree when in his fifties. He died suddenly while attending a wartime reunion at Arnhem just after retiring.

William Raymond (Ray) Haddington 1952-54

Born: Scarborough 18.11.23
5'8" 11st4
Inside forward
FL Apps/Gls 38/12 Total Apps/Gls 40/12
Career: Bradford PA am 10.6.42 [4/- WL], Bradford C. guest 3.44 and 11.44 [2/- WL], Halifax T. guest 2.45 [2/1 WL], York C. guest 1944-45 [1/- WL], Plymouth A. guest 12.45 [3/- WL], Portsmouth guest 1945-46 [3/3 WL], Exeter C. guest 1945-46 [2/1 WL], Bradford C. 7.9.46, Oldham A. 12.8.47 [117/63], Manchester C. 4.11.50 £8000 [6/4], Stockport Co. 15.12.51 £2500 [11/4], Bournemouth & BA 31.8.52 [2/-], Dale 13.10.52 [38/12], Halifax T. 7.11.53 [8/-], Bedford T. 1954-55, Ashton U. 2.56 to 4.56, Juventus (Australia) 1958
Honours: Division 2 promotion 1951

Ray played with a string of Yorkshire sides during the war, before a posting to the south saw him guest for several other sides in 1945-46. He made his FL debut with Oldham in 1947 and accumulated 63 goals at better than one every other game for the Latics, being particularly noted as a devastating striker of a dead ball. He hit 18 goals in 1948-49 and 19 the following season – often from outrageous positions - before a transfer to Manchester City. He scored in each of his first four games for City, but only played a couple more times as City won promotion to the top division. After even briefer stays at Stockport and Bournemouth he arrived at Spotland in the autumn of 1952 and netted eight times in a struggling side, including a hat-trick against Darlington. Figuring equally in the two inside positions, Ray lost his place a year after signing, on the arrival of Jack Haines. Later emigrating to Australia, he could lay claim to having played for Juventus (even if not the Italian one!) and lived for many years in Adelaide. His younger brother Harry was also with the two Bradford clubs and played over 200 games for Walsall.

Mark Radcliffe 1952-53
Born: Hyde 26.10.19
Goalkeeper
FL Apps 1 Total Apps 2
Career: Oldham A. 12.42 [90 WL], Fulham 8.46 [11], Witton Albion 8.48, Dale 11.52 [1], Witton Albion manager 1953, {Ashton U. 10.54?}

Mark was 32 when he joined Dale, but had only played 11 FL games and added just one more whilst with them. Most of his senior appearances had come with Oldham during the war, though after being signed by former Dale boss Jack Peart for Fulham he made a number of appearances in 1946-47. He had a long spell at Witton Albion, returning to manage them after his brief interlude at Spotland.

William (Billy) Morris 1952-53

Born: Radcliffe 1.4.31
Outside right
FL Apps/Gls 4/1
Total Apps/Gls 4/1
Career: Bury jnr, pro 5.48, Derby Co. 10.51, Dale 11.52 [4/1], Corby T. c.1953

Billy's elder brother Johnny became the holder of the British transfer record in 1949, when moving from Manchester United to Derby and Billy joined him at the Baseball Ground a couple of years later. Having failed to break into the first team at Bury or Derby, Billy made his FL debut at inside right immediately after signing for Dale in November 1952. He later played three games at outside right, scoring in the 6-2 defeat of Barrow when regular winger Harry Whitworth moved to centre forward and grabbed a hat-trick.

Stanley (Stan) Marriott 1952-53
Born: Rochdale 21.7.29
Centre forward
FL Apps/Gls 6/2 Total Apps/Gls 6/2
Career: Leeds U. am, Rochdale YMCA, Dale am 1951-52 [6/2], Rossendale U. 1953-54

Signed on amateur terms by Dale in 1951-52, after a similar spell at Leeds, Stan replaced Bert Foulds for a number of games in the middle of the following campaign. He scored at both Mansfield and Darlington though Dale lost each time – indeed they lost 21 of their 23 away games that season.

John Graham 1952-53
Born: Leyland 26.4.26
Winger
FL Apps/Gls 10/1 Total Apps/Gls 10/1
Career: Leyland Motors, Aston Villa 11.46 [10/3], Wrexham 6.49 £2000 [45/7], Wigan Ath. 7.52, Dale 1.53 [10/1], Bradford C. 7.53 (part exchange for J. Anders) [18/1], retired 1954

Recruited to replace Eric Betts on the left wing, John was only with Dale for six months, and like Billy Morris scored his only goal in the 6-2 demolition of Barrow. He was then traded for Bradford City winger Jimmy Anders and decided to retire the following year. Earlier he had played a few games in the top flight for Aston Villa, figuring in various forward positions, and then spent three seasons at Wrexham, mostly at inside forward, without becoming a regular.

Daniel (Dan) Boxshall 1952-54
Born: Bradford 2.4.20
Centre forward
FL Apps/Gls 11/3 Total Apps/Gls 12/3
Career: (army), Salem Ath., Queens Park R. 1.46 [3/1 WL, 30/14], Bristol C. 5.48 [52/10], Bournemouth & BA 7.50 [51/8], Dale 7.52 [11/3], Chelmsford C.
Honours: Division 3 South (north region) second competition winners 1946

Though born in Yorkshire, Danny had played most of his football in the south, accumulating over 130 Southern Section appearances for his three clubs before joining Dale in the summer of 1952. Despite Dale's travails, it wasn't until the following April that he was handed his debut. He played in the last 8 games of the season, scoring three times, as Dale won four times to escape the bottom two places by a single point. Again almost entirely restricted to the reserves the following term he moved to Southern League Chelmsford. During the war he had won the Military Medal when in charge of a bren gun crew in France.

John Graham Cordell 1953-55
Born: Walsall 6.12.28
Goalkeeper
FL Apps 15 Total Apps 19
Career: Hilary St. School, Hilary St. Old Boys, Walsall Star, Aston Villa am 6.49, pro 9.49 [5], Dale 5.53 [15], Brush Sports 1955
Honours: Walsall Schoolboys

A reserve 'keeper at Villa, making a handful of Division 1 appearance over the previous couple of years, Graham had a brief but eventful Dale career. His debut on the opening day of 1953-54, Harry Catterick's first game in charge, ended in a 7-0 defeat at Carlisle and the following year he shared in a defensive mistake riddled 5-4 defeat at Accrington in a howling gale. On the other hand, when given further opportunities over his two seasons at Spotland he kept a total of 6 clean sheets in 15 league games, or one every 2.5 games, giving him the best ratio of any Dale goalkeeper with more than a couple of appearnces. His national service had taken him to Hong Kong and he later worked for the Inland Revenue back in Walsall.

Kenneth (Ken) Rose 1953-54
Born: Eckington 18.3.30
Centre forward/outside right
FL Apps/Gls 11/0 Total Apps/Gls 11/0
Career: Chesterfield 11.50, Exeter C. 6.52 [11/3], Dale 7.53 [11/-], Workington 6.54 [6/2], assistant trainer 1955

Ken travelled the length of the country from Exeter to Workington in search of regular first team football but was never more than an able deputy at any of his clubs. For Dale he started out on the right wing, then switched to centre forward, but played only for the reserves after October. He subsequently joined Workington's training staff, under future managerial legend Bill Shankley, when he was still only 25.

Frederick John (Fred) Evans 1953-54

Born: Petersfield 20.5.23
Right back
FL Apps/Gls 12/0
Total Apps/Gls 13/0
Career: Portsmouth 1.45 [27/19 WL, 9/3], Notts Co. 7.47 [40/14], Crystal Palace 3.51 [52/11], Dale 6.53 (exchange for A. Foulds) [12/-], Biggleswade T. 1954
Honours: Division 3 South champions 1950

Signed by Dale in exchange for Bert Foulds in 1953, Fred had played regularly for Palace in 1951-52 at centre forward or outside right, scoring 10 goals. Top scorer for Portsmouth in the final wartime season, he had also had a decent scoring record in four seasons at Meadow Lane, his best season being 1949-50 when he played about half of County's games when they won the Southern section title. After three games up front for Dale at the start of the season, Fred was tried at right back later in the term, and despite his first game in defence ending in a 6-0 defeat (his debut had been in the 7-0 opening day defeat), he continued in this role for the next couple of months.

Neville Black 1953-56
Born: Ashington 19.6.31
Inside left
FL Apps/Gls 62/13 Total Apps/Gls 67/14
Career: Pegswood, Newcastle U. 9.49, Exeter C. 1.53 [4/-], Dale 7.53 [62/13], Ashington 1956

Neville arrived from his native north east via Exeter (where he had been signed by Dale old boy Norman Kirkman) and spent three seasons in and out of the Dale side before returning home. Left out after the 7-0 first day defeat at Carlisle, he reclaimed the inside left shirt for most of the second half of the 1953-54 campaign but had to share the role with the likes of Haines, Mitcheson, McClelland and Andrews over the next two years, sometimes being used on the left wing.

James (Jimmy) Anders 1953-57
Born; St. Helens 8.3.28   5'4" 10st
Outside left
FL Apps/Gls 123/28 Total Apps/Gls 135/33
Career: Parr Central School, St Helens T., Preston NE am 3.4.45, pro 28.8.45 [1/- WL], Brentford 1.9.48 [12/-], Bradford C. 2.6.51 £1000 [51/11], Dale 2.7.53 (part exchange for J. Graham) [123/28], Bradford PA 10.9.56 [20/4], Accrington St. 25.1.57 [129/30], Buxton 8.60, Bradford PA 5.9.60 £250 [39/8], Tranmere R. 11.61 [8/1], New Brighton 8.62

Jimmy and his almost equally diminutive brother Harry, later of Manchester City and Accrington Stanley, both joined Preston from St Helens Town at the end of the war, Jimmy then moving on to Brentford where he made his FL bow as an inside forward in 1949. After two reasonably productive seasons at Bradford City he was signed in exchange for John Graham, Dale definitely getting the better of the deal as Jimmy went on play well over 100 times for them. Small and stocky, yet "fast moving and tricky", he hardly missed a game in three seasons on the left wing – generally with Arnold Kendall on the other flank – and twice hit double figures in goals. Moving to the other half of Bradford, along with Kendall, he stayed only a few months before teaming up with brother Harry at Accrington, who finished 2nd in the final season of the Third (North), and again making well over a century of appearances. In 1958-59 he became Stanley's highest scoring winger ever, when he netted 20 goals including a treble in the FA Cup against future employers Buxton. Briefly out of the FL, he then had another spell at Park Avenue before finishing in league football through injury when with Tranmere.

Albert Morton 1953-57
Born: Newcastle 27.7.19   6'0"   12st
Goalkeeper
FL Apps 89   Total Apps 94
Career: St Peter's Albion, Sheffield W. 3.38 [78 WL, 40], Dale 7.53 to cs.57 [89]
Honours: League North Cup final 1943

Albert joined Sheffield Wednesday from minor football before the war and was on their books for the next 15 years. His most successful period was probably in wartime football when he appeared quite regularly and played in the 1943 League North Cup Final against Blackpool (when one of his teammates was Wally Reynolds, guesting from Rochdale). In seven post-war seasons, though, he managed only 40 appearances, over half of them in 1947-48, and was largely second string to the even longer serving Dave McIntosh before joining Dale in 1953, when he was already 34. Missing the opening day disaster, he was Dale's regular goalkeeper for two seasons and then reserve to Jimmy Jones for two more.

Zdislaw ('Adam') Wasilewski 1953-54
Born: Poland c.1925
Centre forward
FL Apps/Gls 4/1   Total Apps/Gls 4/1
Career: Altrincham 1951-52, Polish Circle (Blackley), Dale pt 7.53 to 11.53 [4/1], (amateur football) (d. 1956)

Born in Poland in the mid-twenties, Adam, as he was more conveniently known, found his way to Britain and was playing centre forward for a team of Polish expatriates in the Blackley League in Manchester when spotted by the Dale in 1953. He had earlier been with Altrincham at the same time as fellow Pole Konrad Kapler (q.v.). He spent a few months at Spotland as a part-timer and made four FL appearances, scoring in a 1-1 draw at Southport. He then returned to local amateur football and worked for the Mellowhide company in Rochdale, but sadly died only a couple of years later when living in Salford.

Robert Herbert (Bob) Priday 1953-54

Born: Cape Town 29.3.25
5'9"   12st2
Outside left
FL Apps/Gls 5/1
Total Apps/Gls 5/1
Career: Cape Town City, Liverpool 1.12.45 [12/4 WL, 34/6], Blackburn R. 17.3.49 £10000 [44/11], Clitheroe cs.51, Northwich Victoria cs.52, Accrington St. 13.12.52 [5/-], Dale trial 17.8.53 to 10.10.53 [5/1]
Honours: Football League champions 1947, Lancashire Senior Cup winners 1947

The second overseas born player to make their Dale debuts in successive weeks, Bob started with a goal on his debut at centre forward, though in a 5-1 reverse, and played some further games on the left wing during his two month trial. Born in Cape Town, he was one of several South Africans signed by Liverpool at the end of the war – in his case on a liner, as it entered Southampton! He made eight appearances when they won the league title in 1947 and appeared quite regularly on the wing the following term. A neat ball player, noticeable because of his red hair, a big money transfer took him to Blackburn in 1949 and he played a reasonable number of games over the next two years before dropping from the second division to non-league football, later reappearing briefly in the FL with Accrington, where he was unfortunately injured on his debut, and then Dale. He subsequently returned to South Africa.

William Alfred (Bill) Morgan 1953-55
Born: Rotherham 26.9.26
Right half
FL Apps/Gls 28/0   Total Apps/Gls 29/0
Career: Wolverhampton W. jnr 1942, pro 11.43 [4/- WL], Sheffield U. 9.46, Halifax T. 8.48 [109/3], Dale 7.53 to 1955 [28/-]

Bill played a few wartime league games with Wolves while still in his teens but had to wait until joining Halifax in 1948 for his FL debut. He played over 100 times for the Shaymen, being everpresent in 1950-51 but was less used thereafter, also suffering with a knee injury in 1952-53. He then moved to Spotland but again was not able to fully secure his place in the side, appearing regularly at right half in the second half of his first season but only a couple of times the following term.

Harold Arnold Kendall 1953-57
Born: Siddall 6.4.25   5'5"   10st1
Outside right
FL Apps/Gls 111/25 Total App/Gls 121/27
Career: Manningham Mills, East Bierley, Bradford PA am 5.43 [1/- WL], Salts (Saltaire) 5.46, Ossett T. 7.48, Bradford C. am 2.49, pt 2.49 [113/13], Dale 9.53 [111/25], Bradford PA pt 9.56 [90/12], Wigan Rovers 8.59, Wisbech T. 1959, Buxton T. 1960, Skelmersdale U. 1961, Wisbech T. 1962, Goole T. 1962, Bridlington 1962-63
Honours: West Riding FA

Arnold's career tracked that of fellow Dale winger Jimmy Anders to a significant extent, both being with the two Bradford clubs either side of their Spotland stint. After a remarkable season scoring 69 goals for amateurs Salts, Arnold became a part-timer at Valley Parade – he worked as a motor mechanic in a garage owned by a City director – and accumulated well over 100 appearances, as he did in three years as Dale's first choice outside right, twice netting double figure goal tallies. He almost reached the ton at Park Avenue, too, before embarking on an extensive round of the non-league scene, finishing at Bridlington when he was 38. Arnold was also a keen snooker player and golfer and his son Paul was on Bradford City's books as an amateur in the early 'seventies.

Brian Leslie Mottershead 1953-55
Born: Rochdale 13.7.35
Inside right
FL Apps/Gls 1/0 Total Apps/Gls 1/0
Career: Hamer YC, Notts Co. jnr 1950, pt 9.52, Dale 8.53 to 1954-55 [1/-], {Ashton U. 10.54?}, Mossley 1957-58

Though a Rochdale lad, playing youth football with Hamer, Brian was on Notts County's books before signing for Dale as an 18 year old. His one FL appearance came shortly afterwards, at inside right against Wrexham in September 1953.

John Thomas William (Jack) Haines

1953-55
Born: Wickhamford 24.4.20 5'9" 10st11
Inside forward
FL Apps/Gls 60/16
Total Apps/Gls 68/18
Career: Badsey Council School, Evesham GS, Evesham T. 1934, Cheltenham T. 1937, Liverpool 11.37, Swansea T. 6.39 [10/2 WL, 28/7], Worcester C. guest, (RAF), Wrexham 1941-42 [1/- WL], Doncaster R. guest 3.43 [2/- WL], Notts Co. guest 10.42 and 1945-46 [9/2 WL], Lincoln C. guest 1943-44, 1945-46 [12/3 WL], Bradford PA guest 11.43 [1/- WL], Leicester C. 6.47 [12/3], West Bromwich A. 3.48 (exchange for P. McKennan) [59/24], Bradford PA 12.49 £12000 [136/34], Dale 9.53 £2000 [60/16], Chester 7.55 [46/8], Wellington T. 7.57, Kidderminster H. 7.58, Evesham T. 10.58 to cs.59, Bretforton Village 8.60 to 3.61
Honours: RAF XI, England v Switzerland 1948, Division 2 promotion 1949

A well-travelled former England international, Jack was signed for Dale by Harry Catterick for a substantial fee when he was 33. Brought up in Worcestershire and coached by old internationalist Jesse Pennington at school, he signed for Liverpool at 17 but his FL debut with Swansea had to wait until after the war, though in the meantime he had guested for a whole string of clubs while serving in the RAF. Transferred to Leicester and then West Brom a few months later, he proved a big success at the Hawthorns, netting a hat-trick in a 6-0 victory over Bradford soon after signing. Starring at inside forward in the Baggies' side that gained promotion to the top flight, he won his one England cap, scoring twice in a 6-0 success by a somewhat experimental side against Switzerland. Joining Park Avenue for a very sizeable £12,000 in 1949 (the year of the first £25,000 transfers), he played regularly for three and a half seasons, twice netting double figure goal tallies. He managed 11 goals – including a hat-trick against Crewe - in his first season at Rochdale, but was less effective in his second campaign and was allowed to leave for Chester. Going full circle, he ended his career back with his original club Evesham Town when he was 39, 25 years after first joining them on leaving school, and then retired to concentrate on his greengrocers business.

William (Bill) Tolson 1953-55

Born: Rochdale 29.3.31
Inside forward
FL Apps/Gls 10/0
Total Apps/Gls 12/0
Career: St Alban's c.1947, Dale 10.53 [10/-], (Australia 1955)

Another local like Brian Mottershead, Bill followed him into the Dale side, making his FL debut in the 3-0 defeat of Darlington in November 1953 after a previous outing in the Lancashire Cup. He managed a few more appearances as a stand-in for regular inside men Haines and Black over the next 12 months before emigrating to Australia. As a youth he played in the same St Alban's side as future

Manchester U. full back and Bolton manager Ian Greaves and Lancashire cricketer Freddie Moore.

Frank Lord 1953-61

Born: Chadderton 13.3.36
6'0" 12st4
Centre forward
FL Apps/Gls 122/54
Total Apps/Gls 131/56
Career: Chadderton Secondary Modern, Royton Amateurs, Oldham A. am, Dale am cs.53, pro 10.53 [122/54], Crewe A. 7.61 £2500 [108/68], Plymouth A. 11.63 £12000 [69+1/23], Stockport Co. 2.66 £5000 [27/18], Blackburn R. 12.66 £10000 [10/1], Chesterfield 8.67 [12/6], Plymouth A. player-coach 10.67 [6/2], Cape Town City manager, Stoke C. coach, Preston NE caretaker manager 2.73 to 3.73, Crystal Palace coach 4.73 to 7.75, Cape Town City manager, Hereford U. manager 10.79 to 10.82, Penang State (Malaysia) manager 1.83 to 1985, (South Africa), Lincoln C. assistant manager to 9.95, Wigan A. director of football, caretaker manager 1995, Manchester U. South African scout
Cricket for Newhey St Thomas (District Cricket League champions 1961)
Honours: Army v Navy 1956. As manager: South African manager of the year 1977

An amateur on Oldham's and then Dale's books, Frank made an inauspicious debut at centre forward when Dale lost 6-0 at Hartlepools at the end of October 1953. At the time Dale's youngest ever player at 17 years 7 months, he got another chance a couple of months later, scored twice in a 4-0 victory over Chester and kept his place, ending the season with 10 goals including a hat-trick against Wrexham (plus another, in 9 minutes in a floodlit friendly against Third Lanark). However, a broken leg suffered in the first game of the following season, his National Service (during which he represented the Army) and a second broken leg a week after his demob meant that, apart from 1956-57 when he netted 15 goals including two more trebles, it was towards the end of 1959-60 before Frank was able to really revive his career. He netted 16 times in as many games at the start of the following term before his, and the Dale's goals dried up, and after being in dispute with the club for some time he was sold to Crewe. He netted three hat-tricks in his total of 31 goals in his first season and 68 goals in just over two years brought a move to Plymouth which earned Crewe a tidy profit. (While at Home Park, he was Argyle's first substitute, when they became the last club in the FL to use one, in December 1965). A centre forward of the old school, he suffered numerous other broken bones during his career but continued to fire in the goals – 172 in all - as he made regular moves around the league until ending up back at Plymouth as player-coach in 1967. He then went into management with Cape Town City and had various stints managing and coaching in the FL, including three years at Hereford, interspersed with other jobs abroad (winning the South African manager of the year award), eventually settling in South Africa where he acted as Manchester United's local scout.

Desmond (Des) Frost 1953-55
Born: Congleton 3.8.26 5'10" 12st
Centre forward
FL Apps/Gls 16/6 Total Apps/Gls 17/6
Career: Civil Defence Messengers (Congleton), (army), Congleton T. 1946, Leeds U. 4.49 [10/2], Halifax T. 1.51 [117/55], Dale 11.53 (exchange for R. Haddington) [16/6], Crewe A. 9.54 to 1956 (exchange for E. Gemmell) [42/12]
Honours: England v Scotland (services international)

Des was a messenger with the civil defence volunteers in his home town (playing with his colleagues in local football) before his call-up to the Northamptonshire Regiment, subsequently playing for England against Scotland in a services international while with the RASC in Singapore. Despite this he spent three more years in non-league football after the war before signing pro for Leeds. After a few second division games he moved on to become a regular at Halifax, with over 50 FL goals, including 24 when everpresent in 1951-52. Exchanged for Dale's Ray Haddington in 1953 he scored only twice and was soon replaced at centre forward by Frank Lord. Returning the following term after Lord's broken leg, he fared much better with four goals in seven games but was then involved in another exchange deal, heading for Crewe when Eric Gemmell came the other way.

George William Lyons 1953-57
Born: Rochdale 1.5.35 5'6" 11st8
Winger
FL Apps/Gls 29/4 Total Apps/Gls 30/4
Career: Dale 12.53 to 1957 [29/4], Nantile Vale 1961-62

The much younger brother of Eddie, George signed pro for Dale at the same time that the former wartime guest joined them from Crewe, and – despite their 15 year age difference – uniquely for Dale, the brothers made their FL debuts together against Bradford City on Boxing Day 1953 when Harry Catterick was without six of his regulars after the previous day's game. George scored in just his second league game, when remarkably

Eddie also scored, and made a number of appearances, on either wing over the next four years without ever gaining a regular spot, in part because of a serious illness. He later played under former Dale teammate Eric Gemmell at Welsh non-league side Nantile Vale and was suspended following the allegations of fielding another club's player under an assumed name.

Bevil Arthur (Bev) Glover 1953-59

Born: Salford 25.3.26
6'1" 12st5
Centre half
FL Apps/Gls 169/1
Total Apps/Gls 186/1
Career: Cheadle, Stockport Co. 1946, pro 1.48 [137/1], Dale 2.54 £1500 to 1959 [169/1]

Following the retirement of veteran Wally Birch, Dale were in need of a dominating centre half and the £1500 which Harry Catterick paid Stockport for Bev early in 1954 proved money well spent. He had already accumulated nearly 150 senior games for County over the previous six years, missing only one game in 1950-51, and took his overall tally past 300 in five and a half seasons at Spotland. He again had only one absence in 1954-55 (as did his half back partners Lynn and Murphy) as Dale showed a significant improvement compared to the previous few seasons. He was out for a time the following term with appendicitis and was sorely missed when injured in the middle of 1956-57 after Dale had challenged near the top of the table. He left league football when Dale had a clearout after they successfully made the cut for the new national Division 3 in 1958 but then slumped to the bottom of the table the following year. He had a benefit game against a Select XI in April 1959.

George Raymond (Ray) Calderbank 1953-58
Born: Manchester 8.2.36 5'8" 10st
Inside left
FL Apps/Gls 1/0 Total Apps/Gls 2/0
Career: Hyde U., Dale am 8.53 [1/-], Nelson 29.9.57

Another youngster who spent a number of years in the reserves at Spotland, Ray's one FL game came in his first season, when he appeared in the final match, a 1-0 defeat by Bradford Park Avenue. His other Dale appearance was in the Lancashire Cup in 1956 after he returned from his national service. His father had been on Accrington's books.

William Duncan (Billy) McCulloch 1954-58

Born: Edinburgh 25.6.22
5'8" 11st5
Full back/half back
FL Apps/Gls 140/2
Total Apps/Gls 149/2
Career: (RAF), Stockport Co. 2.44 [47/9 WL, 309/4], Manchester U. guest 3.45 [3/- WL], Dale 7.54 [140/2], retired cs.58

Having secured Bev Glover from them the previous term, Harry Catterick returned to Stockport for his main defensive signing in the summer of 1954. Billy had played over 300 FL games for County, and 385 in total in a career dating back to wartime football. An apparently indestructible Scottish defender, he had played at least 40 games in seven of the first eight peacetime seasons and only missed the second half of 1947-48 through a severe concussion sustained when scoring County's extra time winner in a cup tie. Though absent for part of his first Spotland campaign, he then missed only one game in two years, appearing at full back, in his original wing half role or at centre half, as required. He retired at the age of 36, having added another 149 games to his overall tally, after Dale secured a place in the new Division 3 and worked as a travelling salesman. Sadly, soon afterwards he was diagnosed with multiple sclerosis and shortly after his former clubs played a benefit game for him he died at the age of only 39.

Francis John (Frank) Mitcheson 1954-56

Born: Stalybridge 10.3.24
Inside forward
FL Apps/Goals 50/8 Total Apps/Goals 56/9
Career: Droylsden, Doncaster R. 5.44 [50/12 WL, 22/5], Crewe A. 11.48 [181/34], Dale 6.54 [50/8], Stalybridge Celtic, Mossley 7.56 to 1957, caretaker manager 9.56 to 10.56
Honours: Division 3N champion 1947

Frank entered senior football with Doncaster towards the end of the war and made a handful of appearances when Rovers ran away with the Third North title in 1947. His most successful spell was at Crewe where he was a regular for five seasons. Used less frequently in 1953-54 he joined his former boss Harry Catterick at Rochdale and was a consistent performer at inside forward for a season and a half but lost his place following the signing of Andy McLaren, moving into non-league football where he (apparently reluctantly) managed Mossley for a time, losing only one of his 11 games in charge.

George Ronald Underwood 1954-55
Born: Sheffield 6.9.25
Right back
FL Apps/Gls 19/0 Total Apps/Gls 19/0
Career: Sheffield U. 9.46 [17/-], Sheffield W. 10.51, Boston U. Scunthorpe U. 6.53 [8/-], Dale 6.54 to cs.55 [19/-]

George had a somewhat sporadic FL career, making a number of second division appearances at centre half for the Blades in 1949-50 and 1950-51 but not appearing in the first team for neighbours Wednesday. He reappeared in the league when Scunthorpe finished third in the Third North in 1954 before moving to Spotland. Gaining a regular place at right back, he had the misfortune to be one of the three Dale defenders to famously score own goals in the same game, a 7-2 defeat at Carlisle on Christmas Day. Worse was to befall two days later though, as he broke his leg in the return game and did not play in the league again.

Daniel (Danny) Murphy 1954-57
Born: Burtonwood 10.5.22 5'9" 11st3
Left half
FL Apps/Gls 109/0 Total Apps/Gls 119/1
Career: Burtonwood Athletic, Bolton W. 2.43 [98/3 WL, 66/1], Bury guest [2/- WL], Crewe A. 1.52 [106/1], Dale 7.54 [109/-], Macclesfield 7.57, Prescot Cables 3.58
Honours: League North Cup winners 1945, War Cup winners 1945, Army

Approaching the veteran stage when he reached Willbutts Lane, Danny had been with Bolton since 1943, accumulating almost 100 wartime appearances as well as figuring in two cup winning sides. He also played in the 'Burnden Park disaster' cup tie against Stoke in 1946 when a number of spectators were killed when barriers collapsed. He made relatively few appearances in six years of peacetime football, though, and moved on to Crewe. Everpresent in 1952-53, he topped the century of appearances at Gresty Road before becoming another of his former players to follow Harry Catterick to Rochdale. Missing just one match in his first two seasons, he again passed 100 FL appearances before being released in 1957. At Carlisle on Christmas Day 1954 he was one of the three unfortunate Dale backs who all contrived to put the ball past their own 'keeper, Albert Morton. After leaving the game, Danny worked as a milkman.

Brian Geoffrey Green 1954-59

Born: Droylsden 5.6.35
5'11" 12st11
Forward/wing half
FL Apps/Gls 46/8
Total Apps/Gls 54/8
Career: Haggate Lads c.1948, Dale trial 1951, am 23.8.52, (army, Sheffield W. trial), Dale pro 10.5.55 [46/8], Southport 14.3.59 £415 [20/7], Bury trial 27.7.60, Colwyn Bay U. 9.60, Barrow 20.9.60 [3/-], Runcorn 10.60, New Brighton cs.61, Altrincham 12.61, Exeter C. 2.8.62 [9/1], Chesterfield 4.2.63 [2/-], Wisbech T. 1963-64, Mossley 1963-64, Sydney Prague 1.64, Stalybridge Celtic cs.64, Sydney Prague 1.65, Ashton U. cs.65, Wisbech T., Boston U., Glossop 1967, player-manager 1.68, Barrow coach 1968, Halifax T. coach 1970, Kuwait national coach 1971, Southport coach 1972, Chester coach 1973, Australian national manager 1975, Dale manager 5.76, Leeds U. coach 9.77, Blackburn R. asst manager, Stockport Co. asst manager 1979, Bryne (Norway) manager 1981, IK Start (Norway) manager 1986, 1989 and 1991, Egersunde Idretts Klub (Norway) manager, Stockport Co. asst manager 1989, Castleton Gabriels manager 7.93 to 3.94, FA regional tutor 1990s, Ryder University (USA) coach
Cricket for Lancashire Schoolboys.
Honours: Lancashire League champions 1958, Army XI; as coach, Division 4 champions 1973 Division 4 promotion 1975, Coach of the Year 1975, Norwegian Cup winners

Brian played in the Rochdale Amateur League for Haggate Lads (with future England goalkeeper Eddie Hopkinson) from the age of 12, also appearing for Lancashire Schoolboys at cricket, and signed amateur forms at Spotland when he was 17. Making a goalscoring debut at centre forward in September 1954, he was then called up for his National Service and spent most of the next two years playing for the Army. He eventually made around 50 appearances for the Dale in a variety of positions in the forward line or at wing half, also helping the Reserves win the Lancashire League title, and was then sold to Southport for the odd sum of £415, receiving a benefit of just £70 for his seven years effort. He subsequently did the rounds of senior non-league football with a few further stints at FL clubs thrown in (for instance playing for Exeter after spending the summer as a lifeguard at nearby Teignmouth), also figuring with Sydney Prague in Australia. He started in management with Glossop and coached Southport when they won the Fourth Division title in 1973, but really made his name as a coach with Chester, being voted coach of the year when they reached the League Cup semi-final in 1975. He was next appointed national manager of Australia, getting the job ahead of subsequent Arsenal boss Don Howe. Returning to England in the summer of 1976 he took the manager's chair at Spotland, but despite a bright start, by the time he left to coach first division Leeds just over a year later, the impoverished Dale were rooted to the bottom of the league. From 1981 onwards he had a highly successful time managing in Norway, eventually reappearing in Rochdale as an FA regional tutor and manager of Castleton Gabriels. Also running a hotel, Brian spent summers coaching at Ryder University in the USA.

Eric Gemmell 1954-56

Born: Manchester 7.4.21 5'11" 12st
Centre forward
FL Apps/Gls 65/32
Total Apps/Goals 74/35
Career: Manchester U. am, Goslings 1945, Manchester C. 25.3.46 [2/1 WL], Ashton U. loan 4.47, Oldham A. 24.6.47 [195/109], Crewe A. 20.2.54 [15/5], Dale 25.9.54 (exchange for D. Frost) [64/32], Buxton 10.4.56, Nantile Vale player-manager 7.60 to 1961-62
Cricket pro for Levenshulme
Honours: Division 3(N) champions 1953

Oldham's then record goalscorer, Eric made his FL bow with the Latics in 1947 when he was already 26. Over the next seven seasons as a "stylish and strong shooting" centre forward, Eric became one of the most prolific marksmen in the Third North, hitting 23 goals in 1948-49, 22 two years later, 29 in 1951-52 and 25 in only 29 games the year after that as Oldham won the title. When the Latics beat Chester 11-2 in 1952, Eric remarkably notched seven of the goals, and he also recorded six other hat-tricks. Oldham found it much harder going in Division 2 and Eric moved on to Crewe, briefly, and then joined Dale in exchange for Des Frost and showed he had not lost his goalscoring touch with 19 goals in 36 league games, plus two in the cups, adding 13 more the following term when he was again leading scorer. Indeed, even after moving to Buxton he netted a hat-trick on his debut. His short managerial career was less distinguished, as he was suspended sine die by the FA for allegedly fielding another club's player under an assumed name while in charge of Welsh club Nantile Vale. Also a highly proficient cricketer, he played for a time as a pro in the Lancashire leagues.

George Johnson 1954-56

Born: Daveyhulme, Manchester 27.4.36
Outside left
FL Apps/Gls 1/0
Total Apps/Gls 1/0
Career: Gerrards c.1951, Moorside Juniors c.1952, Bolton W. am 5.54, Oldham A. 1954, Dale 13.11.54 [1/-], Buxton 1955-56, Northwich Victoria 1957-58, Witton Albion 1959-60, Wigan Rovers, Mossley 1960-61, Ashton U. 8.61, Southport 29.1.63 [6/-], Altrincham 1963-64, Mossley 1963-64, Ashton U. 1964-65, Hyde U., Curzon Amateurs
Honours: Cheshire League Cup winners 1961

George was on the books of several FL club but played most of his career at senior non-league level. Playing rugby league at school, he came up through works football and once scored four goals for Bolton in the youth cup against Manchester City. His league debut came as an 18 year old in February 1955, playing on the left wing for Dale in a 1-0 victory over Stockport. He also played for them in a friendly against Oldham the following season, but his next league game wasn't until 1963 when he played inside left for Southport. He scored a hat-trick in his first game for Altrincham but surprisingly played only twice more, having much more productive spells with Ashton United and Mossley before finishing because of a knee injury. He worked as a carpenter and joiner and later in the construction industry in South Africa and Spain amongst others.

James (Jim) Storey 1955-57

Born: Rowlands Gill, Co. Durham 30.12.29
5'10" 11st
Full back
FL Apps/Gls 24/1 Total Apps/Gls 28/1
Career: Spen Valley, Spen Black & Whites, Newcastle U. 8.48, Exeter C. 6.53 [9/-], Bournemouth & BA 7.54, Dale 6.55 [24/1], Darlington 12.6.57 [6/-], Macclesfield cs.58, Wigan Rovers 1959

Like Neville Black a couple of years earlier, Jim arrived from Newcastle via Exeter, where he had gained his only previous league experience. With Dale, he took the right back spot in the first three games of 1955-56 and then had a run of games at the end of that season, usually playing when Charlie Ferguson was moved from full back to centre half. He played only six times in 1956-57 and then made the same number of appearances at Darlington the following term. He remained living in Rochdale, though, working as a draftsman, and celebrated his golden wedding there in 2003.

John William (Johnny) McClelland 1955-56
Born: Colchester 11.8.30
Forward
FL Apps/Gls 24/5 FL Apps/Gls 25/5
Career: Colchester U. 9.51, Stoke C. 6.52 [4/-], Swindon T. 6.54 [14/1], Dale 6.55 [26/5], Clacton T. 7.56

The only other significant signing apart from Jim Storey in the summer of 1955, Johnny was also fairly inexperienced at league level. Initially a first choice in one of the inside forward positions, scoring against Grimsby on the opening day of the season, competition from Derek Andrews and new signing Andy McLaren limited his appearances later in the season when he sometimes figured on the wing or at centre forward.

David Raymond Neville 1955-56
Born: Birmingham 8.1.29
Right back
FL Apps/Gls 1/0 Total Apps/Gls 1/0
Career: Paget Rangers, Bournemouth & BA 4.49, Chelsea 7.50, Yeovil T. 1951-52, Burton Albion, Dale 8.55 [1/-], Crewe A. 9.55

David had a somewhat unusual career, at one time moving from Third South Bournemouth to first division Chelsea but without ever playing in the first team for either of them. However, he did play for Yeovil, probably the top non-league side of the day, and finally made his one and only FL appearance during a month's contract with Dale in August 1955, replacing Jim Storey at right back against Accrington.

Harrison Lockhead (Harry) Fearnley

1955-56
Born: Morley, 27.5.23
5'8" 10st6
Goalkeeper
FL Apps 1 Total Apps 1
Career: Bradford PA am, (navy), Leeds U. am 11.41, pro 11.45 [10 WL, 28], Halifax T. 1.49 [3], Newport Co. 7.49 [103], Selby T. 1953, Dale 7.55 [1], Winsford U. 9.55
Honours: Royal Navy v Army

Harry served as a commando during the war, playing in representative games for the navy in services football. He signed pro for Leeds, playing both wartime league and FL games before a brief stint at Halifax. The vast majority of his senior games came in four years with Newport County (where he also worked as a window cleaner), but he had been playing non-league football for a couple of years before his single, if memorable, Dale game. With Harry replacing Albert Morton in goal and Don Partridge playing his first game for a year in front of him at centre half, the match against Oldham ended 4-4, and neither of them played again.

Derek Andrews 1954-57
Born: Bury 14.12.34 5'9" 11st3
Inside forward
FL Apps/Gls 22/4 Total Apps/Gls 25/5
Career: Bamford Road Secondary Modern, Hopwood 1952, (army), Dale am, pro 3.55 [22/4], Altrincham 1957
Honours: Heywood Boys, England youth trial

A local schoolboy star, Derek played in an England youth trial in 1952 at Dunlop's ground, in a side including three future full internationals, Eddie Hopkinson (later Bolton Wanderers), Brian Miller (Burnley) and the legendary Duncan Edwards of Manchester United. After his army service he turned pro with Dale and following a scoring debut in a 5-1 defeat of Barrow in September 1955 he played about half Dale's games for the rest of the season, mainly at inside left, though he sometimes played on the wing. The following season, though, he managed just one FA Cup tie.

John Raymond (Ray) Aspden 1955-67

Born: Horwich 6.2.38
5'11" 11st3
Centre half
FL Apps/Gls 297/2
Total Apps/Gls 346/2
Career: Bolton W. am, Dale 5.55 [297/2], retired injured 1966-67
Honours: Football League Cup final 1962

One of Dale's all time stalwarts, Ray was, at the time, both their youngest ever player and their appearance record holder, despite the most inauspicious of starts when Dale lost his first game 7-2 to Chesterfield in September 1955. He didn't appear again until the following March (at left back) and with his national service in the RAF also intervening it was half way through 1958-59 before he got in the side again, taking over from Bev Glover. Although Dale were relegated, Ray became an automatic choice as a "hard as nails, thou shalt not pass" traditional stopper centre half, rarely beaten in the air and able to 'sort out' much larger opponents than himself. He played in several good Dale sides in the early sixties, figuring in the amazing run to the League Cup Final in 1962 and the promotion near miss of 1965 and eventually clocked up a record 297 FL appearances (or 299 if you count the expunged games against Accrington Stanley) and 346 in all competitions. He was injured in a pre-season game in 1966, and though initially not expected to be out long, in fact never played again. Having been in dispute with the directors more than once in the past – he had put in a transfer request the week before the second leg of the League Cup semi-final - he became disillusioned with football and with the club for his treatment after he was forced to retire and sadly he was never awarded a benefit or testimonial despite his long service. He was eventually reconciled with the club many years later and was one of the 'legends' invited to the centenary celebrations in 2007.

James Alfred (Jimmy) Jones 1955-61

Born: Birkenhead 3.8.27
5'10" 13st
Goalkeeper
FL Apps 177
Total Apps 192
Career: Everton am 7.5.45, pro 1.12.45, Ellesmere Port Town 1946-47, Everton 2.8.48, New Brighton 19.8.50 [32], Lincoln C. 20.8.51 £750 [76], Accrington St. 19.2.54 £550 [46], Dale 13.9.55 £750 [175], retired 6.61. Lincoln C. reserve team trainer 12.65
Honours Division 3(N) champions 1952

Jimmy was already an experienced Third North campaigner with over 150 games to his credit when signed by Dale in September 1955. He was New Brighton's regular 'keeper in their final league campaign and later became their last surviving player in the FL. His debut had been spectacular, as he almost single handedly kept out league leaders Tranmere, saving a penalty and being knocked out diving at a forward's feet. At Lincoln he won a Third North championship medal, his penalty save in the penultimate game guaranteeing the title. Moving on to Accrington, he signed for Dale for £750 when he lost his place at Peel Park to his deputy Tommy McQueen after suffering concussion crashing into a goalpost. He was a regular choice over the next five years, helping them qualify for the new Third Division, though he missed half of the 1958-59 season with eye trouble, subsequently playing in contact lenses. After 192 appearances, the most by a Dale goalkeeper up to that time, he was eventually supplanted by Ted Burgin and retired in 1961 to become a publican in Lincoln, later helping out with the reserve team at Sincil Bank

Ralph Morement 1955-56

Born: Sheffield 24.9.24
Right half
FL Apps/Gls 1/0
Total Apps/Gls 1/0
Career: Hampton's Sports, Sheffield U. 9.46 [2/-], Chester 5.50 to cs.53 [121/19]. Dale 8.55 [1/-]
Honours: Welsh Cup final 1953, Lancashire Senior Cup final 1953

Ralph was another player with a one match Dale career, one of three debutants in the match after the 7-2 thrashing at Chesterfield. Previously he had spent three seasons as a first choice at Chester, skippering the side and playing in seven different positions in 1952-53 when they reached both the Welsh Cup Final and Lancashire Cup Final. His versatility even stretched to playing in goal for most of what turned out to be his final appearance for them (Chester losing 7-0 to Wrexham).

Roderick Calvin Hilgrove (Cal) Symonds

1954-56
Born: Pembroke, Bermuda 29.3.32
Centre forward
FL Apps/Gls 1/0
Total Apps/Gls 1/0
Career: Key West Rangers (Bermuda), Dale 10.54 [1/-], Pembroke Hamilton Club (Bermuda) 10.55
Cricket for St. Georges, Bermuda (1950-69), Pembroke Hamilton Club, coach to Bermuda cricket team 1990s

The wonderfully monikered Cal was Dale's first black player. According to a Bermudan writer, he was "a magnificent football and cricket player ... described as the best captain the island has ever seen". He became only the second Bermudan to become a professional footballer when he signed for Dale and made his debut in a friendly against Bury in November 1954. He played his single FL game at centre forward in a 2-0 defeat at Barrow the following September, but then returned to the Caribbean, where he worked as a taxi driver, rather than be called up for national service in the UK. Retiring from football through injury, he subsequently concentrated on his cricket. Noted as a superb fielder, he played for St. Georges and then the Pembroke Hamilton Club (who he had earlier played football for) for over twenty years and later became coach to the national team, leading them on a tour of England in 1992. "Bummy", as he was known locally, was a major figure in Bermudan life, later writing an autobiography "My Way", as well as being the subject of a biography by the suitably named Bermudan historian and government minister Dale Butler. He also has soccer studentships and a community foundation named in his honour.

Charles (Charlie) Ferguson 1955-59

Born: Glasgow 22.4.30
5'10" 12st1
Right back/centre half
FL Apps/Gls 150/4
Total Apps/Gls 161/5
Career: Tollcross YMCA, Benburb, Heart of Midlothian 1948 [1/- ScL], Hamilton Ac. cs.53 [10/- ScL], Accrington St. 19.5.54 [1/-], Dale 19.9.55 £500 [150/4], Oldham A. 8.7.59 [57/-], Rossendale U. player-coach 8.61
Honours: Lancashire Combination champions and cup winners 1955

After figuring in the top flight in Scotland with Hearts and Hamilton Accies, Charlie became part of Accrington's virtually all Scottish squad. Playing centre half, he skippered their reserves to a league and cup double but surprisingly made just one first team appearance. Requesting a transfer, he moved to Spotland the same week as teammate Jimmy Jones. Strong in the air and a "robust and fearless" tackler, he started at centre half, but subsequently played more at right back and was a regular for the next three years, reaching 150 league appearances. He also famously scored the last minute winning goal when Dale came back from 4-1 down with 30 minutes left to beat Darlington 5-4. He eventually lost his place to the incoming Stan Milburn after Dale made it into the national Division 3 but then found themselves bottom of the table. Granted a free transfer on appeal to the FL, he had two further years in the league with Oldham before becoming player-coach at Rossendale.

Bernard Stonehouse 1954-57

Born: Manchester 23.12.34 5'9" 10st12
Winger
FL Apps/Gls 19/1 Total Apps/Gls 21/2
Career: Cheadlehulme, Crewe A. am 1951, Dale am 3.55, pro 8.55 to 1957 [19/1]. Altrincham 7.65
Honours: England Youth trial, Army

Bernard had been on Crewe's books as an amateur for several years and had a trial for the England youth team before joining Dale following his national service, when he had played for the army in Hong Kong. He played in the friendly against the Army in March 1955, scoring one of the Dale goals, and made his league debut the following November. Nearly all his other senior games came towards the end of that season, alternating between the two wings. Almost a decade later, he was reported to have joined Altrincham.

Andrew Torrance (Andy) McLaren 1955-57

Born: Larkhall 24.1.22
5'6" 10st1
Inside forward
FL Apps/Gls 44/12 Total Apps/Gls 46/12
Career: Larkhall Academy, Larkhall Thistle 1.38, Preston NE am 7.38, pro 2.39 [69/29, 76/49 WL], Carlisle U. guest 1939-40 [1/- WL], (army, RAF), Royal Albert guest 1939-40, King's Park guest 1939-40, Hamilton Ac. guest {1939-40}, 1942-43 [2/- ScWL], Liverpool guest 5.42 [2/1 WL], Blackburn R. guest 8.42 and 3.43 [13/11 WL], Bristol C. guest 1942-43 [3/1 WL], Burnley 12.48 [3/1] (exchenge for J. Knight), Sheffield U. 3.49 [31/4], Barrow 2.51 [155/52], Bradford PA 10.54 [18/7], Southport 21.6.55 [4/1], Dale 23.11.55 [44/12], Fleetwood pt cs.57, Bury scout
Honours: Scotland Schoolboy international (3 caps), Scotland (4 caps), North Regional League champions 1941, War League Cup winners 1941

Andy was the 'star name' signed to boost the Dale's fortunes in 1955-56 after they had failed in an optimistic bid to sign Blackpool legend Stan Mortensen. A Scottish schoolboy international, he made his mark with Preston as a 17 year old drafted into the side alongside the equally youthful Tom Finney in wartime league games. He scored five times when North End hammered Tranmere 12-1 in a cup tie and grabbed all six when they beat Liverpool 6-1 to win the 1941 North Regional League title, totalling 31 in all that year, including one in the War Cup Final from a Finney cross. Subsequently spending three years in the RAF, serving in Egypt, after the war he won his first full Scottish cap after just 11 FL games. Displaying "masterful ball control and a thunderous shot", despite his small stature, he scored four times in his four internationals, including one in a 1-1 draw against the 'auld enemy'. Andy's best peacetime season was 1947-48 when he missed only one first division game and notched 17 goals, but a move to Burnley lasted just a matter of weeks before he switched to Sheffield United where his career was disrupted by a broken leg. Dropping down the divisions, he had three good years at Barrow, registering 20 goals when everpresent in 1953-54. After brief stops elsewhere he spent a season and a half at Spotland before an influx of other inside forwards saw him leave to play part-time for Fleetwood while working for Leyland Motors.

Harry Jackson 1955-56

Born: Shaw 12.5.34
5'10" 11st7
Centre forward
FL Apps/Gls 1/1
Total Apps/Gls 1/1
Career: Oldham A jnrs, pro 5.6.51 [10/3], Dale 19.10.55 [1/1], Northwich Victoria 1956, Stalybridge Celtic 6.56, Mossley 9.2.57 (exchange for R. Garland), Ashton U. 8.58, (amateur football)
Cricket for Lancashire 2nd XI, Crompton CC

Harry was one of the select band of players to score in their only match for the Dale, doing so in a 2-1 victory at Carlisle – not usually a happy hunting ground for Rochdale – in Christmas week of 1955 when Eric Gemmell was missing. Indeed, he had a second effort disallowed. A "hard running assertive forward", he had earlier spent four years at Boundary Park but appeared only 10 times in the FL despite an outstanding scoring record in the junior teams, once scoring eight for the 'A' team and five for the reserves the following week. An allround sportsman, he had been a schoolboy swimming champion and opened the batting for Lancashire Second XI as well as playing in Central Lancashire League cricket. He worked for Oldham Council's landscape department.

Gerard (Gerry) Molloy 1953-60

Born: Rochdale 13.3.36
5'9" 11st6
Left half/outside left
FL Apps/Gls 6/0 Total Apps/Gls 6/0
Career: (junior football), Dale 11.53 to 1960 [6/-]

Gerry was a local lad who had a very long spell in Rochdale's junior and reserve sides. He first played in a friendly against the Army in March 1955 and made three FL appearances at the end of the following campaign, at left half, and three more the following season on the left wing. He appeared in pre-season practice matches in 1957-58 but did not make the first team again and left to run a local newsagents.

John Albert (Jackie) Grant 1956-59

Born: High Spen 8.9.24
5'4" 10st3
Right half
FL Apps/Gls 102/3 Total Apps/Gls 105/3
Career: High Spen Ath., Wolverhampton W. trial, Everton 1941, pro 12.42 [92/4 WL, 122/10], Stockport Co. guest 3.43 [1/- WL], Blackburn R. guest 8.43 [1/1 WL], Tranmere R. guest 1945-46 [2/- WL], Dale 5.56 £6000 (with E. Wainwright and G. Lewis) [102/3], Southport 23.1.59 to cs.61 [40/-], Blackburn scout
Honours: Division 2 promotion 1954, Central League champions 1954, Lancashire Combination Division 2 promotion 1961

In the summer of 1956, Harry Catterick returned to the club where he had made his name to sign Jackie, along with Eddie Wainwright and Gwyn Lewis, for a joint fee of £6000. A "tough little terrier" at right half, though he appeared in seven different positions for them, Jackie had been with the Toffees for 15 years and including wartime games had over 200 appearances to his credit. After being everpresent in 1950-51 - despite Everton's relegation - he did not appear in the first team at all in his last two years, but skippered the Central League side to numerous successes. Noted for his stamina, he missed just two games in two seasons for Rochdale but like several other senior pros was released as Dale struggled at the foot of the new Division 3. Signed by another former teammate Wally Fielding for Southport, he suffered with cartilage problems in 1959-60 and in his final season he skippered Southport's reserves to promotion in the Lancashire Combination. His son David was an England schoolboy international while on Everton's books and played for Wrexham briefly later in the 1960s.

James (Jimmy) McGuigan 1956-59

Born: Addiewell, Midlothian 1.3.24
5'10" 11st13
Left half
FL Apps/Gls 70/2
Total Apps/Gls 77/2
Career: Bonnyrigg Rose, Hamilton Ac. 1942-43, pro 1946-47 [11/2 ScL], Sunderland 6.47 [3/1], Stockport Co. 6.49 [43/9], Crewe A. 8.50 [207/32], Dale 8.56 [70/2], Crewe A. trainer-coach 1959, manager 13.6.60, Grimsby

T. manager 11.64, Chesterfield manager 7.67, Rotherham U. manager 5.73, Stockport Co. manager 11.79 to 4.82, Sheffield U. coach 11.83 to 1987
Honours: as manager, Division 4 champions 1970, Division 4 promotion 1963, 1975, Division 4 manager of the year 1975

Another experienced player recruited in 1956, Jimmy had played the first post-war season at Hamilton before a move to Sunderland, where he played just three first division games in two years. A season as a regular at Stockport was followed by six years at Crewe, making over 200 appearances, originally on the right wing before switching to right half. In January 1955, he was sent off along with three Bradford players, the first instance of four dismissals in a FL game. He closed his playing career with a couple of years sharing the Dale's left half spot with former Alex teammate Danny Murphy and then Tom McGlennon, fading out of the picture during Dale's struggle in Division 3. He then joined Crewe's training staff and in 1960 was appointed their manager, winning promotion with them three years later, a feat he repeated with Chesterfield, who went up as champions in 1970 a year after finishing 20th, and Rotherham in 1975 (being voted manager of the year). He later coached Sheffield United for several years up until his retirement.

Edward Francis (Eddie) Wainwright
1956-59

Born: Southport 22.6.24
5'8" 10st9
Inside right
FL Apps/Gls 100/27 Total Apps/Gls 107/30
Career: High Park (Southport), Everton am 1939, Fleetwood Hesketh, Southport trial cs.42, Everton am 1943, pro 3.44 [66/35 WL, 207/69], Middlesbrough guest 1944-46 [12/2 WL], Dale 6.56 £6000 (with J. Grant and G. Lewis) [100/27] to cs.59
Honours: British Army v French Army, Army v FA XI 1946-47, Football League v Irish League 1950, FA tour to Canada 1950, Division 2 promotion 1954

Signed from Everton with Jackie Grant, Eddie had had an even more impressive career at Goodison Park. After making his debut in 1943 he scored prolifically in wartime games and spent ten seasons in Everton's league side, totting up over 200 FL appearances, twice being leading scorer and netting more than 100 goals in total, including four against Blackpool in 1948-49. During the war he had played for the British Army against their French counterparts and before being demobbed played in the Army team which beat an FA Select XI 8-3. An "intelligent player with a fierce shot", generally playing at inside right, Eddie had a particularly fine season in 1949-50 when he starred in Everton's run to the FA Cup semi-final (where they were beaten by Liverpool) and was chosen both for the Football League side to play the Irish and for the post-season FA tour to Canada, where he netted hat-tricks in 9-0 and 9-2 victories. Sadly, a broken leg in December 1950 ruled him out for 2 years and it wasn't until 1953-54 that he recaptured a fairly regular spot for Everton, quite often playing on the right wing. At Spotland he was the regular inside right for two seasons and also managed to survive through most of the dire 1958-59 campaign, heading the scoring charts with 10 in total. He reached exactly 100 league appearances for Dale before retiring to enter the licensing trade.

Thomas Bell (Tommy) Todd 1956-57
Born: Stonehouse, Lanark 1.6.26 5'11" 11st9
Centre forward
FL Apps/Gls 5/1 Total Apps/Gls 5/1
Career: Burnbank Ath., Motherwell 11.44, Airdrieonians 10.48 [4/- ScL], Stonehouse Violet 1949, Hamilton Ac. 1.51 [65/25 ScL], Crewe A. 8.55 [13/3], Derby Co. 11.55 [4/3], Dale 4.5.56 [5/1]
Honours: Scottish Division 2 promoted 1953

Tommy played for a variety of clubs in Scotland, with his most successful spell coming either side of the Accies' promotion to the top flight in 1953. Short stays at Crewe and Derby produced a decent goal return but only limited appearances – at the Baseball Ground he had to compete for the centre forward spot with the up and coming Ray Straw - while at Spotland all his appearances came in the first month of the 1956-57 campaign.

Gwynfor (Gwyn) Lewis 1956-57
Born: Bangor 22.4.31 5'7" 10st6
Centre forward/inside left
FL Apps/Gls 27/11 Total Apps/Gls 28/11
Career: Everton jnr, pro 5.48 [10/6], Dale 6.56 £6000 (with J. Grant and E. Wainwright) [27/11], Chesterfield 2.57 £3500 [123/59], Heanor T. 1961
Honours: Wales Youth international, Army, Division 2 promotion 1954, Central League champions 1954

A Welsh youth international who also represented the Army during his national service, Gwyn was the inexperienced member of the trio of Evertonians recruited by Harry Catterick in 1956, though he had netted six times in his ten games for them, with two on his debut in March 1952 as stand-in for Dave Hickson. He was quickly into his stride at Rochdale with three goals in the first two games and after switching from inside left to centre forward scored seven times in five matches as Dale garnered six wins and three draws from nine games. Unfortunately neither Gwyn nor the team could keep this up, but Gwyn had done enough to earn a transfer to Chesterfield where he again made a terrific start with five goals in four games and took his combined tally for the season to 21. He exceeded this with 24 the following campaign and though, like his colleagues still at Spotland, he found it harder in the new Division 3, he continued to score at nearly a goal every other game for two more seasons, fading out of the picture when the Spireites were relegated in 1961.

Joseph (Joe) Devlin 1956-58

Born: Cleland, Lanarkshire 12.3.31
5'6" 11st2
Outside left
FL Apps/Gls 38/7
Total Apps/Gls 39/7
Career: Cleland St. Michael, Albion Rovers 10.47 [16/1 ScL], Falkirk 1950 [22/2 ScL], Accrington St. 23.7.53 [114/18], Dale 22.9.56 £2000 [38/7], Bradford PA 4.11.57 [34/3], Carlisle U. 18.7.59 [5/-], Nelson cs.60, Northwich Victoria 1961, Accrington St. 9.2.62 to 16.3.62 [1/-], Northwich Victoria, Netherfield
Honours: Scottish Division 2 promoted 1948, 1952

A "strong, sturdy little winger", Joe was another experienced Scot who had twice been in promoted sides north of the border. He was with Accrington for three seasons, figuring in their all-Scottish team in 1955-56 and being able to continue playing for them during his national service as he was a miner working in nearby Huncoat pit. After over a century of appearances, he was sold to Rochdale for £2000 following the departures of their regular wing men Anders and Kendall to Bradford. Noted for his "pace, accuracy and footcraft", Joe spent just over a year at Spotland before also following the trail to Park Avenue. After a couple of years in non-league football, he returned to Peel Park just before Stanley's demise, playing in their last home game, against the Dale. After retiring from the game with a knee injury, he became an electrical contractor in Accrington.

Reginald (Reg) Tapley 1956-57
Born: Nantwich 2.11.32
Outside left
FL Apps/Gls 1/0 Total Apps/Gls 2/0
Career: Crewe A. 9.53, Bangor C., Dale 10.56 [1/-]

Another of the players with the briefest of FL careers, Reg had not made the senior side in three years at Crewe and did so just twice for Dale. He was one of four reserves brought in for a Lancashire Cup tie against Chester in November 1956 and stood in for Joe Devlin in the 1-1 draw at Bradford City the following week.

Cyril Frank Lello 1956-57

Born: Ludlow 24.2.20
Left half/inside left
FL Apps/Gls 11/0
Total Apps/Gls 11/0
Career: Ludlow T., Hereford U., Shrewsbury T. 1939, Norwich C. guest 1940-41 [5/1 WL], Lincoln C. am 10.43, pro 2.44 [17/21 WL], Millwall guest 1944-45 [2/- WL], Shrewsbury T. 1946, Everton 9.47 [236/9], Dale 11.56 [11/-], Runcorn player-manager 3.6.57, New Brighton manager
Honours: Division 2 promotion 1954

Another of the ex-Everton contingent at Spotland in 1956-57, Cyril had first come to prominence with a remarkable scoring record with Lincoln during the war, netting seven times in a game against Notts County in 1943. At Goodison he became a goal maker rather than goal scorer and soon moved back to a wing half role. Despite missing the entirety of 1950-51 – when Everton were relegated – through injury, he totalled 254 senior appearances, being everpresent when they were promoted again and in their first season back in the top flight, also figuring in the FA Cup semi-final defeat by Bolton in 1953. After his brief spell with Dale, Cyril, by then aged 37, moved into non-league management, but actually turned out once for New Brighton in 1962-63. He later ran an electrical goods shop. A biography, 'From Dinham Mill to Goodison Park; The Story of Cyril Lello, A Craftsman Footballer' was published in 2001.

Stephen Valentine (Steve) Parr 1956-58

Born: Bamber Bridge 22.12.26
5'10" 12st
Full back
FL Apps/Gls 16/1 Total Apps/Gls 16/1
Career: Farrington Villa, Leyland, Liverpool am 1947, pro 5.48 [20/-], Exeter C. 5.55 [8/-], Dale 12.56 [16/1], Burscough player-coach 1958
Honours: Lancashire Senior Cup final 1954

A long serving Liverpool reserve – nearly all his league appearances were in 1951-52 – Steve did represent them in the Lancashire Cup Final in 1954. After a stint with Exeter, again mostly spent in the reserves, he returned north to join Dale in December 1956 and played fairly regularly for the remainder of the season in either full back spot when Charlie Ferguson or Billy McCulloch were absent or moved to half back. He made just one appearance the following term, though, becoming player-coach of Burscough and working in engineering.

Edward (Eddie) Moran 1956-59

Born: Cleland, Lanarkshire 20.7.30
5'6" 12st
Inside left
FL Apps/Gls 43/13
Total Apps/Gls 44/13
Career: Cleland Juniors, Coltness, Leicester C. 9.47 [8/1], Stockport Co. 10.51 £5000 [110/52], Dale 13.2.57 [43/13], Crewe A. 9.58 (exchange for C.W.T. Finney) [22/8], Flint Town United 8.59, Glossop player-coach 11.63

Coincidentally a native of the same Lanarkshire village as Joe Devlin, Eddie became Devlin's inside partner at Spotland. Unlike him, though, all of Eddie's senior football was played south of the border. Used sparingly by Leicester, they nevertheless placed a fee of £15,000 on his head when he asked for a transfer and it took three appeals to the FL before it was reduced to a level where Stockport were able to afford him. A "talented, ball-playing inside forward", he frequently played alongside Jack Connor (q.v.), making over 100 appearances and scoring more than 50 goals, 13 of them in 26 games in 1954-55. Although out of the County side for most of the next season, he hit a purple patch at the end of the campaign, netting eight times in the last five games (as did Connor, County notching 27 in all). He then hit seven in the first nine games of the following season, but later in the campaign was allowed to join Dale. His arrival, and the return from injury of Bev Glover, prompted a remarkable upturn in form, Dale hammering Southport 6-1 in his first match and, after only one win in the previous 15 games, won eight of the last 15. In 1957-58 he was again involved in some high scoring games - partnering Dave Pearson when he netted four against Halifax and Jim Dailey when the latter went one better against Workington - but at the start of the next season (when Dale didn't actually have a manager) he was swapped for Crewe's Bill Finney. Forced to retire from the FL through knee ligament problems at only 28, he played and coached at lower levels and worked for British Aerospace.

Terrence John (Terry) Mulvoy 1955-60

Born: Manchester 2.12.38 5'6" 9st8
Inside forward
FL Apps/Gls 2/0 Total Apps/Gls 2/0
Career: Dale 2.56 to 1960 [2/-]

Terry had a lengthy, but fairly unproductive association with the Dale, first appearing in a friendly against a Star XI after the end of the 1955-56 season when he was 17. He appeared twice at inside forward in the league side towards the end of the following term – Dale picking up a draw and a win - and played in pre-season practice and a friendly in 1957-58, but after being posted to Carlisle on his national service had no further senior opportunities. He had earlier played rugby league for St Patrick's and Rochdale Schools.

David Thomas (Dave) Pearson 1956-58

Born: Dunfermline 9.11.32
5'7" 12st8
Centre/inside forward
FL Apps/Gls 32/17 Total Apps/Gls 33/17
Career: Comrie Colliery, Blackburn R. 28.11.49, Ipswich T. 12.5.54 £2000, Darwen 1955-56, Oldham A. 10.8.56 [25/12], Dale 16.2.57 [32/17], Crewe A. 31.5.58 (exchange for D. Whiston) [9/2], Chorley 1959, Third Lanark trial 2.61

Despite his Scottish background, like Eddie Moran, all Dave's senior football was played in England. Failing to break into the first team in seven years at Blackburn and Ipswich, he was playing for Darwen while on the transfer list at Ipswich when signed by Ted Goodier for Oldham and made up for lost time with a hat-trick on his league debut. Later in the season, though, Goodier let him go to Rochdale, where he again made a scoring start at inside right. Playing all across the forward line, he netted 13 times in 1957-58 but was never an automatic selection despite scoring four against Halifax in September and was traded for Crewe's Don Whiston the following summer. Yet again netting on his debut, he didn't appear after November and his league career was thus compressed into just over two years during which he scored 31 times.

James (Jim) Brown 1956-61
Born: Manchester 5.10.35 5'4" 9st2
Winger
FL Apps/Gls 52/4 Total Apps/Gls 60/5
Career: Dale am 1956, pro 4.57 [53/4], Altrincham 1961, Droylsden 7.65

Perhaps rather lightweight for the Third North, Jim was gradually eased into the side, playing in the last four games of 1956-57 but only once the following term. He figured fairly frequently on the right flank in the Dale's single season in Division 3 and was first choice, on the left wing, at the start of 1960-61 before moving to Altrincham. He was Dale's 12th man (in the days before substitutes) on his wedding day in 1959.

Harold Rudman 1957-58

Born: Whitworth 4.11.24
5'10" 12st7
Left back
FL Apps/Gls 21/1
Total Apps/Gls 23/1
Career: Burnley jnr, pro 12.42 [76/5 WL, 71/-], Manchester U. guest 4.44 [1/- WL], Blackburn R. guest 12.44 [1/- WL], Dale 7.57 to cs.58 [21/1]
Honours: Central League champions 1949

Harold was a great club man at Burnley over a 15 year period. He played numerous games at right half as a youngster during the war but made only 16 FL appearances in the first eight post-war seasons, eventually getting a run in the side at right back during 1954-55 and 1955-56. He spent a single season at Rochdale, sharing the left back spot with the other veteran Bill McCulloch as Dale made the cut for the new Third Division. His most famous contribution – his only goal in a 12 year FL career - came when Dale recovered from 4-1 down to Darlington to win 5-4 with Harold and full back partner Charlie Ferguson both scoring in the last three minutes.

Thomas (Tom) McGlennon 1957-59
Born: Whitehaven 20.10.33 5'8" 11st6
Left half/outside left
FL Apps/Gls 61/2 Total Apps/Gls 69/2
Career: Blackpool jnr, pro 11.50, Dale 5.57 [61/2], Burton Albion cs.59, Barrow 11.59 [60/6], Toronto City (Canada) 1961 to 1965
Honours: Eastern Canada Professional League champions 1961, 1964

Tom had also been a long standing reserve, in his case at Blackpool, before joining Dale. Though making his FL debut on the first day of 1957-58, Jimmy McGuigan soon regained the left half slot and Tom's games later in the season were mostly on the left wing. The following year, in the new Division 3, he was probably Dale's most consistent performer, making 40 league appearances, but was still one of the numerous players released. He later had considerable success in Canadian football and in 1961 played for Toronto against a touring Real Madrid side including Puskas and di Stefano.

Crichton ('Jock') Lockhart 1957-58
Born: Auchterarder, Perth 6.3.30 5'7" 10st7
Outside right
FL Apps/Gls 40/11 Total Apps/Gls 42/11
Career: Chertsey, Southend U. 8.50 [45/11], Dale 6.57 [40/11], Gravesend & Northfleet 1958

Notwithstanding his origins, Jock spent most of his career in the area around London. The exception was a season at Spotland when he was an automatic choice at outside right, playing almost as many games as in his seven years at Southend. He scored twice on his debut in a 4-2 win at Mansfield and ended with the excellent tally for a wingman of 11. Earlier he had scored a hat-trick on his home debut for Southend in 1953, though oddly this was three years after his first away game for them.

Bernard Thomas (Benny) McCready

1957-59
Born: Dumbarton 23.4.37
6'2" 12st9
Goalkeeper
FL Apps 29 Total Apps 34
Career: Dumbarton St Patricks, Renfrew Juniors, St Mirren trial 2.55, Hibernian trial 4.55, Celtic 8.5.55 [1 ScL], Dale 28.5.57 [29], Oldham A. 16.3.59 [7], Clyde trial 8.59 to 9.59, {Buxton}, (USA 1960)

Benny had played one game for Scottish giants Celtic (where his height earned him the nickname 'Big Ben'), keeping a clean sheet against Aberdeen, before arriving at Spotland as understudy to

Jimmy Jones in 1957. He was thrust into the side for the second game of the season when Jones was injured, starting with a clean sheet. He also deputised when Jones suffered eye problems the following year but was transferred to Oldham on the same evening as playing his final game, against Colchester, in March 1959. Away from the game, he was a trained chartered accountant but after finishing playing moved first to the USA and then to Indonesia where he worked in the building trade, remaining in Jakarta after retirement.

Colin John Vizard 1957-59
Born: Newton-le-Willows 18.6.33 5'7" 11st
Outside left
FL Apps/Gls 41/7   Total Apps/Gls 42/7
Career: Everton jnr, pro 9.51, Dale 5.57 [41/7], Wigan Ath. cs.59
Honours: England Youth international

Following the success of Gwyn Lewis the previous year, Harry Catterick again raided Everton's Central League side to sign Colin, a former England youth international. He started out at inside left, scoring on his debut, before gaining a reasonably regular place on the left wing for the next two seasons, though he did actually play in all five forward positions.

George Syme Torrance 1957-58
Born: Glasgow 27.11.35 6'0" 12st8
Goalkeeper
FL Apps 2   Total Apps 2
Career: Thorniewood U., Leicester C. 31.7.54, Oldham A. 11.8.56 [4], Dale 6.9.57 [2], Albion R. cs.58 to 1959 [9 ScL]

George, another Scot, was Dale's third 'keeper in 1957-58, signed when both Jones and McCready were injured, and played in a 4-2 defeat at Darlington and then a 3-0 win at Stockport. He had played four games for Oldham the year before and returned to Scotland to turn out for Albion Rovers in 1958. Off the field, he was one of the first footballers also involved in the new pop music business.

James Augustine (Jim) Dailey 1957-59

Born: Airdrie 8.9.27
5'8" 11st12
Centre forward
FL Apps/Gls 53/25
Total Apps/Gls 57/25
Career: St Margaret's Boys' School (Airdrie), St. Joseph's Boys Guild, Wolverhampton W. am 8.43, Third Lanark 9.45, Sheffield W. 10.46 [37/24], Birmingham 2.49 £10,000 [51/14], Exeter C. 8.52 [45/14], Workington 12.53 [176/74], Dale 10.57 [53/25], Weymouth 7.59, Bath C. 1961, Poole T., Bridport, Portland U. manager, Dorchester T. manager
Honours: Scottish schoolboy international

A schoolboy international in Scotland during the war, Jim played his first senior games with Sheffield Wednesday in 1946-47 and though not an automatic choice had a remarkable scoring record with 13 goals in 17 games, including a hat-trick against Spurs, followed by 10 in 15 the year after, five of them in a game against Barnsley. Following a big money transfer to Birmingham he actually played even fewer games per season, but after dropping down the leagues, first at Exeter and then especially at Workington, scored consistently over an extended period. Ever present at Borough Park for three seasons, he hit successively 19, 23 and 26 goals and had scored 15 times in the first 15 games of 1957-58 when Harry Catterick remarkably managed to prise him away. He added 19 more in Dale colours, 15 of them in a run of 10 games, including the second five goal haul of his career in a 7-0 thrashing of Hartlepools which equalled Bert Whitehurst's record for a game at Spotland. Like the rest of the side he struggled in Division 3 but on moving to the Southern League netted 42 times in a couple of seasons with Weymouth. Opening a sports outfitters in the town, he played for and managed a number of other non-league sides in the vicinity.

George Patrick P. Newell 1957-58
Born: Rochdale 17.3.36 5'10" 11st13
Centre half
FL Apps/Gls 1/0   Total Apps/Gls 2/0
Career: {Hamer 1952}, Dale 4.57 to 1958 [1/-]

Arriving from local football, George was another one game man at FL level. He appeared in the 1957-58 pre-season practice games and played his one senior game, deputisng for Bev Glover at centre half in a 2-0 victory over Southport that November.

Kevin Barber 1953-58
Born: Rochdale JAS.36 5'9" 11st
Right half
FL Apps/Gls 0/0   Total Apps/Gls 1/0
Career: {St. Clements 1952-53}, Bolton W. cs.53, Dale 3.54, Buxton 1958, Ashton U. 10.58 to 1960-61
Honours: Army XI 1954-55

Another local lad who had been on Bolton's staff, Kevin signed pro for Dale after playing in a friendly against Swindon in 1954, and, along with Brian Green, he played for the Army against the Dale in a friendly the following season while doing his National Service. After figuring in the pre-season practice games in 1957, his sole competitive first team game was a Lancashire Senior Cup tie against Manchester City later that year. He did, though, play approaching 100 games in three seasons at Ashton. {Earlier he had played for local amateurs St Clements when they beat touring Danish side Frederica 5-4 in March 1953.}

Leslie (Les) Spencer 1957-60
Born: Manchester 16.9.36 5'6" 9st11
Inside forward
FL Apps/Gls 74/17 Total Apps/Gls 86/20
Career: Dale pt 24.1.58, Luton T. 7.60 £3000, retired 3.61 [7/1]

Les came into the Dale side not long after signing part-time terms, appearing seven times at inside or outside right near the end of 1957-58 when Dale made it into the new Division 3 despite not winning any of the last 11 games. A regular choice at inside forward for the next two seasons and joint top scorer in the relegation campaign, albeit with eight league goals, he was sold to Luton for £3000 in 1960 but had to retire because of a hip injury after only a handful of games for the Hatters. Indeed, in 1962 he had two long spells in hospital with an arthritic hip before being able to walk properly again.

John Collins (Jock) Wallace 1957-60
Born: Glasgow 11.1.36 5'10" 11st5
Left back
FL Apps/Gls 7/0 Total Apps/Gls 8/0
Career: Falkirk, St Roch's, Dale 26.2.58 £500 to 1960 [7/-]. Hamilton Ac. 1961-62 [24/- ScL], Petershill

Jock had a somewhat eventful, if brief, league career with Dale. He was bought from Scottish side St Roch's with a donation from the supporters club in 1957, but broke his leg in 1958, was suspended by the club for missing a reserve match to get married in 1959 and was released in 1960. In between, he managed just seven FL appearances and one in a Lancashire Cup tie. He later figured quite regularly for Hamilton in the Scottish Second Division.

Donald (Don) Whiston 1958-59
Born: Chesterton 4.4.30 5'10" 12st5
Left back
FL Apps/Gls 14/0 Total Apps/Gls 17/0
Career: (Boys Brigade football), Stoke C. jnr, pro 12.49 [30/4], Crewe A. 2.57 [52/9], Dale 5.58 to cs.59 [14/-]

Don was a junior with Stoke and made his debut for them immediately after turning pro in a 2-1 victory over Sunderland in front of a 41,000 crowd. At the time a centre forward, he scored in two of his four Division 1 games that season, but only had a real run in the side in 1955-56, by which time he was playing at right back. He moved to Crewe the following year and was a regular, alternating between the two roles and in fact being joint top scorer, albeit with just six goals as the Alex finished bottom of the league. He joined Dale for the first season of the new Division 3 but though given the left back slot at the start of the season was replaced by Dai Powell a couple of months later and retired at the end of the season.

Gordon Archibald McBain 1958-59
Born: Blantyre 4.12.34 5'8" 11st
Winger
FL Apps/Gls 10/1 Total Apps/Gls 12/1
Career: Shotts Bon Accord, Kilmarnock c.1956 [1/- ScL], Dale 21.5.58 to 11.58 (registration retained until cs.60) [10/1], Third Lanark 1960-61, Cowdenbeath 1960-61 [35/16 ScL], Hamilton Ac. trial 1961-62 [3/2 ScL], Brechin C. 1962-63 [21/4 ScL], Stirling Albion 1963-64 [9/7 ScL]

Gordon joined Kilmarnock from Bon Accord and made one top flight appearance before joining Dale. He played in the first two games of 1958-59 and then had another spell in the side in September and October, playing on either wing. However, in November he walked out and returned to Scotland, Rochdale suspending him though retaining his registration. He eventually resumed his career in Scotland in 1960 and did the rounds of Division 2 sides over the next four years.

James Smith (Jim) Maguire 1958-59
Born Eaglesham 3.2.32 5'10" 12st
Outside left
FL Apps/Gls 15/0 Total Apps/Gls 18/0
Career: Cambuslang Rangers, Dumbarton trial 1953-54 [3/2 ScL], Glasgow Ashfield 1954, Queen of the South 1955 [21/2 ScL], Dale 8.58 [15/-], Alloa Ath. 1959 [3/- ScL], Coleraine 1959-60, Brechin C. 1959-60 [6/1 ScL]

Another Scot recruited in 1958, Jim started on the opposite wing to McBain but his appearances became less frequent as Dale's dismal season ran its course and nine other players were tried on the left flank at some point. He figured both back in Scotland and in Ireland the following year.

David Morgan (Dai) Powell 1958-61

Born: Swansea 19.1.35
5'10" 12st
Left back
FL Apps/Gls 76/1
Total Apps/Gls 89/1
Career: Blackpool 12.52, Dale 7.58 [76/1], Rochdale Police cs. 61 to 11.62, Mossley 1.63 to cs.63
Honours: British Police XI

Dai had spent six seasons at Blackpool without making the first team, but despite playing for Dale in 1958-59 when they turned out to be outclassed in the new Division 3, he survived the general clear out and was their regular left back for a further 18 months. After losing his place to fellow Welshman Jack Edwards he decided to join the local constabulary and played for a British Police representative side in a friendly against the Dale. He also played semi-pro for Mossley briefly and was an expert in judo.

Charles William Thomas (Bill) Finney
1958-59
Born: Stoke 5.9.31 5'8" 11st
Forward
FL Apps/Gls 31/1   Total Apps/Gls 35/2
Career: Crewe A. am 1947, Stoke C. 5.49 [57/14], Birmingham 11.55 [14/-], Queens Park R. 5.57 [10/1], Crewe A. 7.58 [1/-], Dale 9.58 (exchange for E. Moran) [31/1], Macclesfield cs.59 to 1961

Like Don Whiston, Bill had spent several seasons with Stoke. He made a scoring debut at centre forward against Manchester United in October 1952, but Stoke ended the season relegated. He also played quite frequently the following term but was less used thereafter, joining Arthur Turner, who had also signed him for Crewe and Stoke, at Birmingham. Though making only a few league appearances, Bill did have the honour of being one of the first British players to figure in a European competition when he played in the Inter Cities Fairs Cup. By 1958 he had arrived back at Crewe but played only once before being traded for Dale's Eddie Moran, oddly enough, while Dale were between managers. He appeared regularly for the rest of the season, playing all across the forward line, but was unable to help steer them away from the foot of the table (indeed he scored less goals for his other four clubs put together than he had in his first three games for Stoke).

Herbert (Bert) Thomson 1958-60
Born: Glasgow 18.2.29 5'10" 11st9
Right half
FL Apps/Gls 55/1 Total Apps/Gls 59/1
Career: Springburn U., Partick Thistle 1948 [91/1 ScL], Yeovil T. 1957-58, Dale 6.58 [56/1], San Francisco Scots (USA) cs.60

Yet another Scot in the Dale line-up, though in his case arriving from Yeovil, Bert had spent seven seasons in and out of the Partick side. He took over as the regular right half from Jackie Grant half way though 1958-59 and was in turn replaced by Norman Bodell a year later, also figuring at right back for a spell. He then emigrated to the USA to play for San Francisco Scots.

George Heyes 1956-60

Born: Bolton 16.11.37
5'10" 11st
Goalkeeper
FL Apps 24
Total Apps 25
Career: (Bolton junior football), Dale 6.56 [24], Leicester C. 7.60 £7000 [25], Swansea T. 9.65 [98], Barrow 7.69 [26], Hereford U. cs.70, Bedford T. 8.70 to 1971. Goalkeeping scout for Blackburn R., Aston Villa, Leicester C., Nottingham F.
Honours: Welsh Cup winners 1966, final 1969

George made his Dale debut in a friendly against Walsall in December 1957, but his FL debut came the following September, when he had the misfortune to fumble Southend's goal over the line. Left out after a 6-1 defeat at Bury a couple of week's later and also doing his national service, he eventually gained a regular spot in goal when Jimmy Jones was out of action in the second half of 1959-60. Snapped up by Leicester that summer for a decent fee, he spent five years at Filbert Street as Gordon Banks' understudy before the emergence of Peter Shilton. Despite letting in 12 goals in his first two away games for Swansea, due to the timing of his transfer, he had the unusual record of playing 48 FL games in 1965-66. While with the Swans he played in two Welsh Cup Finals and appeared in the European Cup Winners Cup. Trained as a telephone engineer, he worked for BT after retiring from semi-pro football and later owned his own company. He also acted as a specialist scout for goalkeepers for several league clubs.

Alan Moore 1958-59
Born: Hebburn 7.3.27 5'8" 10st10
Outside right
FL Apps/Gls 11/2 Total Apps/Gls 12/3
Career: Sunderland am 1944, pro 5.46, Spennymoor 1948, Chesterfield 12.48 [66/3], Hull C. 7.51 £7000 [13/4], Nottingham F. 1.52 [101/39], Coventry C. 12.54 £10,000 [58/11], Swindon T. 7.57 [19/3], Dale 11.58 [11/2], Wisbech cs.59, Cambridge C. player-manager 12.59 to 10.63. Cambridge University coach 1967 to 1969

Alan made his league bow with Chesterfield immediately after joining the second division side from Spennymoor, playing outside right with Stan Milburn behind him at right back. A relatively expensive move to Hull proved short lived, but he made over a century of appearances for Notts Forest. The best season of his career was undoubtedly 1953-54 when he was everpresent and leading scorer with 19 goals from the wing, including a hat-trick against Stoke, as Forest just missed promotion to the top flight, finishing 4th. Sold to Coventry the following term, he was never an automatic choice for his later clubs, including Dale after he became Jack Marshall's first signing. Moving to Cambridge, he opened a sports shop and was player-manager of Cambridge City for several seasons, later coaching the University side.

Stanley (Stan) Milburn 1958-65

Born: Ashington 27.10.26
5'9" 11st4
Right back/centre half
FL Apps/Gls 238/26
Total Apps/Gls 275/27
Career: Ashington, Newcastle U. am, Ashington, Chesterfield 1.47 £1000 [179/-], Leicester C. 3.52 £20,000 [174/1], Dale 1.59 to 5.65 [238/26], (local football), Spotland Meths 1979-80, T.B.A. 1980-81, coach
Honours: Division 2 champions 1954, 1957, FA XI v Army 1949-50, Football League v Irish League 1950, 1951, England 'B' 4 caps 1950 to 1957, FA tour to Canada 1950, Canadian Tour XI v World Cup XI (Charity Shield) 1950, Football League Cup final 1962

A true Dale legend, Stan was a member of the famous Milburn clan from Ashington, his brothers Jack (Leeds and Bradford City), George (Leeds and Chesterfield) and Jim (Leeds and Bradford Park Avenue) all being long serving FL fullbacks, while 'Wor Jackie' of Newcastle and England fame was a cousin and Stan's sister Cissie was mother of England's World Cup heroes Jack and Bobby Charlton. He first appeared with Chesterfield in the first post-war season, partnering brother George – 16 years his senior – at full back. Quickly making his mark, in 1949-50 he was selected for the England 'B' international against Holland played at Newcastle and appeared for the Football League, cousin Jackie scoring a hat-trick in a victory over the Irish League. He toured Canada with the FA side the following summer and played in the Charity Shield game between the Canada tourists and the 1950 World Cup team. (The tourists had beaten the USA in a game prior to the World Cup which ended with England's senior side knocked out by the American no-hopers). He was sold to Leicester in 1952 for the huge fee of £20,000, only just short of the record for a full back of £21,000 which Spurs had paid for Alf Ramsey. He accumulated over 170 league appearances, as he had for the Spireites, twice winning the second division championship, as well as making further appearances for the England 'B' squad, indeed "good judges in the game considered him unlucky not to become a full international". A unique incident occurred in December 1954 when Stan and fellow defender Jack Froggatt officially 'shared an own goal', when their simultaneous attempt at a clearance ended with the ball in their own net. Arriving at Spotland when already 32, Stan amazingly became one of their longest serving players, appearing in 275 senior games. A right back by trade, he also played a number of games at centre half, but more remarkably also turned his hand to centre forward, netting a hat-trick on his first appearance there against Barrow in September 1959 (having scored just one career goal in 350 games for his previous clubs!) and ending the season as top scorer with 15, eight of them from the penalty spot. He was also the man to call on to go between the sticks if the 'keeper was injured. He played throughout Dale's amazing run to the League Cup Final in 1962 and having already had benefits at Chesterfield and Leicester, was also awarded one in his final season at Spotland when Dale just missed promotion in 1964-65. He then turned out in local football, playing in a cup final for Spotland Methodists in 1980, when he was 53! A warehouseman at Turner Bros, he also played for and coached their football team in the early eighties. A regular attendee at club events such as the Centenary celebrations and the 'Legends' dinner, Stan died just after the Dale regained their place in the third tier in 2010 and a minute's silence was observed in his honour.

George Cooper 1958-60
Born: Kingswinford 1.10.32 5'7" 10st11
Inside/centre forward
FL Apps/Gls 32/9 Total Apps/Gls 33/9
Career: Brierley Hill Alliance, Crystal Palace 1.55 [69/27], Dale 1.59 [32/9], Stourbridge 1960

George spent four years in a Crystal Palace side struggling at the wrong end of the Third South, his best season coming in 1957-58 when he netted 17 goals in only 25 games before unfortunately being injured. He appeared only once the following term before a move to Spotland, his debut coming in a rare victory. He figured quite frequently, at centre forward or inside left, in the first half of the following campaign, netting five goals in five games, but subsequently lost his place back to Les Spencer.

Norman Bodell 1955-63
Born: Royton 29.1.38 5'9" 10st11
Wing half
FL Apps/Gls 79/1 Total Apps/Gls 94/3
Career: Rochdale am 1955, pro 9.56 [79/1], Crewe A. 3.5.63 [108+1/2], Halifax T. 11.66 [36/-], Altrincham 1968, Barrow coach 1968, manager 2.69 to 2.70, Wolverhampton W. reserve team coach, Preston NE coach 1974, Blackburn R. coach, assistant manager 6.75, caretaker manager 3.78, Birmingham C. coach 1978, acting manager 2.82, chief scout to 1983, West Bromwich A. chief scout
Honours: Football League Cup final 1962

Norman was with Dale for eight years, though it took him three to break into the first team, first appearing after completing his national service in February 1959 when manager Jack Marshall made five changes to the side beaten 6-1 at Southampton. Down in Division 4, Norman gained a fairly regular spot at wing half, though on occasion he played at full back or up front (he had been a centre forward as a junior), playing in about half the games over the next three seasons, including both legs of the League Cup Final in 1962. With Stan Hepton the regular choice at right half the following season, and dissatisfied with the terms offered, he moved to Crewe, managed by Jim McGuigan (q.v.), and made over 100 appearances for them before finishing his league career at Halifax as a central defender, following the advent of the 'back four'. Appointed coach at Barrow, he shortly afterwards became the youngest manager in the FL, at the age of 31, but with the side heading for relegation lasted only a year. Returning to coaching he had spells with several top clubs, also working in Zambia at one point, and was twice acting manager, at Blackburn and Birmingham, replacing Jim Smith both times. He later became chief scout for Birmingham and then rivals West Brom.

Robert Peter (Bob) Entwistle 1958-60
Born: Bury 6.10.38
Centre forward
FL Apps/Gls 1/0 Total Apps/Gls 2/0
Career: Bury jnr, Macclesfield 1958, Dale am 7.2.59 [1/-], Accrington St. 9.60 [2/-], Llandudno 1961-62, Bangor C. 1962-63, East Lane U. (Johannesburg, SA) 5.64, Hartlepools U. 17.10.64 [14/3], Chesterfield trial 3.8.65, Scarborough 11.65 to 1970, Shepton Mallett manager (3 months)
Honours: South Africa XI v Southern Rhodesia, South African XI v Real Madrid

Despite a modest FL career, Bob played against some of the world's top stars. His sole Dale FL appearance was at No.9 in a goalless draw with Chesterfield in March 1959 (notable mainly for Milburn having to play in goal when Jones was injured), though he played a Lancashire Cup game the following season. He only just beat that at Accrington where he figured twice on the wing. However, in 1962-63 he played in Europe for Bangor City when they sensationally beat Napoli at home, to draw 3-3 on aggregate with the Italian cup winners, eventually going down 4-2 in a play-off at Highbury (under modern rules they would have gone through on away goals). Then, while one of the first British pros to appear in South Africa, he played for their national side against Southern Rhodesia and in a representative side which faced a touring Real Madrid including Puskas, Santamaria and Gento. A return to England saw him score his only FL goals, netting in his first two games for Hartlepools. After his footballing career he turned to horse training, also riding in a couple of races at Ascot and Newbury in the early eighties, and running an equestrian centre in Bury. He subsequently took over the Church Inn adjacent to the Dale's ground and in the early nineties owned a horse called Spotland Lass.

Frederick Malcolm Hussey 1958-59
Born: Darfield 11.9.33 5'11" 12st8
Right half
FL Apps/Gls 1/0 Total Apps/Gls 1/0
Career: Rotherham U. jnr, pro 4.52 [24/-], Scunthorpe U. 8.56 [23/-], Dale 3.59 [1/-]

Malcolm signed pro for Rotherham when he was 18 and appeared in a few games in each of the next four seasons. He then figured fairly regularly at centre half for Scunthorpe early and late in the 1956-57 season but hadn't played any senior football for 18 months when he joined Dale. His single appearance for them came as replacement for Bert Thomson at right half in a goalless draw at Mansfield, one of their better away performances of the season, given that they registered just 5 draws and 18 defeats.

Alan Bushby 1959-61

Born; Doncaster 15.1.32
5'9" 11st2
Left half
Apps/Gls 66/0 Total Apps/Gls 76/0
Career: Scunthorpe U. 8.52 [218/10], Dale 7.59 [65/-], Goole T. player-manager 7.61, New York Generals (USA) coach 11.67 (d.11.67)
Honours: Division 3 North champions 1958

Alan was a stalwart for Scunthorpe through the 1950s, playing left half in the Iron's sides which twice finished 3rd before winning the final Third North championship in 1958, also beating Newcastle to reach the 5th round of the FA Cup the same season. However, Alan missed the end of that season though injury and appeared only once in Division 2. At Spotland he was an automatic choice, missing only one game, in 1959-60, but played only half the games the following term and was released when Dale bought Jim Thompson. Player-manager of non-league Goole Town, he had the opportunity to coach the New York Generals, under Freddie Goodwin, but tragically died of a heart attack just a week after arriving in the US, at the age of only 35.

Charles Ronald (Ron) Barnes 1959-61

Born: Bolton 21.2.36
5'10" 11st6
Outside right
FL Apps/Gls 91/7 Total Apps/Gls 105/10
Career: Blackpool jnr, pro 5.54 [9/-], Dale 6.59 £1000 [91/7], Wrexham 7.61 £4000 [88/24], Norwich C. 8.63 [21/1], Peterborough U. 7.64 £5000 [39/6], Torquay U. 1.66 [110+4/25], Cape Town City (SA) 5.69
Honours: Welsh Cup final 1962, Division 4 promotion 1962

A long-term understudy to Stanley Matthews at Blackpool, Ron's career took off when Rochdale bought him for a modest fee in 1959. He missed only one game of any sort in his two years with them, garnering the remarkable total of 105 appearances for such a short stay. Transferred to Wrexham for a tidy profit, he again missed just a handful of games in two years and in addition displayed previously unsuspected goalscoring form, hitting double figures each time and netting a hat-trick (as did two of his teammates) when Wrexham amazingly trounced Hartlepools 10-1 on the way to promotion in 1962. After a season at Norwich he moved to Peterborough, where he played in their remarkable run to the FA Cup quarter-final, beating Arsenal along the way. Besides his own goals, Ron also made them for a succession of famous centre forwards of the day, Wyn Davies at Wrexham, Ron Davies at Norwich and Derek Dougan with the Posh. He played well over 100 games for Torquay before moving to South Africa, working in the printing trade there after retiring from playing.

Ronald (Ron) Cairns 1959-64

Born: Chopwell 4.4.34
5'8" 10st6
Inside forward
FL Apps/Gls 195/66
Total Apps/Gls 233/78
Career: Chopwell Juniors, Consett, Blackburn R. 9.53 [26/7], Dale 6.59 £2500 [195/66], Southport 9.7.64 [34/13], Wigan A. 5.65, Hyde U., Darwen c.1967
Honours: Division 2 promotion 1958, Football League Cup final 1962, Lancashire Senior Cup final 1965

Ron had spent six years working his way through the ranks at Blackburn, his best spell coming in 1957-58 when he netted six times in 15 games during Rovers promotion to the first division. He became Rochdale's record signing when Jack Marshall spent £2500 on him in 1959 and it proved an excellent investment, Ron playing well over 200 senior games for Dale and netting 78 goals, a post-war record at the time. Small and lightweight, Ron was one of the new breed of goal poacher. Most often figuring at inside left, though he sometimes played in the other inside positions, his best seasons were 1960-61, when he netted 20 league goals and two in the cup, and 1961-62 when he totalled 21 including the crucial third in the home leg of the League Cup semi-final against his former club. He also netted 14 when Dale finished 7th in 1963, but appeared less the following term,. However, he did net the crucial penalty on the last day of the season to beat champions Gillingham and escape the re-election places, before moving on to Southport where he figured in their surprise run to the Lancashire Cup final. After suffering back trouble while at Wigan he played some games at a lower level and became a sales rep for Trebor.

John Lockhart (Johnny) Anderson 1959-60

Born: Glasgow 5.4.28
5'9" 10st12
Centre forward/inside left
FL Apps/Gls 28/5 Total Apps/Gls 33/6
Career: Glasgow Benburb, Partick Thistle 1951 [12/- ScL], Northampton T. 6.53 [14/3], Exeter C. 7.54 [7/-], Dundee 1955 [3/1 ScL], Wrexham 6.56 [98/27], Dale 7.59 [28/5], Chester 7.60 [17/2], Wrexham 8.61 [1/-], reserve team player-coach 1961-62, Colwyn Bay U. 2.65, Colchester U. coach, Aldershot coach cs.69, trainer c.1973 to c.1989
Honours: Welsh Cup final 1962, Division 4 promotion 1962

Johnny was a well travelled Scottish inside forward with experience on both sides of the border, but whose most successful seasons were actually spent in Wales, with Wrexham. He missed only two games in 1956-57 and hit 18 goals, by far the best return of his career. He joined Dale in 1959, initially figuring in his usual inside left position, but in the continued absence of Frank Lord played for much of the term at centre forward, albeit in a deep lying role, a tactical disposition dubbed the 'Marshall plan' following the 'Revie plan' at Manchester City. After a spell at Chester, he returned to Wrexham at the start of a long career as coach or trainer. Though only playing once in the league for Wrexham in his second spell, he did figure in their Welsh Cup Final side. He later spent 20 years with Aldershot.

Anthony Norman (Tony) Collins 1959-61

Born: Kensington 19.3.26
5'11" 10st12
Outside left
FL Apps/Gls 47/5
Total Apps/Gls 51/6
Career: Brentford am, Sheffield W. 11.47, York C. 7.49 [10/1], Watford 8.50 [90/2], Norwich C. 7.53 [29/2], Torquay U. 7.55 [89/17], Watford 7.57 [17/3], Crystal Palace 11.57 [54/14], Dale 6.59 [47/5], manager 6.9.60 to 9.67, Bristol C. scout 12.67 to 1972, Leeds U. scout, England staff 1974, Bristol C. assistant manager 1976, caretaker manager 9.80, Leeds U. chief scout 1980, Manchester U. scout 1.82 to 1988, Queens Park R. scout, Newcastle U. chief scout 1.89, Millwall scout, Aston Villa scout, Derby Co. scout
Honours: Southern Professional Floodlit Cup final 1959. As manager: FL Cup final 1962

Another of the experienced men signed by Jack Marshall in the attempt to regain third division status at the first attempt, Tony had made his FL debut 10 years earlier at York, but the rest of his career had been spent in the Third South. Quite tall for a winger, his most productive spells had been at Watford – he was an everpresent in 1952-53 – and Torquay, where he missed only 3 games in two years as well as netting 17 goals. In 1958-59 he played regularly with Palace in the new Division 4, and he did likewise at Spotland. A cartilage operation in the summer of 1960, kept him out at the start of the following term, but when Jack Marshall left in September to manage Sheffield Wednesday, Tony was promoted to player-manager. With part Afro-Carribean heritage, he thus predated the next generation of black managers such as Keith Alexander by three decades. He picked himself for a number of games in the second half of the season, but then retired to concentrate on the management. His greatest triumph was to mastermind Dale's run to the League Cup Final in 1962, making them the only side from the fourth level of English football to contest a national final until Bradford City also did so over 50 years later. Not afraid to experiment, he was one of the first managers in the FL to play what would become known as 4-2-4, dropping a nominal forward, Stan Hepton, back alongside his centre half when facing superior opposition in cup ties. He later took this a step further by picking an actual defender at No. 9, but after Dale's successful 1964-65 season when they finished 6th with a best ever 58 points (enough to have gained promotion in any other fourth division campaign), the manager's permanent switch to 4-2-4 the following season proved something of a disaster, Dale having to seek re-election. They again finished 21st in 1967 and with the following season going the same way, Tony resigned. Working next as a scout, his job with Leeds led to a position within the England set up, studying future opponents, when Don Revie became England manager. He then had four years as assistant manager at Bristol City before returning to scouting, working for Manchester United and Newcastle amongst others.

William John (Jack) Edwards 1959-61

Born: Risca 6.7.29
5'9" 11st
Full back
FL Apps/Gls 68/1 Total Apps/Gls 75/1
Career: Cardiff C. am, Lovells Ath., Crystal Palace 9.49 [223/-], Dale 7.59 [69/1], Ashford T. player-coach cs.61, Exeter C. trainer cs.62, manager 2.63 to 1.65, Torquay U. trainer 1965 (caretaker manager 12.68 to 1.69),

manager 10.71, Exeter C. trainer 1.73, Plymouth A. assistant manager 11.73, Leeds U. scout
Honours: Army Cup final 1948. As manager: Division 4 champions 1964

Jack Marshall's sixth experienced signing in the summer of 1959 (probably uniquely, no further players were signed during the season), Jack joined Dale from Crystal Palace just after Tony Collins, but had been at Selhurst Park much longer, having accrued well over 200 FL appearances in ten years, mostly in a struggling side and had a benefit game in 1955. At Spotland he generally had to share the left back slot with fellow Welshman Dai Powell unless the ubiquitous Milburn was being used in some other role, in which case Jack took over at right back. Moving into coaching at Southern League Ashford Town, he soon obtained a post with Exeter and after only a few months was promoted to manager, leading them to the fourth division title in 1964. A similar scenario followed at Torquay and he completed a tour of Devon when appointed assistant manager of Plymouth. At the start of his career, during his national service, he had played in the Army Cup final when two players were tragically killed by lightning.

Thomas D. (Roy) Anchor 1959-60
Born: Salford AMJ.35
Right back
FL Apps/Gls 0/0 Total Apps/Gls 1/0
Career: (Salford local football), Dale 14.6.59

Roy was a reserve full back for Dale in 1959-60 when manager Jack Marshall set a record by using only 17 players in FL games. Hence, Roy's only outing came in the Lancashire Cup, against Preston.

Ronald James (Ron) Phoenix 1960-62

Born: Stretford 30.6.29
5'8" 11st3
Half back
FL Apps/Gls 64/0
Total Apps/Gls 81/0
Career: Humphrey Park, Manchester C. 3.50 [53/2], Dale 6.60 [64/-], Altrincham cs.62

Noticeable because of his red hair, Ron spent a decade at Manchester City, scoring on his debut in a 2-2 draw at Arsenal in January 1952 and playing in all the last 14 games of that season, mostly at left half. City only won once in that time, though, and Ron was largely consigned to the reserves thereafter, only getting another decent run in the side in 1958-59.

One of only two major signings by Jack Marshall in the summer of 1960, he missed just a handful of games in his first season, generally playing at right half but also appearing at left half and inside right and even filling in at centre half and left back. He also played regularly for the first half of the following season and was particularly unfortunate not to appear in either leg of the League Cup Final, playing in the first leg of the semi-final and in all the league games around the final.

Stanley (Stan) Hepton 1960-64

Born: Leeds 3.12.32
5'8" 10st3
Forward/wing half
FL Apps/Gls 149/21
Total Apps/Gls 180/28
Career: Leeds Ashley Road, Blackpool 3.50 [7/3], Huddersfield T. 8.57 [6/1], Bury 6.59 [14/3], Dale 7.60 [149/21], Southport 7.64 [22/2], Northwich Victoria 5.65, MOD (Leeds) am
Honours: Lancashire Senior Cup winners 1954, League Cup final 1962

Like Ron Barnes, Stan had been a long serving reserve at Blackpool, managing just seven games in seven years as a back-up to centre forward Stan Mortensen, though he did score on his debut in front of a 53,000 crowd at Sunderland in 1953 and figured in the 1954 Lancashire Cup Final. Indeed, it was only on arriving at Spotland that he made his mark, missing only three games and netting a total of 16 goals, mostly from inside right, in 1960-61. One of these was the winner at Scunthorpe in the League Cup which gave the Dale their first victory over higher division opposition (except in the Lancashire Cup) since they joined the FL. This proved the prelude to the amazing exploits the following season when Dale made it all the way to the final, Stan sometimes being deputed by Tony Collins to drop back alongside centre half Ray Aspden in a forerunner of a 4-2-4 formation. He also bagged the crucial goal, with a long range strike, in the away leg of the semi-final with Blackburn which gave Dale the tie on aggregate. He continued with Dale for two further seasons, largely at right half, though he could turn his hand to almost any position - indeed he missed only centre half and outside left during his time at Spotland. A dispute over his club house led to him moving to Southport where his season was cut short when he tore a calf muscle. He later worked for the Ministry of Defence in Leeds and appeared for their football team as a permit player. His son Russell was a well known racing cyclist.

Joffre McKay 1960-63
Born: Connah Bridge, Inverness 21.1.37 6'0" 11st
Goalkeeper
FL Apps 9 Total Apps 16
Career: Ross County, Bury 12.58, Dale 7.60 [9]

Signed from the Highland League, Joffre spent a season and a half in the reserves at Bury before joining Dale as understudy to Jimmy Jones following the sale of George Heyes. Handed his debut in the League Cup replay at Scunthorpe, he kept a clean sheet to earn Dale their first victory over a higher division club in a major cup tie for 40 years. He kept his place for the next couple of months, until the arrival of Ted Burgin, but with the latter becoming a permanent fixture in the side his only further appearances were in the Lancashire Cup in 1961-62 and as a substitute in a friendly against Stockport the year after.

John (Jack) Pollitt 1960-61

Born: Farnworth 29.3.37
6'0" 11st7
Centre forward/outside left
FL Apps/Gls 6/1 Total Apps/Gls 8/2
Career: (Bolton junior football), Bolton W. 3.1.55, Bury 19.8.58 [4/-], Accrington St. 4.3.60 [3/1], Dale 17.8.60 [6/1], Winsford U. 1961, Stalybridge Celtic, Mossley 1961-62

Despite 60 games and a good scoring record for their reserves, Jack managed just four senior games for Bury before a somewhat doomed move to bottom of Division 3 Accrington. Stanley conceded 12 goals in his three games and scored just one, which Jack himself netted. Though making a scoring debut on the left wing in the FA Cup at Crewe, Jack was otherwise reserve to centre forward Frank Lord in his year at Spotland and subsequently moved onto the Cheshire League circuit.

Kenneth Francis (Ken) McDowall 1960-61
Born: Manchester 6.5.38
Outside left
FL Apps/Gls 6/0 Total Apps/Gls 8/0
Career: Rhyl, Manchester U. 9.59, Dale 10.60 £1250 [6/-], Rhyl 1961, Bangor, Caernarvon 1965-66
Honours: Lancashire Senior Cup winners 1960, Welsh League (North) champions 1966, North Wales Coast FA Cup winners 1966

Tony Collins' first signing, when he arrived from Manchester United for a sizeable fee by Dale standards, Ken played a few games on the left wing before the manager regained fitness after his cartilage operation and selected himself. Indeed, even when Collins did not play, he subsequently preferred Jim Brown to Ken and he drifted off to play in Wales, winning a number of honours. While at Old Trafford he had played in United's reserve side in the Lancashire Cup final.

Bryn Owen 1960-63
Born: Rochdale 25.4.39 5'9" 11st2
Right back
FL Apps/Gls 6/0 Total Apps/Gls 11/0
Career: Turf Hill, Dale 8.60 [6/-], Mossley 1963 to 1965

A reserve for Dale for three seasons, Bryn played in two Lancs Cup ties before making his FL debut in the final game of 1960-61, against Aldershot. He played a handful of games the following season as cover for Milburn and Winton, but appeared only in a friendly against Bradford in 1962-63. His spell at Mossley wasn't much more productive, with just eight Cheshire League outings in two years.

John Alan Hardman 1960-67

Born: Bury 17.12.40
5'10" 10st9
Half back/right back
FL Apps/Gls 40/2
Total Apps/Gls 51/2
Career: Bess's Boys, Dale 8.60 [40/2], Witton Albion 1967

A long standing, and long suffering, squad member at Spotland, John arrived from local football in 1960 and like Bryn Owen made his debut in a Lancashire Cup game against Manchester City. His FL debut at wing half followed shortly after and he also played four games at right back at the end of the season, though Dale didn't win any of them. He stood in for Ray Aspden for a spell the following term, figuring in Dale's shock defeat of Charlton Athletic in the League Cup. He scored his first senior goal when selected at No. 9 against Exeter in September 1962 and was Dale's first named substitute on the opening day of 1965-66. However, the game which put him in the record books for the wrong reasons came two weeks later when he broke his leg for the second time in seven months to become the first Dale player replaced by a sub. He played his final nine games early the following season, the longest run in the side that he ever managed.

James Charles Alfred (Jim) Sanders

1960-61
Born: Marlborough 15.10.32
6'0" 11st9
Left half
FL Apps/Gls 0/0 Total Apps/Gls 1/0
Career: Bristol C. 11.51, Crystal Palace 17.3.55 [37/-], Dale 10.60 to 11.60, Cheltenham T., Exeter C. 8.62 [20/1]

Jim had been with Crystal Palace at the same time as Tony Collins, being their regular left half in 1957-58, and was offered a month's trial by Collins when he was freed by Palace. He figured in just the Lancashire Cup victory over Manchester City in November 1960, before deciding that he did not want to move from his home in Bristol. After a spell with non-league Cheltenham, he later played some further FL games with Exeter.

Joseph Arthur Searles (Joe) Richardson

1960-65
Born: Liverpool 17.3.42
5'7" 11st
Inside forward
FL Apps/Gls 115/31
Total Apps/Gls 136+1/41
Career: Birmingham 9.59, Winsford U., Sheffield U. 1.60, Dale 10.60 £1250 [115/31], Tranmere R. 7.65 (d. 1966)
Honours: League Cup final 1962

Obtained from Sheffield United for a significant fee for an untried 18 year old, and the fourth debutant in the Manchester City Lancs Cup tie, Joe played and scored in the League Cup tie with first division Blackburn a week later and made a few league appearances over the rest of the season. He gained a regular place at inside forward from December 1961 and played in the later stages of Dale's run to the League Cup Final, scoring two brilliant goals in the first leg of the semi-final against Blackburn. Having to share the inside position with George Morton the following term when Dale finished 7th, he regained a regular place, at the expense of Ron Cairns, in 1963-64, netting his best ever tally of 16 goals in all games. The arrival of Reg Jenkins saw Joe moved to outside right the following year, when Dale put together a strong challenge for promotion, eventually finishing 6th. Moving on to Tranmere, he tragically never had the chance to play for them, being killed in lorry accident while working for Whitbreads.

Edward (Ted) Burgin 1960-66

Born: Sheffield 29.4.27
5'9" 11st7
Goalkeeper
FL Apps 207
Total Apps 246
Career: Alford T., Sheffield U. 3.49 [281], Doncaster R. 12.57 £3000 [5], Leeds U. 3.58 [58], Dale 1.61 [207], Glossop player-manager 7.66, Oswestry T., Wellington, Buxton c.1972
Honours: England 'B' v Germany B, Yugoslavia B 1954, FA tours to Australia 1951 (3 'tests') and to South Africa 1956 (24 appearances), reserve for England v Austria 1951, England squad 1954 World Cup, FA v Army 1950-51, 1953-54, v RAF 1953-54, Division 2 champions 1953, League Cup final 1962

One of the top goalkeepers in the country in the 1950s, Ted became a Rochdale great when well into his thirties. Earning his place in the Sheffield United side in 1949-50, despite a 7-0 thrashing at champions Spurs, United missed promotion on goal average by just one goal. In the following three seasons Ted missed only three games, already making it onto the FA tour to Australia and being reserve for the England side in 1951. After the Blades won the second division title in 1953 he was twice selected for England 'B' – helping them beat West Germany 4-0 - and was included in the World Cup party to travel to Switzerland. Despite collecting numerous injuries over his career, including two broken legs, he played nearly 300 games for the Blades before Doncaster bought him to replace Harry Gregg, who had just left for Manchester United. However, he broke his collar bone soon after – earning him the tag of one of the most injured men in football - and when fit again signed for Leeds, playing regularly in 1959-60 when they were relegated. Joining Dale towards the end of the next campaign when nearly 34, he went on to add another 200 FL games to his tally, passing 600 senior games during his career. Indeed, he played 170 consecutive games from his debut, including the run to the League Cup Final. Initially pensioned off at the end of 1963-64, before Tony Collins had a change of heart, he was again everpresent when Dale came close to promotion the following year, becoming the appearance record holder for a Dale 'keeper before eventually being forced into retirement by a finger injury. Dale played a benefit for him against Leeds, by then one of the top sides in the country, and Ted made a farewell appearance playing outside left in the second half! He actually continued playing at lower levels until he was 45 and worked in the Cleansing Department in Rochdale. Believing in keeping himself fit, he coached schoolboys and, having moved to the Fylde coast, helped out at Blackpool into his seventies and was still working out in his own gym in his loft when he reached 80. His brother Eric was also on Sheffield United's books and appeared in the FL with York, but was better known as a Yorkshire cricketer.

Oliver P. (Ollie) Norris 1960-61

Born: Londonderry 1.4.29
5'9" 11st7
Centre forward
FL Apps/Gls 2/1 Total Apps/Gls 3/1
Career: Middlesbrough jnr, pro 7.48 [12/2], Bournemouth & BA 7.55 [96/34], Northampton T. 9.58 [14/1], Gloucester C., Ashford T. 1959, Dale 4.60 [3/1], Ashford T. 1961, SC Croatia (Australia) 1964

Ollie was one of the few Irishmen to figure for Dale in his era, arriving in the middle of a somewhat nomadic career. He played a few Division 1 games for Middlesbrough, alongside Wilf Mannion, in 1952-53, but had his most productive spell at Bournemouth. Playing either centre or inside forward, he netted 15 league goals in two successive seasons. He also grabbed seven in six FA Cup ties in 1956-57, including one in Bournemouth's famous defeat of Spurs on their amazing run to the quarter finals, where they lost narrowly to Manchester United. His career at Spotland was rather brief, just three games as stand-in for Frank Lord in February 1961, scoring in the victory over Doncaster. He was later considered one of the top players in the fledgling Victoria State Football Federation and continued to live in Australia after he finished playing. He was noted for his habit of jumping up and down in front of the thrower at opposition throw-ins, a tactic which was not then against the rules.

James (Jim) Thompson 1960-66

Born: Chadderton 26.11.35 6'0" 11st7
Left half
FL Apps/Gls 199/15
Total Apps/Gls 239/17
Career: Oldham A. am 9.52, pro 28.1.54 [110/19], Exeter C. 13.12.58 (part-exchange for R.C. John) [104/9], Dale 16.3.61 £3000 [199/15], Bradford C. 24.12.65 [23+1/1], Hyde U. player-coach 1966, Buxton player-manager
Honours: Chadderton Schoolboys, Football League Cup final 1962

Though still only 25, Jim was already an experienced lower league wing half with over a century of appearances for both Oldham and Exeter to his credit when he became Tony Collins' third important signing during his first season in charge, costing Dale around £3000, a new record. Also the possessor of a fierce shot and deadly from the penalty spot, Jim had once scored 9 goals in 9 games for the Latics. At Spotland he was undisputed first choice left half for four years, playing in every match on the way to the League Cup Final – in fact scoring the winner against York – and missing only one game when Dale just missed promotion in 1965. However, after being left out of the side in November 1965 he asked for a transfer and soon moved on to Bradford City. He spent only a few months there, though, before going into non-league football and subsequently running a guesthouse in Blackpool. Jim's son Steve played for Leicester against Dale in the League Cup in 1993-94 during a career spanning over 600 games, half of them for Bolton.

Brian Birch 1960-62

Born: Salford 18.11.31
5'7" 11st6
Inside left
FL Apps/Gls 11/0
Total Apps/Gls 13/0
Career: Manchester U. jnr 5.46, pro 7.5.49 [11/4], Wolverhampton W. 19.3.52 £11,000 [3/1], Lincoln C. 5.12.52 £5500 [56/16], Boston U. 1955, Barrow 21.6.56 £2500 [60/27], Exeter C. 22.9.58 £2500 [19/2], Oldham A. 11.1.60 £800 [35/10], Dale 16.3.61 £750 [11/-], Philippines coaching 6.62, Boston U. 8.63, Mossley 9.63, Sydney coaching 2.64, Ellesmere Port 1966 to 1.67, Blackburn R. junior coach 11.67, coach 1968-

69, Australia coaching c.1970, Galatasaray (Turkey) coach 1970 to 1974, Egypt coaching, Sweden coaching c.1977, Galatasaray coach 1980-1982
Honours: Salford Schools, England Schools, Great Britain Schools, England youth international 1949, Lancashire Senior Cup winners 1951. As coach: Turkish champions (three times)

After a brief halt at Spotland, Brian became a globe trotting coach, spending time everywhere from Sweden to Australia via Turkey and the Philippines, coaching Galatasaray to three successive league championships. A schoolboy star, he joined United as a 15 year old and, after playing for the England youth team, made his debut at 17. A "brainy little inside forward" with clever ball control, he played a few games in 1950-51 when United finished second in the league before Stan Cullis paid a very large fee to take him to Wolves. Unable to break into the team he soon moved to Lincoln, scoring twice on his debut. The only season he was an automatic choice, though, was 1957-58 when he scored 20 goals in 44 games for Barrow. Dale were the eighth club of his 12 year career when he arrived for a modest fee towards the end of 1960-61 and he left after just one game the following term.

George Douglas (Doug or 'Jock') Winton

1961-64
Born: Perth 6.10.29
5'9" 10t9
Left back
FL Apps/Gls 119/0
Total Apps/Gls 146/0
Career: Jeanfield Swifts, Burnley 9.47 [182/1], Aston Villa 1.59 [37/-], Dale 6.61 £1500 [119/-], retired cs.64
Honours: Scotland 'B' v England 'B' 1957, Lancashire Senior Cup final 1957, Division 2 champions 1960, League Cup final 1962

Doug, generally known as Jock, spent over a decade with Burnley, making his debut in April 1952 and gaining a regular place at left back towards the end of 1953-54. Over the next four years or so he took his tally to 182 first division games and appeared for Scotland 'B' against the English (as well as missing a penalty in a 9-0 win over New Brighton in the cup), before being transferred to Villa. He was unable to help prevent their relegation and only played in the first game when Villa came back up the following year, but did play quite regularly in the top flight in 1960-61. Perhaps surprisingly then bought by fourth division Dale, he had three excellent seasons at Spotland, missing only a handful of games. He played a major role in Dale's progress to the League Cup Final in 1962, not least when clearing off the line in the last minute in the 1-0 victory over Charlton. (Villa had reached the final the previous year, but Jock only played up to the quarter final). He later worked as a coalman back in Burnley.

Douglas (Doug) Wragg 1961-64

Born: Nottingham 12.9.34
5'8" 10st4
Outside right
FL Apps/Gls 103/15
Total Apps/Gls 128/17
Career: West Ham U. 6.53 [16/-], Mansfield T. 3.60 [46/12], Dale 7.61 £2000 [103/15], Chesterfield 7.64 [17/4], Grantham 1965, Alfreton T. 1966
Honours: England Schools, Division 2 champions 1958, League Cup final 1962

The most expensive of Tony Collins' four major signings in 1961, Doug had had an excellent previous year at Mansfield, scoring 11 goals. Earlier he had been a schoolboy international and signed for West Ham as a teenager, playing a few games either side of their promotion to the top division in 1958. Prematurely balding, he was a popular figure as Dale's regular outside right in his first two seasons, when they reached the League Cup Final and then finished 7th in the league, but was less used in 1963-64 when they slipped down the table. While at Chesterfield the following year, he was injured in the car crash in which his team-mate Ralph Hunt was tragically killed.

James Louis (Lou) Bimpson 1961-63

Born: Rainford 14.5.29
6'1" 12st2
Centre forward
FL Apps/Gls 54/16
Total Apps/Gls 70/21
Career: Burscough, Liverpool 28.1.53 [94/39], Blackburn R. 11.59 £6000 [22/5], Bournemouth & BA 2.61 [11/1], Dale 8.61 [54/16], Wigan A. cs.63, Burscough am cs.65
Honours: FA Cup final 1960, League Cup final 1962, Lancashire Senior Cup winners 1956

Lou was already 23 when he moved from non-league to Division 1 Liverpool. He started 1953-54 in style with a hat-trick in the second game, a 4-4 draw with Manchester United, and four against Burnley, and despite losing his place at centre forward later in the season when the Reds finished bottom, was still joint top scorer with 13. Never a regular, he nevertheless earned a transfer back up to Division 1 with Blackburn, where, despite his height, he mostly figured on the right wing and played there in the 1960 Cup Final, before heading off briefly to Bournemouth and arriving at Spotland only a year after playing at Wembley. The regular No. 9 in his first season when Dale in turn reached a cup final, he bagged 16 goals in all, but was in and out of the side that finished 7th in the league the following term and by 1965 he had gone full circle back to Burscough. He also worked as a fork-lift truck driver.

Colin Whitaker 1961-63

Born: Leeds 14.6.32
5'10" 11st8
Outside left
FL Apps/Gls 54/11
Total Apps/Gls 72/14
Career: Leeds U. jnr, Farsley Celtic, Bradford C. am, Sheffield W. 28.11.51 [1/-], Bradford PA 19.6.53 [49/10], Shrewsbury T. 11.7.56 [152/59], Queens Park R. 15.2.61 [8/-], Dale 19.5.61 [54/11], Oldham A. (part exchange for P. Phoenix) 6.10.62 [72/29], Barrow 7.8.64 [12/-], Ashton U. 6.11.64, Buxton 1965, Heanor T. 8.66, Stalybridge Celtic player-manager 6.67, Droylsden manager, Buxton manager, Droylsden manager, Buxton manager 1977 to 1980, Stalybridge Celtic manager
Cricket for Pudsey St. Lawrence, Castleton Moor, Shropshire
Honours: Division 4 promotion 1959, League Cup final 1962

Colin came up through the ranks in Yorkshire football, managing a reasonable number of games for Park Avenue – scoring on his debut, against Bradford City – and would have won an England under-23 cap in 1954-55 but for being posted to Germany with the RAF during his National Service. He had a highly productive stint with Shrewsbury, being everpresent and scoring 15 times when the Shrews were promoted in 1959, remarkably netting four times from the wing when they beat Southport 6-2. Everpresent again the following term, he netted 19 times as Shrewsbury rose to 3rd in Division 3, as well as setting up many of player-manager Arthur Rowley's 70 goals over the two seasons. He signed for Dale in the summer of 1961 and was the final member of the 11 which set a record by playing unchanged though the first eight games of the season. Indeed he was outside left in every match in the league and in the run to the League Cup Final. He moved to Oldham early the next season, Peter Phoenix moving in the opposite direction, and totalled 20 goals for the two sides during the season. While with Oldham, he again demonstrated his liking for Southport by scoring a hat-trick against them in the Latics amazing 11-0 win. (Altogether in his career, he scored eight hat-tricks). He subsequently had a lengthy spell playing and managing in the non-league game. A part-time sports teacher while with Dale, he was also a cricketer good enough to play in the Minor Counties championship for Shropshire, as well as in the Lancashire leagues. A keen golfer, he later had a job building golf courses and lived in Spain for a time. An odd footnote to his career came when he was about 70 and auctioned off the crutch Matt Busby had used after the Munich disaster, Busby having given it to him when he was having treatment at Old Trafford during his days with Oldham.

Peter Whyke 1961-62

Born: Barnsley 7.9.39 5'5" 9st6
Winger
FL Apps/Gls 5/0 Total Apps/Gls 10/0
Career: Smithies FC, Barnsley am 1957, pro 1.58 [27/1], Dale pt 7.61 [5/-], Scarborough cs.62, Wombwell player-manager

Restricted to the reserves for almost all his season as a part-timer at Spotland, Peter nonetheless made an appearance in a national cup final, when he replaced the injured Doug Wragg at outside right for the second leg of the League Cup Final against Norwich. He had earlier played a number of third division games for his home town club Barnsley, also working there as a bricklayer, as he continued to do for 45 years.

Donald (Don) Watson 1962-64

Born Barnsley 27.8.32
5'8" 11st5
Centre/inside forward
FL Apps/Gls 58/15 Total Apps/Gls 65+1/17
Career: Worsborough Bridge MW, Sheffield W. 9.54 [8/1], Lincoln C. 11.56 £4250 [14/2], Bury 11.57 £2250 [172/65], Barnsley 1.62 £2850 [9/1], Dale 7.62 [58/15], Barrow 7.64 [17/1], Buxton 10.66
Honours: Division 3 champions 1961

The majority of Don's league experience came during four years at Bury, his best campaign undoubtedly being 1960-61. Often used previously at inside right, he played in every game at centre forward and scored 23 league goals in a powerful attack (the five regular forwards netting 99 between them) as the Shakers won the third division title. The following term proved much tougher for the whole side and Don was sold to Barnsley, arriving at Spotland just a few months later. He appeared fairly regularly as Dale finished 7th, their best for some time, playing inside or centre forward or, for a spell, right half. In and out of the side the following term when Dale slipped to 20th, he was released and joined Barrow where he had the unfortunate experience of scoring in the League Cup at Workington but being on the wrong end of a 9-1 scoreline. (His FL debut for Wednesday 10 years earlier had been somewhat similar, as he scored in a 7-2 defeat by Spurs).

John G. (Jack) Martin 1962-64

Born: Dundee 20.8.35
5'9" 10st13
Full back
FL Apps/Gls 24/1 Total Apps/Gls 28+1/1
Career: Dundee St. Stephens, {Dundee NE}, Sheffield W. 2.54 [63/-], Dale 6.62 [24/1], Alfreton T. 1964

Like Don Watson, an ex-Wednesday man, Jack made a reasonable number of appearances in four of his nine seasons at Hillsborough. He didn't have the chance to figure more prominently at Spotland, either, spending two years as the stand-in for the vastly experienced full back pairing of Milburn and Winton.

George Edmund Morton 1962-66

Born: Liverpool 30.9.43 5'8" 11st
Inside forward
FL Apps/Gls 146+1/51
Total Apps/Gls 164+1/57
Career: Everton groundstaff, pro 1.10.60, Dale 7.62 [146+1/51], New Brighton cs.66, Bangor C. cs.67, Witton Albion, Collegiate Old Boys
Honours: Youth Cup final 1961

Having appeared in the 1961 FA Youth Cup Final, George was still only 18 when signed from Everton, then managed by former Rochdale boss Harry Catterick. Making his debut at inside right a month into the 1962-63 season, he scored twice in his second match, a 6-0 trouncing of Barrow and went on to be joint leading scorer with 14 as Dale managed a 7th place finish. Dale struggled the following term, but when they mounted another promotion challenge in 1964-65, George, with 17 in the league, was second highest scorer behind Reg Jenkins, despite missing a couple of months through injury. During Dale's slide down the table the following season he asked for a transfer but the club turned down a bid of £5000 for him from Torquay before perversely giving him a free transfer at the end of the season. Though only 22, and with 50 FL goals to his credit, he only played non-league football thereafter. In 1972 he played against Dale when they lost to Bangor in the cup.

Peter Patrick Phoenix 1962-64

Born: Manchester 31.12.36
5'10" 11st2
Outside left
FL Apps/Gls 36/4 Total Apps/Gls 39/5
Career: Stretford Boys FC, Lostock Gralam, Oldham A. 24.2.56 [161/26], Dale (part exchange for C. Whitaker) 5.10.62 [36/4], Exeter C. 10.10.63 [15/1], Southport 24.1.64 [10/-], Stockport Co. 27.7.64 [19/1], Wigan A. 8.65, Witton Albion 1965-66, Bangor C., Altrincham

Oldham's top scorer in 1958-59, his first full season, when he netted 13 times as a "quick and go-ahead" wingman, Peter was later transformed into a wing half as the Latics recovered from two seasons in the re-election places. He moved to Rochdale in exchange for Colin Whitaker, taking the latter's place on Dale's left wing, during the successful 1962-63 campaign but lost his place to Dave Storf the following season and soon moved to Exeter and then Southport and Stockport in quick succession.

Anthony (Tony) Moulden 1962-63, 1966-67

Born: Farnworth 28.8.42
5'8" 11st1
Inside left
FL Apps/Gls 6/1 Total Apps/Gls 9/1
Career: Smith's XI (Bolton Federation), Blackburn R. am, Bury 5.60 [4/-], Dale 6.62 [5/1], Peterborough U. 14.11.62 £3000 [62/9], Notts Co. 5.65 [23/1], Dale 9.66 [1/-], Buxton 1967

Tony had played a few games for Bury before joining Dale, and after just five games as stand-in for leading scorer Ron Cairns in October 1962 was sold to Peterborough, Tony agreeing to the move as Dale needed the money. He was reasonably successful with the Posh, playing over 60 games in two and a half seasons before moving to Notts County and then back to Spotland for an even briefer stay than his first. His son Paul also came up through Bolton Federation football, in his case to play for Manchester City, and later appear at Spotland, too.

David Alan (Dave) Storf 1963-67

Born: Sheffield 4.12.43
5'9" 11st
Outside left
FL Apps/Gls 138/19 Total Apps/Gls 154/23
Career: Sharrow Road School, Sheffield W. jnr, pro 12.60, Dale 6.63 [138/19], Barrow 7.67 £7500 [154+4/26], Fleetwood cs.72, Stockport Co. trial 1973
Honours: Sheffield Boys, Lancashire Senior Cup final 1970

Signing pro with Wednesday when he was 17, Dave moved to Spotland a couple of years later, immediately becoming first choice on the left wing. Indeed, the only game he missed in his first season was the last one, which Dale won to avoid re-election. Dale had a much better time the following season, finishing 6th, but Dave missed the second half of the campaign with a broken ankle. Restored to the side just after the start of 1965-66, he played regularly, sometimes in the new 'link man' role in a 4-2-4 formation, and despite putting in a transfer request missed only three games the following year, though Dale finished in the bottom four each time. With over 150 games to his credit, he was sold to Barrow, just promoted to Division 3, for their record fee of £7500. Over the next five seasons, until Barrow lost their league status, he again accumulated over 150 senior games, though latterly suffering with a persistent knee injury. After a comeback with Fleetwood, he later worked as a salesman.

David Thomas (Dave) Kerry 1963-64

Born: Derby 6.2.37 5'9" 11st1
Centre forward
FL Apps/Gls 12/4 Total Apps/Gls 15/5
Career: Derby Co. am, Preston N.E. 5.55, Chesterfield 7.61 [55/21], Dale 7.63 [12/4], Kettering T. cs.64, {Belper T.?}
Honours: Derbyshire Schools, England Youth international 1955

Though a youth international, Dave spent six years at Preston without making the first team. Making his mark at Chesterfield, he was top scorer with 16 goals in 29 games in his first season, but after a less successful second term, he was allowed to move on and joined Dale. He played a number of games early in the season, mostly at centre forward, and netted in each of his first four games but figured only once after October, on the right wing.

William David (Dave) Wells 1963-64

Born: Eccleston 16.12.40
Full back
FL Apps/Gls 8/0 Total Apps/Gls 10/0
Career: Blackburn R. jnr, pro 5.62, Dale 7.63 [8/-], Margate 8.64
Honours: Youth Cup winners 1959

A promising junior at Blackburn, Dave played in the FA Youth Cup Final of 1959, Rovers beating a West Ham youth team containing a certain Bobby Moore and Geoff Hurst. However, his only senior appearance for them was in the Lancashire Cup and by the time his Youth Cup opponents became World Cup winners, Dave's FL career was already over, consisting as it did of just eight games in a Dale shirt in October and November 1963, covering at full back when Stan Milburn had to replace Ray Aspden at centre half.

Simon Christopher Jones 1963-67

Born: Nettlesham, Lincs 16.5.45 5'10" 11st
Goalkeeper
FL Apps 47
Total Apps 51+1
Career: Gainsborough Trinity, Dale 6.63 [47], Bangor C. cs.67, Chester 10.67 [3], Stalybridge Celtic

Simon was recommended to Rochdale by namesake and former Dale 'keeper Jimmy Jones (who was then based in Lincolnshire) and made his debut in a Lancashire Cup tie at Chester in November 1963. He also played half a dozen league games near the end of the season, but with the otherwise permanent fixture Ted Burgin in possession of the 'keeper's jersey, it was 1965-66 before he appeared again. Back in the reserves following the signing of Bob Williamson, he played the last 12 games of the next campaign. He later played a few league games for Chester but remained living in Rochdale where he ran a record shop.

Brian Taylor 1961-68

Born: Manchester
29.6.42 6'2" 12st
Half back
FL Apps/Gls 131+1/7
Total Apps/Gls 145+1/8
Career: (Rusholme Sunday League), Dale am, pt 3.62, pro 7.63 [131+1/7], Altrincham cs.68 to cs.74
Honours: Northern Premier League Cup winners 1970, Cheshire Senior Cup final 1970

Brian took some time to break into the Dale first team after joining them from Sunday League football, Dale only deciding to put him on part-time terms when Stalybridge Celtic wanted to sign him. Like Simon Jones, his debut came in the Lancs Cup at Chester and his FL bow came in February 1964, at right half. He made occasional appearances the following season, often at inside forward, becoming a regular only in November 1965 when he took the left half spot from the departed Jimmy Thompson, Dale subsequently turning down a £5000 bid from Doncaster for him. This was the era of the change to a genuine back four defensive system, and as a 6'2" wing half, Brian was a natural to play alongside the centre half, though he could still play as an attacking wing-half, or 'link-man' if required. He missed only a couple of games in the next campaign but was less certain of his place after Bob Stokoe became manager. A stalwart at Altrincham, he appeared in a total of 290 games for Alty in a stay spanning the Cheshire League to the creation of the Northern Premier League from all the foremost non-league sides in the north and midlands.

Donald Alexander (Don) McKenzie 1963-65

Born: Prescott 30.1.42
5'7" 9st4
Winger/inside left
FL Apps/Gls 41/7
Total Apps/Gls 43/7
Career: Everton 1.63, Dale 10.63 [41/7], New Brighton 5.65

Briefly a professional at Goodison Park before signing for Dale, Don played regularly following a scoring debut in December 1963, either on the right wing or at inside left. (Interestingly, for the third season in a row, no further players made debuts in the second half of the campaign). In the final game of the season, he scored in the first minute against champions Gillingham, who had the best defence in the division, to set up the win which enabled Dale to avoid the bottom four. He also played regularly in place of Dave Storf on the left wing in the second half of the following campaign when Dale came close to promotion, but wasn't retained.

Roy Ridge 1964-66

Born: Wortley, Sheffield
21.10.34 5'8" 12st6
Right back
FL Apps/Gls 85/0
Total Apps/Gls 97/0
Career: Ecclesfield, Sheffield U. 11.51 [11/-], Dale 10.8.64 [85/-], Worksop T. 7.66

Signed as a 17 year old by Sheffield United, Roy spent nearly 13 years with them, yet, in an era when the top clubs could retain complete professional reserve and 'A' teams in case they needed a stand-in, he appeared just 11 times in the league team, 9 of those appearances coming in 1953-54. Roy's particular misfortune was to be in the queue for a full back spot behind Cec Coldwell and Graham Shaw, each of whom made more than 400 FL appearances for the Blades. In contrast he was an automatic choice at Spotland, usually at right back though sometimes on the opposite flank, as they made a strong promotion challenge in 1964-65 but then surprisingly fell away the following term. Away from the game he was a steelworker in Sheffield.

Laurence John (Laurie) Calloway 1964-68

Born: Birmingham
19.6.45
5'10" 12st
Left back
FL Apps/Gls 161+1/4
Total Apps/Gls 184+1/6
Career: Queen's Colts YC, West Bromwich A. jnr, Wolverhampton W. app 1961, pro 10.62, Dale 9.7.64 [161+1/4], Blackburn R. 3.68 £5500 [17+7/1], Southport 8.70 (exchange for A. Russell) [45/7], York C. 6.71 £6000, [54+1/3], Shrewsbury T. 12.72 [77+5/3], San Jose Earthquakes 4.74 to 1977 [75/3

NASL], South California Lazers coach 1978 , San Jose Earthquakes player-coach 1979 [4/- NASL], California Surf coach 1981, Seattle Sounders coach 1983, San Jose Earthquakes coach 1984 to 1988, Salt Lake Sting coach 1990, San Francisco Bay Blackhawks coach 1991 and 1992, San Jose Clash coach 1996 and 1997, US Brazilian Youth Soccer Association 1998, Des Moines Menace coach 2001 and 2002, Syracuse Salty Dogs coach 2003 and 2004, Rochester Raging Rhinos coach 2005 to 2007, Rochester Futbol Club program coach 2008, McQuaid soccer program technical director 2009
Honours: Staffordshire Schools, Youth Cup final 1962. As coach; Western Soccer Alliance champions 1985, APSL champions 1991, US 4th Division coach of the year 2002

Laurie had a lengthy playing career and has since had an even more impressive catalogue of appointments as a coach and administrator in the USA. He played outside left for Wolves in the Youth Cup Final of 1962, but did not make his FL debut until playing for Dale, at left back, on the opening day of 1964-65. Missing only one game as Dale finished 6th, he continued through the following three depressing campaigns as a hard-tackling full back who fell foul of referees on occasion, before being sold to second division Blackburn. After four seasons back in the lower leagues, captaining Southport from midfield, he left Shrewsbury as they headed for relegation along with the Dale in 1974, Laurie instead heading for the North American Soccer League. A key man for San Jose Earthquakes – winning an 'All Star Honourable Mention' in his first season - he played against the likes of George Best and was in the Earthquakes side which beat New York Cosmos, Pele and all, in 1976. Moving into coaching, he was with a string of clubs in the various American soccer leagues over the next 30 years, winning several titles, before becoming technical advisor on youth soccer programs and Executive Vice President of the US Brazilian youth Soccer Association.

James Graham Cunliffe 1964-65

Born: Hindley 16.6.36
5'9" 10st7
Right half
FL Apps/Gls 36/0
Total Apps/Gls 41/0
Career: Bolton W. 1.55 [25/-], Dale 1.7.64 [36/-], retired 5.65

Another player who spent many years in the reserves at a top side, Graham was with Bolton for 10 seasons but managed only 25 FL games, having significant runs in the side at left half only in 1959-60 and 1960-61. He beat that tally in one excellent season as Dale's regular right half but then retired to run his newsagents business in Wigan.

John Turley 1964-65

Born: Bebbington 26.1.39 5'10" 11st7
Centre forward
FL Apps/Gls 22/5
Total Apps/Gls 26/7
Career: Ellesmere Port, Sheffield U. 5.56 [5/3], Peterborough U. 6.61 [32/14], Dale 26.5.64 [22/5], Cambridge U. 5.65

John was yet another ex-Sheffield United reserve to arrive at Spotland in the early sixties, having scored in each of his first three games for the Blades when he was 18, but only appearing twice more. He again scored three in three games for Peterborough as stand-in for centre forward Terry Bly in 1961-62 but despite a decent scoring rate over the next two years never became a regular. He started 1964-65 as Dale's first choice at No. 9, but despite Dale's excellent season found goals hard to come by and was replaced by new signing Bert Lister later in the campaign.

Reginald (Reg) Jenkins 1964-73

Born: Millbrook, Cornwall 7.10.38
5'10" 13st7
Inside left
FL Apps/Gls 294+11/119
Total Apps/Gls 346+13/141
Career: Millbrook, Truro C., Plymouth A. 10.57 [16/3], Exeter C. 12.60 [19/6], Torquay U. 7.61 [88/23], Dale 27.6.64 £2250 [294+11/119], Millbrook player-manager 1973, later manager, Bodmin T. manager 7.80, Millbrook manager until 1993, Plymouth Civil Service manager
Honours: Division 3 champions 1959, Division 4 promotion 1969, Lancashire Cup winners 1971

Quite simply Rochdale's greatest ever player according to various polls (and anyone of the generation of Dale fans who saw him play!), the burly Cornishman set a goal scoring record for

Rochdale that shows no sign of ever being beaten. Starting his FL career in Plymouth, his first goal came in March 1959 when he beat an up and coming Chesterfield goalkeeper by the name of Gordon Banks, and Reg became one of the few players to figure for all three Devon clubs. He had three useful seasons at Torquay as a deep lying inside forward before a proposed transfer to Bristol Rovers prompted Dale boss Tony Collins to make a counter offer of £2250 and Reg headed for Rochdale instead, getting 10% of the transfer fee and the offer of a club house in Passmonds. Possessor of a thunderous shot often compared to Bobby Charlton's, he immediately repaid the fee, scoring 25 times, a post-war record, as Dale gathered their best ever 4th division points tally, but just missed out on promotion. He soldiered on though the following depressing seasons as Dale slumped into the re-election places, scoring 20 times in all games, including a FA Cup hat-trick against Fleetwood, in 1965-66, but missing the first part of the following season through injury. In 1967-68 he spent nearly half the season at centre half as Dale just scraped clear of a third consecutive bottom four finish. However, after a slow start to the next term he was returned to his favourite No. 10 shirt and scored both goals in a victory at Workington on Boxing Day. He added a hat-trick the following week as Dale began the run that took them to promotion, with Reg fittingly scoring twice in the final day victory over Southend. Up in Division 3, Reg netted 20 goals in the league and 24 in total and despite various injuries he was top scorer with 19 in all games - and helped Dale lift the Lancashire Cup - in 1970-71. He top scored again in his final season, albeit with just 8 league goals, taking his tally past that of Bert Whitehurst and up to 119 in the league and 141 in all games. His 305 FL appearances also set a new club record, though unlike his goals record, that was soon beaten by long time team-mate Graham Smith. When given a free transfer, while Dale were between managers, Reg was offered the job as Jimmy Frizzell's assistant at Oldham, but instead he headed back to Cornwall, taking over as player-manager of his local club Millbrook and steering them to the relative heights of the South Western League. Working as a shipwright in Plymouth docks until 1990, Reg later had a hip replacement but was accorded a hero's welcome whenever he returned for various club events and was on hand to celebrate with the next Dale side to gain promotion in 2010. After he passed away on holiday in Tenerife in January 2013, the Dale faithfull held a minute's applause in his memory at the next home game, and 'Sir Reg' must be one of few players with careers spent entirely in the lower divisions to have their obituary published in the Independent. Millbrook FC subsequently renamed their ground Jenkins Park in his honour.

Brian Birch 1964-66

Born: Southport 9.4.38
5'8" 10st5
Outside right/right half
FL Apps/Gls 60+1/6
Total Apps/Gls 70+1/16
Career: Bolton W. jnr 1953, pro 4.55 [165/23], Dale 7.64 [60+1/6], Bangor C. 1966
Honours: England Youth international, FA XI v RAF 1957, 1958, FA Cup winners 1958

The second player of the same name to turn out for Rochdale in four years, Brian had had a long and quite productive career in the top flight with Bolton. An England youth international, he made his Bolton debut at outside right aged just 16 years and 5 months and was a regular when he was 19, figuring in the Bolton side that beat a post-Munich Manchester United in the Cup Final. He had three further seasons as a first choice and was in the Bolton side for the first FL game to be televised live in 1960. Released after Bolton were relegated in 1964, he initially found it hard to break into the Dale side battling for promotion and played a few games on the left wing, at inside forward and even right half as well as his normal outside right position. The following season, as Dale tried to adapt to a 4-2-4 system, he frequently operated as one of the 'link-men', wearing the No. 4 shirt. He had a business in Rochdale after retiring and his grandson Will Johnson also became a footballer, playing in the USA for Real Salt Lake.

Herbert Francis (Bert) Lister 1964-67

Born: Manchester 4.10.39 5'9" 10st9
Centre forward
FL Apps/Gls 56/16
Total Apps/Gls 65/20
Career: Manchester C. am 25.12.54, pro 16.11.57 [2/-], Oldham A. 1.10.60 (£10,000 for two players) [135/81], Dale 29.1.65 £2250 [56/16], Stockport Co. 5.1.67 [16/11], Altrincham 12.67 to 1969
Honours: Manchester Schoolboys, Division 4 promotion 1963, champions 1967

Signed as a pro by Manchester City when he was 18, Bert really flourished after joining Oldham three years later along with Ken Branagan for a joint fee of £10,000, scoring 14 times in his first half season. In 1961-62 he had a hat-trick expunged from the records when Accrington resigned from the league, but he netted 32 times as Oldham won promotion the following year, including a sensational double hat-trick in the 11-0 demolition of Southport and a goal after just 10 seconds against Chesterfield. In January 1965, with 95 goals for the Latics to his credit, Bert was signed up to join Reg Jenkins and George Morton to boost Dale's promotion challenge. Unfortunately, though the two inside forwards continued to prosper with Bert leading the attack, his own goal tally was just three in 16 games as Dale finished three points short of the promotion places. He was also sent off, still then a fairly rare occurrence, for fighting with the Brighton centre half. He totalled 15 in all games the following year, though, and half way through 1966-67 was transferred to Stockport, this time succeeding in firing his new club to promotion with 11 goals in 16 games. He didn't figure the following year though and dropped out of league football when still only 28, having scored 108 FL goals. He was later a taxi driver in Blackpool.

Brian Hardman 1963-67
Born: {Preston 1945?}
Outside left
FL Apps/Gls +0/0 Total Apps/Gls 2/0
Career: Dale am 1963 to 1967
Honours: Lancashire FA v Cumberland FA 1963-64, v East Riding FA 1966-67, Lancashire League Supplementary Cup winners 1966

Brian was on Dale's books as an amateur for several years and twice appeared for Lancashire in amateur representative games, captaining them in 1967. His two first team appearances for the Dale were in the Lancashire Cup in 1964-65, on the left wing, and 1966-67 at left half. He was also selected as substitute for the league side but without getting on. For the reserves, he scored in the 2-0 victory over Everton 'A' to gain the Lancashire League Supplementary Cup.

Neville Bannister 1965-66
Born: Briersfield 21.7.37
5'5" 10st2
Winger
FL Apps/Gls 18+1/2
Total Apps/Gls 22+1/2
Career: Bolton W. jnr, pro 7.54 [26/4], Lincoln C. 3.61 £4000 [68/16], Hartlepools U. 8.64 [41/8], Dale 1.7.65 to 5.66 [18+1/2]
Honours: Charity Shield 1958

Following former Burnden Park colleagues Brian Birch and Graham Cunliffe to Rochdale, Neville had had a couple of seasons as Birch's understudy on the right wing, playing in the 1958 Charity Shield game in his absence. He was a regular at Lincoln in 1961-62, but despite netting a hat-trick against Torquay was relatively little used as the Imps completed a dramatic slide from Division 2 to the re-election places in Division 4 in successive seasons. After a productive year at Hartlepools he joined Dale, where he played a number of games on each wing, though his main claim to fame was as their first substitute to be used, against Torquay in September 1965.

George Robert (Bob) Stephenson 1965-67
Born: Derby 19.11.42
5'8" 11st
Forward
FL Apps/Gls 50+1/16
Total Apps/Gls 57+1/18
Career: Derwent Sports, Derby Co. jnrs, pro 9.60 [11/1], Shrewsbury 6.64 [3/-], Dale 21.7.65 [50+2/16], Lockheed Leamington 7.67, Worcester C. 10.67, Buxton 8.68, retired cs.69
Cricket for Castleton Moor, Derbyshire 1967 and 1968 (9 games), Hampshire 1969 to 1980 (263 games)

The son of George, the pre-war Aston Villa, Derby and England inside forward, Bob started out with the Rams but had only a few FL games to his credit when he signed for Dale in 1965. A frequent performer in his first term, mainly at inside forward but also playing on the wing, he was joint top scorer in the league with 13, scoring twice in each of three late seasons wins, though Dale still finished 21st. Freed a year later he had a couple of seasons in non-league football but mainly concentrated on his cricket. Having figured with Castleton Moor while with the Dale, he had a couple of years at Derbyshire but really made his mark as Hampshire's wicket keeper, making over 650 dismissals over his career and figuring alongside the likes of Malcolm Marshal and Barry Richards. Hampshire won the county championship in 1973 and Bob later captained them for a couple of years. After retiring he became a sports teacher and coached another future Hampshire captain, Jimmy Adams. As well as his father, two uncles were prominent footballers, Clem playing for Villa, Huddersfield (winning three league championships) and England and Jim for Villa and Watford.

James Barrie Ratcliffe 1965-66

Born: Blackburn 21.9.41 5'7" 10st8
Winger
FL Apps/Gls 12/1
Total Apps/Gls 19/2
Career: Bolton W. jnr, Blackburn R. 9.58 [36/4], Scunthorpe U. 5.64 [26/7], Dale 1.7.65 to 5.66 [12/1]
Honours: Youth Cup winners 1959, Lancashire Senior Cup final 1961, Anglo-French Friendship Cup winners 1961-62

A member of Blackburn's Youth Cup winning side of 1959 (along with other future Dale men Dave Wells and Vinny Leech), Barrie also figured for a reserve Rovers side in the Lancashire Cup Final a couple of years later. He played quite regularly on either wing in 1961-62, appearing in the League Cup semi-final against the Dale, but in 1964 moved to Scunthorpe (missing another Lancashire Cup Final appearance as the game had been delayed until the start of the new season). He arrived at Spotland a year later and, like Neville Bannister, played a number of games on either wing, though apart from a Lancs Cup tie didn't appear again after the cup defeat by Altrincham.

George Edgar Smollet Sievwright 1965-66

Born: Broughty Ferry 10.9.37 5'9" 11st4
Wing half/right back
FL Apps/Gls 31+1/1
Total Apps/Gls 39+2/2
Career: Broughty Ferry Ath., Dundee U. 1957 [8/- ScL], Oldham A. 25.6.63 £500 [37/4], Tranmere R. 16.6.64, Dale 22.7.65 [31+1/1], Macclesfield 8.66, Mossley player-manager 11.72 to 1.74, Stalybridge Celtic manager, Emley coach
Honours: FA Trophy winners 1970, Northern Premier League champions 1969, 1970

A "dour, craggy Scot", George made a number of top flight appearances north of the border before a season at Oldham where he made his mark as a hard as nails wing half. Not used at all by Tranmere, he had a year at Spotland, figuring in the new defensive role alongside the centre half, as well as a more traditional wing half, and at right back. He had a very successful spell at Macclesfield, appearing in a total of 270 games, twice winning the new Northern Premier League and collecting the FA Challenge Trophy at Wembley. Less successful as a manager, he then worked for a lighting company.

Ian David McQueen 1965-67
Born: Manchester 4.2.46
Centre forward
FL Apps/Gls 14+2/4 Total Apps/Gls 16+2/4
Career: Dale am 1965, pro 1.66 [13+2/4], Hyde U. 1967

Ian was promoted to the professional ranks just after making his FL debut at centre forward in a 6-2 defeat at Tranmere in December 1965 and then grabbing his first goal in a 6-0 victory over Wrexham. He never managed a substantial run in the side, though, and had odd games in other forward positions before being released. Sadly, he died at the early age of 39.

John Heath 1965-66

Born: Heywood 5.6.36 6'0" 11st
Goalkeeper
FL Apps 6 Total Apps 8
Career: Blackburn R. am, Bury am, pro 9.56 [8], Tranmere R. 1.62 [58], Wigan A. 7.64, Dale 1.66 [6], Buxton 6.66, Chester 1966-67, Mossley 1966-67

John had been reserve 'keeper at Bury for several seasons, leaving when Chris Harker (q.v.) was signed. He had more employment at Tranmere, sharing the jersey with Harry Leyland, but had been out of the FL for a while when signed as cover for Simon Jones following the retirement of Ted Burgin early in 1966. He made his bow in a Lancs Cup success against Chester and played in the next six league games, from which Dale gathered just one point.

Kevin Holland Connor 1963-67

Born: Radcliffe 12.1.45
Right back
FL Apps/Gls 21+2/1
Total Apps/Gls 25+2/1
Career: Dale am 1963, pro 1.66 [21+2/1], Warley 1967
Honours: Lancashire County FA v Cumberland 1963

Kevin played for Lancashire County while an amateur in Dale's reserves, eventually tuning pro at the same time as Ian McQueen. He made his debut at right back in a Lancashire Cup tie in February 1966 when Roy Ridge was injured and kept his place for the next couple of league games. He also had a decent run in the team the following year when new right back Graham Smith was switched to centre half, and managed his one career goal when getting a game on the right wing.

Brian Handley 1965-66
Born: Barnsley 21.6.36   6'1" 12st
Centre forward
FL Apps/Gls 3/0 Total Apps/Gls 3/0
Career: Wakefield T., Goole T., Aston Villa 9.57 [3/-], Torquay U. 9.60 [80/33], Bridgwater T. 1964-65, Dale loan 2.66 to 3.66 [3/-]

Brian had brief top flight experience with Villa but had played, and scored, regularly for Torquay, where he was a clubmate of Reg Jenkins. His best campaign there was undoubtedly 1962-63 when he hit 20 goals in 40 league games, plus 4 more in cup ties, as the Gulls missed promotion by a single point. However he was playing for Bridgwater Town when borrowed by Dale in 1966. Unfortunately Dale were in the middle of a run of eight league games without a win and Brian was unable to do enough to earn a longer engagement.

Paul Crossley 1965-67

Born: Rochdale 14.7.48 5'8" 11st6
Outside right
FL Apps/Gls 17/2
Total Apps/Gls 19/2
Career: Heybrook School, St. Clements, Dale 9.65 [17/2], Preston NE 11.66 £8000 [3/-], Southport loan 9.68 [10/2], Tranmere R. 6.69 [186+17/37], Seattle Sounders summer 1975 [21/4 NASL], Chester 9.75 [93+6/26], Seattle Sounders 1977 to 1979 [58/12 NASL], Baltimore Blast 1980 to 1982 (indoor soccer), Baltimore Sports Complex manager 1987, Loyola University (Chicago) assistant coach, Shoreline Community College coach 1991, Lynwood High School coach 1994-95 (d. 1996)
Honours: Rochdale Schools 1962: as coach; NWAACC North coach of the year 1993

Appearing for Rochdale Schools when he was 14, Paul made his FL bow for the Dale at 17, playing in the final three games of 1965-66 as Dale failed to escape the bottom four. First choice on the right wing the following season, after only two months he was sold to second division Preston for a sizeable fee. Though never breaking through with North End, he went on to a lengthy career in the lower divisions with Tranmere, where he played over 200 games, and Chester, also demonstrating a decent strike rate for a winger, with more than 60 league goals. He had his first taste of soccer in the USA in 1975 and subsequently emigrated permanently, playing in the NASL and then in major league indoor soccer. He ran the sports complex in Baltimore and coached college soccer at various levels until dying suddenly in Washington at the age of only 48. His son Brad played for US Schools.

Robert (Bob) Williamson 1966-68

Born: Edinburgh 6.12.33 6'0" 12st
Goalkeeper
FL Apps 36 Total Apps 39
Career: Rosewell Rosedale, Stenhousemuir trial 1954-55 [1 ScL], Arbroath 1954-55 [188 ScL], St. Mirren 1960-61 [43], Barnsley 8.63 [46], Leeds U. 6.65, Dale 7.66 [36], Chorley 1968
Honours: Scottish Division 2 promotion 1959

Bob had a successful time in the lower divisions in Scotland in the late fifties, helping Arbroath reach the top flight in 1959 and then moving on to St. Mirren. First arriving in the FL with Barnsley, despite them finishing bottom of Division 3 he was signed by Division 1 runners up Leeds in 1965 as back up to Gary Sprake and namesake Brian Williamson. He spent one season as the regular 'keeper at Rochdale but was subsequently reserve to Les Green.

Graham Leslie Smith 1966-74

Born: Pudsey 20.6.46
5'9" 10st7
Right back
FL Apps/Gls 316+1/3
Total Apps/Gls 371+2/6
Career: Leeds U. jnr, pro 2.64, Dale 31.5.66 [316+1/3], Stockport Co. 7.74 [147+4/2], Buxton 7.79, Ashton U. player-coach cs.80, Thackley coach 1982-83, assistant manager 1985-86, Southampton scout
Honours: Division 4 promotion 1969, Lancashire Cup winners 1971

Graham had been a junior with Leeds and turned pro the year they won promotion to Division 1. He joined Dale two years later and though starting out at right back spent much of his first two seasons with the club, as Dale battled to avoid the re-election places, at centre half, missing only four games over the two campaigns. Losing his place at the start of 1968-69, he deputised in several positions before replacing Vince Ratcliffe at right back just as Dale started their run to promotion from Boxing Day onwards. He was everpresent in Dale's first season back in Division 3, forming a terrific full back partnership with Derek Ryder, and the following season played in Dale's Lancashire Cup Final victory over Oldham and in the famous FA Cup defeat of Coventry, as well as netting a rare goal in the League Cup against another first division side, Crystal Palace. Virtually everpresent again between 1971 and 1973, he was the only member of the promotion team to have the misfortune to still be around for the catastrophic season which saw then plunge back to Division 4 with only two wins to their name. However, during the season Graham did surpass the record of his long time teammate Reg Jenkins and took his appearance tally to 317 in the FL and 373 in all games (just surpassing the record of his namesake from pre-FL days, Albert Smith), before joining Stockport. Still only 28 when he left the Dale, he added another 150 FL games while at Edgeley Park before moving into coaching at non-league level. He later ran his own plumbing business back in Yorkshire and worked as a scout for Southampton.

Brian William Richardson   1966-67

Born: Sheffield 5.10.34
5'9" 11st9
Half back
FL Apps/Gls 19/1 Total Apps/Gls 21/1
Career: Wincobank School, Sheffield U. 12.54 [291/9], Swindon T. 1.66 £4000 [11/-], Dale 7.66 to cs.67 [19/1]
Honours: Sheffield Boys, Sheffield v Glasgow 1958

A stalwart at Sheffield United for over a decade, Brian accumulated around 300 senior appearances for the Blades. Indeed, he missed just two games between 1960 and 1964, playing on the right of an almost unchanging half back line alongside Joe Shaw and Gerry Summers. After being sold to Swindon in 1966 he quickly moved on again to Spotland. He played in all the games until November playing at centre half as well as in both roles now being taken by the old time wing halves, either in the back four or in midfield. However after being carried off against Bradford City he made only two further appearances and retired at the end of the season.

Graham Frank Collins   1965-67
Born: Bury 5.2.47
Left half
FL Apps/Gls 7/0 Total Apps/Gls 8/0
Career: Dale jnr, pro 2.9.65 [7/-], Witton Albion 1967

A regular in Dale's reserves for a couple of seasons as a teenager, Graham played a few league games as a defensive wing half early in 1966-67 when Brian Taylor moved to centre half to cover for the injured Ray Aspden.

William (Billy) Russell   1966-68

Born: Hounslow 7.7.35
5'8" 10st
Forward/midfield
FL Apps/Gls 60+1/8
Total Apps/Gls 69+1/9
Career: Rhyl, Sheffield U. am 8.57, pro 11.57 [145/55], Bolton W. 3.63 £10,000 [22/2], Dale pt 7.66 [60+1/8], Scarborough 1968
Honours: England Amateur international v Finland, Wales 1957

Yet another of the string of former Sheffield United players to turn up at Spotland in the mid-sixties, Billy first came to notice in 1957, after leaving university, when Rhyl knocked Notts County out of the FA Cup. Also a school teacher, he made his Sheffield United debut while still an amateur, scoring three times in his first two outings at inside forward, and then appeared twice for the England amateur team, scoring twice each time. Turning pro, he ended his first season with 14 goals and surpassed that in 1960-61 when he missed only one game and bagged 18 league goals, half of them while playing on the right wing, and netted another 7, including a hat-trick against Newcastle, during the Blades run to the FA Cup semi-finals. A big money move to Bolton was unproductive, though, as all bar eight of his appearances came in the first few weeks of his three year stay. Joining Dale as a part-timer, he played both as an old style inside (or even centre) forward and in the new midfield positions, as well as figuring on the wings, so that in all he wore seven different shirt numbers during his two seasons in the side.

Barry Wheatley 1966-67

Born: Sandbach 21.2.38
5'10" 11st7
Inside left
FL Apps/Gls 13/4 Total Apps/Gls 17/4
Career: Liverpool 3.56, Crewe A. 9.57 [242/49], Dale 7.66 [13/4], Witton Albion 6.67

Barry was another experienced new signing for Dale in 1966 having spent nine years, six of them as a regular choice, at Crewe. Though basically an inside forward, later in his career he also turned out quite often on the flanks. Having partnered many former and future Dale players from Eddie Moran to Peter Gowans, while at Gresty Road, Barry himself really only figured in the Dale side until the October of his single season. Despite scoring in three of his first four games he was left out when they picked up only two points from a run of six games.

James (Jim) Pennington 1966-67

Born: Golborne 26.4.39 5'6" 10st11
Winger/midfield
FL Apps/Gls 14/0 Total Apps/Gls 15+1/0
Career: Manchester C. am 6.12.55, pro 21.8.56 [1/-], Crewe A. 11.3.61 [34/2], Grimsby T. 6.4.63 £2000 [89/8], Oldham A. 7.7.65 [23/-], Dale 2.7.66 [14/-], Northwich Victoria cs.67

Jim played one first division game for City before moving to Crewe where he played alongside Barry Wheatley. However he had a much shorter stay than Wheatley, being sold to Grimsby where he became the regular outside right for a couple of seasons, noted for his speed off the mark. In and out of the side at Oldham, his initial games for the Dale were in midfield before reverting to the wing.

William Carson (Bill) Calder 1966-67

Born: Greenock 28.9.34
5'9" 12st5
Forward
FL Apps/Gls 7+1/1 Total Apps/Gls 8+1/1
Career: Port Glasgow Ath., Leicester C. 8.55 [3/-], Bury 5.59 [174/67], Oxford U. 11.63 [66+1/28], Dale 11.66 [7+1/1], Macclesfield T. 1967, Nantwich T. cs.68, Chorley, Nantwich T. player-manager to cs.71, manager to 12.72

Honours: Division 3 champions 1961, Division 4 promotion 1965

A Scottish forward brought south by Leicester, Bill really made his mark during a stint at Bury. Originally usually a right winger, he was everpresent and scored a remarkable 21 goals in 1960-61, including a hat-trick in a 6-0 defeat of Torquay, when the Shakers ran away with the Division 3 title. He almost matched that two years later, when he hit 18, by now from the centre forward position, as Bury came within 5 points of promotion to the first division. He continued to score regularly for FL newboys Oxford, netting for them in their giant-killing victory over Blackburn in 1964 when they reached the FA Cup quarter-finals despite finishing 18th in Division 4. He hit an opening day hat-trick the following term as Oxford went on to gain promotion and scored four in the Cup against Walsall but played relatively little thereafter. He scored the winner against Hartlepools on his Dale debut, but his other six starts, in various forward positions, brought just a single point. He later went into non-league management and worked for a building company.

Roger {H.} Cutler 1966-67

Born: {Heywood AMJ.44}
Goalkeeper
FL Apps 0 Total Apps 1
Career: Dale am 1966-67, Mossley 1966-67, Prestwich Heys
Honours: Lancashire County FA

Roger was Dale's amateur third team 'keeper and one of seven players to be given their senior debuts in the Lancashire Cup tie against Bury in December 1966. While several of his teammates went on to greater things, it proved to be his only appearance at that level, though he did later represent the Lancashire FA and played in the Cheshire league for Mossley.

Stephen Thomas (Steve) Melledew

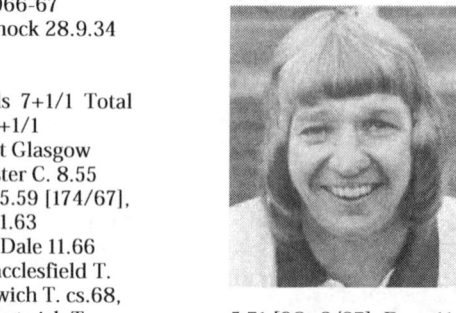

1964-70, 1976-78
Born: Rochdale 28.11.45
5'10" 11st7
Midfield/striker
FL Apps/Gls 164+11/35 Total Apps/Gls 185+12/40
Career: Whipp & Bourne, Dale am 1964, pro 5.12.66 [88+9/23], Everton 12.9.69 £15,000, Aldershot 5.71 [90+2/27], Bury 11.73 [14+6/2], Crewe A. 10.74 [49+7/2], Boston Minutemen loan summer 1975 [23/7 NASL], Dale 7.76 [76+2/12], Kiffen

(Finland) 4.78, Hillingdon Borough 8.78, Leatherhead, Kiffen (Finland), Wallingford T. player-coach 1982-83, Marlow manager 1984, Wallingford T. manager 1986-87, Enfield assistant manager 1989, Chertsey manager 1993, Thatcham T., Newbury T., Reading assistant youth coach, chief development officer c.1999
Honours: Division 4 promotion 1969, 1973, 1974, FA XI 1979

Dale's top local discovery of his era, Steve was playing for factory team Whipp & Bourne and completing his engineering apprenticeship when spotted by Dale. Signing on pro terms in December 1966 he made his senior debut with a string of his reserve team colleagues in the Lancashire Cup defeat by Bury. Making his FL bow three weeks later, his whole hearted style earned him the nickname 'Wild Bull' and he became a fixture in the side, playing in midfield for the rest of the season. Appearing regularly in 1967-68 he had a spell at right back during which he netted three goals, finishing as joint second highest scorer and being played up front. At the start of 1968-69 he had probably the most remarkable scoring streak of any Dale player – Dale drew 1-1 five times in succession and Steve scored the goal every time. He also netted in the 6-0 victories over both Bradford clubs and ended the promotion season again tied for second place in the goal scoring charts with Reg Jenkins, netting the opener in the final day victory over Southend. At the start of the following campaign Steve starred in a friendly victory over a full strength Everton side and a few weeks later Everton signed him for £15,000, easily a new club record. Unlucky to be injured the week he was to have been included as sub, he never played in the first team at Goodison Park but had a successful spell at Aldershot, being everpresent and scoring 18 goals in 1972-73 when they were promoted, also going up with Bury the following year. He played with Eusebio and against Pele while with Boston in the NASL and further travel saw him arrive back at Spotland as skipper under Brian Green in 1976. Despite a bright start Dale were in decline and by the time Steve left two years later they were rooted to the foot of the league. Steve had expected to be offered the manager's job when Green left, but chairman Fred Ratcliffe apparently had a last minute change of mind and gave the job to Mike Ferguson instead. Steve subsequently had a lengthy coaching career in non-league football around the southern area, coincidentally acting as assistant to Ferguson at Enfield. He also worked for Reading's youth development staff as well as running a transport company and a sports coaching business.

Raymond (Ray) Daubney 1966-68
Born: Oldham 7.12.46
5'8" 11st
Outside right
FL Apps/Gls 12/2 Total Apps/Gls 14+1/2
Career: Dale 12.66 [13/2], Stalybridge Celtic 1968

Ray was another Lancashire Cup debutant in December 1966, the day before his 20th birthday, and a couple of weeks later he made his first FL start when preferred to the much more experienced Pennington and Calder on the right wing (Paul Crossley having been sold the previous month). Despite a decent initial run in the side, when the Dale won four games out of six, he was subsequently returned to the reserves and played only once the following season.

Hughen William (Hughie) Riley 1966-72
Born: Accrington 12.6.47
5'9" 10st8
Midfield/winger
FL Apps/Gls 81+11/12 Total Apps/Gls 100+13/13
Career: Dale 29.11.66 [81+11/12], Crewe A. 16.12.71 [116+5/9], Bury 12.74 [47+4/4], Bournemouth 4.76 [69+3/7], Dorchester T., Weymouth
Honours: Division 4 promotion 1969

After writing to request a trial at Spotland, Hughie also made his debut in the Lancs Cup at Bury in December 1966 but had to wait until the first game of the following season to make his league debut as a left winger, following the departure of Dave Storf. He managed 20 games that term, some of them on the other flank, but during Dale's promotion season played just once, in the temporary absence of Norman Whitehead. Retained nonetheless, Hughie became an important member of the squad, taking Vinny Leech's place in midfield when Leech was injured. In January 1971 he became the first non-forward to net a hat-trick for Dale and he missed only four games that season. A terrier of a midfielder, nicknamed 'Tiger', he ran into trouble with increasingly strict referees and a long suspension at the start of 1972-73 cost him his place in the side and led to him moving to Crewe. A regular for three years he made well over 100 appearances before shorter spells at Bury, where he again played alongside Billy Rudd, and then Bournemouth. Remaining living in Dorset he played non-league football before becoming a licensee and running a hotel.

Joseph Michael (Joe) Fletcher 1966-69

Born: Manchester 25.9.46
5'10" 11st
Forward
FL Apps/Gls 55+2/21
Total Apps/Gls 66+2/22
Career: Manchester C. am, Dale am 1966, pro 31.12.66 [55+2/21], Grimsby T. 7.69 [11/1], Barrow 10.69 [7+1/1], Chorley 1970, Wigan A., Hakoah (Australia), Mossley 1975-76, Macclesfield T. £250 cs.78, player-coach 1979-80

Another reserve handed a chance in the Lancs Cup, Joe made his FL debut in April 1967, playing centre forward. He managed four goals in nine games in a struggling side and the following season became a regular. Playing up front or on the right wing, he was easily top scorer with 15 league goals as Dale just avoided a third consecutive re-election application. He played a few games at the start of 1968-69 but with the promotion winning front line now in place, he did not appear at all in the second half of the season and was one of only three squad members not retained. Short stays with other league clubs were fairly unproductive, but Joe had a long career in senior non-league football, particularly with Mossley for whom he scored 20 goals in 105 NPL games, and he also spent some time in Australia.

Francis Kevin (Frank) McEwan 1966-68
Born: Dublin 15.2.48 5'7" 10st8
Midfield/forward
Total Apps/Gls 17/2 Total Apps/Gls 20/2
Career: Manchester U. app, pro 5.65, Dale 12.66 [17/2], Drogheda 1968
Honours: League of Ireland, Republic of Ireland under-23s

Frank came over from Dublin to sign as an apprentice at Old Trafford and played in the same youth team as George Best, once scoring four goals (to Best's three) when United beat Barrow 14-1 in the Youth Cup. He did not make the first team, though, and joined Dale, going straight into the side, when he was 18. However, with Dale struggling in the league he was not able to make much impression, either at inside right where he initially played or later on the right wing. He returned to Ireland after just over a year subsequently playing representative football for both the Irish under-23s and the League of Ireland.

David J. Dow 1965-68
Born: Manchester 10.6.47
Central defender
FL Apps/Gls 8/0 Total Apps/Gls 10+1/0
Career: Avorton FC, Dale am 2.66 [7/-], Ellesmere Port 1968

The final debutant in the Lancs Cup tie with Bury – he came on as substitute for Hughie Riley – David had to wait until the end of March for his first league game. With Stewart Holden injured, a reshuffle gave him his chance at centre half but the game ended in a 5-0 defeat by Port Vale. His next game, the following season turned out even worse, when Dale lost 7-0 in the Lancashire Cup to Manchester United, but he did play seven further league games in the back four later that term.

James Stewart Holden 1966-67
Born: Grange Moor 21.4.42 5'8" 11st12
Midfield/right back
FL Apps/Gls 21/0 Total Apps/Gls 21/0
Career: Huddersfield T. jnr, pro 23.4.59 [28/2], Oldham A. 22.7.65 [39+3/6], Dale 14.1.67 [21/-], Wigan A. cs 67, Hyde U. 12.67, Stalybridge Celtic 8.68
Cricket for Heyside

Originally a wing half, Stewart managed a few second division games for Huddersfield before moving to Oldham where he played at inside forward and at left back. Losing his place early in his second season there, he made the short trip to Spotland in January 1967. Initially figuring in midfield, he was switched to right back when Kevin Connor was injured and remained in that position for most of the remaining games. Subsequently moving into the northern non-league circuit, he was also a useful club cricketer and worked as manager of a tyre company in Oldham.

David Gerald (Dave) Crompton 1966-68
Born: Wigan 6.3.45
Outside left/midfield
FL Apps/Gls 15+2/0 Total Apps/Gls 15+2/0
Career: Dale am 11.66, pro 4.67 [15+2/-], Rossendale U. c.1968. Wigan A. youth team coach c.1980, reserve coach 1985, director of youth football to 2001

Dave made his debut on the left wing when he turned pro in April 1967, but then played the remaining games of the season in midfield. He again played a few games on the wing the following term before leaving for non-league football. In 1971-72, he figured in Rossendale's amazing FA Cup run when they defeated NPL champions Stafford Rangers 6-3 to reach the first round proper, where they overcame Altrincham before going out to Bolton Wanderers. He went into coaching quite early and was on Wigan's staff for around 20 years.

Leslie (Les) Green 1967-68

Born: Atherstone 17.10.41
5'9" 11st9
Goalkeeper
FL Apps 44
Total Apps 51
Career: Atherstone BC, Mancetter, Baddesley Colliery, Atherstone T., Arsenal trial, Hull C. 8.60 [4], Nuneaton Borough 7.62, Burton A. 6.65, Hartlepools U 11.65 [34], Dale trial 4.67, signed 5.67 [44], Derby Co. 5.68 £8500 [107], Durban C. (SA) 8.71 to 1974, later assistant manager. Nuneaton Borough commercial manager 1989, manager 8.89 to 1.91, Hinckley T. manager 4.91 to cs.91, Tamworth manager 1993, Bedworth U. manager 1995
Honours: Division 2 champions 1969, Champion of Champions (S.A.) 1971, NFL champions (S.A.) 1972, Coca Cola Shield (S.A.) 1972

Judged too small to be a top class goalkeeper early in his career, Les went on to star under Brian Clough at Derby. He first played for Clough at Hartlepools in 1965 but really made his mark in a season at Rochdale when already 25 years old, missing only two games and helping steer them clear of the re-election zone. In May 1968 he was sold to Derby for £8500 and went on to play over 100 times as they won the second division title – conceding only 32 goals in 42 games - and established themselves in the top flight. He then played for South African champions Durban City, but suffered a broken leg in a match against local rivals Durban United and subsequently became their assistant manager. Back in England he was commercial manager at Nuneaton Borough before making the unusual sideways move to managing the football club. He managed several other midlands sides before working as a salesman in Derby.

John Reid 1967-68
Born: New Mains, Lanarkshire 20.8.32
5'10" 11st6
Midfield/left back
FL Apps/ Gls 37+2/3 Total Apps/Gls 42+2/3
Career: Kelso Rovers, Hamilton Ac. 1954 [74/17 ScL], Bradford C. 12.57 £2700 [147/32], Northampton T. 11.61 £5000 [85/14], Luton T. 11.63 £13,000 [109+2/7], Torquay U. 6.66 £ [21+2/1], Dale 7.67 [37+2/3] retired cs.68. Market Rasen T. manager 5.80
Honours: Division 3(N) v Division 3(S) 1958, Division 3 champions 1963

Making his Dale debut the day before his 35th birthday, John had seen service with a number of clubs since starting out with the Accies back in 1954. Bought by Bradford City, he was a regular for four seasons and was considered one of the most skilful inside forwards in the third division, representing the Northern Section against their Southern counterparts in 1958. He was sold to Northampton in time to help them win promotion to Division 2 but an even larger fee then took him to Luton, where he became skipper and played virtually every game for two and a half seasons, despite their relegation in 1965, latterly at wing half. At Spotland he was a regular choice, though wearing six different shirt numbers and playing in midfield, on the wing and eventually at left back. After retiring with almost 500 senior games to his credit, he kept in touch with the game and later managed at minor non-league level.

Brian Eastham 1967-68
Born: Bolton 26.4.37 6'0" 11st11
Central defender/left back
FL Apps/Gls 13/0 Total Apps/Gls 16/0
Career: Chorley, Bury 9.58 [188+1/3], Toronto Falcons (Canada) summer 1967, Dale 7.67 [13/-], Sligo Rovers 1968

Brian had a rather chequered association with the Dale after earlier being a stalwart at Bury, playing almost 200 games over nine seasons and being everpresent when they finished as high as 8th in Division 2 in 1963. Leaving when they finished bottom in 1967, he played for Toronto Falcons in the unsanctioned National Professional Soccer League, causing him to be suspended by the FA after he signed for the Dale. He played a number of games either in central defence or at left back but his career came to an abrupt halt after his former Bury boss Bob Stokoe took over at Spotland. Having played only once in the previous two months he was brought back to play in a Lancashire Cup tie against Manchester United Reserves, but United won 7-0 at Spotland and Stokoe sacked him for a claimed lack of effort.

Jack Winspear 1967-68
Born: Leeds 24.12.46
Outside right
FL Apps/Gls 15+1/3 Total Apps/Gls 17+1/3
Career: Leeds U. 10.64, Cardiff C. 6.66 [1/-], Dale 7.67 [15+1/3], Port Elizabeth (SA) cs.68

Jack had been in the same Leeds junior sides as Graham Smith, and had played against Rochdale in Ted Burgin's testimonial game, but spent a year at Cardiff, where he made his FL debut, at inside left, before joining Smith at Spotland. Initially given a run on the right wing by Tony Collins, he faded out of the picture after Bob Stokoe arrived and decided to go with the new 4-3-3 formation. After being released Jack tried his luck in South Africa.

Victor Herbert (Vic) Cockroft 1967-68

Born: Birmingham 25.2.41
5'9" 10st12
Full back
FL Apps/Gls 42/0 Total Apps/Gls 44/0
Career: Wolverhampton W. jnr, pro 12.59, Northampton T. 7.62 [45+1/1], Dale 6.67 [42/-], Kidderminster Harriers cs.68
Honours: England Youth international 1959, Division 3 champions 1963, Division 2 promotion 1965

Vic had played for England at youth level while at Wolves, but did not make his FL debut until joining Northampton, playing a few games (alongside future Dale team-mate John Reid) when they won the third division title in 1963 and then amazingly gained promotion to the top level two years later. He was actually used more in their one season in Division 1, making 18 appearances, the first two in draws against Arsenal (when he was Northampton's first ever substitute) and Manchester United. Released after the Cobbler's second successive relegation he joined Dale and was their regular right back, partnering their other ex-Wolves man Laurie Calloway, before switching to the left side when Calloway was sold.

James Barry Hutchinson 1967-68

Born: Sheffield 27.1.36
6'0" 12st2
Forward
FL Apps/Gls 27/3
Total Apps/Gls 30/5
Career: Bolton W. am, Chesterfield 4.53 [155/15], Derby Co. 7.60 (£2025 + two players) [107/51], Weymouth 7.64, Lincoln C. 7.65 [24/18], Darlington 2.66 (£5000 + K. Allison) [24+2/14], Halifax T. 11.66 £2500 [25/14], Dale 7.67 £2850 [27/3], Bangor C. 8.68, Hyde U. 9.68
Honours: Division 3N v Division 3S 1956-57, Division 4 promotion 1966

Barry was signed as a wing half by veteran Chesterfield manager Teddy Davison who had signed his father Jimmy for Sheffield United before the war, Hutchinson senior later marking his mark at Lincoln. After over 150 games for the Spireites and representing the Third North against the Third South, Barry was part of a cash plus players deal which took him to Derby County in 1960. Converted to an inside left, he netted 16 times in his first season and in 1962-63 upped that to 20. Even so, 1964-65 saw him playing in the Southern League, but 45 goals for Weymouth soon saw him back in the league with his father's old club Lincoln where he hit 18 goals in just half a season, despite the Imps being in the re-election places. This prompted a transfer to Darlington at the other end of the table, his combined tally for the season being 30 goals in 41 games, making him the third highest scorer in the FL. However when the Quakers struggled in the higher division he was soon sold to Halifax and after a good second half of the campaign, netting 19 goals for the Shaymen, was bought by Rochdale the following summer. Dale's poor form, which led to the departure of long serving manager Tony Collins, and a couple of injuries meant that Barry made relatively little impact and he was one of the large number of players freed by Bob Stokoe at the end of the season.

Leslie (Les) Harley 1967-68
Born: Chester 26.9.46 5'9" 10st4
Outside right
FL Apps/Gls 5/0 Total Apps/Gls 7/0
Career: Chester jnr, pro 9.64 [22+3/3], Blackpool 7.67, Dale loan 2.68 [5/-]
Honours: Welsh Cup final 1966

Les came up through the ranks at Chester and though never a regular played for them in the Welsh Cup final. Despite only starting 10 games when Chester just avoided the re-election zone in 1967 Les was then signed by second division Blackpool, but after failing to make the first team joined Dale on loan in the latter part of the season., playing five games on the right wing. His elder brother Albert had a long league career, notably for Shrewsbury and Stockport, and nephew Lee followed them both in joining Chester.

Dennis Anthony Butler 1967-73

Born: Macclesfield 26.4.44
5'6" 10st3
Outside left
FL Apps/Gls 152+4/36
Total Apps/Gls 177+6/41
Career: Leigh GS, Atherton Collieries, Bolton W. jnr, pro 6.61 [61+4/11], Dale 15.2.68 £3000 [152+4/36], coach 1973, Bury coach, reserve team manager 1976, Port Vale coach 11.77, manager 5.78 to 9.79, Swindon T. assistant manager
Honours: Atherton Schoolboys, Division 4 promotion 1969, Lancashire Cup winners 1971

The nephew of pre-war Bolton and England star Billy, Dennis also turned pro with the Trotters and made his debut in December 1962. Two months later Bolton appeared on the new Saturday sports programme on the BBC and it was reported that "Butler's terrific shot for Bolton at Highbury is possibly the best goal seen on the programme all season". Playing on either wing he made a number of appearances over the next four seasons but had been little used for eighteen months when Bob Stokoe made him his first permanent signing for Rochdale for a £3000 fee. An automatic choice on the left wing, always keen to cut inside and have a crack at goal, he went on to be top scorer during Rochdale's promotion campaign, scoring the crucial goal in the 1-0 victory over Halifax in front of a massive 12,806 crowd at Spotland two weeks from the end of the season. Again a first choice up in Division 3, he hit a hat-trick in a 4-1 win at Halifax on Boxing Day 1970 and then struck the winner against first division Coventry in the famous cup giant killing a couple of weeks later. Back and knee injuries took their toll though, and Dennis was rarely able to string together long spells in the side thereafter, though he did play in the Lancashire Cup Final victory. Finishing playing in 1973 he moved onto the coaching staff and later had coaching jobs with Bury and Port Vale before becoming the latter's manager. After a spell with Swindon, Dennis returned to Rochdale to run a post office and later worked for Rochdale education department.

William Thomas (Billy) Rudd 1967-70

Born: Manchester 13.12.41
5'7" 10st10
Midfield
FL Apps/Gls 108/8
Total Apps/Gls 120/8
Career: Manchester U. am 1956-57, Arsenal trial, Stalybridge Celtic 1958, Birmingham 10.59 [24/3], New York All Stars (USA) loan summer 1961, York C. 11.61 [193/30], Grimsby T. 7.66 [59+1/9], Dale 16.2.68 £1500 [108/8], Bury 13.6.70 (£5000 + A. Arrowsmith) [174+15/18], player-coach 1975, coach 1977, Blackpool reserve coach 5.78, Dale coach 12.79, Aston Villa scout
Honours: Manchester Boys, Lancashire Boys, Division 4 promotion 1965, 1969, 1974

Billy played for Lancashire Boys with Nobby Stiles and joined him as an amateur at Old Trafford, but it wasn't until giving up his job as a cabinet maker to join Birmingham (and make his debut against United) that his career took off. He played nearly half of the league games in 1960-61, either on the left wing or at inside left, and scored against Ujpesti Dozsa in the Fairs Cup. During a long spell with York he played around 200 games and skippered the side to promotion in 1965, though they immediately went back down again. In February 1968 he was Bob Stokoe's second important signing on successive days and like Dennis Butler went on to play a crucial role in Dale's promotion the following season, forming the midfield engine room with Vinny Leech. Everpresent again the following year – indeed he played in every one of Dale's 120 games while he was with the club – he was surprisingly traded to Bury - without his knowledge - in exchange for Alf Arrowsmith plus cash (reports varying between £5000 and £20,000). Despite a broken leg, he went on to make the best part of 200 appearances for the Shakers, winning promotion again in 1974, before retiring in 1977 to be full time coach under Bob Stokoe again. He left Bury when overlooked for the manager's job following Stokoe's departure and briefly coached at Spotland during Stokoe's second spell in charge, later working as a decorator. Billy's father, Billy senior, played the odd game for Dale during the war and his uncle Jimmy was a regular for York and Rotherham.

Kenneth (Ken) Bracewell 1967-68

Born: Colne 5.10.36
5'11" 11st12
Centre half
FL Apps/Gls 5/0
Total Apps/Gls 5/0
Career: Trawden, Burnley am 1955, pro 4.57, Tranmere R. 5.59 [28/1], Nelson 1961-62, Toronto Italia (Canada) 1963, Norwich C. 10.63, Lincoln C. 11.63 [12/1], Margate 5.65, Bury 12.66 [1/-], Toronto Falcons (Canada) 1967, Dale 3.68 [5/-], Toronto Falcons (Canada) 4.68 [27/1 NASL], Atlanta Chiefs (USA) 1969 [65+/1 NASL], Atlanta Apollos (USA) player-coach 1973 [12/- NASL], Fleetwood manager, Toronto Mapleleafs (Canada) manager, Denver Dynamos (USA) player-manager 1974 [3/- NASL], Oakland Stompers (USA) manager 1978, San Francisco Scots (USA) manager 1983. Tranmere R. chief executive 7.84 to 2.87, coaching in North California, Colne Dynamos committee c.1992, acting manager 10.96
Honours: NASL final 1971

Originally working as an engineer, until encouraged to go for a trial at Burnley during his national service with the RAF, Ken had a rather stop start career in England but was a leading figure in North America, both as player and coach. His FL debut came in 1959 for Tranmere, but after dropping into non-league football made his first transatlantic move to join Toronto Italia in 1963. A few further league games at Lincoln, where he suffered a broken leg in a reserve game, were followed by a successful spell with Margate where he operated as a "strong, mobile fullback", figuring 63 times in the SL and scoring eight goals. He then returned to Toronto to play for the Falcons, with a very brief stint as Dale centre half before the start of the 1968 American season. Remaining in the NASL when he entered coaching, he was the player-manager of Denver Dynamos when they signed Stan Horne, Jim Grummett and Mick Poole from the Dale in 1975. In 1984 he became chief executive of Tranmere when they became the first club taken over by American owners; but then resumed his coaching career in California, suffering a broken collarbone during the San Francisco earthquake of 1991. He was later involved with the short lived attempt to turn Colne Dynamos into a FL club.

Ernest Stanley (Ernie) Wilkinson 1967-68
Born: Chesterfield 13.2.47 6'0" 12st3
Central defender
FL Apps/Gls 9/0 Total Apps/Gls 9/0
Career: Arsenal app, pro 2.64, Exeter C. 6.66 [59+1/-], Dale loan 3.68 to 4.68 [9/-], Rhyl 1968
Honours: Youth Cup final 1965

A rarity as a Dale player with Arsenal connections, Ernie played centre half in the 1965 Youth Cup Final for the Gunners. The majority of his senior football came in two years at Exeter – he was everpresent in his first season - but ended when he was loaned out to Dale for the last couple of months of the 1967-68 season, figuring in the back four or as a defensive midfield player.

Christopher Joseph (Chris) Harker

1968-70
Born: Shiremoor 29.6.37
5'10" 12st10
Goalkeeper
FL Apps 92
Total Apps 102
Career: Backworth Welfare, West Allotment Celtic, Newcastle U. am 1954, pro 3.55 [1], Consett loan 11.58, Aberdeen loan 11.59 to 11.61 [23 ScL], Bury 12.61 £1000 [178], Grimsby T. 6.67 [10], Dale 2.7.68 [92], Darlington trainer cs.70, Stockton player-manager 1971-72
Honours: Division 4 promotion 1969

Chris appeared in the Scottish League for Aberdeen while on his National Service but had managed just one game for Newcastle, in April 1958, when clubmate Bob Stokoe took him to Bury when he became their player-manager. Missing only one game in three and a half years, he helped the second division Shakers reach the League Cup semi-finals in 1963. He was also involved in the collision which led to the retirement of Sunderland centre forward Brian Clough and set him on his legendary managerial career. Rejoining Stokoe at Spotland in July 1968, Chris was everpresent, as Dale gained their first ever promotion, keeping an impressive 20 clean sheets, including a run of five in succession, and conceding just 35 goals all season. He was also everpresent the following year as Dale established themselves in Division 3 under Len Richley, before following the latter to Darlington. He later worked as a fitter.

Vincent (Vince) Radcliffe 1968-69
Born: Manchester 9.6.1945 5'8" 11st6
Defender
FL Apps/Gls 26/1 Total Apps/Gls 32/1
Career: Portsmouth app 1961, pro 6.63 [10/-], Peterborough U. 7.67 [2/-], Dale 2.7.68 [26/1], Kings Lynn cs.69, Western Suburbs (Australia) 5.73, Kingsway Olympic (Perth), Sorrento (Australia) player-coach 5.79, coach to c.1999
Honours: Division 4 promotion 1969

Though he had played a few games for his previous league clubs, Vince's main claim to fame was as a member of Dale's 1968-69 promotion winning squad. He was the regular right back for the first half of the season but was used only as a stand-in for the central defenders later in the campaign and was one of only two first team players to be released that summer. He later emigrated to Australia, living in Dianella and combining football with a job as a confectionary sales manager.

Derek Francis Ryder 1968-72
Born: Leeds 18.2.47
5'8" 11st4
Left back
FL Apps/Gls 168/1 Total App/Gls 203/1
Career: Pudsey Juniors, Leeds U. jnr 1962, pro 2.64, Cardiff C. 6.66 [4/-], Dale 4.7.68 [168/2], Southport 20.7.72 £2000 [80+2/2], retired cs.74
Honours: Leeds Schoolboys, Division 4 promotion 1969, Division 4 champions 1973, Lancashire Cup winners 1971

Terry Cooper's understudy at Leeds, Derek had played just four FL games for Cardiff (the last a 7-1 defeat) and been sidelined with cartilage trouble before arriving at Spotland. He was everpresent at left back in a defence which conceded just 35 goals on the way to Dale's promotion, and again in Division 3 the following term. He eventually made 124 consecutive appearances, 96 of them partnering Graham Smith in the fullback positions. Indeed he had passed 200 games for the club, including an appearance in the Lancashire Cup Final, when, after being in dispute with the club for some time, he was sold to Southport, helping them to win the fourth division championship in his first season. He was later a sales rep for S&N and then a confectionary firm before becoming a landscape gardener.

Vincent Graham (Vinny) Leech 1968-71

Born: Facit, Lancashire 6.12.40
5'8" 11st
Midfield FL Apps/Gls 59+1/1 Total Apps/Gls 68+1/1
Career: Roch Valley Boys, Littleborough, Whitworth Valley, Burnley am, Facit Parish, Blackburn R. 4.59, Bury 7.61 [108+3/-], Dale 2.7.68 [59+1/1], retired injured 20.3.71. Fleetwood 8.71
Honours: Youth Cup winners 1959, Lancashire Senior Cup final 1961, Division 3 promotion 1968, Division 4 promotion 1969

While playing in local football, Vinny was offered part time terms by Dale (at £3 a week) before first division Blackburn signed him. He played at left half in the Rovers side which beat West Ham in the Youth Cup Final, when two of the opposition half backs were Bobby Moore and Geoff Hurst. He went on to play a century of matches for Bury, latterly at full back, most of them under Bob Stokoe who signed him for his new look Dale side in 1968. Forming the engine room of the side with midfield partner Billy Rudd as Dale won promotion, he played in Dale's amazing run of eighth victories that took them to the top of Division 3 early the following term but then suffered a knee injury in a game against his former club on his 29th birthday. Although attempting a comeback in 1970-71, this effectively ended his career and he became an insurance man, later running a guest house in Blackpool.

Colin Parry 1968-72

Born: Stockport 16.2.41
6'1" 12st11
Centre half
FL Apps/Gls 154+2/1 Total Apps/Gls 181+2/1
Career: Vernon Park Amateurs, Stockport Co. 7.62 [132+1/-], Bradford C. loan 9.65 [5/-], Dale 2.7.68 [154+2/1], Macclesfield 7.72, retired injured cs.74
Honours: Division 4 champions 1967, Division 4 promotion 1969, Cheshire Senior Cup winners 1973

Colin was a stalwart of a struggling Stockport side of the mid-sixties, playing when they remarkably held Liverpool 1-1 in the FA Cup in 1965 despite being bottom of the league, but only played once when they were promoted two years later. Just the sort of dominating centre half Dale needed, he was one of the seven new signings who appeared on the opening day of 1968-69 and went on to earn promotion the following May. He missed only one game in his first two seasons and despite subsequent injuries totalled 183 appearances before being released. His one career goal came in a 3-2 defeat of Halifax in his 164th game for the club. He later worked for many years in a flour mill.

Joseph Matthew (Joe) Ashworth 1968-72

Born: Leeds 6.1.43
6'1" 12st
Central defender
FL Apps/Gls 133/3
Total Apps/Gls 161/5
Career: Ashley Road Methodists, Bradford PA jnr 1959, pro 1.60 [3/-], York C. 5.62 [57/-], Bournemouth & BA 6.65 [60/2], Southend U.7.67 [36/2], Dale 2.7.68 [133/3], Chester 29.12.71 [5/-], Stockport Co. 6.72 [14/-], retired injured cs.73
Honours: Division 4 promotion 1965, 1969, Lancashire Cup winners 1971

Originally an inside forward and then wing half noted as an excellent passer, with the evolution of the game, Joe was transformed into a tough tackling central defender. He was a well known performer in the lower divisions through the sixties, winning promotion with York. At Spotland he formed a tremendous defensive partnership with Colin Parry, Dale conceding only 35 goals on their way to promotion. He missed just one game as Dale settled into life in Division 3 and also scored a rare goal in the Lancashire Cup Final victory over Oldham in 1971, but was sent off on the opening day of the next term as a referees' 'get tough' policy took hold. Joe was displaced by the arrival of Len Kinsella later that year and moved on to Chester and then Stockport without much success due to an achiles injury. His son Neil joined Dale in 1983, but without his father's success. Joe worked for the prison service at Hull and Strangeways before having to retire in 1997 with arthritis and a subsequent hip replacement, sadly dying when only 59.

Norman John Whitehead 1968-72

Born: Liverpool 22.4.48
5'9" 10st9
Outside right
FL Apps/Gls 154+2/11
Total Apps/Gls 189+2/14
Career: Everton jnr 1964, Bury am 1965, Skelmersdale 12.66, Southport am 25.10.67, pro 16.12.67 [7+1/-], Dale 4.7.68 [154+2/11], Rotherham U. 26.2.72 (£10,000 + L. Brogden) [29+4/2], Chester 24.8.73 £8000 [66+8/5], Blackpool trial 7.76, Grimsby T. 8.76 [3+1/-], Bangor C. 9.76, Poulton Victoria 1978, Rhyl 12.78, Rockvile 1980-81
Honours: FA Amateur Cup final 1967, Division 4 promotion 1969, 1975, Lancashire Senior Cup winners 1971

The seventh Dale debutant on the opening day of 1968-69, Norman had only turned pro at Southport during the previous season, following an appearance in the Amateur Cup Final at Wembley with Skelmersdale as a 19 year old. He soon became an automatic choice on the right wing as Dale stormed to promotion, and though not a prolific goalscorer himself, was provider in chief for Reg Jenkins, Steve Melledew, Terry Melling and later Tony Buck in the middle. A star performer up in Division 3 (and voted the supporters' player of the year in 1970-71), Manchester City's Malcolm Allison reputedly made a "name your own price" bid to get the tricky winger to Maine Road. However, with Dale in a relegation battle at the time, this was turned down and when Norman did leave it was in an exchange deal for Rotherham's Lee Brogden plus cash. A broken ankle restricted his time at Millmoor and despite further moves and another promotion while with Chester, he was back playing non-league football when he was 28 and worked for the Mersey ferry company.

Stephen (Steve) Lee 1968-69
Born: {Birmingham JAS.48?} 5'10" 11st8
Right back
FL Apps/Goals 0/0 Total Apps/Goals 1/0
Career: {Birmingham C. 1967}, Dale trial cs.68

Steve had a trial with Dale in the summer of 1968 and played at right back in the Rose Bowl game, but was not taken on, Vince Radcliffe taking the number 2 shirt at the start of the league campaign.

Terence (Terry) Melling 1968-69
Born: Billingham 24.1.40 6'0" 12st
Centre forward
FL Apps/Gls 20/8 Total Apps/Gls 23/8
Career: Army, Slough T., Tooting & Mitcham, Maidstone U., Tow Law Town am, Newcastle U. 12.65, Watford 5.66 [23+1/5], Newport Co. 1.67 £2500 [34/14], Mansfield T. 12.67 £3000 [31/7], Dale 18.9.68 £1000 [20/8], Darlington 11.3.69 £1000 [21/6], Scarborough 1969-70, Tow Law Town
Honours: Durham Schoolboys, Army XI

Terry spent six years in the Coldstream Guards, captaining the Army XI, and figuring in amateur football both in the south east and back in his native north east, before signing professional at Newcastle. He made his FL debut for Watford in May 1966, before being bought by Newport, scoring against the Dale and netting a hat-trick against Wrexham early in 1967-68. After another short lived move to Mansfield, he was Bob Stokoe's last signing for the Dale, where he replaced the temporarily out of favour Reg Jenkins at centre forward. The high spot of his stay was a hat-trick at Bradford when the tough ex-squaddie, who had not been expecting to play, appeared with his head bandaged, reputedly the result of falling off a bus the night before. When Dale added Tony Buck to their squad, they recouped some of the transfer fee by selling Terry to rivals Darlington, his fifth club in less than three years. Later working in the building trade, he was disabled following a work accident in 1986.

Anthony Rowland (Tony) Buck 1968-73

Born: Clowne, Derbyshire 18.8.44 5'11" 11st
Forward
FL Apps/Gls 73+11/29
Total Apps/Gls 90+13/33
Career: Seaford BC, Eastbourne T., Headington/Oxford U. 1959, pro 8.62 [34+5/6], Newport Co. 1.68 [49/18], Dale 14.2.69 £5000 [73+11/29], Bradford C. loan 1.72 [3/-], Aldershot loan 10.72, Northampton T. 23.1.73 £2000 [16+1/3], Bedford T. 6.74
Honours: Division 4 promotion 1965, 1969, (Lancashire Senior Cup winners 1971), Southern League First Division North champions 1975

The final piece in Dale's promotion jigsaw, added by Len Richley for a club record £5000, Tony had hit 13 goals for Newport in the first part of the season, including all five against Bradford, and added 8 more for Dale. The following term the blonde striker had scored 15 more, including a hat-trick at Bristol Rovers, before tragically breaking his leg on an icy pitch at Reading in February 1970, when Dale still harboured hopes of a second successive promotion. (Tony was voted the club's first ever player of the season at the end of the campaign). Although he made a brief comeback the following season, playing in the famous cup win against Coventry, and figured in a number of games in 1971-72, he was never able to recapture his old form and after a couple of spells out on loan was sold to Northampton. He retired completely when still only 30, due to knee trouble, after scoring 12 goals to help Bedford Town win the Southern League first division north title. He was subsequently a service manager for Ford.

Paul Stewart Clarke 1969-72
Born: Chesterfield 25.9.50 6'1" 13st6
Centre half
FL Apps/Gls 10+1/0 Total Apps/Gls 12+1/0
Career: Liverpool app 1966, pro 10.67, Dale 16.6.69 [10+1/-], Matlock T. cs.72
Honours; England Schools international (5 caps), England youth team trial

Despite his background as a schoolboy international, coming through the junior ranks at Liverpool, Paul was unable to translate this into a league career. One of only three signings by Len Richley to boost the squad for Division 3, Paul played in the Rose Bowl game at the start of the campaign but appeared just twice in the league as stand-in for Joe Ashworth in his first year. He again replaced Ashworth or Parry on occasion over the following two years, but the versatile Ronnie Blair was more often used as the defensive cover and Paul totalled just 10 FL starts.

Robert David (Bobby) Downes 1969-74

Born: Bloxwich 25.8.49
5'10" 11st5
Midfield/left back
FL Apps/Gls 164+10/10
Total Apps/Gls 192+12/12
Career: West Bromwich A. jnr, pro 8.66, Peterborough U. 9.67 [24+2/3], Dale 1.7.69 [164+10/10], Watford 24.5.74 £10,000 [192+7/19], Barnsley 3.80 £10,000 [43/1], Blackpool cs.82 [27+1/3], n/c player-coach cs.84, coach 1985, Aston Villa youth coach 7.87, Port Vale youth team manager, Wolverhampton W. coach, director of youth football, Watford coach, Blackburn R. coach 1997, academy director c.1999 to 2009
Honours: Division 4 champions 1978, Division 3 promotions 1979 and 1981, Lancashire Senior Cup winners 1971

Bobby was a key signing for Dale in 1969, partnering Billy Rudd in midfield when Vinny Leech missed the start of the season, and became an established member of the side after Leech was forced to retire and Rudd was sold. He was also used on the left flank as Dick Connor moved towards three or four man midfield formations, and was a capable stand-in left back. He broke his leg in a challenge with Manchester City's Rodney Marsh in the League Cup in 1972 but returned later in the season and was one of the few players to come out of the disastrous 1973-74 campaign with any credit, earning a transfer to Watford. He had made just over 200 appearances for the Dale and repeated that at Vicarage Road, playing in the side that won successive promotions n 1978 and 1979. He also gained promotion with Barnsley, later going into coaching while with Blackpool, before a lengthy career at several top clubs as youth coach or director of youth football.

David (Dave) Cross 1968-72

Born: Bury 8.12.50
5'11" 12st
Centre forward
FL Apps/Gls 50+9/20 Total Apps/Gls 62+12/26
Career: Heywood GS, Heywood GSOB, Dale as 1966, pt 6.1.69, pro 5.8.69 [50+9/20], Norwich C. 6.10.71 £40,000 [83+1/21], Coventry C. 13.11.73 £150,000 [90+1/29], West Bromwich A. 16.11.76 £140,000, [38/18], West Ham U. 13.12.77 £180,000 [178+1/78], Manchester C. 11.8.82 £135,000 [31/12], Vancouver Whitecaps 4.83 £80,000 [26/19 NASL], Oldham A. 6.10.83 [18+4/6], Vancouver Whitecaps [23/10 NASL], West Bromwich A. 26.10.84 [16/2], Bolton W. 2.7.85 [19+1/8], Bury loan 30.1.86 [12+1/-] Blackpool n/c 26.7.86, Aris Salonika (Greece), AEL Limasol (Cyprus) player-coach, Altrincham coach. Later Oldham A. coach, youth team manager c.1998, assistant manager 2002, West Ham U. scout
Cricket for Heywood
Honours: Heywood Schools, Lancashire Senior Cup winners 1971, Division 2 champions 1972, 1981, Football League Cup final 1973, 1981, FA Cup winners 1980, Tennant Caledonian Cup winners 1977

Dave came through the junior sides at Spotland to become one of their greatest ever discoveries. His debut, as substitute, was in the first game up in Division 3 and he became a regular at centre forward the following term, scoring a famous header in the FA Cup win against Coventry as well as two goals in the Lancashire Cup Final. Ten goals in 13 games at the start of 1971-72 led to a record £40,000 transfer to Norwich, with whom he earned promotion to the top division and played in the League Cup Final. Even bigger money moves took him to fellow Division 1 sides Coventry and West Brom before he reached West Ham where he was a fixture for four and a half seasons. He played in their surprise 1980 FA Cup Final victory over Arsenal and in a second League Cup Final before helping them regain their top flight status in 1981, winning the Golden Boot in the process, with a total of 34 goals, four of them in a game against Grimsby. (An odder hat-trick came when West Ham beat Castilla 5-1 behind closed doors to win 6-4 on aggregate, in the European Cup Winners Cup). Playing on, both in the FL and in the NASL until he was 35, Dave subsequently went into coaching and also sold pensions and worked as a finance broker. In his younger days Dave had played cricket for Heywood and was at one time their president (as his father had been), while son Bobby also played for them, as well as graduating to Lancashire 2nd XI. Daughters Jennifer (also a netball superleague player) and Katie played cricket for Lancashire, the latter playing for England in the successful Women's Ashes series in 2014, taking six wickets on her debut at the WACA.

David (Dave) Tennant 1969-71

Born: Walsall 13.6.45
5'11" 12st11
Goalkeeper
FL Apps 16
Total Apps 24
Career: Aston Villa jnr cs.61, Walsall am cs.62, pro 8.63, Worcester C. 7.65, Grimsby T. trial 8.66, Lincoln C. 9.66 [40], Dale 7.69 [16], Corby T. 8.71 to cs.73, Lincoln C. 8.74, Lincoln U. 3.75, Skegness T. cs.75, Ruston Bucyrus 1977-78

Dave was on the books of several league clubs but played in the first team only for Lincoln and Dale. He was signed as Chris Harker's deputy and his only appearance before Harker's departure was in the Lancashire Cup. One of the few players of his day to sport a beard, in his second season he shared the 'keeper's jersey with Tony Godfrey and was in goal for the famous giant killing defeat of Coventry, making a number of heroic interventions. Leaving to join the police, he played on at non-league level and did make one appearance back at Lincoln City, albeit in a pre-season friendly. He later worked as a bricklayer.

Ronald Victor (Ronnie) Blair

1969-72, 1982-83
Born: Coleraine 26.9.49
5'10" 11st7
Utility player
FL Apps/Gls 69+5/3 Total Apps/Gls 92+7/4
Career: Coleraine 6.65, Oldham A. am 20.7.66, pro 6.10.66 [74+2/1], Preston NE trial 12.69, Dale loan 28.2.70, signed 6.4.70 £1300 [69+5/3], Oldham A. 28.7.72 (exchange for K. Bebbington) [275+10/22], Colorado Caribous loan summer 1978 [18/1 NASL], Blackpool 4.8.81 [35+1/3], Dale 6.8.82, n/c 28.9.82 to 10.82 [3/-], Milton to 1988-89, Castleton Gabriels manager 1990-91 to 3.92, Bacup Borough manager 5.92 to 12.92
Honours: N. Ireland schools, youth international, 5 full caps 1974 to 1976, Lancashire Senior Cup winners 1967, 1971, Division 3 champions 1974

There were 12 years between Ronnie's first and last Dale games, but in fact he spent most of his career at Oldham. Dick Conner's first signing when he borrowed him from the Latics in February 1970, he soon signed permanently and became the side's utility man, figuring in midfield, in central defence and at fullback. Indeed, the only outfield shirt that he didn't wear over the next two years was the No. 7. He appeared in Dale's Lancashire Cup Final defeat of Oldham but was then traded back to them in exchange for Keith Bebbington. Ronnie made around 300 further first team appearances at Boundary Park, scoring 11 times when they were Division 3 champions in 1974, and won five full caps for Northern Ireland. He had a testimonial game between Oldham and a All-Ireland Select XI in 1979. Despite not missing a second division game in 1980-81 he then spent the following season at fourth division Blackpool before Dale signed him for a second time. However, after three league games he cancelled his contract because of clashes with work outside football (he ran a printing firm). He was subsequently involved with local football, winning manager of the month for the North West Counties League Division 2 in November 1991.

Anthony (Tony) Godfrey 1970-72

Born: Pangbourne 30.4.39 5'7" 12st
Goalkeeper
FL Apps 71
Total Apps 83
Career: Norwich C. am, Basingstoke, Southampton 4.58 [140], Aldershot 12.65 [172], Dale 1.7.70 [71], Aldershot to 7.72 [68], Andover cs.76
Honours: Division 3 champions 1960, Division 4 promotion 1973, Lancashire Senior Cup winners 1971

A very experienced goalkeeper when he reached Spotland, Tony had played when Southampton beat Dale 6-1 in the first season of the new Division 3, but also when Dale beat the Saints on the way to the 1962 League Cup Final. Following his seven seasons with Southampton, mostly in Division 2, he spent five with their neighbours Aldershot, twice being everpresent, before joining former Shots coach Dick Conner at Spotland. Left out after a 5-1 defeat he reclaimed his place from Dave Tennant in the second half of the season and despite the signing of Rod Jones played the majority of games the following season, being voted player of the year. Rejoining Aldershot, he was again everpresent as they won promotion for the first time ever in 1973.

Alfred William (Alf) Arrowsmith 1970-72

Born: Ashton-under-Lyne 11.12.42 5'9" 11st8
Centre forward
FL Apps/Gls 40+6/14
Total Apps/Gls 48+7/21
Career: St Charles (Hadfield), Tintwistle Villa 1959-60, Ashton U. 8.60, Liverpool 9.60 £1250 [43+4/20], Bury 12.68 £25,000 [45+3/11], Dale 12.6.70 (exchange for W. Rudd) [40+5/14], Macclesfield cs.72 to cs.73
Honours: Division 2 champions 1962, Division 1 champions 1964 and 1966, Charity Shield 1964, Lancashire Senior Cup final 1962

A remarkable goalscorer in minor football – he hit 96 goals for Tintwistle in 1959-60 - he made the move straight from Ashton United to Liverpool, playing once during their promotion campaign. Though generally below the likes of Roger Hunt and Ian St John in the pecking order, Alf actually had his most productive season the year Liverpool claimed the league championship for the first time, when he replaced Jimmy Melia at inside left, netting 15 goals in 20 league appearances, including one in the 5-0 victory over Arsenal that clinched the title, and four in the FA Cup against Derby. Signed from Bury in exchange for Billy Rudd, Alf managed 17 goals in his first season for the Dale yet was never an automatic choice up front before heading for the non-league game.

Peter Taylor Gowans 1970-74
Born: Dundee 25.5.44 5'10" 11st
Midfield
FL Apps/Gls 136+8/21
Total Apps/Gls 160+10/23
Career: Shamrock Boys Club (Dundee), Celtic 1960-61, Crewe A. 2.7.63 [141/43], Aldershot 6.7.67 £3000 [111+2/27], Dale 1.7.70 [136+8/21], Southport 19.7.74 to 17.10.74 [3+1/1], Crewe A. trial 1974, Nantwich T. 1974-75, Whitchurch 1976, Nantwich T.
Honours: Lancashire Senior Cup winners 1971

Peter left Scottish giants Celtic for English minnows Crewe when he was 19 and had an excellent record as a goalscoring right winger or inside forward, netting 17 times in 1964-65. By then operating on the left flank, he was similarly productive at Aldershot before his former Shots' coach Dick Conner signed him for the Dale. He again made well over a century of appearances in midfield, striking a number of long range goals, not least the one at Brighton that guaranteed Division 3 survival in 1972, when his nine goals made him the leading scorer in league games. His league career ended when he fell out with Alan Ball at Southport and he later worked on the railways in Crewe, where, in the 1990s, he was coaching the Jumping Frog pub team.

David Aubrey John (Dave) Pearson 1970-71
Born: Shotton 13.10.47 5'8" 12st
Right back
FL Apps/Gls 3/0 Total Apps/Gls 4/0
Career: Everton app 22.7.63, pro 20.10.65, Southport 25.8.67 [91+1/-], Dale 2.9.70 [3/-], Morecambe cs.71, Netherfield 1976, South Liverpool 1977, Chorley trial 1977, Burscough 1977-78, Southport 9.79
Honours: Flintshire Schools, Welsh Schoolboy international (5 caps), Wales under-23s v Scotland 1970, FA Youth Cup final 1965, FA Challenge Trophy winners 1974, Lancashire Senior Cup final 1974

Dave had a very brief Dale career as understudy to Graham Smith, all three games he played ending in defeats, but was much more successful elsewhere. He had captained Flintshire Schools and scored nine times in five games for Wales Schools (as an inside forward), then played for Everton in the Youth Cup Final and while at Southport appeared for the Welsh under-23s. At Morecambe he made more than 300 appearances in all games, gaining an FA Trophy winners medal at Wembley in 1974, as well as Morecambe surprisingly making it all the way to the Lancashire Cup Final, beating Everton and Manchester United reserve sides. He also worked in a garage.

Andre (Andy) Mandzuk 1969-72
Born: Rochdale OND.53
Right back
FL Apps/Gls +0/0 Total Apps/Gls +0/0
Career: Kingsway School, Dale app 14.4.69 to 5.5.72, Dicken Green 1972, St. Albans c.1975
Honours: Rochdale Schools 1967, Rochdale Sunday League XI 1975

Andy was an all-round sportsman as a junior, figuring for a schools under-14 basketball side which reached the national semi-finals in London as well as playing football for Rochdale Schools. One of Dale's first two apprentices in April 1969, along with Brian Ashworth, Andy was unused substitute for the away game with league leaders Preston in November 1970, when both regular full backs were out injured, the match attracting a 13,000 crowd.

Rodney Ernest (Rod) Jones 1971-74

Born: Ashton 23.9.45
6'1" 12st8
Goalkeeper
FL Apps 19 Total Apps 28+1
Career: Manchester U. jnr, Ashton U., {Burnley 6.65?}, Rotherham U. 9.65 [35], Burnley 5.67 £8000 [9], Dale 28.5.71 £4000 [19], Barrow cs.74, Mossley 1976-77
Honours: Lancashire Senior Cup winners 1970, final 1968

Uniquely, Dale made only one signing in the summer of 1971, obtaining Burnley reserve Rod for £4000, a record for a Dale 'keeper. Although playing in two Lancashire Cup Finals, he had made only nine league appearances in four years and lost his place in the Dale goal after only four games. Freed at the end of 1972-73, he was re-signed by new manager Walter Joyce at the start of the following term only to be shortly replaced by youngster Mick Poole. All his Northern Premier League appearances for Barrow came in 1975-76.

Leonard (Len) Kinsella 1971-74
Born: Alexandria, Dumbarton 14.5.46
5'10" 12st10
Midfield/central defender
FL Apps/Gls 82+3/4 Total Apps/Gls 95+3/4
Career: Saltaire, Burnley app 1962, pro 5.63 [7+5/-], Carlisle U. 9.70 £12,000 [9+4/-], Dale 16.9.71 £6000 [82+3/4], retired 5.74
Honours: Scotland Schoolboys, Bradford Boys 1961, Lancashire Senior Cup winners 1965, 1966, 1970, final 1968

Scots born but brought up in Yorkshire, Len was another long serving Burnley reserve and played in no fewer than four Lancashire Cup Finals, scoring in two of the three which the Clarets won. A sizeable fee took him to Carlisle but he only became a league regular after he (briefly) became Dale's most expensive signing just after the 1971-72 season got underway. Originally a midfielder, he was soon transformed to a centre back by Dick Conner and later often played as part of essentially a five man back line in an increasingly defensive formation. A regular for two years he was soon left out by new boss Walter Joyce and decided to retire from the game.

Malcolm Darling 1971-74

Born: Arbroath 4.7.47
5'7" 10st
Forward
FL Apps/Gls 82+4/16
Total Apps/Gls
91+6/21
Career: Errol, Luncarty Juniors, Blackburn R. 10.64 [114+13/20], Norwich C. 5.70 (part exchange for B. Conlon) [16/5], Dale 6.10.71 (part exchange for D. Cross) [82+4/16], Bolton W. 27.9.73 £14,000 [6+2/-], Chesterfield 8.74 [100+4/33], Stockport Co. loan 3.77 [11/2], Sheffield W. 8.77 [1+1/-], Hartlepool 9.77 [2+2/-], Morecambe 1977-78, Bury n/c 3.78 [1+1/-], Morecambe cs.78, California Sunshine (USA), Lancaster C., Workington, Macclesfield 1.81, Darwen c.1981, manager c.9.83

After scoring twice on his Blackburn debut on the right wing in a 9-0 Lancashire Cup demolition of Oldham, Malcolm also scored on his first division debut. He played well over 100 games for Rovers, later switching to a striking role and top scoring for Rovers in 1968-69 when he netted an FA Cup hat-trick against Portsmouth. A short spell at Norwich ended when he was part of the deal that took Dave Cross (q.v.) to Carrow Road. He missed only one game in 1972-73 and was Dale's top scorer, albeit with only eight league and four cup goals. Scoring in the first two games the following season, he was sold to second division Bolton for a sizeable fee, but almost all his further FL games came in a stint at Chesterfield where he scored 18 times in 1975-76. He later had an extremely brief spell as manager of Darwen, who lost all their games while he was in charge and got through five managers before Christmas in 1983-84!

Arthur Marsh 1971-74
Born: Dudley 4.5.47 5'11" 11st5
Central defender
FL Apps/Gls 89+1/0 Total Apps/Gls 99+2/1
Career: Brierley Hill, Bolton W. jnr 1963, pro 7.64 [73+2/-], Dale 2.12.71 £7000 [89+1/-], Darlington 7.74 to cs.75 [23/1]

Though only a regular during 1969-70, Arthur made a number of second division appearances for Bolton over a five year period before becoming Dale's most expensive signing. Originally a full back, he had later played at centre back and this was the role he largely adopted at Spotland, often playing as one of three central defenders with Colin Blant and Len Kinsella. Distinguished by his goatee beard, after Dale's relegation season he had a year at Darlington before joining the police.

Jack Howarth 1971-73

Born: Crook 27.2.45
6'0" 13st6
Centre forward
FL Apps/Gls 40/12
Total Apps/Gls 46/13
Career: Esh Winning, Crook Town, Stanley U., Chelsea 10.63, Swindon T. 10.64 [2/-], Aldershot 7.65 [258+1/113], Dale 12.1.72 £8000 [40/12], Aldershot 23.11.72 £8000 [163/58], Bournemouth 12.76 [39+3/6], Dorchester T. loan, Southport n/c 2.3.78 [9/1], South California Lazers (USA) summer 1978, Farnborough T. cs.78, Andover 12.78, player-coach 1979-80, Basingstoke T. 1.81, Andover, Salisbury C., Andover, Romsey T. 1983, manager 1985
Honours: Division 4 promotion 1973

An all time great at Aldershot, Jack played 422 league games for the Shots and scored a staggering 171 league goals for them, easily a club record. An old fashioned centre forward, he was one of the best headers of the ball in the lower divisions, his power in the air contributing to a record which saw him net at least 14 league goals in eight of his nine full seasons with Aldershot, 25 of them in 1973-74, the Shots first season up in Division 3. This came after he had spent less than a year away from the Recreation Ground when he became Rochdale's third record signing in four months, his dozen goals at Spotland being a decent return in a low scoring side. He later did the rounds of non-league football back in Hampshire and after becoming a postman played for the Post Office team in Sunday football.

Lee Brogden 1971-74

Born: Leeds 18.10.49
5'7" 10st4
Outside right
FL Apps/Gls 48+9/7 Total Apps/Gls 54+10/9
Career: Leeds Ashley Road, Rotherham U. 12.67 [79+8/16], Dale 25.2.72 (part exchange for N. Whitehead) [48+9/7], Denver Dynamos summer 1974 [18/2 NASL]

Lee had a relatively short FL career, but nevertheless played around 150 games. He arrived at Spotland from Rotherham as part of the deal which took fellow right winger Norman Whitehead in the opposite direction and played fairly regularly for about a year, scoring against Walsall to send Dale to the top of Division 3 at the end of September 1972. Despite scoring five times in a run of seven games he was little used by new manager Walter Joyce as Dale were relegated and Lee headed off to play in the NASL, settling in the USA after playing for Denver. On returning later to the UK he became an insurance man.

Charles William P. (Charlie) Simpson
1971-73
Born:Rochdale 11.7.54 5'7" 10st4
Midfield
FL Apps/Gls 1/1 Total Apps/Gls 2/1
Career: Sacred Heart, Dale app 25.5.71, pro 8.72 [1/1], Rochdale Nomads cs.73, Mossley 1973-74. Whitworth Valley c.1982 (+ Tim Bobbin 1979-80 to 1989, Free Trade 1990-91 in Sunday football). Rochdalians under-17s manager c.2001
Honours: Rochdale Sunday League XI 1980, Greater Manchester Inter League Trophy winners 1981, Rochdale Sunday League Cup winners 1981, Rochdale Sunday League Division 1 champions 1991

Charlie is one of the few Dale players to score in their sole league appearance – albeit when an attempted clearance cannoned off him into the net - in a 2-1 defeat at Chesterfield in March 1973, when he played instead of Bobby Downes. He had previously been an unused substitute while still an apprentice and had made his first team debut in the Lancashire Cup. After playing in the Northern Premier League with Mossley, Charlie became a stalwart of Sunday league football in Rochdale, appearing with several other ex-Dale players for the successful Tim Bobbin side amongst others.

Richard (Dick) Renwick 1972-74

Born: Gilsland 27.11.42
5'11" 12st9
Left back
FL Apps/Gls 48+1/0
Total Apps/Gls 56+1/0
Career: Grimsby T. jnr, pro 12.59, Aldershot 7.63 [203+2/5], Brentford 2.69 [96/5], Stockport Co. 10.71 [30/1], Dale 3.7.72 [48+2/1], Darlington loan 2.74 [19/-]

A red haired left back, Dick had played well over 300 league games, 200 of them in six seasons with Aldershot, when he joined ex-Shots coach Dick Conner and former teammates Peter Gowans and Jack Howarth at Spotland in 1972. He formed part of a robust back line for Dale as they topped the table briefly but the following season was one of the losers as new boss Walter Joyce went for youth over experience, ending his career with a loan spell at Darlington who were now managed by Conner.

Colin Blant 1972-74

Born: Rawtenstall 7.10.46
6'1" 13st4
Centre half
FL Apps/Gls 51/0
Total Apps/Gls 57/0
Career: Rossendale U., Burnley 8.64 [46+6/7], Portsmouth 4.70 [64/1], Dale 6.7.72 £7000 [51/-], Darlington 1.74 [89/-], Grimsby T. 8.76, [9/-], Workington T. 11.76 [21/-], Horwich RMI cs.77. Dale School of Excellence coach 1996-97
Honours: Lancashire Senior Cup winners 1966

Colin started out as a centre forward at Burnley, scoring twice in his second match in the first division. Converting to centre half he had a couple of seasons as a regular for Portsmouth before signing for Rochdale for £7000 in the summer of 1972. An ultra-physical defender nicknamed 'Garth' after the comic strip hero, even in the days of relatively lenient referees he chalked up nine bookings during the season, second only to Leeds hard man Norman Hunter. After rejoining Dick Conner at Darlington he managed to earn a suspension during a loan spell, but after signing permanently made more appearances for the Quakers than for any of his other league clubs. After retiring he worked as a newsagent and a school caretaker and had a spell working in the Dale's youth set up with another old school centre half, Keith Hicks.

Richard Keith Bebbington   1972-74
Born: Nantwich 4.8.43   5'8"   11st
Winger/midfield
FL Apps/Gls 57+3/6   Total Apps/Gls 68+4/6
Career: Northwich Victoria trial, Stoke C. jnr 1958, pro 19.8.60 [99+2/17], Oldham A. 20.8.66 (£25,000 for two players) [237/38], Dale 28.7.72 (exchange for R. Blair) [57+3/6], Winsford U. cs.74 to 1978
Honours: Division 2 champions 1963, Division 4 promotion 1971, Football League Cup final 1964, Lancashire Senior Cup winners 1967

Having joined Stoke at 15, Keith made just over a century of appearances for the Potters, often playing on the opposite wing to Stanley Matthews, 28 years his senior. He scored in Stoke's remarkable 9-1 victory over Ipswich in 1964 and in the first leg of the League Cup Final, which Stoke lost 4-3 on aggregate to Leicester. He was also their first ever substitute (for Dennis Violet) on the opening day of 1964-65. He had an even lengthier spell at Oldham before the Latics exchanged him for their former player Ronnie Blair. A regular on the left wing for much of his first season at Spotland, he was one of the few experienced players to remain in the side, in midfield, after Walter Joyce took over.

Gordon Raymond Morritt   1972-74

Born: Rotherham 8.2.42
6'4"   14st1
Goalkeeper
FL Apps 31   Total Apps 33
Career: Kimberworth Secondary School, Steel Peach & Tozer, Rotherham U. 6.61 [77], Durban C. (South Africa) c.3.66, Doncaster R. 9.67 [40], Northampton T. 8.68 [42], York C. 10.69 [41], Dale 27.7.72 [31], Darlington 21.9.73 £1000 [34], North Yorkshire Police cs.74

Honours: Rotherham Boys, North Regional League champions 1963, British XI (in South Africa), Division 4 promotion 1971

A massively proportioned 'keeper – he was also an amateur boxer and briefly a pro fighter during his spell playing in South Africa – Gordon joined second division Rotherham from his factory team, where he was originally a centre half, and when not keeping goal played centre forward in the Millers' reserves (scoring 22 goals in 1962-63). After playing for a 'British XI' in a representative game while in Durban, he was a regular in seasons at Doncaster and Northampton but largely a reserve at York. His penalty save against Walsall took Dale to the top of Division 3 in September 1972, but the following week he broke his leg. Though he was back in the side by January, he was ignored by Walter Joyce when the latter took over as manager and Gordon quickly beat what became a well travelled trail to Dick Conner's new club Darlington. After serving in the police he became a security manager, later returning to the sporting environment as a greenkeeper at a golf club in York and acting as kit man for York RLFC.

Barry Bradbury   1972-74
Born: Castleton 5.8.52   5'9"   11st4
Defender
FL Apps/Gls 12+2/0   Total Apps/Gls 16+2/0
Career: Matthew Moss, Dale am 1970, pro 16.7.72 [12+2/-], St Gabriels cs.74, {Barrow 1975-76?}

Barry was an amateur defender in Dale's reserves after leaving school, signing pro in the summer of 1972. He was on the bench a few times before making his debut as a defensive midfielder in a line-up that already included three other centre backs, Blant, Kinsella and Marsh, for a match against Chesterfield which was televised on ITV. He played a number of games at full back the following term.

William Harold (Harry) Wainman   1972-73

Born: Hull 22.3.47
6'0"   13st11
Goalkeeper
FL Apps 9   Total Apps 10
Career: Hull C. jnr, Ainthorpe Old Boys, Grimsby T. jnr 1963, pro 7.64 to cs.80 [420], Dale loan 5.10.72 to 28.11.72 [9], Grimsby T. n/c player-youth team coach 2.81
Honours: Hull Schools, England youth international 1964, Division 4 champions 1972

An England youth international just after turning pro at Grimsby, Harry went on to be a tremendous stalwart at Blundell Park, spending the best part of 20 years on Grimsby's playing staff. He was their player of the year in 1972 when they won the fourth division title, but was temporarily out of the side in September of that year when Dale 'keeper Gordon Morritt broke his leg in a game at Grimsby and Dick Conner immediately arranged a loan move for Harry. Back with the Mariners, he won their player of the year again in 1976 and despite a broken arm the following year made a massive 420 league appearances before finishing in 1980. He returned as youth team coach and was registered as a non-contract player, being awarded a second testimonial in 1981 against Leeds, being stretchered off with cut ear!

James McAvoy (Jim) Bowie 1972-73
Born: Howwood, Renfrew 11.10.41 6'2" 11st7
Midfield
FL Apps/Gls 1+2/0 Total Apps/Gls 3+2/0
Career: Neilston Waverley, Third Lanark am 1958, Arthurlie 1960, Oldham A. am 1961, pro 20.7.62 [331+3/38], Dale 8.10.72 to 16.11.72 [1+2/-]
Honours: Division 4 promotion 1963 1971, Lancashire Senior Cup winners 1967, final 1971

Originally an inside forward - scoring in four successive games in his first season, when Oldham were promoted – 'Big Jim' later turned wing half and with the development of modern formations became a "languid, elegant" midfielder. Having also figured at full back, by the time the Latics won promotion again in 1971 (but were beaten in the Lancashire Cup Final by Dale) he was everpresent in central defence. After well over 300 games, he was released in 1972 and was signing on at the labour exchange in Oldham when offered a month's trial at Spotland. He played in two Lancashire Cup ties, but only started one league match before deciding to give up the game.

David (Dave) Hunt 1972-73
Born: Swinton AMJ.54
Forward
FL Apps/Gls 0/0 Total Apps/Gls 2+1/0
Career: Dale am 4.10.72 to 9.73

Dave was a promising amateur striker in Dale reserves and made his senior bow alongside Jack Howarth and Reg Jenkins in the Lancashire Senior Cup in November 1972 when Dale beat Manchester City 4-2, also figuring in two games against Bury in the next round.

Paul Anthony Fielding 1971-76
Born: Rochdale 4.12.55 5'8" 10st
Midfield
FL Apps/Gls 65+7/5 Total Apps/Gls 69+8/5
Career: Dale app 23.9.71, pro 12.73 [65+7/5], Southport trial 8.76, Sligo Rovers 1976, (Australia), Sligo Rovers player-manager 1982, Glenavon
Honours: League of Ireland champions 1977. As manager; FA of Ireland Cup winners 1983

A local lad, Paul signed apprentice forms at Spotland when he was only 15 and made his FL debut as substitute for Barry Bradbury in the televised game against Chesterfield in November 1972, 9 days before his 17th birthday, making him their youngest ever senior player. With Walter Joyce preferring to go with youth, Paul had further opportunities the following season and became a regular in midfield half way through 1974-75. Indeed, by the time he was 18 and a half, he was the longest serving player at the club. He was later a noted player in Ireland, playing in the European Cup against Red Star Belgrade after Sligo won the League of Ireland. He returned to become their player-manager when he was only 26, the youngest manager in senior football in the British Isles, and steered them to qualification for Europe again.

Kenneth (Ken) Williams 1971-73
Born: {Lancashire c.1955}
Defender
FL Apps/Gls +0/0 Total Apps/Gls +0/0
Career: {Sacred Heart?}, Dale app 10.4.71 to 22.5.73. Castle (Sunday League) 1975

Ken was an apprentice at Dale and was named as substitute the week after Paul Fielding had made the bench, but in his case was not used. He wasn't selected again and left at the end of his apprenticeship, returning to local football.

Michael David (Mick) Poole 1972-78, 1981-82

Born: Morley 23.4.55
6'0" 12st7
Goalkeeper
FL Apps 219
Total Apps 252+1
Career: Pudsey Juniors, Leeds Ashley Road, Coventry C. app 1971, Dale 16.10.72 [192], Denver Dynamos loan summer 1974 [17 NASL], Portland Timbers loan summer 1977 [21 NASL],

Portland Timbers 2.78 to 1980 £15,000 [85 NASL], (+ Houston Summit 1979-80, Portland Timbers 1980-81, indoor soccer), Dale 1981 to cs.82 [27], (Baltimore Blast 1982-83 indoor soccer)
Honours: National Conference final (NASL) 1978

Mick joined Dale as a 17 year old, making his debut in the Lancashire Cup, and became their regular keeper half a dozen games into the following season. Despite conceding 91 goals in 43 games as Dale sank to relegation, he won the player of the year award, winning it a second time in 1977. He made over 200 appearances, with several interludes in the North American Soccer League, before a permanent transfer to Portland Timbers where he was rated one of the best performers in the one-on-one US style shoot-outs (and wore a squad number of 00!). He also played in the Major Indoor Soccer League before reappearing at Spotland for one further campaign, when he took his overall tally past 250 games thus surpassing Ted Burgin's record for a Dale 'keeper. On the down side, he was the first Dale keeper to be sent off, for squaring up to the opposition centre forward, who was also dismissed, in a defeat at Brentford in 1975.

William Mark (Bill) Atkins 1972-74

Born: Solihull 9.5.39
6'2" 12st7
Centre forward
FL Apps/Gls 25/7
Total Apps/Gls 27/8
Career: Birmingham GPO, Aston Villa 5.58, Swindon T. 6.59 [75/27], Halifax T. 8.65 (part exchange) [74/34], Stockport Co. 3.67 £4500 [92/37], Portsmouth 3.69 £10,000 [11/2], Halifax T. 12.69 £9000 [123+2/37], Dale 9.12.72 £1750 [25/7], Darlington 27.9.73 £1000 [41+3/12], trainer 11.74
Honours: Division 3 promotion 1963

A veteran centre forward signed by Dale to replace Jack Howarth, when the latter returned to Aldershot, Bill had had a successful start to his league career as an inside forward at Swindon in the early sixties. He maintained a good strike rate for his subsequent clubs and was a particular favourite at Halifax where he scored over 70 goals in 200 games in two spells. A regular in the second half of 1973-74, he was then one of the experienced players moved on by Walter Joyce and followed Dick Conner to Darlington along with Gordon Morritt and then Colin Blant and Dick Renwick.

Leopold Anthony (Leo) Skeete 1972-75

Born: Liverpool 3.8.49
6'1" 12st3
Striker
FL Apps/Gls 39+1/14
Total Apps/Gls 46+1/15
Career: Burscough, Ellesmere Port T. £250, Dale 4.4.73 £1500 [39+1/14], Mossley loan 1.75, signed 14.3.75 £500, Runcorn cs.81 £3500 [51+4/18 Conf], Altrincham 1983-84 [30/8 Conf]
Honours: England semi-professional international, Northern Premier League champions 1979, 1980, Alliance League champions 1983, NPL cup winners 1979, FA Trophy final 1980, FA XI 1977-78, Northern Premier League XI

One of the top non-league strikers of his generation, Leo was spotted by Dale while with Ellesmere Port and scored in each of his first three games at the end of 1972-73. Easily top scorer with just 10 goals the following term when Dale were relegated, despite being used in only half the games he moved to Mossley where he attained legendary status. Nicknamed the 'Dusky Destroyer', he hit 45 goals in all games in 1976-77, captained the side, twice won the player of the year award as Mossley took the NPL championship, played for the England semi-professional side, and was voted a Non-League Player of the Year in 1980 when Mossley also won the FA Trophy at Wembley. Awarded a testimonial game against Manchester United in 1980, he eventually totalled 188 goals in 351 games before a late career move to Runcorn where he won the Alliance League (subsequently renamed the Conference). He had worked for the Mossley chairman's engineering company and later became a company director. Leo's brother Steve also played for Mossley and Runcorn.

INDEX TO PLAYERS

		Page	Season	To	FL	FAC	FLC	LSC	ExpL	WL	Other	Total
Harold	Acton	45	1944-45							2/1		2/1
Alf	Ainsworth	15	1939-40	1944-45						16/3		16/3
Walter	Ainsworth	44	1944-45							7/3		7/3
Bob	Ancell	32	1941-42							1/1		1/1
Roy	Anchor	105	1959-60					1/0				1/0
Jimmy	Anders	83	1953-54	1956-57	123/28	6/2		6/3				135/33
Alex	Anderson	65	1947-48		4							4
Alfie	Anderson	13	1939-40					1/0		10/1		11/1
Eddie	Anderson	66	1947-48		1/0							1/0
Johnny	Anderson	104	1959-60		28/5	4/1		1/0				33/6
Derek	Andrews	90	1955-56	1956-57	22/4	2/0		1/1				25/5
Alf	Arrowsmith	131	1970-71	1971-72	40+6/14	2/3	1/0	4+1/3			1/1	48+7/21
Jackie	Arthur	63	1946-47	1953-54	170/25	12/2		9/0				191/27
Ken	Ashbridge	57	1945-46							3		3
Joe	Ashworth	128	1968-69	1971-72	133/3	8/1	8/0	8/1			4/0	161/5
Ray	Aspden	90	1955-56	1966-67	297/2	9/0	20/0	13/0	2/0		5/0	346/2
Bill	Atkins	137	1972-73	1973-74	25/7		1/1	1/0				27/8
Kenneth	Atkinson	45	1944-45							2/0		2/0
Arthur	Bailey	50	1944-45							1/0		1/0
Alan	Ball	79	1951-52		5/1							5/1
John	Banner	43	1943-44	1944-45						2/0		2/0
Neville	Bannister	116	1965-66		18+1/2		1/0	2/0			1/0	22+1/2
Eric	Barber	75	1950-51	1951-52	17/2							17/2
Kevin	Barber	98	1957-58					1/0				1/0
Tommy	Barkas	60	1946-47	1947-48	44/17	3/1		4/1				51/19
Jeff	Barker	30	1941-42	1942-43						3/0		3/0
Ron	Barnes	103	1959-60	1960-61	91/7	6/1	4/2	4/0				105/10
Roly	Bartholomew	33	1941-42	1942-43						11/6		11/6
James	Bate	50	1944-45							1/0		1/0
Sam	Baum	59	1945-46							1/0		1/0
David	Bebb	37	1942-43							5/1		5/1
Keith	Bebbington	135	1972-73	1973-74	57+3/6	4/0	3/0	4/0			+1/0	68+4/6
Alf	Bellis	21	1940-41	1941-42						9/2		9/2
Eric	Betts	78	1951-52	1952-53	52/8	4/2						56/10
Lou	Bimpson	109	1961-62	1962-63	54/16	1/0	8/4	3/0	2/1		2/0	70/21
Brian(1)	Birch	108	1960-61	1961-62	11/0	1/0		1/0				13/0
Brian(2)	Birch	115	1964-65	1965-66	60+1/6	4/0	2/0	4/0				70+1/6
Wally	Birch	57	1945-46	1953-54	243/10	14/2		12/1		11/0		280/13
Neville	Black	83	1953-54	1955-56	62/13	1/0		4/1				67/14
Ronnie	Blair	131	1969-70	1982-83	69+5/3	3+1/1	7/0	12/0			1+1/0	92+7/4
Colin	Blant	134	1972-73	1973-74	51/0	1/0	3/0	1/0			1/0	57/0
Jack	Blood	39	1942-43							3/0		3/0
Norman	Bodell	102	1958-59	1962-63	79/1	3/0	6/0	4/2	1/0		1/0	94/3
Arnold	Bonell	67	1948-49		5/0			1/0				6/0
Les	Boulter	28	1941-42							1/0		1/0
Jim	Bowie	136	1972-73		1+2/0			2/0				3+2/0
Dan	Boxshall	82	1952-53	1953-54	11/3			1/0				12/3
Harry	Boyle	74	1950-51	1955-56	175/0	9/0		6/0				190/0
Ken	Bracewell	126	1967-68		5/0							5/0
Barry	Bradbury	135	1972-73	1973-74	12+2/0	3/0		1/0				16+2/0
Lew	Bradford	34	1942-43	1943-44						72/0		72/0
Jack	Bradley	45	1944-45							1/0		1/0
Jack	Bradshaw	45	1944-45							2/0		2/0
Tom	Breakwell	38	1942-43	1943-44						20/0		20/0
Jack	Breedon	53	1945-46							4		4
Charlie	Briggs	63	1946-47	1947-48	12			1				13
Jack	Brindle	54	1945-46	1947-48	1/0	6/1		1/1		17/8		25/10
Jack	Brinton	49	1944-45							2/1		2/1
Jimmy	Britton	65	1947-48	1948-49	20/0	1/0		1/0				22/0
Lee	Brogden	134	1971-72	1973-74	48+9/7	4/2		2+1/0				54+10/9
Cyril	Brown	68	1948-49	1950-51	61/11	4/1		4/0				69/12
Jim	Brown	97	1956-57	1960-61	52/4	3/1	3/0	2/0				60/5
	Brown	36	1942-43							2/0		2/0
Alistair	Buchan	75	1950-51	1954-55	107/2	3/0		3/0				113/2
Tony	Buck	129	1968-69	1972-73	73+11/29	5+1/2	2+1/0	7/1			3/1	90+13/33
Tom	Burdett	18	1939-40							2/2		2/2

		Page	Season	To	FL	FAC	FLC	LSC	ExpL	WL	Other	Total
Ted	Burgin	107	1960-61	1965-66	207	10	17	6	2		4	246
Billy	Burnicle	39	1942-43							1/0		1/0
Alan	Bushby	103	1959-60	1960-61	66/0	5/0	4/0	1/0				76/0
Dennis	Butler	125	1967-68	1972-73	152+4/36	6/1	7/2	7+1/1			5+1/1	177+6/41
	Byrne	40	1942-43							1/0		1/0
Bill	Byrom	16	1939-40	1947-48	30/0	3/0				85/0		118/0
Les	Bywater	64	1947-48	1948-49	34	2		3				39
Ron	Cairns	103	1959-60	1963-64	195/66	10/4	15/3	8/2	2/1		3/2	233/78
Bill	Calder	120	1966-67		7+1/1	1/0						8+1/1
Ray	Calderbank	87	1953-54	1957-58	1/0			1/0				2/0
Laurie	Calloway	113	1964-65	1967-68	161+1/4	6/1	7/0	5/1			5/0	184+1/6
Bill	Carey	13	1939-40	1940-41				1/0		22/0		23/0
Roy	Carrick	42	1943-44							1/0		1/0
Alex	Carruthers	61	1946-47		13/4	3/2		1/0				17/6
Don	Carter	17	1939-40							3/1		3/1
Norman	Case	79	1951-52		2/0							2/0
Cliff	Chadwick	14	1939-40							1/0		1/0
James	Chambers	48	1944-45							1/0		1/0
Alfred	Chaney	45	1944-45							1/0		1/0
Jimmy	Cheetham	69	1948-49					1/0				1/0
Tommy	Chester	13	1939-40							5/0		5/0
Arthur	Chesters	33	1941-42	1945-46		6				69		75
Jackie	Chew	26	1940-41							1/0		1/0
Trevor	Churchill	70	1948-49	1952-53	110	1		4				115
Paul	Clarke	129	1969-70	1971-72	10+1/0		1/0				1/0	12+1/0
	Clarke	26	1940-41							1/0		1/0
J.	Clive	54	1945-46							1/0		1/0
Harry	Cload	38	1942-43							8/4		8/4
Davy	Cochrane	46	1944-45							2/1		2/1
Tom	Cochrane	46	1944-45							4/1		4/1
Vic	Cockroft	124	1967-68		42/0	1/0					1/0	44/0
Doug	Cole	46	1944-45							2/0		2/0
Ossie	Collier	63	1946-47	1947-48	6/0							6/0
Albert	Collinge	40	1942-43							1/0		1/0
Graham	Collins	119	1966-67		7/0		1/0					8/0
Tony	Collins	104	1959-60	1961-62	47/5	3/1		1/0				51/6
Duncan	Colquhoun	15	1939-40	1942-43						41/7		41/7
Hugh	Colvan	66	1947-48		1/0							1/0
Jack	Connor	19	1940-41							17/0		17/0
Jack T.	Connor	70	1948-49	1950-51	82/42	3/3		6/3				91/48
Kevin	Connor	117	1965-66	1966-67	21+2/1	1/0		3/0				25+2/1
S.	Connor	43	1943-44							1/0		1/0
Jimmy	Constantine	47	1944-45					1/1		13/7		14/8
George	Cooper	102	1958-59	1959-60	32/9			1/0				33/9
Graham	Cordell	83	1953-54	1954-55	15	1		3				19
Wally	Cornock	64	1947-48		1							1
Ellis	Cornwell	40	1942-43	1944-45						33/0		33/0
Joe	Coupe	78	1951-52		8/0							8/0
Dave	Crompton	122	1966-67	1967-68	15+2/0							15+2/0
Dave	Cross	130	1969-70	1971-72	50+9/20	4+1/1	5+1/2	2/2		1+1/1		62+12/26
Paul	Crossley	118	1965-66	1966-67	17/2		1/0				1/0	19/2
Ken	Crowther	75	1950-51		2/0							2/0
Arthur	Cunliffe	44	1944-45	1946-47	23/5	9/3		2/0		32/5		66/13
Graham	Cunliffe	114	1964-65		36/0	1/0	2/0	1/0			1/0	41/0
Jim	Cunliffe	19	1940-41	1946-47	2/0					90/47		92/47
Frank	Curran	35	1942-43							1/0		1/0
Roger	Cutler	120	1966-67					1				1
Stan	Cutting	33	1941-42	1942-43						13/1		13/1
Jim	Dailey	98	1957-58	1958-59	53/25	2/0		2/0				57/25
Malcolm	Darling	133	1971-72	1973-74	82+4/16	2/0	3/2	4+1/2			+1/1	91+6/21
Ray	Daubney	121	1966-67	1967-68	12/2			2+1/0				14+1/2
Andrew	Davenport	27	1941-42							5/0		5/0
Alec	Davies	27	1941-42							1/0		1/0
Bob	Davies	43	1943-44	1944-45						2/0		2/0
Robert	Delaney	31	1941-42							1/0		1/0
Joe	Devlin	95	1956-57	1957-58	38/7			1/0				39/7
Jack	Dobson	58	1945-46							5/0		5/0
Tom	Dooley	29	1941-42	1943-44						21/1		21/1
David	Dow	122	1966-67	1967-68	8/0			1+1/0			1/0	10+1/0

		Page	Season	To	FL	FAC	FLC	LSC	ExpL	WL	Other	Total
Bobby	Downes	129	1969-70	1973-74	164+10/10	8+1/2	9/0	10/0			1+1/0	192+12/12
Eric	Downes	75	1950-51	1953-54	54/0	4/0		2/0				60/0
Jim	Drury	77	1951-52		4/1							4/1
Tommy	Dryburgh	68	1948-49	1957-58	82/17	4/1		10/4				96/22
Bertie	Duffy	37	1942-43							13/1		13/1
Sam	Earl	16	1939-40	1947-48	4/1	2/0				1/0		7/1
Brian	Eastham	123	1967-68		13/0		1/0	1/0			1/0	16/0
George	Eastham	67	1948-49		2/0	1/0		2/0				5/0
Eric	Eastwood	18	1940-41							3/0		3/0
Jack	Edwards	104	1959-60	1960-61	68/1	4/0		3/0				75/1
Jack	Ellis	12	1939-40							2		2
Bob	Entwistle	102	1958-59	1960-61	1/0			1/0				2/0
Fred	Evans	83	1953-54		12/0			1/0				13/0
George	Farrow	25	1940-41							1/0		1/0
Harry	Fearnley	90	1955-56		1							1
Micky	Fenton	22	1940-41							1/0		1/0
Charlie	Ferguson	92	1955-56	1958-59	150/4	6/0		5/1				161/5
Bill	Fielding	40	1943-44							12		12
Paul	Fielding	136	1972-73	1975-76	65+7/5	3/0	1+1/0					69+8/5
Bill	Finney	100	1958-59		31/1	3/1		1/0				35/2
Fred	Fisher	76	1951-52		1/0			1/0				2/0
Joe	Fletcher	122	1966-67	1968-69	55+2/21	1/1	2/0	4/0			4/0	66+2/22
Wiliam	Folds	36	1942-43							1		1
Bert	Foulds	73	1950-51	1952-53	61/24	4/0		2/0				67/24
Jack	Foxton	48	1944-45							1/0		1/0
Frank	France	34	1941-42	1942-43						2/0		2/0
Des	Frost	86	1953-54	1954-55	16/6	1/0						17/6
Con	Gallacher	66	1947-48		6/1							6/1
Frank	Gallimore	36	1942-43							6/0		6/0
Jack	Gallon	44	1943-44	1944-45						23/5		23/5
Arthur	Garfoot	36	1942-43							1/0		1/0
Harry	Gee	38	1942-43	1943-44						44/19		44/19
Eric	Gemmell	89	1954-55	1955-56	65/32	5/2		4/1				74/35
Jimmy	Gemmell	50	1944-45							3/0		3/0
Bobby	Gilfillan	77	1951-52	1953-54	62/11	1/0		2/0				65/11
Bev	Glover	87	1953-54	1958-59	169/1	9/0		8/0				186/1
Tony	Godfrey	131	1970-71	1971-72	71	3	4	3			2	83
Ted	Goodall	35	1942-43							3		3
Willie	Gorman	26	1941-42							8/0		8/0
Peter	Gowans	132	1970-71	1973-74	136+8/21	4+1/0	6/1	13/1			1+1/0	160+10/23
Billy	Graham	20	1940-41							2/0		2/0
John	Graham	82	1952-53		10/1							10/1
Jackie	Grant	93	1956-57	1958-59	102/3	2/0		1/0				105/3
Brian	Green	88	1954-55	1958-59	46/8	1/0		7/0				54/8
Les	Green	123	1967-68		44	1	1	2			3	51
Albert	Griffiths	45	1944-45							1/0		1/0
Robert	Griffiths	54	1945-46							1/0		1/0
Walker	Grimsditch	45	1944-45							7		7
Ray	Haddington	81	1952-53	1953-54	38/12	1/0		1/0				40/12
George	Haigh	41	1943-44	1945-46				1/0		60/3		61/3
Jack	Haines	85	1953-54	1954-55	60/16	5/1		3/1				68/18
Harry	Hall	48	1944-45							2		2
Jack	Hall	15	1939-40	1941-42						38		38
Bill	Hallard	59	1946-47		17/2	3/0		2/0				22/2
Reg	Halton	18	1939-40							1/0		1/0
W.	Hamilton	57	1945-46							2/0		2/0
Brian	Handley	118	1965-66		3/0							3/0
S.	Hanna	27	1941-42							1/0		1/0
Alf	Hanson	48	1944-45	1945-46				2/0		17/11		19/11
Brian	Hardman	116	1964-65	1966-67	+0/0			2/0				2/0
John	Hardman	106	1960-61	1966-67	40/2	2/0	2/0	5/0			2/0	51/2
Joe	Hargreaves	55	1945-46	1947-48	35/24	9/8		1/1		23/18		68/51
Tommy	Hargreaves	60	1946-47		7/0							7/0
Chris	Harker	126	1968-69	1969-70	92	3	2	3			2	102
Jack	Harker	38	1942-43	1945-46						40/38		40/38
Willie	Harker	12	1939-40	1940-41						12/1		12/1
Les	Harley	124	1967-68		5/0						2/0	7/0
James	Harrison	23	1940-41	1944-45						22/5		22/5
Alex	Hawson	69	1948-49		1/0							1/0

		Page	Season	To	FL	FAC	FLC	LSC	ExpL	WL	Other	Total
Eric	Hayton	77	1951-52		12/0			1/0				13/0
Jimmy	Hazzleton	77	1951-52		11/1			1/0				12/1
John	Heath	117	1965-66		6			2				8
Billy	Heaton	74	1950-51		5/0	1/0						6/0
Bill	Henderson	60	1946-47		17	3		2				22
Stan	Hepton	105	1960-61	1963-64	149/21	7/1	16/5	4/1	1/0		3/0	180/28
Albert	Hesketh	49	1944-45							1		1
Cyril	Heydon	67	1948-49		1/0							1/0
George	Heyes	100	1958-59	1959-60	24			1				25
Kenneth	Heyes	24	1940-41							1		1
Jack	Higham	51	1944-45	1945-46						2/0		2/0
Tom	Hindle	79	1951-52		6/1							6/1
Charlie	Hogan	81	1952-53		3/0							3/0
Stewart	Holden	122	1966-67		21/0							21/0
Ron	Hood	69	1948-49		9/1							9/1
Walter	Horrabin	24	1940-41	1942-43						20/10		20/10
Jimmy	Horton	29	1941-42							8/0		8/0
Les	Horton	25	1940-41	1949-50						15/0		15/0
Jack	Howarth	133	1971-72	1972-73	40/12	1/0	2/0	2/1			1/0	46/13
Jack	Howshall	59	1945-46							1/0		1/0
Harry	Hubbick	71	1948-49	1950-51	90/0	2/0		7/0				99/0
A.	Hughes	24	1940-41							1/0		1/0
Archie	Hughes	73	1950-51		9			1				10
Arthur	Hughes	50	1944-45							1/0		1/0
Dave	Hunt	136	1972-73					2+1/0				2+1/0
George	Hunt	19	1940-41							5/0		5/0
Charlie	Hurst	57	1945-46	1946-47	4/1					5/0		9/1
Malcolm	Hussey	102	1958-59		1/0							1/0
Barry	Hutchinson	124	1967-68		27/3			2/1			1/1	30/5
Dennis	Isherwood	22	1940-41							1/0		1/0
Harry	Jackson	93	1955-56		1/1							1/1
Len	Jackson	55	1945-46	1946-47	61/0	6/0		3/0		5/0		75/0
Reg	Jenkins	114	1964-65	1972-73	294+11/119	10+1/5	16/5	16+1/9			10/3	346+13/141
Bill	Jennings	76	1951-52		3/1							3/1
Roy	John	32	1941-42							2		2
George	Johnson	89	1954-55	1955-56	1/0							1/0
Jack	Johnson	23	1940-41							1/0		1/0
Ron	Johnston	65	1947-48		17/7	2/0						19/7
A.	Jones	36	1942-43							1/1		1/1
Arthur	Jones	52	1945-46	1946-47	1/0	2/0		1/0		12/3		16/3
David	Jones	28	1941-42							9/7		9/7
David L.G.	Jones	37	1942-43							15/3		15/3
Jimmy	Jones	43	1943-44	1944-45						16/2		16/2
Jimmy A.	Jones	91	1955-56	1960-61	177	8	1	6				192
John	Jones	58	1945-46							2		2
Ossie	Jones	34	1941-42							1/0		1/0
Rod	Jones	132	1971-72	1973-74	19	1	3	4			1+1	28+1
Simon	Jones	112	1963-64	1966-67	47		2	1			1+1	51+1
Tom	Jones	21	1940-41	1944-45						59/1		59/1
Tom A.	Jones	69	1948-49					1/0				1/0
Verdun	Jones	29	1941-42	1942-43						15/5		15/5
Wally	Jones	61	1946-47		2/2							2/2
Arthur	Joseph	41	1943-44							1/0		1/0
Konrad	Kapler	71	1949-50		4/0							4/0
Joe	Keddie	56	1945-46							1/0		1/0
Walter	Keeley	78	1951-52		4/0	1/0						5/0
Ike	Keen	22	1940-41							19/0		19/0
Arnold	Kendall	85	1953-54	1956-57	111/25	5/1		5/1				121/27
Dave	Kerry	112	1963-64		12/4	1/0	2/1	2/0				17/5
Vince	Kershaw	21	1940-41							5/1		5/1
John	Kindred	59	1945-46							1/0		1/0
Len	Kinsella	133	1971-72	1973-74	82+3/4	2/0	3/0	7/0			1/0	95+3/4
John	Kirk	56	1945-46	1946-47			1			5		6
Norman	Kirkman	24	1940-41	1947-48	53/0	3/0		4/0		6/0		66/0
Cyril	Lawrence	63	1946-47	1949-50	44/5	1/0		4/0				49/5
Steve	Lee	128	1968-69								1/0	1/0
Vinny	Leech	127	1968-69	1970-71	59+1/1	3/0	1/0	4/0			1/0	68+1/1
Les	Leivesley	42	1943-44							1/0		1/0
Cyril	Lello	95	1956-57		11/0							11/0

		Page	Season	To	FL	FAC	FLC	LSC	ExpL	WL	Other	Total
Gwyn	Lewis	94	1956-57		27/11	1/0						28/11
Bert	Lister	115	1964-65	1966-67	56/16	3/2	4/1	1/1			1/0	65/20
Sandy	Lister	80	1952-53		2/0							2/0
Jack	Livesey	55	1945-46	1950-51	113/36	6/1		5/1		1/1		125/39
Archie	Livingstone	17	1939-40							2/2		2/2
Jock	Lockhart	97	1957-58		40/11	1/0		1/0				42/11
Bert	Lomas	72	1950-51		9	3						12
Charlie	Longdon	65	1947-48		2/0							2/0
Frank	Lord	86	1953-54	1960-61	122/54	3/0	3/2	3/0				131/56
Harry	Lowe	46	1944-45							5/0		5/0
George	Lunn	53	1945-46							1/0		1/0
Joe	Lynn	76	1951-52	1955-56	193/23	10/1		5/0				208/24
Eddie	Lyons	49	1944-45	1954-55	19/1	3/0		2/0		5/0		29/1
George	Lyons	86	1953-54	1956-57	29/4			1/0				30/4
J.	Macauley	44	1943-44	1944-45						2/0		2/0
Willie	MacFadyen	31	1941-42							2/0		2/0
Jim	Maguire	99	1958-59		15/0	3/0						18/0
Sammy	Makin	47	1944-45	1946-47	5/1	2/1		2/0		30/7		39/9
Albert	Malam	50	1944-45							2/0		2/0
Andy	Mandzuk	132	1970-71		+0/0							+0/0
Willie	Mangham	31	1941-42	1944-45						3/0		3/0
James	Manning	36	1942-43							1/0		1/0
Stan	Marriott	82	1952-53		6/2							6/2
Arthur	Marsh	133	1971-72	1973-74	89+1/0	3/1	1+1/0	5/0			1/0	99+2/1
Frank	Marsh	39	1942-43							1/0		1/0
Jack	Martin	111	1962-63	1963-64	24/1		2/0	2/0			+1/0	28+1/1
Richard	Maudsley	41	1943-44							4/0		4/0
Gordon	McBain	99	1958-59		10/1			2/0				12/1
Johnnny	McClelland	90	1955-56		24/5			1/0				25/5
Joe	McCormick	52	1945-46	1947-48	66/0	10/0		5/0		28/1		109/1
Benny	McCready	97	1957-58	1958-59	29	2		3				34
Bill	McCulloch	87	1954-55	1957-58	140/2	3/0		6/0				149/2
Ken	McDowell	106	1960-61		6/0		1/0	1/0				8/0
Frank	McEwan	122	1966-67	1967-68	17/2	1/0		2/0				20/2
John	McGahie	41	1943-44							1/0		1/0
George	McGeachie	69	1948-49	1950-51	90/6	5/0		6/0				101/6
Tom	McGlennon	97	1957-58	1958-59	61/2	4/0		4/0				69/2
Jack	McGowan	18	1939-40							1/0		1/0
Jimmy	McGuigan	93	1956-57	1958-59	70/2	4/0		3/0				77/2
Joffre	McKay	106	1960-61	1962-63	9	2	3	2				16
Don	McKenzie	113	1963-64	1964-65	41/7			1/0			1/0	43/7
Andy	McLaren	92	1955-56	1956-57	44/12	1/0		1/0				46/12
Alex	McNichol	75	1950-51		17/3							17/3
Ian	McQueen	117	1965-66	1966-67	14+2/4			1/0			1/0	16+2/4
Gordon	Medd	73	1950-51		5/1							5/1
Joe	Meek	53	1945-46							4/1		4/1
Steve	Melledew	120	1966-67	1977-78	164+11/35	7/0	7+1/2	5/2			2/1	185+12/40
Terry	Melling	129	1968-69		20/8			3/0				23/8
Alan	Middlebrough	68	1948-49	1951-52	47/25	7/2		3/2				57/29
John	Middleton	30	1941-42							1/0		1/0
Stan	Milburn	101	1958-59	1964-65	238/26	13/1	18/0	1/0	2/0		3/0	275/27
N.	Miller	35	1942-43							1/0		1/0
Willie	Miller	41	1943-44							7/0		7/0
Harry	Mills	76	1950-51		1/0							1/0
Frank	Mitcheson	87	1954-55	1955-56	50/8	5/1		1/0				56/9
Gerry	Molloy	93	1955-56	1957-58	6/0							6/0
Paddy	Molloy	53	1945-46					1/0		4/0		5/0
Alan	Moore	101	1958-59		11/2			1/1				12/3
Alan	Moorhouse	61	1946-47	1947-48	17/3							17/3
Eddie	Moran	96	1956-57	1958-59	43/13	1/0						44/13
Ralph	Morement	91	1955-56		1/0							1/0
Bill	Morgan	84	1953-54		28/0			1/0				29/0
Billy	Morris	82	1952-53		4/1							4/1
Ernest	Morris	42	1943-44	1944-45						20/10		20/10
Gordon	Morritt	135	1972-73	1973-74	31		2					33
Albert	Morton	84	1953-54	1956-57	89	4		1				94
George	Morton	111	1962-63	1965-66	146+1/51	6/0	8/4	2/0			2/2	164+1/57
Jackie	Moss	62	1946-47	1948-49	58/17	3/0		3/0				64/17
Brian	Mottershead	85	1953-54	1954-55	1/0							1/0

		Page	Season	To	FL	FAC	FLC	LSC	ExpL	WL	Other	Total
Tony	Moulden	111	1962-63	1966-67	6/1	2/0		1/0				9/1
Reg	Mountford	20	1940-41							4/0		4/0
Matthew	Muir	45	1944-45							15/0		15/0
Robert	Muir	52	1945-46							1/0		1/0
Edward	Mulligan	41	1943-44							3/1		3/1
Terry	Mulvoy	96	1956-57	1957-58	2/0							2/0
Danny	Murphy	88	1954-55		109/0	5/0		5/1				119/1
George	Murphy	38	1942-43	1943-44						6/3		6/3
Les	Murray	81	1952-53		16/3							16/3
Albert	Mycock	51	1944-45							2/0		2/0
Dick	Neilson	56	1945-46							3/0		3/0
David	Neville	90	1955-56		1/0							1/0
George	Nevin	12	1939-40							1/0		1/0
George	Newall	98	1957-58		1/0			1/0				2/0
Jimmy	Nicholls	77	1951-52		50	3		2				55
Benny	Nicol	71	1949-50		5/1			2/0				7/1
Ollie	Norris	108	1960-61		2/1			1/0				3/1
Harry	Nuttall	59	1945-46							1/0		1/0
Jack	Oakes	62	1946-47		1/0							1/0
Hugh	O'Donnell	62	1946-47		40/14	2/1		2/1				44/16
Fred	Olive	51	1944-45	1945-46				1		3		4
Tommy	Olsen	12	1939-40					1/0		13/1		14/1
Michael	O'Mahoney	42	1943-44	1945-46						3/0		3/0
Bryn	Owen	106	1960-61	1962-63	6/0			4/0			1/0	11/0
Herbert	Palfreyman	40	1942-43							3/0		3/0
Steve	Parr	96	1956-57	1957-58	16/1							16/1
Colin	Parry	127	1968-69	1971-72	154+2/1	9/0	4/0	10/0			4/0	181+2/1
Don	Partridge	54	1945-46	1955-56	103/2	10/0		8/0		14/0		135/2
Samuel	Patton	31	1941-42							3/0		3/0
Dave	Pearson	96	1956-57	1957-58	32/17			1/0				33/17
Dave A.J.	Pearson	132	1970-71		3/0			1/0				4/0
Jim	Pennington	120	1966-67		14/0	1/0					+1/0	15+1/0
Peter	Phoenix	111	1962-63	1963-64	36/4	2/1	1/0					39/5
Ron	Phoenix	105	1960-61	1961-62	64/0	4/0	8/0	3/0	1/0		1/0	81/0
Stanley	Pickstock	47	1944-45							1/1		1/1
Cliff	Pitt	30	1941-42							7		7
Jack	Pollitt	106	1960-61		6/1	2/1						8/2
Syd	Pomphrey	52	1945-46	1946-47	9/0	4/0		4/0		29/0		46/0
Mick	Poole	136	1972-73	1981-82	219	20	10	3			+1	252+1
Harry	Potter	80	1952-53		52/0	2/0		2/0				56/0
Dai	Powell	100	1958-59	1960-61	76/1	9/0	2/0	2/0				89/1
Walter	Price	67	1948-49		1/0							1/0
Bob	Priday	84	1953-54		5/1							5/1
Mark	Radcliffe	82	1952-53		1	1						2
Vince	Radcliffe	127	1968-69		26/1	2/0	1/0	3/0				32/1
Alf	Radford	76	1951-52		27/0	3/0		1/0				31/0
Barrie	Ratcliffe	117	1965-66		12/1	3/0	2/0	2/1				19/2
Syd	Rawlings	16	1939-40	1940-41						22/6		22/6
Doug	Redwood	16	1939-40	1943-44						7/3		7/3
Maurice	Reeday	24	1940-41							1/0		1/0
Dave	Reid	66	1947-48	1950-51	36/2			2/0				38/2
John	Reid	123	1967-68		37+2/3	1/0	1/0	1/0			2/0	42+2/3
John M.	Reid	47	1944-45	1945-46						13/7		13/7
Dick	Renwick	134	1972-73	1973-74	48+1/0	1/0	2/0	4/0			1/0	56+1/0
Harry	Revell	48	1944-45							1/0		1/0
Arthur	Richardson	14	1939-40							15/15		15/15
Brian	Richardson	119	1966-67		19/1		1/0				1/0	21/1
Joe	Richardson	107	1960-61	1964-65	115/31	2/2	11/5	5/1	1/0		2+1/2	136+1/41
Norman	Richardson	57	1945-46							1/0		1/0
Gil	Richmond	33	1941-42	1942-43						14/0		14/0
Norman	Richmond	36	1942-43							1/0		1/0
Roy	Ridge	113	1964-65	1965-66	85/0	3/0	5/0	2/0			2/0	97/0
Hughie	Riley	121	1966-67	1971-72	81+11/12	5/0	4/0	7+2/1			3/0	100+13/13
Bill	Roberts	58	1945-46	1948-49	43	3		2		5		53
Syd	Roberts	47	1944-45							2/1		2/1
Alick	Robinson	17	1939-40							3/0		3/0
Jack	Robinson	23	1940-41							1/0		1/0
Ernie	Robson	14	1939-40	1941-42						12		12
Joe	Rodi	58	1945-46	1946-47	9/3					7/5		16/8

		Page	Season	To	FL	FAC	FLC	LSC	ExpL	WL	Other	Total
Ken	Rose	83	1953-54		11/0							11/0
B.	Rothwell	23	1940-41							1/0		1/0
Ron	Rothwell	62	1946-47	1953-54	48/0	2/0		4/0				54/0
Billy (snr)	Rudd	41	1943-44							2/0		2/0
Billy	Rudd	125	1967-68	1969-70	108/8	3/0	2/0	4/0			3/0	120/8
Harold	Rudman	97	1957-58		21/1	1/0		1/0				23/1
Billy	Russell	119	1966-67	1967-68	60+1/8	2/0	2/0	2/0			3/1	69+1/9
Derek	Ryder	127	1968-69	1971-72	168/1	9/0	8/0	14/0			4/0	203/1
Jim	Sanders	107	1960-61					1/0				1/0
	Schofield	39	1942-43							1/0		1/0
Harry	Seddon	23	1940-41	1944-45						8/1		8/1
John	Shadwell	14	1939-40							1/0		1/0
	Shaw	38	1942-43							1/0		1/0
Jimmy	Shields	30	1941-42							3/0		3/0
Tom	Sibley	42	1943-44	1947-48	23/3	2/0		1/0		3/3		29/6
Wally	Sidebottom	20	1940-41							17/11		17/11
George	Sievwright	117	1965-66		31+1/1	3/1	2/0	3/0			+1/0	39+2/2
Charlie	Simpson	134	1971-72	1972-73	1/1			1/0				2/1
Leo	Skeete	137	1972-73	1974-75	39+1/14	4/0	3/1					46+1/15
Mike	Skivington	66	1947-48		1/0							1/0
Clem	Smith	59	1945-46							1/0		1/0
Fred	Smith	29	1941-42							11/1		11/1
Graham	Smith	118	1966-67	1973-74	316+1/3	15/0	13/1	19/1			8+1/1	371+2/6
Jack	Smith	27	1941-42							1		1
Tom	Smith	35	1942-43							2/0		2/0
Bob	Smyth	74	1950-51		3/1			1/0				4/1
Les	Spencer	99	1957-58	1959-60	74/17	7/2		5/1				86/20
Wally	Stanners	72	1949-50	1950-51	5	1		1				7
Alan	Steen	72	1950-51	1951-52	45/8	3/1		1/0				49/9
Bob	Stephenson	116	1965-66	1966-67	50+1/16	1/0	2/1	3/0			1/1	57+1/18
Bernard	Stonehouse	92	1955-56	1956-57	19/1			2/1				21/2
Jim	Storey	89	1955-56	1956-57	24/1	1/0		3/0				28/1
Dave	Storf	112	1963-64	1966-67	138/19	5/1	6/2	2/0			3/1	154/23
Donald	Strachan	46	1944-45							6/0		6/0
Jim	Strong	34	1942-43							28		28
Harry	Sutherland	21	1940-41							1/0		1/0
Brian	Sutton	81	1952-53	1955-56	13							13
Fred	Sweeney	39	1942-43							1/0		1/0
Tom	Swinburne	27	1941-42							5		5
Cal	Symonds	91	1955-56		1/0							1/0
Reg	Tapley	95	1956-57		1/0			1/0				2/0
Brian	Taylor	113	1963-64	1967-68	131+1/7	3/0	4/0	3/1			4/0	145+1/8
Fred	Taylor	54	1945-46					1/0		1/1		2/1
J.	Taylor	14	1939-40							7/0		7/0
Jimmy	Taylor	51	1944-45							1/0		1/0
Joe	Taylor	20	1940-41							2/0		2/0
Percy	Taylor	23	1940-41	1944-45						40/9		40/9
Dave	Tennant	130	1969-70	1970-71	16	3		5				24
Jim	Thompson	108	1960-61	1965-66	199/15	9/0	19/2	5/0	2/0		5/0	239/17
	Thompson	37	1942-43							1/0		1/0
Bert	Thomson	100	1958-59		55/1	2/0		2/0				59/1
James	Thorpe	33	1941-42	1942-43						6/0		6/0
Walter	Thorpe	50	1944-45							1		1
Tommy	Todd	94	1956-57		5/1							5/1
Bill	Tolson	85	1953-54	1954-55	10/0	1/0		1/0				12/0
Frank	Tomlinson	79	1951-52		20/2	2/2						22/4
George	Torrance	98	1957-58		2							2
Ernie	Toseland	56	1945-46					1/0		3/2		4/2
Ernie	Toser	28	1941-42							1/0		1/0
Jim	Treanor	26	1941-42	1944-45						44/1		44/1
John	Turley	114	1964-65		22/5	1/0	1/1	1/0			1/1	26/7
Les	Turner	24	1940-41							4/0		4/0
George	Underwood	88	1954-55		19/0							19/0
Colin	Vizard	98	1957-58	1958-59	41/7			1/0				42/7
Harry	Wainman	135	1972-73		9			1				10
Eddie	Wainwright	94	1956-57	1958-59	100/27	5/3		2/0				107/30
Frank	Walkden	25	1940-41	1946-47	1/0					1/0		2/0
Jock	Wallace	99	1957-58	1959-60	7/0			1/0				8/0
John	Walmsley	58	1945-46							1		1

		Page	Season	To	FL	FAC	FLC	LSC	ExpL	WL	Other	Total
Bill	Walsh	31	1941-42							3/0		3/0
George	Walton	34	1942-43							5/0		5/0
Arthur	Warburton	13	1939-40	1943-44				1/0		30/0		31/0
Jack	Warner	80	1952-53		21/0	1/0						22/0
Adam	Wasilewski	84	1953-54		4/1							4/1
Bill	Watson	67	1948-49		200/0	7/0		7/0				214/0
Don	Watson	110	1962-63	1963-64	58/15	4/1	2/1	1/0			+1/0	65+1/17
	Webb	40	1942-43							1/0		1/0
Dick	Webster	27	1941-42							7/1		7/1
Dave	Wells	112	1963-64		8/0	1/0		1/0				10/0
Tom	West	60	1946-47		4/2			2/0				6/2
Harold	Whalley	3	1942-43							1/0		1/0
Jackie	Wharton	43	1943-44							3/1		3/1
Barry	Wheatley	120	1966-67		13/4	1/0	1/0	1/0			1/0	17/4
Don	Whiston	99	1958-59		14/0			3/0				17/0
Colin	Whitaker	110	1961-62	1962-63	54/11	2/0	11/1	1/0	2/1		2/1	72/14
Norman	Whitehead	128	1968-69	1971-72	154+2/11	9/1	8/1	14/1			4/0	189+2/14
Jim	Whitehouse	73	1950-51	1951-52	46/13	2/2		2/0				50/15
Bill	Whittaker	28	1941-42							2/0		2/0
Fred	Whittaker	49	1944-45							7/0		7/0
William	Whittle	52	1944-45	1945-46						5/0		5/0
Harry	Whitworth	29	1941-42	1952-53	70/9	2/0		2/0		1/0		75/9
Peter	Whyke	110	1961-62		5/0	1/0	1/0	3/0				10/0
Tom	Wildsmith	38	1942-43	1945-46						21/0		21/0
Ernie	Wilkinson	126	1967-68		9/0							9/0
Bert	Williams	71	1949-50		8/3			1/0				9/3
Ken	Williams	136	1972-73		+0 0							+0/0
Bob	Williamson	118	1966-67	1967-68	36	1	1				1	39
Charles	Wilson	48	1944-45							1/0		1/0
Charles	Windle	42	1943-44							1/0		1/0
Jack	Winspear	123	1967-68		15+1/3			1/0			1/0	17+1/3
Doug	Winton	109	1961-62	1963-64	119/0	6/0	14/0	3/0	2/0		2/0	146/0
Dick	Withington	64	1947-48		32/6	3/0		2/1				37/7
Eric	Wood	37	1942-43	1950-51	148/15	12/1		13/0		93/39		266/55
John	Wood	24	1940-41	1941-42						5/1		5/1
Ron	Wood	29	1941-42							2/0		2/0
Billy	Woods	51	1944-45	1949-50	28/2	5/6		3/0		13/1		49/9
James	Wotherspoon	49	1944-45							1/0		1/0
Doug	Wragg	109	1961-62	1963-64	103/15	4/0	12/0	4/0	2/0		3/2	128/17
Frank	Wright	28	1941-42							3/1		3/1
Robert	Yates	58	1945-46							1		1
James	Young	47	1944-45							2/1		2/1

ADDITIONS AND CORRECTIONS TO WHO'S WHO 1907 TO 1939

Since the first part of the Who's Who was published, further details of some early players have emerged.

Christian names have been found or confirmed for the following (in date order); Christopher Wynn (born Manchester 1883), Robert Barlow, William Aspinall, Harold Chadwick Meadowcroft (born Workington JFM.1889, k.i.a. on the Somme 1.7.16), Thomas Albert Gledhill (born Farnworth AMJ.1885), Ernest Clark, Walter Buckley (born Rochdale AMJ.1883), John Taylor, Harry Parkinson, Thomas Henry Thornley, James William Willcock (born Worsley JFM.1884), Clifford McCormack (born Crumpsall AMJ.1886), Ernest Stansfield, Herbert Barnes, Frank Greenhalgh, John Henry Jones, William Wright, Jesse Robinson, Samuel Matthews, Joseph Mills, Joseph Thorp (not James), Robert Marcroft (born Rochdale JFM.1888), Arthur Harding (born Ashton OND.1898), Herbert Harrison Butterworth (born Oldham 1890), Frederick Chadwick (born Patricroft OND.1891), Frank Herbert Herring (born Chorlton AMJ.1899), Percy Gibson Jeffcott (born Derby OND.1889), Arthur Bussy (born Rochdale OND.1895).

Additional, confirmed or corrected dates of birth; J.T. Tolley Todmorden AMJ.1882, M. Kingsley OND.1874, E. Petty Farsley JFM.1885, P. Galvin Glossop OND.1882, F. Pearson 18.5.1884, J. Carthy Liverpool JFM.1880, R. Reeves Littleborough JAS.1885, D. Cunliffe 11.6.1875, P. Hardy delete Hebden Bridge JAS.1889, W.E. Bamford Rochdale 16.10.1888

There are significant changes/additions to the following entries:
W. Davidson with West Ham 7.06 not 1902-03, then Stalybridge Rovers 10.06.
W.H. Martin, born Grays, Essex JFM.1891. Career: Workington 5.09, Bristol C., Bristol R., Dale 5.11 [1/0 CL], Merthyr T. 6.12, Halifax T. 7.13, South Liverpool 6.14, Bristol R. 10.14, Halifax T. 1919, Bridgend 7.20.
'W.' Davies 1912-13 should be Alfred (Alf) Davies, born Manchester c.1889, 5'10", 12st. Career: Alderley Edge, Dale 11.12 [4/1 CL], Hurst 12.13, (Dukinfield guest 8.15), Manchester U. 9.15 [25/2 WL], Manchester C. 9.16 [18/1 WL], Bolton W. 12.17 [41/7 WL; 8/1], Bury cs.21 [3/-], Hurst 8.22, Macclesfield cs.27. Alf played over 250 games as a half back for Hurst.
J.W. Yarwood is probably John William, born Wigan AMJ.1889. Early career Hindley Central, Appleby Bridge, Southport Central 6.12, Bolton W. 9.13.
H. Tierney probably born Birtle, Bury AMJ.1885. Early clubs Bury St. Thomas, Freetown, Unsworth.
Gordon Best, born Wigan AMJ.1885. Career: St. George's School (Wigan), Ince Athletic, Brynn Central 11.06, Hindley Central 7.07, Northwich Victoria 9.07, Hindley Central 12.07, Altrincham 5.08, Nelson 3.09, Preston NE 1.10, Macclesfield 5.10, Hyde U. 5.12, Chester 12.12, Heywood U. 7.13, South Shields 1.14, Denton 5.14, Altrincham, Dale 1918 [4/1 WL], Altrincham 8.19, Witton Albion 11.19.
T. Hampson, early clubs Woolfold Ath., Elton, Accrington St.

Other correction:
The photograph shown for John Reynolds is actually of the earlier John Reynolds of Aston Villa.

BY THE SAME AUTHOR:

ROCHDALE AFC WHO'S WHO 1907-1939

In a companion volume to the one you are holding, Steven Phillipps traces the career of 665 men who played for the club up to 1939. Starting in the Manchester League, the club also had spells in the Lancashire Combination and the Central League, before becoming a founder member of the Football League Division Three Northern Section in 1921. Steven's book also includes biographies of players that played in the Football League's Lancashire Section during the First World War.

Illustrated with many photographs, the book can be obtained from the publisher at the address on the title page. The price is £12. The ISBN is 978-1-905891-64-1.

All Rochdale's players, team line-ups, and goal scorers will be found in the English National Football Archive at www.enfa.co.uk